ICONS OF THE MIDDLE AGES

Recent Titles in
Greenwood Icons

Icons of Unbelief: Atheists, Agnostics, and Secularists
Edited by S. T. Joshi

Women Icons of Popular Music: The Rebels, Rockers, and Renegades
Carrie Havranek

Icons of Talk: The Media Mouths That Changed America
Donna L. Halper

Icons of African American Protest: Trailblazing Activists of the Civil Rights
Movement
Gladys L. Knight

Icons of American Architecture: From the Alamo to the World Trade Center
Donald Langmead

Icons of Invention: The Makers of the Modern World from Gutenberg to
Gates
John W. Klooster

Icons of Beauty: Art, Culture, and the Image of Women
Debra N. Mancoff and Lindsay J. Bosch

Icons of Mystery and Crime Detection: From Sleuths to Superheroes
Mitzi M. Brunsdale

Icons of Black America
Matthew C. Whitaker, Editor

Icons of American Cooking
Victor W. Geraci and Elizabeth S. Demers, Editors

Icons of African American Comedy
Eddie Tafoya

Icons of African American Literature: The Black Literary World
Yolanda Williams Page, Editor

ICONS OF THE MIDDLE AGES

Rulers, Writers, Rebels, and Saints

Volume 1

Lister M. Matheson, Editor

GREENWOOD

AN IMPRINT OF ABC-CLIO, LLC
Santa Barbara, California • Denver, Colorado • Oxford, England

Copyright 2012 by Lister M. Matheson

All rights reserved. No part of this publication may be reproduced, stored in a retrieval system, or transmitted, in any form or by any means, electronic, mechanical, photocopying, recording, or otherwise, except for the inclusion of brief quotations in a review, without prior permission in writing from the publisher.

Library of Congress Cataloging-in-Publication Data

Icons of the Middle Ages : rulers, writers, rebels, and saints / Lister M. Matheson, editor.
        p. cm. — (Greenwood icons)
    Includes bibliographical references and index.
    ISBN 978-0-313-34080-2 (hardcopy : alk. paper) — ISBN 978-1-57356-780-0 (ebook) 1. Biography—Middle Ages, 500-1500. 2. Civilization, Medieval. 3. Europe—History—476-1492—Biography. I. Matheson, Lister M.
    CT114.I36 2012
    940.1—dc23   2011020938

ISBN: 978-0-313-34080-2
EISBN: 978-1-57356-780-0

16 15 14 13 12   1 2 3 4 5

This book is also available on the World Wide Web as an eBook.
Visit www.abc-clio.com for details.

Greenwood
An Imprint of ABC-CLIO, LLC

ABC-CLIO, LLC
130 Cremona Drive, P.O. Box 1911
Santa Barbara, California 93116-1911

This book is printed on acid-free paper ∞

Manufactured in the United States of America

Wha's like us? Damn few, and they're a' deid!
[Old Scottish Toast]

Contents

Series Foreword

Worshipped and cursed. Loved and loathed. Obsessed about the world over. What does it take to become an icon? Regardless of subject, culture, or era, the requisite qualifications are the same: (1) challenge the status quo, (2) influence millions, and (3) impact history.

Using these criteria, ABC-Clio/Greenwood introduces a new reference format and approach to popular culture. Spanning a wide range of subjects, volumes in the Greenwood Icons series provide students and general readers a port of entry into the most fascinating and influential topics of the day. Every title offers an in-depth look at up to 24 iconic figures, each of which captures the essence of a broad subject. These icons typically embody a group of values, elicit strong reactions, reflect the essence of a particular time and place, and link different traditions and periods. Among those featured are artists and activists, superheroes and spies, inventors and athletes, the legends and mythmakers of entire generations. Yet icons can also come from unexpected places: as the heroine who transcends the pages of a novel or as the revolutionary idea that shatters our previously held beliefs. Whether people, places, or things, such icons serve as a bridge between the past and the present, the canonical and the contemporary. By focusing on icons central to popular culture, this series encourages students to appreciate cultural diversity and critically analyze issues of enduring significance.

Most importantly, these books are as entertaining as they are provocative. Is Disneyland a more influential icon of the American West than Las Vegas? How do ghosts and ghouls reflect our collective psyche? Is Barry Bonds an inspiring or deplorable icon of baseball?

Designed to foster debate, the series serves as a unique resource that is ideal for paper writing or report purposes. Insightful, in-depth entries provide far more information than conventional reference articles but are less intimidating and more accessible than a book-length biography. The most revered and reviled icons of American and world history are brought to life with related sidebars, timelines, fact boxes, and quotations. Authoritative entries are accompanied by bibliographies, making these titles an ideal starting point for further research. Spanning a wide range of popular topics, including business, literature, civil rights, politics, music, and more, books in the series provide fresh insights for the student and popular reader into the power and influence of icons, a topic of as vital interest today as in any previous era.

Preface

Icons of the Middle Ages: Rulers, Writers, Rebels, and Saints is the result of a quickie conception, an elephantine gestation (with intermittent health problems), and a difficult birth. Nevertheless, we believe that the resultant offspring will prosper and go on to serve a useful role in life and society.

The present two volumes describe the lives and afterlives of a wide variety of larger-than-life medieval men and women who have affected and influenced deeply the modern world and the imaginations of those who live in it, whether we realize it or not. Many of these outstanding characters have exerted lasting significance and presence in the popular imagination (in literature, film, television, art, and so on). Some, such as Saint Francis of Assisi, have become powerful symbols of good for many people; others, such as Vlad Dracul of Wallachia and King Richard III of England, have become archetypal symbols of evil. An iconic physical artifact—the castle—and an iconic military practice—siege warfare—have also been included as important symbols of life in the Middle Ages. The castle is a once-proud manifestation of power that is still visible throughout Europe, although often much decayed or ruined. The siege of a castle or stronghold was a common military operation during the Middle Ages; it had its own equipment, rules, and procedures that were well known to and widely practiced by medieval warriors.

The 18 biographical chapters treat individual characters, with the exception of three cases in which two individuals are so closely or inextricably linked that they "go together like bread and butter"—Abelard and Heloise, Robert the Bruce and William Wallace, and King Arthur and Merlin. Each biographical chapter is longer than the usual journal article, averaging about 15,000 words, but shorter than a full-length biography. The contents of each biographical essay vary somewhat according to the topic, but all chapters focus on the iconic quality of the figure(s). Almost all the essays deal first with the "real" life and deeds of its chosen character(s), before moving on to the afterlife and influence of the character(s) in society, literature, film, and other media. The exceptions are "King Arthur and Merlin" and "Robin Hood," who stand apart as primarily literary/cultural rather than historical figures—though we must remember that King Arthur was generally accepted as historically real, with a factual biography, until the mid-seventeenth century and that Robin Hood may be the only figure in the *Dictionary of National Biography* who never existed (currently in the online version under "Hood, Robin [*supp. fl.* late 12th–13th cent.], legendary outlaw hero."

The two chapters "Castles: Medieval Icons of Power, Wealth, and Authority" and "The Siege: An Iconic Form of Medieval Warfare" are longer, about 25,000 words, and provide detailed discussions of the development and evolution of their subject in the Middle Ages. The two chapters illustrate why castles and sieges can also be considered iconic symbols of the medieval centuries.

Although some chapters do include endnotes for those interested in accessing the scholarly literature, we have deliberately kept the tone of the essays conversational because these volumes are intended to be accessible to general readers, advanced high school students, and introductory college undergraduates. We hope to capture the imaginations of our readers sufficiently that they would like to know more about the remarkable people included in *Icons of the Middle Ages*. To this end, "Further Reading" suggestions are usually given after each chapter, offering details of important studies and texts that are generally available in print or online. *Icons of the Middle Ages* also includes an introduction discussing what is meant by the term "icon" and a detailed subject index to allow readers to access information within the chapters quickly and easily.

Acknowledgments

The preparation and assembly of *Icons of the Middle Ages* have been eye-openers in several respects. As always in collaborative projects, the prime acknowledgments are to the individual contributors, a mixture of seasoned old pros and up-and-coming younger scholars (they can each decide to which category they belong), all cheerful, reliable, and professional.

John Wagner of ABC-Clio deserves particular mention for his constant encouragement, assistance, and occasional whip-cracking during the preparation of these volumes, especially when the editor was paraphrasing Émile Littré's comments in 1880 after the publication of his monumental—indeed *iconic*—*Dictionnaire de la langue française* (published 1863–73; completed in 1873 after nearly 30 years of work): "Combien de fois, quand j'étais au plus fort de mes embarras, n'ai-je pas dit, moitié plaisantant, moitié sérieux: 'O mes amis, ne faites jamais de dictionnaire!'"

Finally, let me thank my partner and colleague, Tess Tavormina, for listening to my concerns, offering valuable advice, and hitting upon the brilliant subtitle of this work.

Lister M. Matheson

Introduction

ICONS

The constituent parts of the title of this book, *Icons of the Middle Ages: Rulers, Writers, Rebels, and Saints*, bear some explication and close reading. In its use here, "icons" is a very new term indeed and reflects the modern age, its psyche, and its fascination with celebrity. Consider some recent instances of "icon" in the press: "Then there is [Barry] Bonds, 46, never a media darling and hardly a sympathetic figure, but a looming icon in this city" (*New York Times*, March 21, 2011);[1] "An icon of old and new Hollywood, she [Elizabeth Taylor] defined modern celebrity—and America couldn't take its eyes off her" (sub-headline, *USA Today*, March 24, 2011, 1A); "PopEater's Rob Shuter recently reported that Lindsay Lohan wants to drop the 'Lo' in 'LiLo' and transform into a new pop icon known simply as Lindsay" (online post at PopEater.com);[2] "A great track . . . leads out onto an astonishing landscape, one that over the years has, deservedly, achieved iconic status" (*Scotland Magazine* 54, Paragraph Publishing Ltd., March 2011).

These excerpts represent very new senses of the noun *icon*, covered by what the *Oxford English Dictionary Online* defined in a draft addition of March 2001 as: "A person or thing regarded as a representative symbol, esp. of a culture or movement; a person, institution, etc., considered worthy of admiration or respect. Freq. with modifying word."[3] The first quotation for this sense in the *OED* is from a magazine article of spring 1952 ("a national icon . . . the American Mr. Moneybags"), followed by five further illustrative quotes, all from newspapers or magazines (1975: "institutional icons such as the ICC and CAB"; 1980: "Defining his *icons* as cultural phenomena, Wolfe [etc.]"; 1988: "an icon for young Indian intellectuals, the 32-year-old Ramanujan"; 1995: "An American icon, the pickup truck"; 2000: "Hollywood's female gay icons Jodie Foster, Susan Sarandon and Jamie Lee Curtis." This sense of the noun is paralleled in the adjective *iconic,* first quoted from *Newsweek* in 1976, with three later magazine and newspaper instances.

The quotations in the *OED* are positive in connotation, but it is clear from the recent citations given above that the sense is expanding: Barry Bonds and Lindsay Lohan are difficult to be "considered worthy of admiration or respect." Wikipedia tries hard to distinguish all sorts of sub-varieties of the modern celebrity sense of *icon*: "pop icon" is distinguished from "cult icon," and has its own entry, as do "cultural icon," "secular icon," and "gay icon," while "political icon" cannot be far behind. And we haven't even touched on the second widespread, new, late twentieth-century sense in computing: "A small symbolic picture of a physical object on a computer screen, *esp.* one that represents a particular option and can be selected to exercise that option" (see *OED Online*)! The earliest, original senses of *icon*—"an image; a portrait; an illustration in a book," "a solid image; a statue," "a simile"—have become obsolete. A philosophical sense of "a sign that represents its object by sharing some common character" is surely restricted at best. Apart from its recently acquired senses, only the sense of "a representation of a sacred personage" in the context of the Greek or Russian Orthodox Church has survived in common parlance.

The lesson is that *icon* and *iconic* have indeed become overused terms, often used indiscriminately and gushingly to denote "a famous (or, by extension, an infamous or even a notorious) person or thing." The expansion in meaning and use are largely driven by the advertising and entertainment industries through print media and the Internet. But such is the development of language, reflecting societal changes and tastes; the *icon*, so to speak, once out of the bottle will never be put back in again.[4]

ICONS OF THE MIDDLE AGES

Very strictly speaking, the term "the Middle Ages" refers to Europe and denotes the historical period between the decline in the fifth century and fall in succeeding centuries of the Roman Empire in the West to the fall of Constantinople to the Islamic Ottoman Turks in 1453, or to the beginning of the Renaissance in the fourteenth century. The dates, however, are elastic and have ranged widely between circa 500 and, in the case of England, the accession of Henry VII in 1485 or even Henry VIII in 1509. Other subsections have been introduced: the emotive term Dark Ages for the period between the decline of the Roman Empire and the appearance of vernacular written documents; the Early Middle Ages (the fifth century to ca. 1000); the High Middle Ages (ca. 1000 to the end of the thirteenth century); and the Late Middle Ages (ca. 1400 to around the end of the fifteenth century).

Our present set of icons lived in that medieval age, though not all in the European West. The dates of their historical lives range from King Arthur and Merlin (seen as "real" figures) in the late fifth to mid-sixth century to Sir Thomas More, born in 1478 and executed in 1535, a man who spans and links the medieval and early modern ages. The set is necessarily very selective, and many other figures might have been included, such as Alfred the Great, Thomas

Aquinas, Attila the Hun, Augustine of Hippo, Avicenna and Averroës, Roger Bacon, Frederick Barbarossa, Elizabeth Bathory, El Cid, Giotto, Pope Innocent III, Pope Joan, Kubilai Khan, Murasaki Shikibu, Nostradamus, Saint Patrick, Prester John, Richard the Lionhearted and Saladin, and Minamoto Yoritomo. All can be considered as icons—our limited selection is representative and not all-inclusive.

RULERS, WRITERS, REBELS, AND SAINTS

Our icons are a mixed bag of the good, the bad, and the downright ugly (at least in behavior). All are highly complex characters, and it is sometimes difficult to pigeonhole them. King Arthur, Robert the Bruce, Charlemagne, Chinggis Khan, Eleanor of Aquitaine, Richard III, and Vlad III Dracula were all rulers, but Robert the Bruce and, arguably, Richard III and Vlad Dracula could be viewed as rebels. Abelard and Heloise, Geoffrey Chaucer, Dante, Hildegard of Bingen, Maimonides, and Thomas More were all writers, but all might also be considered rebels against political, societal, and/or literary norms and conventions. William Wallace was a rebel (though one person's insurgent and rebel is another person's freedom fighter and patriot), as were Joan of Arc and Leif Eriksson the adventurer. Thomas Becket, Francis of Assisi, and Joan of Arc were rebels but also saints. Although the alliterative subtitle does not stretch that far, Richard III and Vlad Dracula, both rulers, became the archetypal rogues and ruffians of history and legend. The castle could be a symbol of pride and security, but it could also be a symbol of domination and oppression: the whitewashed walls and colorful heraldic banners versus the oubliette, dungeon, and torture chamber. The siege was a common event in medieval warfare, as rulers and armies sought to capture castles and other strong, fortified places that were common aspects of medieval life.

All of our human icons are remarkable characters whose lives, deeds, and legends have outlasted them. Even though they lived (or, in some cases, were thought to live) many centuries ago, all remain potent and viable in the present age.[5] They deserve to be remembered, celebrated, and pondered as role models, good and bad, for modern times. An interviewee in the *Times of India* remarked in 2009 that "Today's kids don't actually know the relevance of a Che Guevara or even a Jim Morrison for that matter. T-shirts are sold in plenty emblazoned with these icons. But, how many of these teens know the real story? How many of them know why these icons are who they are?"[6] The present work is an attempt to rectify that situation for our "Icons of the Middle Ages."

COVERAGE IN THE CHAPTERS

The individual chapters give the basic outlines of the lives and careers of their various figures and an overview of their subsequent reputations, influence, and appearances in high or popular culture. Lives and careers can usually be summarized pretty effectively, but we have had to be very selective with regard to later impact and manifestations. There are simply too many instances, already existing and appearing daily, to be listed or described, and every reader will be able to add more examples from personal knowledge. Random illustrations are as follows: John Wayne, hopelessly miscast as Genghis Khan, in *The Conqueror* (directed by Dick Powell, 1956);[7] an episode of the TV drama *House* titled "Brave Heart" (2009); "Camelot," a new Starz 10-episode series started April 1, 2011 ("Sword, Sex and Sorcery," *Vogue*); the made-for-TV "Beyond Sherwood Forest" (directed by Peter DeLuise, 2009);[8] John Steinbeck's *The Acts of King Arthur and His Noble Knights* (1976), his retelling of Malory's *Morte Darthur*; Robert Nye's scabrous tour-de-force *Merlin: Darkling Child of Virgin and Devil* (1978); Joan of Arc in Nye's *The Life and Death of My Lord Gilles de Rais* (1990); a made-for-TV version of *The Lion in Winter,* starring Patrick Stewart and Glenn Close (directed by Andrey Konchalovskiy, 2003); the King Arthur Flour Company; the fact that Ivan the Terrible admired Vlad Dracula, and Josef Stalin admired Ivan, *ergo.* . . . We encourage you to come up with your own examples of the ongoing modern engagement with these "Icons of the Middle Ages."

NOTES

1. Online ed.: http://www.nytimes.com/2011/03/22/sports/baseball/22rhoden.html.
2. http://www.popeater.com/2011/03/28/lindsay-lohan-last-name/#comments.
3. Second edition, 1989; online version March 2011. http://www.oed.com.proxy2.cl.msu.edu/Entry/90879 (accessed 1 April, 2011). Earlier version first published in *New English Dictionary,* 1899.
4. See Suzy Freeman-Greene's article, "Nothing and no one are off limits in an age of iconomania," *The Age* (Melbourne, Australia), online ed., September 15, 2009: http://www.theage.com.au/opinion/society-and-culture/nothing-and-no-one-are-off-limits-in-an-age-of-iconomania-20090914-fntq.html.
5. In the style of the TV show *Deadliest Warrior*: Could Vlad Dracul make (literal) mincemeat of Muammar Gaddafi? Could Leif Eriksson sell a bridge in Vinland to Donald Trump? Could Chinggis Khan outgeneral George S. Patton? Does Richard III outshine Richard Nixon for villainy (though both came to a bad end)? Does Francis of Assisi outsaint Mother Teresa? Do Geoffrey Chaucer and Dante Alighieri outwrite Peter Ackroyd and Matthew Pearl?
6. July 1, 2009. Online ed.: http://timesofindia.indiatimes.com/Potpourri/The-past-beckons/articleshow/4720309.cms.
7. "John Wayne—An American Icon Collection" is coincidentally but unsurprisingly advertised on the same webpage: http://www.imdb.com/title/tt0049092/. We should also mention the Russian-made film *Mongol: The Rise of Genghis Khan* (dir. Sergey Bodrov, 2007), a far more accurate retelling of the khan's story.
8. From a plot summary by Anonymous: "A cursed girl who can change into a ferocious dragon is used to find and pacify Robin Hood," http://www.imdb.com/title/tt1331323/plotsummary.

An illustration from a fourteenth-century French manuscript depicts theologian Peter Abelard tutoring his student, Heloise. Abelard was a scholastic philosopher during the late eleventh and early twelfth centuries. He and Heloise developed an illicit love affair that produced a child. Heloise eventually retreated to a convent, and Abelard was castrated by representatives of her uncle, the canon Fulbert. (The British Library/StockphotoPro)

Abelard (1079–1142) and Heloise (ca. 1090–1164)

Jan Bulman

INTRODUCTION

Abelard and Heloise are among the most famous figures of the Middle Ages. Their lives intersected with many of the preeminent persons of their day, some of whom were their supporters, and many of whom were not. We have a record of their lives that is most uncommon in its detail for any medieval person—we even know some of their most intimate personal feelings. Most of this knowledge comes from Abelard's famous autobiography, *Historia calamitatum* (*The Story of My Misfortunes*), written around 10 years before his death. In it, we read of his arrogant confidence in his intellectual abilities, the sharply competitive world of the twelfth-century schools, his passionate affair with Heloise that resulted in Abelard's brutal castration at the hands of Heloise's relatives, the subsequent separation of the two lovers, and the condemnation of Abelard's theological work on the Trinity at the Council of Soissons in 1121. The most well-known collection of letters from the Middle Ages are the eight letters (including the *Historia calamitatum,* which was also in the form of a letter), written in Latin, exchanged between Heloise and Abelard after they were forced to separate following Abelard's brutal mutilation. For many, the lives of the famous couple seem to embody classic dichotomies: faith versus reason; free inquiry versus church repression; carnal lust versus divine love; novelty versus tradition. Yet, to simplify their story by putting it in terms of simple sets of opposites is to consign them to triteness. The lives of Heloise and Abelard encompass many aspects of what some historians identify as the twelfth-century renaissance, a period on the cusp of the high Middle Ages that witnessed cultural, political, and economic transformations spurred by an intellectual revitalization that produced the zenith of medieval culture.

ABELARD'S EARLY LIFE AND EDUCATION

Abelard was born in 1079 in the small village of Le Pallet, about 10 miles from Nantes in the Duchy of Brittany. Baptized Peter, he received the name Abelard only as an adult, perhaps as something of a jest that referred to his large size and girth. His father, Berengar, was a knight and a landholder, and although it cannot be determined whether his family was of Breton origin, Berengar was probably a minor Breton noble, perhaps a castellan or a knight who guarded the castle of Le Pallet in exchange for a small landholding. Rather than accept his inheritance as the eldest son, Abelard rejected the privileges and military glory that his heritage might have brought him and did not become a knight, but instead pursued his intellectual interests as a cleric. For young Abelard, the path to fame was through learning, and he describes himself as using the arms of dialectical reasoning, rather than the conflict of warfare, to gain trophies.

Le Pallet was near the boundary with Anjou; as such, it was not too far from the towns in the Loire valley where a tradition of learning and composition of Latin poetry flourished. In Abelard's day, schools taught a curriculum that consisted of the trivium (grammar, dialectic, and rhetoric) and the quadrivium (arithmetic, music, geometry, and astronomy). The trivium was dominated by dialectic, a discipline that stressed the science of discourse, commonly thought of as logic. In the first half of the twelfth century, the study of logic was based on the first two treatises of Aristotle's work *Organon*, called *Categories* and *Interpretation*, and Porphyry's *Isagoge*, along with a commentary by Boethius. Most of the *Organon*, which was important to the development of medieval theology known as scholasticism, was unknown in Western Europe during Abelard's day. Although he would not be the first to do so, Abelard's goal was to fuse human logic with Christian revelation to understand Christ as the *logos*, the ultimate logical truth. He believed that through logical discourse directed toward the most logical of religions, all humankind would embrace Christianity.

Determined to pursue the study of dialectic, Abelard left his small village while in his teens. By the 1090s, Abelard was in Loches, where he studied with one of the foremost masters of logic of the time, Roscelin of Compiègne (ca. 1050–ca. 1125). Because there is only one letter to Abelard that can be positively attributed to Roscelin, most of what historians know about Roscelin's thought comes to us indirectly, from what others wrote about him. Roscelin was involved in a controversy with another leading intellectual of his day, Anselm of Canterbury, that mirrored to some extent the intense dispute between Abelard and Bernard of Clairvaux some years later. Anselm attacked Roscelin for his Trinitarian theology, which attempted to apply logic and grammar to understanding the Trinity. Based on what others wrote about his thought, it seems that Roscelin held that universals were mere words with no reality and that when we speak of the Trinity as one nature in three persons—that is, as a universal—we speak out of habit of thought. Therefore, the single unity of the divine trinity has no reality because universals have no reality beyond words. To Anselm and others, even if Roscelin's ideas could not be proven explicitly heretical, his methods were. Anselm wrote a refutation of Roscelin in 1092, after which Roscelin went to England and then perhaps to Rome. By 1098, Anselm had provided a revised version of the refutation to Pope Urban II, claiming that it was heresy to use logic as a tool of theology and that dialecticians who believed universal substances were only words should be silenced. Roscelin's ideas about understanding ancient texts as words, not as things, influenced Abelard's own thought, although, later in his life, Abelard wrote contemptuously of Roscelin's logic and theology. Perhaps because Abelard disagreed with Roscelin's interpretation of universals, or perhaps because Roscelin wrote a contemptuous letter (his only surviving work) to Abelard mocking his castration, Abelard does not acknowledge that he studied under Roscelin; he fails to mention Roscelin at all in his *Historia calamitatum*.

What Are Universals, and Why Do They Matter?

Although the problem of universals was not addressed solely by medieval philosophers, the question of universals drew sophisticated and extended debates in the Middle Ages at a level of intellectual rigor not equaled since that time. Universals are signs common to several things or natures signified by a common term. For instance, think about two red balls. Redness of the red balls is a universal term because it signifies a repeatable entity with certain natures or characteristics predictably found in all red balls. Nominalism holds that all universals are mere names, not realities, and that only particular entities or events have reality. Realism, on the other hand, holds that universals have reality. The problem of universals arose from the third-century neo-Platonist philosopher Porphyry. Porphyry wrote a work called the Isagoge, *an introduction to Aristotle's* Categories *in which he asks, are universals independent of the mind or are they conceptions of the mind? Furthermore, if universals are independent of the mind, are they corporeal or incorporeal? If they are incorporeal, do they exist separate from physical things or within them? To use the example of the red balls, is the redness something that exists independent of the mind, and, if so, is redness a tangible entity or does it exist within the ball?*

In the Middle Ages, difficulties arose when the problem of universals was applied to understanding of the Trinity. Based on what others wrote about his thought, Roscelin subscribed to a nominalist view, holding that mere habit of speech prevented us from describing the Trinity as three entities or three substances. If the three substances were truly one entity, we also would have to believe that the Father and the Holy Spirit had become incarnate with the Son.

*Abelard wrote a commentary on Porphyry in which he asked whether universals were things (*res, *in Latin) or words (*verba). *It seems that Abelard tried to seek a middle position between nominalism—like that of Roscelin—and realism—like that of William of Champeaux—holding that both particular objects and universal concepts are real.*

ABELARD'S EDUCATION IN PARIS

Around 1100, at about 21 years of age, Abelard made his way to Paris to study in the great cathedral school of Notre Dame under William of Champeaux (ca. 1070–1122). At this time, Paris was not yet the intellectual center of Europe, a position it would enjoy from about the thirteenth century as the great medieval university of Paris came to dominate the disciplines of higher learning, especially theology. In fact, for Abelard, Paris comprised little more

than the Île de la Cité, the small island in the Seine River that would eventually hold both Notre Dame Cathedral and the royal palace and tower of King
Louis VI. In 1100, one would be hard-pressed to describe Paris as a city at all;
large town would be a more accurate description. Orleans, in the Loire valley,
was more important than Paris was; it was larger, with a cathedral school of
its own that was better known for Latin literary studies than for the study of
dialectic. No doubt this was why Abelard did not remain in the Loire valley
but instead traveled northward to the valley of the Seine, or as he writes in his
Historia calamitatum, into France. (Just as Paris was a fraction of its present
size, twelfth-century France was limited to the region immediately around
Paris in the Seine valley, a region known as the Île-de-France.) Abelard was
drawn to Paris because, he said, the discipline of logic flourished there and
William of Champeaux—archdeacon of Paris, canon of Notre Dame, and
counselor to King Philip I (1052–1108)—was its most famous teacher.

Paris in Abelard's Day

*Paris had been a Roman foundation of the first century B.C.E. called Lute-
tia, which had been built near the site of an even older Celtic settlement of
the Parisii tribe. Lutetia was typical of most towns in the Roman Empire,
with a bathhouse, aqueducts, and a theatre, and as a prosperous trading
center it spread southward from the Île de la Cité up to what is now the
Sorbonne on the Left Bank. However, the decline of the Roman Empire in
Western Europe brought stagnation, contraction, and decay to its cities.
When Abelard arrived in Paris, he would have found a town that had
pulled back into a much more defensive position. Much of the landscape
was still in ruins after a particularly ferocious Viking raid in 885 that had
left the town burned and scarred. Fortified houses and walled monasteries became the dominant architecture. The royal palace at the west end
of the island was still being rebuilt during Abelard's lifetime. The impressive cathedral of Notre Dame de Paris that dominates the Île de la Cité
today was not begun until 1163, 21 years after Abelard's death. A large
Romanesque cathedral of Saint Stephen that was located just behind the
site of the present-day cathedral lay in ruins, never to be rebuilt as the
influence of Notre Dame increased.*

*To the south, the Petit-Pont bridge, rebuilt in stone around 1120, linked
the Île de la Cité with the Left Bank. To the north, a new bridge, called
the Grand-Pont, and a fortified gate, called the Châtlet, connected the
Île to the Right Bank. The old northern bridge was demolished by about
1116. On the Right Bank of the Seine was an emerging commercial quarter, and on the Left Bank was the student quarter. Today, only two buildings from Abelard's day survive. One is the tower of the church at Saint*

*Germain-des-Prés and the other is the chapel of Saint Aignan, north of
Notre Dame cathedral on the Île de la Cité.*

As a cathedral canon, William of Champeaux was allowed to collect revenue from his own property. A canon was a considered minor clergy, and in the twelfth century, the church was involved in an ongoing reform movement to ban clerical marriage and enforce celibacy among the minor clergy, although recurring papal decrees on the subject suggest that reform had not been fully realized. William of Champeaux was a champion of papal efforts of reform, and in the early 1120s, he worked on behalf of Pope Innocent II to resolve the conflict between the church and the German emperor over papal reforms that resulted in a settlement called the Concordat of Worms. William was the head of the cathedral school; he had studied under one of the great masters of the day, Anselm of Laon (ca. 1055–ca. 1117). During Abelard's lifetime, "master" was a title denoting respect that was often attached before the names of those who had graduated from prestigious schools, or the men who taught at those schools, although use of the title was quite fluid and it may have been applied to a master craftsman as well. Master William of Champeaux adhered to the system of thought called realism, because he believed that universals are real.

Abelard was drawn to William of Champeaux at the cathedral school in Paris because his fame and mastery in logic were well known. Abelard seems to concede William's eminent reputation indeed was merited when he writes that William was the supreme master both by reputation and by fact. Yet, rather than apply himself to learn at his teacher's knee, Abelard pursued a course that would become a lifelong pattern of behavior for him; his seemingly relentless and reckless disregard for prudence repeatedly overturned his hard-won victories. Abelard never seemed to lack self-confidence, and perhaps it was never his intention to learn from William, but rather he meant to engage him in intellectual combat, defeat him, and enjoy the spoils of victory, which in this case would be to oust William and become a master at the school of Notre Dame. Nonetheless, Abelard seems to grasp that his habit of acquiring enemies, whom he claims were jealous of his superior intellect and growing reputation, cost him dearly, and, in fact, he sees his conflict with William as the beginning of his misfortunes.

The arena in which Abelard fought was the classroom, where instruction was carried out by two methods: *lectio* and *disputatio*. With *lectio* (from which we get the English word "lecture"), students heard the master read from recognized authorities. *Disputatio* favored dialogue and debate, with masters and students working through difficult problems through logical argumentation that relied on established authorities to uncover truths and eliminate contradictions. *Disputatio* was not an empty exercise in logic; its effective intellectual goal was not merely to tear down an opposing argument, but also to erect a stronger one that could bring the mind closer to the truth and eliminate error and contradiction. Abelard, never one to downplay his abilities, writes that he excelled at *disputatio*—both as a student, when he challenged and defeated his masters in dialectical combat; and as a teacher, when he stimulated lively debate among his avid students. In Paris, Abelard refuted William's arguments, earned what he described as the master's violent dislike, and alienated his follow students, who saw Abelard as a disrespectful young upstart. In his *Historia calamitatum* Abelard writes that he defeated his master in dialectical disputation by presenting a clear logical argument that forced William to modify his views on universals. Abelard forced William to amend his position, which held that the fundamental nature of all humanity was essentially the same and individuals were distinguished only by "accidents" or differentiated modifications beyond their common nature. Abelard handed William a humiliating defeat by arguing the absurdity of this position, which did not allow that individuals could be genuinely different from one another. Abelard had arrived in Paris as a virtual unknown and severely tarnished the great master's reputation; he writes that the master's lectures fell into disrepute.

Yet, the conflict with William of Champeaux does more than prefigure Abelard's combative nature that would set so many against him; it also anticipates Abelard's preoccupation with logic as a means of linguistic analysis. In Abelard's view, one that was not shared by William of Champeaux, logic should be directed toward understanding how *concepts* were expressed in words, not toward *things*, which should be addressed by physics or metaphysics. The dual purpose of logic was the study of language and the study of the relationship between language and the things it tried to express. For instance, for William of Champeaux and many of his contemporaries, descriptions such as "red" had an independent reality that all red things share. Abelard rejected that notion, but he did not go so far as to claim that descriptions were mere words without meaning beyond themselves. Instead, Abelard held that universals such as redness do not exist on their own but that descriptive words like *red* have a real, unchanging meaning, just as matter has a form, but form cannot exist without matter. Therefore, for Abelard, language was both psychological and physical; it vocalized a sound, but also what that sound signified, both as a concept and as a thing (in Latin, *sensus* and *res*).

Abelard's ability to challenge and to defeat his master in dialectical contests earned him the open hostility of William and the jealous resentment of other, more experienced—though less gifted—students. Although William was not vanquished entirely, his reputation as a teacher never again held the same preeminence, and Abelard's career was launched.

ABELARD THE TEACHER

In about 1102, Abelard left Paris to establish his own school at Melun, just south of Paris, but far enough away to reduce the likelihood that William could obstruct his goal of establishing himself as a master. Abelard described Melun as a fortress and royal seat of the king, but it seems likely that Abelard had other reasons for locating his school in Melun. Although he does not mention it in his autobiography, Abelard secured the support of Stephen of Garlande (ca. 1070–ca. 1148). Like William, Stephen was a canon of Notre Dame de Paris, but unlike William, he occupied a less canonically pure status, for he was both a knight and a cleric. Stephen also appears to have had the support of the king; he had been nominated by King Philip to the episcopal see of Beauvais in 1101, but his nomination was blocked by the powerful Ivo of Chartres (ca. 1040–1115) who complained to the pope that Stephen was unfit for the position because he was an adulterer, an excommunicate, and an illiterate layman. Ivo, much like William, was a vigorous supporter of the papal reform movement that sought to end clerical marriage and concubinage and to reduce the role of the laity in church administration. Although Ivo's accusations should not be taken completely at face value, they draw a portrait of a man who benefited from royal favor and enjoyed lay and clerical privileges. With the security of royal authority behind him, Stephen protected Abelard and saw to it that the school in Melun was established, despite the antagonism of William, thereby extracting a small measure of revenge against the reformers who had blocked his episcopal nomination. It was not the last time that these two powerful men would wrestle, with Abelard as an incidental participant and beneficiary.

Abelard remained in Melun until about 1104. The young, irreverent teacher's prestige attracted many students. The brilliant reputation of young Master Abelard lured former rivals and enemies in Paris away from the school of William of Champeaux. In the highly competitive world of the twelfth-century schools, reputation of the master was the central attraction for students; the prestige of the master, rather than the institution of the cathedral school itself, drew them. No doubt emboldened by success, Abelard decided to move to Corbeil, which was nearer to Paris and the site of another royal residence. He was creeping steadily closer to his rival, William, and to his ultimate goal of becoming the master of the cathedral school in Paris. However, he seems not to have stayed there for long because he suffered a sort of breakdown—an illness, in his words—from overwork. He abandoned his teaching, left France, and returned to Brittany. Now in Brittany, distant from the intellectual center of Paris, Abelard writes that some of his students followed him; such was the extent of his reputation.

Reputation of Masters and the Cathedral Schools

In the twelfth century, learning was on the rise in Europe. At the forefront of the wave of new learning were the cathedral schools. In the early Middle Ages, teaching was usually done by monks in a monastic setting. However, beginning around 1100, mirroring a shift that was taking place within the church as a whole, cathedral schools more often than not became the leading centers of intellectual activity. The transfer of intellectual leadership from monasteries to cathedrals came about for a number of interrelated reasons. First, in general, monasteries were tradition-bound institutions with long histories dedicated to preserving existing knowledge through activities such as copying of texts, but by the twelfth century many people regarded monasteries as out of touch with the new commercial and urban life that was developing across Europe. Beginning in the twelfth century, the most innovative minds were turned toward speculative theology, logic, and legal studies, and the proponents of the various approaches to these disciplines were often fierce intellectual rivals. Although there were exceptions, such as the monastery of Saint Victor in Paris, monastic learning was concerned with maintaining liturgical purity and piety, clearly out of step with the new vitality of the cathedral schools.

The teachers at the cathedral schools, the masters, were scholars who attached themselves to an episcopal church that was wealthy enough to support their educational endeavors by providing a regular stipend. In the expanding urban centers of the early twelfth century, some cities in northern France became centers of learning where students came to study the trivium and the quadrivium, drawn by the reputation of the master, not the city in which they studied. For instance, often a student would write that he had studied with a particular master, but fail to mention the place in which those studies occurred. Because reputation of a master was critical to attracting students, the cathedral schools of Abelard's day can be said to be de-institutionalized—they were not attached to institutions as the monastic schools had been, but rather a school thrived or failed by virtue of the master and his reputation. This situation does not last for long. By the beginning of the thirteenth century, new institutional ties were being created, as teaching came to be licensed and eventually attached to an institution called the studium, *known today as the university.*

His illness and retreat to Brittany was only a temporary setback. Abelard returned to Paris around 1108, ready to begin again as William of Champeaux's student. In his absence, William had joined the canons regular at the monastery of Saint Victor outside the Île de la Cité, where he had established a school to continue teaching. Although Abelard suggests that William joined Saint Victor only to increase his reputation for piety and thereby gain promotion to a higher prelacy, there is no evidence that William's motive was quite so self-serving. The canons regular of Saint Victor followed a reformed rule of Saint Augustine, and perhaps William's goal had been to pursue a reformed clerical life. In any case, the school at the abbey of Saint Victor became quite influential, contrary to the overall trend through the twelfth century in which the most important sites of learning were cathedral, not monastic, schools. William's departure for the abbey of Saint Victor may have seemed like a victory for Abelard, but their rivalry, and the pattern of adversarial interaction between them, continued. Abelard once again engaged and defeated his teacher in at least one contest of disputation. The ebb and flow of their struggle continued as Abelard was placed at the head of the study of dialectic at the Paris cathedral school, only to have William of Champeaux undercut his position there through his considerable influence. Once again Abelard had to depart for Melun, but in 1109 William withdrew from Paris for Saint Victor's and Abelard rushed back to Paris hoping, he writes, to be reconciled with William. If peace was truly his goal, Abelard was to be disappointed. William used his influence once again to block Abelard from acquiring a teaching position at Notre Dame and installed a handpicked master to take his place there after leaving for Saint Victor's, so Abelard was obliged to establish a school and teach at Montagne Saint Geneviève on the south bank of the Seine. The dean of the abbey of Saint Geneviève was Abelard's patron, Stephen of Garlande. Students from Saint Geneviève and Saint Victor engaged one another in contests of disputation.

Abelard and the Garlande Family:
The Enemy of My Enemy Is My Friend

Abelard never mentions the Garlande family in his Historia calamitatum. *Yet, it seems likely that this influential family acted as his protector and patron during the hostilities centering on the twelfth-century cathedral schools. There were four Garlande brothers, and all of them were influential at the highest levels in secular and religious governments. In particular, Abelard probably made an alliance with Stephen of Garlande (ca. 1070–ca. 1148), who was a close advisor first to King Philip I (1052–1108) and then to King Louis VI (1081–1137). Stephen held the positions of chancellor (an administrative head, similar to a cabinet minister) and seneschal (a top military office and head of the royal household) to the king, but at other times, he and his family were out of favor with the monarch. Therefore, the fortunes of Abelard's career mirrored the vicissitudes of Stephen of Garlande's political career.*

The Garlande family's rise to prominence came about in spectacular fashion, because King Philip had marital difficulties. Philip had set aside his wife Bertha of Holland, mother of the future king Louis VI, and in a fit of passion married Bertrada of Montfort even though at the time she was married to Count Fulk V of Anjou (1043–1109). Bertrada's brother, William of Montfort, was the bishop of Paris between 1096 and 1103. There was fierce opposition from many prominent churchmen. The powerful Abbot Suger of Saint Denis vilified Bertrada as a seductress, and others hurled accusations of sorcery. Ivo of Chartres, who had written important compilations of canon law that were instrumental in the Church's evolving definition of marriage in the twelfth century, led the official opposition to the marriage. In fact, Ivo refused to officiate at the bigamous marriage, and the royal displeasure with the churchman's opposition was expressed by having Ivo imprisoned for a time. The Garlandes, on the other hand, were in support of the king's marriage arrangements, and they benefited handsomely from royal gratitude. By 1105 Stephen was Philip's chancellor.

When Abelard came to Paris for the first time, Stephen was an archdeacon of Paris, which carried responsibilities for revenue collections but not many clerical duties. He was also a knight. He had a large chapel and a house near the cloister of Notre Dame. But it was after his nomination by Philip I to the episcopal see in Beauvais that Stephen's enemies emerged. The nomination was blocked by Ivo of Chartres, who objected to Rome that Stephen was unsuitable for the episcopate because he was an adulterer, an excommunicate, and an illiterate layman. Although there is no evidence to confirm or discredit these salacious accusations, Ivo's charges certainly stem from his support for the papal reform movement that since the last century had affected relations between church and state. Born from the desire of the papacy to remove lay interference in what it regarded as church matters, papal reform was particularly concerned with eliminating lay nomination to high clerical positions such as archbishops and bishops and clerical marriage, and these concerns are reflected in the charges that Ivo levied against Stephen. William of Champeaux also was closely associated with the reform movement, and he was an ally of Ivo. Therefore, the rivalries between Stephen of Garlande and William of Champeaux were often played out in arenas peripheral to that of papal reform, such as in the career of Peter Abelard.

Many of the central events in Abelard's life correspond to political successes, failures, and machinations of his patron. So, when Abelard to set up his school at Melun, where the king also had a residence, he writes that he had the help of certain powerful enemies of William. The time when Abelard moved his school from Melun to Corbeil corresponded to the period when the Garlande family had broken ties with the king. Abelard's retreat to Brittany due to illness—brought on, he says, by overwork—was also the period when the Garlandes were out of royal favor; when he returned to Paris from Brittany and William had left for Saint Victor's, the Garlandes once again were enjoying royal esteem. Stephen of Garlande was the dean at the church of Saint Geneviève, where his family owned vineyards and where Abelard established his school. On the outskirts of Paris, Saint Geneviève answered to the king, not to the canons of Notre Dame. When Abelard achieved his goal and became the master at Notre Dame in Paris after 1109, it coincided with the zenith of the Garlande family's influence. When Abelard went to study theology at Laon, the bishop of Laon owed *his office to Stephen. By 1127, Stephen had spent his royal favor and was dismissed from all his royal offices, and although he managed to earn the good graces of the king once again, he fell permanently from power in 1137 with the death of Louis VI. Stephen retired to the abbey of Saint Victor around 1140, around the time that Abelard was prosecuted for heresy at the Council of Sens.*

Although Abelard provides no direct insight into the political intrigues that may have directed the success of his career, it seems likely that the intense hostility between William of Champeaux and Abelard can be interpreted within the context of competing political factions. Certainly, Abelard did not agree with William on the matter of universals, but he does not attack William's intellectual abilities with the same contempt that he reserves for Roscelin of Comiègne and Anselm of Laon. Therefore, while they were certainly rivals, the level of Abelard's disagreement with William did not rise to the same level as that of Anselm, whom he rudely disrespected, claiming he was completely lacking intellectual merit.

Once again, Abelard returned to Brittany, this time because his mother was about to enter a convent. His father had already entered a monastery. It was not an uncommon practice for the laity, as they neared the end of their lives, to enter a monastery, often motivated by the desire to ease their transition to the next world through dedication to a spiritual rather than a secular life. Furthermore, in this way parents could retire to monastic life and supervise the distribution of their property to their heirs during their lifetimes. Abelard does not comment on his parents' motives, but for a child to return to his parents' former home on the occasion of their leaving for a monastic life, as Abelard returned to Le Pallet, also was a common practice. Although he had forsworn any claim to familial property when he left Le Pallet for a life of study, confirmation by anyone who might also have a claim to the property was prudent.

ABELARD THE STUDENT OF THEOLOGY

Abelard returned to France in 1113—not to Paris, but to Laon, where he turned from studying dialectic to studying theology. At this time, Abelard was about 33 years old, and essentially, he was starting over again. Although it was often applied to interpretation of scripture, dialectic was essentially a secular discipline, while theology (*divinitas,* in Latin) was dedicated to understanding religion and could lead to a career in the higher clergy. Abelard began to hear the lectures of Anselm of Laon (ca. 1055–ca. 1117), who along with his brother Ralph was master at the cathedral school. Anselm was a powerful man. Because of his renown as a master (he had taught William of Champeaux), and because he was the dean and chancellor of the cathedral, important church offices gave him control of the cathedral's business concerns. Once again, Abelard's familiar pattern emerged; as he had with William of Champeaux, Abelard developed intense contempt for Master Anselm. The audacious Abelard disrespected the prestige of his master by skipping lectures and complaining that the master lacked active critical intelligence and could give students only practiced and memorized responses. In fact, Abelard anticipates the modern phrase "the lights are on, but nobody's home" when insulting his teacher: he writes that the fire Anselm kindled filled his house with smoke, but shed no light.

The study of theology at the school of Anselm of Laon was undertaken in ways that were just beginning to become systematized. Anselm's school pointed the way that eventually led to the systematization of the *Glossa ordinaria,* a multivolume compilation of commentaries on the Bible produced at the end of the twelfth century. The *Glossa ordinaria* (Standard Gloss) was a compilation of excerpts from the church fathers and other authorities that were inserted in the lines between scriptural texts or in the margins. The *Glossa* served as a kind of condensed running commentary on scripture, especially the passages that were difficult to interpret. Anselm of Laon was especially dedicated to commenting—that is, glossing—on the Psalms and the Epistle to the Romans, which were copied and distributed throughout Europe as analytical tools for biblical study.

In schools like the one in Laon, students heard the master lecture while they took notes. Of course, medieval learning was based on manuscript sources, and the taking of adequate notes—or any notes at all—must have been challenging indeed. Students might employ a wax tablet and a stylus for this purpose. A wax tablet was made by hollowing out an indentation or trough in a wooden (or perhaps ivory, if one were wealthier than the average student) board and then filling it with wax. The wax was sufficiently soft so that a stylus could be used to scratch notes that were intended to be of a temporary nature, as opposed to the more permanent medium of parchment and ink. When the notes were no longer needed, the top layer of wax could be scraped away with the broad end of the stylus, leaving enough wax underneath to begin a new set of notes. Typically, two or more tablets were joined together to form a diptych, and students were generally said to carry a diptych in their belts. Despite the wide use of wax tablets, writing in classrooms must have been difficult; there were no facilities at the schools approaching the dedicated copying centers of the monasteries known as *scriptoria.*

Teaching methods at Laon can be discerned in Abelard's description of his lecture on Ezekiel. Fed up with what he regarded as the pedestrian level of lecture provided by Anselm, Abelard allowed himself to be persuaded by other students to provide his own lectures on the ambiguous and complex prophecy of Ezekiel. Abelard writes that all who heard his first lecture and gloss acclaimed it, so much so that students appealed to him for two more lectures. Abelard writes in the *Historia* that students clamored to hear his lectures and to write notes on his insights into the difficult text, such was the pinnacle of his scholarship. Two of Anselm's senior students, Alberic of Reims and Lotulf of Lombardy, were not impressed with Abelard's erudition, however. They both would have successful careers of their own, but throughout their lives, they never had Abelard's effrontery to lecture on theology without what they considered proper training. They would pursue Abelard throughout his life; Alberic was the prosecutor at Abelard's condemnation in Soissons in 1121. However, in 1113, Alberic had to be content with simply convincing Anselm to expel Abelard from his school, which he did on the pretext that if Abelard, unschooled as he was in biblical exegesis, should err in his theological interpretation, then Anselm would be held responsible. Nonetheless, Abelard had demonstrated that he could deliver lectures on theology superior to those of Anselm, even though his specialized training was much more limited than the master's was.

Although Abelard was once again at odds with a master whom he ridiculed through his arrogant self-confidence, his reputation as a master of exceptional abilities was now well established. Furthermore, his ambition to be placed in charge of the school at Notre Dame was within reach. William of Champeaux had taken up residence as the bishop of Châlons-sur-Marne in 1113; this was significant because as bishop of Châlons he became the patron and supporter of the reform-oriented Cistercian monastery of Clairvaux and its famous abbot Bernard of Clairvaux. No doubt Bernard had learned of Abelard's fierce insubordination from William, and Bernard would become one of Abelard's most intense and powerful critics. However, Bernard's opposition was in the future. From about 1114 until about 1116, Abelard had realized his goal. He became a canon and chair of the faculty at the cathedral school at Notre Dame de Paris; as a teacher of logic, he was at the apex of his fame and renown. Yet, throughout his life, Abelard did not take care to protect his hard-won triumphs, and, through his own rash actions, he seemed to throw away his achievements. It was about this time that he met and fell in love with Heloise.

HELOISE

Heloise had come to Paris from the royal convent of Saint Marie in Argenteuil, where she had been raised, about six miles northwest of Paris. In Paris, she lived under the guardianship of her maternal uncle Fulbert—a canon of Notre Dame, as Abelard newly was. Little is known about her birth family, although she wrote in her letters that she was of low social standing. Yet, when a girl entered a convent such as the one at Argenteuil, a sizable dowry was usually paid, which would have excluded most girls of modest means. Rather than being from a family of humble standing, it seems more probable that Heloise was of illegitimate birth. In the necrology of the convent of the Paraclete, where Heloise died, her mother's name is recorded as Hersindis, but her father's name is not noted, although he may have been from the Montmorency or the Beaufort family. Heloise was probably born around 1090, in which case she would have been about 11 years younger than Abelard was. Heloise came to Paris around the same time that Abelard became a canon and head of the school at Notre Dame; she may have been drawn to Paris and the household of her uncle by Abelard's reputation, which was quite far-reaching. Living with her uncle within the cathedral cloister would have put her in close proximity to an important intellectual center and to one of the most illustrious masters of the day. Although it was quite uncommon for women to be educated at all, Fulbert intended to continue her education in Paris and Heloise acquired a reputation for her extensive knowledge of Latin, Greek, and Hebrew. Abelard calls her *nominatissima,* "the most renowned," for her exceptional abilities in reading and writing.

In his *Historia,* Abelard acknowledges that his pride and overconfidence caused him to give in to his physical desire for Heloise. Events leading up to his success in Paris suggest that Abelard flourished in times of crisis and, at least for the moment, he had vanquished his rivals, and his students followed him with enthusiastic devotion. Perhaps he longed for the stimulation of an adversarial challenge. Whatever the case, Fulbert was anxious to give his niece access to the best teacher available, and so he agreed to allow Abelard to reside in his house and to tutor Heloise. Never lacking in self-confidence, Abelard makes it clear he resided in Fulbert's house fully intending to seduce Heloise, who, he was certain, would find his intellect and physical attractiveness irresistible.

HELOISE AND ABELARD

Heloise and Abelard became passionate lovers, and although Abelard had previously been dedicated to philosophy, intellectual pursuits became tedious, and in his infatuation with Heloise he composed love songs that celebrated his passion for her. None of these love songs survive, although some historians believe that some of the songs written by Abelard—and perhaps Heloise as well—are preserved in the *Carmina Burana,* a collection of poems and dramatic texts from the early thirteenth century. Many of these love songs circulated, and Heloise recalls later that the compositions were "on the lips of everyone" because of their sweetness and melody, which was hardly conducive to keeping their affair a secret. Recklessly driven by what he later describes as lustful desire rather than selfless devotion, Abelard neglected his students, and soon their clandestine affair was widely known. As a result, Fulbert learned of their affair and had them separated. Nevertheless, the lovers thwarted his efforts to keep them apart and they continued to meet in secret. When Heloise became pregnant, Abelard brought her to his family in Le Pallet disguised as a nun, and there she bore a son, whom she named Astralabe, after the scientific instrument the astrolabe.

Astrolabe: What's in a Name?

In about 1118, Heloise gave birth to a son, whom she named Astralabe; Abelard writes that Heloise selected the name. The astrolabe was an instrument used to locate and predict the positions and risings of the sun, moon, planets, and stars and to tell time. Astrolabes were known in ancient times, and they were introduced into Western Europe from Islamic Spain during the eleventh century. The device consists of a metal disk (called a mater) that holds one or more smaller plates (called climates) that are of latitude-specific design. The plate is engraved with a stereographic depiction of circles marking the azimuth and altitude and the celestial sphere above the local horizon. The rim of the largest disk is usually engraved with the hours of the day and degrees of arc. Above the disks is a rotating framework with the projection of the ecliptic plane and several bright stars (called a rete). As the rete is rotated, the stars and ecliptic move across the projection of the coordinates over the climate. In other words, the astrolabe is a flat representation of the celestial sphere that imitates the motion of the heavenly bodies as seen from a representation of a particular horizon and horizon coordinates. To name a child after this instrument was unusual at a time when children typically were named after saints. Some historians have suggested that the name was intended to reflect the desire on the part of the boy's parents to understand the universe, to evoke the lovers who called each other the sun and the moon, or simply to draw attention to their nonconformity. Unless heretofore-unknown evidence emerges, we will never know what was intended by the choice of this unconventional name.

As for the course of Astralabe's life, a bit more is known. A Latin poem offering advice to Astralabe is attributed to Abelard. When Heloise returned to Paris from Le Pallet, she left the child with Abelard's sister, who likely raised him. In 1144, as the abbess of the Paraclete, Heloise wrote to Peter the Venerable asking him to find Astralabe a prebend, which was a stipend or portion of the revenues from a cathedral allocated to a canon for his support. Because of the unusual name, there are few Astralabes in surviving twelfth-century documents, and therefore, when the name appears, it stands out. An Astralabe appears as a canon at Nantes Cathedral in 1150 and as an abbot of the Cistercian monastery of Hauterive in the modern Swiss canton of Fribourg from 1162 to 1165. The death of a "Peter Astralabe, son of our master Peter" is inscribed in the necrology of the Paraclete.

Abelard tried to defuse Fulbert's anger over the affair by apologizing and claiming that he was powerless before the supremacy of love. These must have seemed like lame excuses, since Abelard himself acknowledges that he had planned to reside in Fulbert's house for the very purpose of seduction. To further reduce Fulbert's anger, Abelard offered to marry Heloise, but he proposed a secret marriage, in order to not jeopardize his present and future career prospects. Abelard writes in his *Historia calamitatum* and Heloise confirms in her own correspondence with Abelard many years later that she was strongly opposed to the idea of marriage. She cogently argued against the marriage, demonstrating sophisticated analysis and argumentation—enhanced, no doubt, by the study of logic and philosophy with her tutor. She asserted—rightly, as it turned out—that Fulbert's anger would not be appeased by a marriage, and therefore, the union would hinder Abelard's stellar career trajectory and not pacify her uncle. As a master of the school of Notre Dame, Abelard was a cathedral canon, and while canon law did not explicitly prohibit marriage, for a master to marry would have been quite unusual and an insurmountable obstacle to higher church office. Furthermore, Heloise drew on her extensive knowledge of classical literature—from authors like Pythagoras, Socrates, and Seneca—to support her opinion that married life, with its attendant domestic obligations of parenting, cleaning, and drudgery, was not compatible with the elevated life of a philosopher and a scholar. To tarnish the bright star of Abelard with the dirt of a common life, she wrote, would be obscene, and she implored him to live as the ancient philosophers did: in purity of intellectual pursuit, as a cleric and a canon. Furthermore, in a well-known passage from a letter she wrote to Abelard after his castration, she declares that even if the Roman emperor Augustus (63 B.C.E.–14 C.E.) proposed to marry her, she still would prefer to be Abelard's whore, because wedlock represents chains, and love should be freely given and received, based only on the lovers' devotion. In other words, her love for Abelard was based on love only, and the legality of marriage could add nothing to the strength of her feeling.

MARRIAGE AND ITS CONSEQUENCES

Despite her opposition, Heloise and Abelard were married, although to maintain the secrecy of the marriage, the couple remained apart and rarely saw each other. Fulbert had agreed to keep the marriage a secret, but he began to speak openly about the union, which Heloise continued to deny vehemently, no doubt hoping to protect Abelard. Realizing that Heloise would not corroborate his (true) story, Fulbert reacted angrily. To protect Heloise from her uncle's abuse, Abelard suggested that Heloise flee to the convent of Argenteuil where she had been educated and that she should be clothed as a nun, although he is careful to point out in his *Historia* that she did not wear a veil. To retreat to a monastery, but not as a nun who had taken monastic vows, was not unusual. Men and women in religious houses often were of diverse status; some lived within the walls and followed the rules of the monastery, but they need not have taken monastic vows and perhaps never intended to do so. While she was thus safely away from her uncle's anger, Abelard continued to visit her in Argenteuil, although privacy was not afforded to the couple and Abelard discloses in a later letter that at one time they made love in a corner of the refectory, the hall where the community took their meals. He also writes that he forced himself upon her against her will.

In Paris, Fulbert was enraged because he believed that Abelard intended to set Heloise aside by forcing her into the convent, thereby freeing himself of the inconvenient marriage. In 1117, Fulbert sought vengeance for the perceived insult. He arranged to have Abelard attacked by a group of men while he slept. Abelard was brutally beaten and castrated, in effect ending his luminous career in Paris as a master. The brutality of the act, not to mention its illegality, was shocking even in those times. Abelard writes in his *Historia* that his own reaction was one of shame, because he had given over to lust and carnal pursuits, and humiliation, because he was now a eunuch. He was certain that God was justified in delivering the severe punishment. The attackers were men closely associated with Fulbert; two of them were subsequently caught, castrated, and blinded. After the crime, Fulbert himself suffered a brief period of disgrace and forfeited his property temporarily. With their marriage effectively ended by the castration, Abelard asked Heloise to become a nun at the convent in Argenteuil, where she eventually became the prioress. Out of shame rather than religious conviction, Abelard became a monk.

ABELARD'S TRIAL AND CONDEMNATION AT SOISSONS

After his castration, at about 40 years of age, Abelard left Paris and entered monastic life at the monastery of Saint Denis; at Abelard's command, Heloise became a nun at Argenteuil. Abelard writes in his autobiography that he desired to withdraw from the world that had bestowed so much acclaim and animosity upon him. If this was indeed his intention, Saint Denis was hardly a remote place to find seclusion. It was a wealthy monastery, very near to Paris, with close ties to the monarchy. In the twelfth century, the monastic ideal of withdrawal from the world to seek a secluded life of prayer was contrasted with actual practice, in which monks and abbots were often respected and prominent men. In fact, three of the most influential abbots of the twelfth century were Suger the abbot of Saint Denis, Peter the Venerable the abbot of Cluny, and Bernard the abbot of Clairvaux. All three men are connected with Abelard, although when Abelard came to Saint Denis, Suger was not yet the abbot there. It is not clear why Abelard chose to enter Saint Denis; perhaps it was the monastery's close connection with the French crown, which was favorably disposed toward Abelard's patrons at the time. Perhaps he desired a close proximity to Heloise at Argenteuil. However, it seems unlikely that Abelard sought the peaceful retreat from worldly affairs that he suggests in his *Historia*.

Whatever his purpose may have been, the peaceful life in the cloister eluded him, and he returned to learning. He reopened a school at a priory belonging to the monastery, and the throng of students, still enthralled by his scholarship and now with an almost devotional dedication, followed him as they had done before in Paris. Abelard provides several reasons for his return to teaching. He claims that Adam the abbot of Saint Denis begged him to resume teaching for the glory of God and to help the poor, rather than for money and prestige, as he had done before. Moreover, he writes that once again, he had made enemies of those around him by condemning the lax and degenerate lifestyle of the abbot and monks at Saint Denis, and so they were anxious to divest themselves of the troublesome critic. Abelard had not lost his proclivity for antagonism.

Moreover, Abelard was not finished with controversy, and the enemies he made earlier in his life proved to be lasting ones. Around 1120, Abelard's first master, Roscelin of Compiègne, wrote a highly critical letter to Abelard, mocking his castration (for example, Roscelin refused to address him by the masculine name of Peter, since he wrote that he was no longer of that gender) and criticizing his theological teaching. Furthermore, Roscelin claims that after putting the monks of Saint Denis through a great deal of trouble to find suitable accommodations for his new school, Abelard took the money he earned there and delivered it personally to Heloise. No evidence exists that Abelard visited Heloise at this time, who had taken the veil at Argenteuil, and Roscelin's accusation cannot be verified. Likely the bitterness in Roscelin's tone can be attributed to Abelard's request to Gilbert the bishop of Paris, who had punished Fulbert after Abelard's attack by having Fulbert's property seized, to convene an assembly to judge whether Abelard's writings on the Trinity were heretical, as Roscelin had charged. Abelard asked that the council decide the matter and discipline either Roscelin or Abelard. It seems, however, that Abelard's strategy against Roscelin failed, because Abelard, not Roscelin, was put on trial—not in Paris, but in Soissons in 1121.

Abelard describes the trial in his *Historia,* but he makes no mention of Roscelin; instead, he lays the blame for the trial at the feet of the enemies he had made in his rise to fame: Alberic of Reims and Lotulf of Novara, the pupils of Anselm of Laon whom Abelard had encountered some eight years earlier while studying theology. The work for which he was put on trial was his first treatise on theology, his analysis of the Trinity known as *Theologia summi boni.* Exposition of the nature of the Trinity was a topic fraught with potential for heretical drift. In fact, Roscelin himself had been condemned in 1092, also at Soissons, because he had apparently suggested that the three elements of the Trinity, the three persons as theologians refer to them, were separate deities. The conceptual nature of the Trinity requires a subtle and careful mind to stay within the bounds of Christian orthodoxy, which states that the godhead comprises three persons: the Father, the Son, and the Holy Spirit. The three persons are equal, and compose a single deity, as Christian monotheism demands. The central element of Christianity is the belief that the Incarnation of God the Son on earth was when Jesus took on a human body and nature, living and suffering as a man to conquer human sin. Thus, the nature of Jesus and the Trinity is a complex topic, and even with careful exposition, one ran the risk of falling afoul of the ecclesiastical authorities.

Yet, the exercise of caution was never part of Abelard's nature. In *Theologia summi boni* he uses logic, his sharpest intellectual tool, to address the problem of the Trinity. He writes that only dialectic and philosophy can lead to a full understanding of the complex subject. He posits that Christ can be understood by distinguishing names, which is in keeping with his understanding of Christ as *logos* or word. He assigns the Father, the Son, and the Holy Spirit different natures: power, wisdom, and goodness, respectively. Abelard was most open to criticism with his allocation of power to the Father, which his enemies suggested assigned a superior role to that person and was, therefore, heretical. In Abelard's day, the legal framework for defining and trying heresy was not yet fully developed, and so those who sought to attack Abelard at the Council of Soissons for his controversial use of logic in theological exposition had to resort to a strategy that would prevent the most gifted logician of the day from gaining the upper hand.

In March 1121, Abelard was summoned to appear before the Council of Soissons, which was convened by Cardinal Cono of Palestrina, a papal legate, or representative from the pope to France and Germany. The cardinal was a supporter of the papal reform movement and a close colleague of William of Champeaux. In his *Historia,* Abelard makes it clear that Alberic and Lotulf were behind the summons, because they were now masters themselves and they used their influence over Ralph the archbishop of Reims, who presided over the council. Alberic and Lotulf served more or less as prosecutors during the council, although getting the charge of heresy to stick proved difficult. Using logic in the service of theology was not inherently heretical, so Abelard writes that the two began their attack before he even arrived in Soissons, by spreading the false rumor that Abelard was expounding that there was more than one God. The strategy of disinformation was sufficient to stir up anger among the clerics and people of Reims, and Abelard and a few students narrowly escaped being stoned by the populace upon their arrival in Soissons. However, Abelard had prepared a strategy of his own. He went immediately to Cono, the papal legate, and gave him a copy of the *Theologia,* stating that if, after reading the book for himself, Cono had found anything in it that was wrong, he was prepared to be corrected. Cono demonstrated his antagonism to Abelard by refusing his request and was instructed to go before the council, or, as Abelard writes, before his enemies. Abelard writes in his *Historia* that he sought to influence the outcome in his favor by preaching in public about the Trinity before the council met, and that all who heard him were impressed by his interpretation.

Many high-ranking ecclesiastics, including Geoffrey the bishop of Chartres, Thierry of Chartres (master of the school of the same city), and Adam the abbot of Saint Denis, attended the Council of Soissons. William of Champeaux may have been present, although the surviving records do not verify his presence. The accusations of heresy against Abelard were not the only business of the council, which was convened primarily to promote and to implement further the papal reform agenda of wresting control of ecclesiastical offices away from the laity and the prohibition of clerical marriage to churchmen above the rank of subdeacon. The charges against Abelard were put off until the final day. Abelard writes that the council could find nothing objectionable in the *Theologia*. He must have felt particularly vindicated when Alberic of Reims believed he had found a passage in the book that was heretical, only to have Abelard soundly refute his accusation by pointing out that the passage was, in fact, a quote from the magisterial church father Augustine of Hippo. Geoffrey the bishop of Chartres, who was an ally of Abelard's patrons in the Garlande family, spoke in support of the logician, first proposing that Abelard be allowed to defend his ideas. When this was not allowed, Geoffrey proposed the time-honored strategy of all committees: that the matter should be postponed until another committee at Abelard's monastery of Saint Denis could examine the issue. Although Cono at first agreed to this proposal, Alberic and Lotulf saw this for what it surely was: a move to defuse the situation and to bring the matter to a favorable resolution on Abelard's behalf in his own diocese. Saint Denis was in the diocese of Sens, and the archbishop Henry Sanglier was a cousin of Stephen of Garlande. Unwilling to let this happen, Alberic and Lotulf sought out Ralph the archbishop of Reims, who presided over the council, and the legate Cono, whom Abelard describes as not as learned as he should have been. Perhaps not Abelard's equal in logic, Alberic and Lotulf were adept at behind-the-scenes maneuvers, and they tailored their persuasion to the egotism of each man. To the archbishop, they spoke of the shame that would be cast on him if the case were moved to another set of judges and the danger that would result if Abelard escaped in this manner. To Cono, they maintained that Abelard should be condemned because, at the very least, he had read publicly from his book and allowed for it to be copied without papal or other ecclesiastical approval. Cono was convinced to condemn the treatise and have Abelard imprisoned in a monastery.

Geoffrey of Chartres informed Abelard of the decision. Abelard was summoned before the council, and without any further debate on the matter, he was ordered to throw his treatise into the fire, an act that was intended not so much to suppress the *Theologia* as to symbolically discredit the work and humiliate its author. Abelard writes that Master Thierry of Chartres shouted out in protest, but the archbishop ordered him to be silent. To further his humiliation, Abelard was ordered to recite the Athanasian Creed like a schoolboy—and even given a copy of the text should he not remember it—because it contained a statement about the equal omnipotence of the three persons of the Trinity. Furthermore, he was confined to the nearby monastery of Saint Médard.

About ten years earlier, when Abelard was a master at Saint Geneviève, a student named Goswin challenged Abelard over his irreverence for established authority, and the two entered into a heated disputation. Goswin went on to become the prior of Saint Médard. Goswin's biographer wrote of the confrontation with Abelard, the only source for the encounter, claiming that Goswin got the better of Abelard in disputation. The biographer's purpose is to present his subject in a favorable light, and the incident cannot be confirmed elsewhere, so the veracity of the account is unknown, but it suggests that a there was a history of hostility between the brash logician and Goswin abbot of Saint Médard. Nonetheless, Abelard's confinement at Saint Médard lasted only a few days, and he was allowed to return to Saint Denis—where Abelard writes that he was widely detested.

ABELARD'S RETURN TO THE MONASTERY OF SAINT DENIS

Back at Saint Denis, Abelard applied himself to the monastery's renowned library. The sizable library and scriptorium (the writing room where monks copied texts by hand) at Saint Denis offered him an enhanced opportunity to access a comprehensive collection of texts that had influenced the development of religious doctrine, especially the Latin church fathers; the collection at Saint Denis exceeded even that of the school at Notre Dame in Paris. These authorities had shaped religious thought since the earliest days of the church, forming a body of scriptural interpretation that was second in authority only to the Bible itself. Abelard's command of these works likely was started at the extensive library of Saint Denis; his facility with these authorities is demonstrated clearly in his famous work *Sic et non* (*Yes and No*), which he probably began at Saint Denis. This work shows Abelard's logical mind striving to resolve the inevitable contradictions among these authorities. In effect a work of comparative scholarship, *Sic et non* presents sets of disputed theological and scriptural propositions and then puts forward quotations and citations arguing contrasting positions—hence, the title *Yes and No,* or, as we might say today, "on one hand, but on the other hand." Abelard proves, and then disproves, about 158 questions by citing the church fathers, scripture, church councils, and reason. For instance, he proposes a problem, such as "that God can do all things and against this," and then systematically presents authorities supporting each side of the proposition. Abelard writes in the preface that his purpose is not to undermine authority by pointing out contradictions, which can arise from any number of benign reasons such as words with different meanings, shifts in meaning when texts are taken out of context, or even scribal errors. Abelard does not try to reconcile the conflicting authorities, and *Sic et non* is, effectively, a sort of notebook in which he has collected sentences to illustrate two sides of difficult questions. It seems likely that following his condemnation at Soissons, Abelard realized that henceforth he would have to support his arguments not simply with logic and reason but with past authorities' opinions as well—in effect, precedent.

Abelard describes in his *Historia* how once again he invited controversy when he disputed the identity of the presumed founder of the monastery of Saint Denis. Saint Denis was among the most prestigious monasteries in France, owing in large part to its presumed illustrious founder. It was believed that a third-century bishop of Paris, Saint Denis, was martyred in 270 and the abbey of the same name was founded on the site where the famous martyr was believed to have been buried. Over time, the martyred saint came to be known as the patron saint of France, and his tomb became an important pilgrimage site, generating considerable income, as well as prestige for the monastery. The name Denis is rendered in Latin as Dionysius. In the Middle Ages, knowledge of ancient history often was quite sketchy, and Dionysius the early bishop came to be confused with another famous Dionysius from the Acts of the Apostles. This Dionysius was converted to Christianity by Saint Paul and then believed to have become the first bishop of Athens, the site of his conversion. In fact, the two were separated by more than two centuries, but the misidentification endured. The situation was complicated further by a third Dionysius, this one known today as an anonymous theologian and philosopher from the late fifth or early sixth century called Pseudo-Dionysius the Areopagite, but in Abelard's day he was believed to be the same Dionysius who was converted by Saint Paul. Therefore, medieval scholars had conflated the first-, third-, and sixth-century Dionysiuses as the same person. Abelard, who had been working his way through Saint Denis's extensive monastic library, came across a sentence in a work called *The History of the English Church and People* (by the eighth-century English scholar known as the Venerable Bede) that he claimed contradicted the monks' belief that Dionysius had been the bishop of Athens. To the annoyance of the monks, Abelard claimed that Bede had placed Dionysius not as the bishop of Athens, but as the bishop of Corinth. The outraged monks claimed their belief was based on the findings of their ninth-century abbot Hilduin, and they flatly declared that Bede was a liar. Abelard, now most willing to rely on authority to support his position, asserted that Bede carried much more weight than Hilduin and was recognized by the entire Church. As the dispute continued to grow, Adam the abbot of Saint Denis viewed the incident as an attack on France and seemed to be preparing to send Abelard before the king on a charge of treason. Abelard writes in his *Historia* that he endured the blows of fortune and the wickedness of the monks, and, declaring that the entire world had conspired against him, he fled Saint Denis in secret under cover of night, resolving to remove himself from France (the Île-de-France).

THE PARACLETE

Abelard's flight from Saint Denis was spurred by the animosity of the monks and Abbot Adam, but also by his rejection of what he considered their disregard for the austerity demanded by the Benedictine Rule. Writing in the

Historia that he was horrified by the monks' wickedness and feeling that the whole world had conspired against him, Abelard arrived at the priory of Saint Ayoul in the town of Provins in the county of Champagne. He probably chose Saint Ayoul because its prior, Radulphus, was a friend of his, and the count of Champagne, Thibaud II, was an acquaintance as well. Abelard's goal was to set up a school and monastery in Champagne, and he no doubt had hoped that these allies would help him. Champagne was already home to the monastery of Clairvaux, which under its famous abbot Bernard was bringing prestige, money, and people to the county. Another monastery headed by a well-known abbot would have raised the profile of the already wealthy county even further. However, as was the pattern his entire life, Abelard had left a trail of enemies behind him, and his former abbot Adam of Saint Denis would not absolve him for running away, nor would he allow the troublesome Abelard to live as a monk wherever he chose, despite Thibaud's petition to Adam on Abelard's behalf. A monk took a vow of obedience to his abbot, and Abelard was left without options. Adam demanded that Abelard return to Saint Denis under pain of excommunication. Yet, shortly afterward, on February, 19, 1122, the abbot of Saint Denis died and was succeeded by Suger, who, like Bernard of Clairvaux, Peter the Venerable, and Abelard himself, would become a seminal figure of the twelfth century. Abbot Suger also was not inclined to grant Abelard's request, but the intervention of Abelard's powerful patron, Stephen of Garlande, at this time the seneschal of France, secured the permission he sought. Confirmed in the presence of the king, Abelard was allowed to quit Saint Denis and to place himself under the authority of another monastery, and in fact go to any solitary place he wished, as long as he did not bring disrepute upon Saint Denis.

And so, Abelard relocated once again, this time to a secluded site in the parish of Quincey, near Nogent-sur-Seine, still within the county of Champagne. Abelard busied himself constructing a small dwelling from mud, sticks, and reeds, with the intention of living as a hermit. He dedicated the primitive structure to the Holy Trinity, surely a reference to his condemnation at Soissons. However, Abelard writes that his fame and the enthusiasm of his students would not allow his withdrawal. They flocked to him en masse from Paris, and the tents and huts of his adoring students destroyed the seclusion he had sought. Although Abelard asserted that he sought comfort in the solitude of a hermit, he soon resumed teaching students again because of his acute poverty. If this was the case, his fortunes were reversed by the influx of students, and a new oratory made of stone and wood replaced the original oratory of mud and wattle. He consecrated the new oratory to the Paraclete. "Paraclete" was an unusual, but surely a personally significant, name for the oratory. Paraclete is a Greek word, meaning one who helps or assists; but in the Bible, it is used to mean the Holy Spirit as comforter (in Latin, *consolator*). Paraclete often figures in theological discussions about the Trinity to describe how God is revealed in the world and his part in salvation. Paraclete, or Holy Spirit, is the third person of the Trinity. Abelard may well have chosen the name as a show of defiance for the condemnation at Soissons, but he writes in the *Historia* that the Oratory of the Paraclete was an outward manifestation of the Holy Spirit that he believed resided within him.

Moreover, although many of Abelard's works are difficult to date with certainty, it seems that his time at the Paraclete was one of the most prolific periods in his life. He defiantly reworked the book that he had been forced to burn at Soissons, this time calling the work *Theologia Christiana*. He may also have written *Sic et non* (his work presenting conflicting theological quotations), *Tractatus de intellectibus* (glosses on the late third- or early fourth-century philosopher Porphyry of Tyre), the *Soliloquium* (an internal dialogue between Peter and Abelard), the *Collationes* (dialogues between a philosopher and a Jew, and between a philosopher and a Christian), and works on grammar and rhetoric that do not survive. Clearly, Abelard was better suited to the life of a writer and teacher than to that of a hermit, and he remained teaching and writing at the Paraclete from about 1122 to about 1127, one of the longest periods of sustained scholarship in his life. To allow him more time to study, his students took over the running of the Paraclete. Abelard writes that pupils were drawn by his superior reputation as a teacher, igniting the jealousy and criticism of his rivals once again.

However, these attacks mark a departure from past criticisms, which had come from rival schoolmasters or students. Now, they originated with those whom Abelard contemptuously refers to as those who boasted that they had restored the purity of the lives of monks and canons regular. Most historians believe that Abelard is referring to Bernard of Clairvaux as the monastic reformer and Norbert of Xanten as the reformer of the canons regular. Both men were associated with the reform movement, and Abelard writes that they preached avidly against him and his supporters. It does seem that the winds of change were blowing against Abelard and, perhaps more importantly, his patrons. Stephen of Garlande, who was the seneschal of King Louis VI and an archdeacon of the cathedral of Notre Dame in Paris, once again had fallen out of royal favor. He had intervened on Abelard's behalf to secure permission to leave Saint Denis, thereby helping to make the Oratory of the Paraclete a reality. Although it is difficult to trace precisely what led to Stephen's fall from grace, it seems likely that he had attracted the hostility of many of the reformers who objected to his personal wealth and temporal power, which they saw as inconsistent with the office of archdeacon of Notre Dame. Stephen's fall resulted in his removal as the seneschal; his property was confiscated, his great house on the Île de la Cité was demolished (though the chapel was spared), and his vineyards near the abbey of Saint Geneviève on the Left Bank, where he was dean and Abelard had established a school, were uprooted. Although Abelard was in Champagne and, as a supporter of the Garlande faction, Count Thibaud could accord him a certain amount of security, sometime between 1125 and 1127 Abelard left the sanctuary of the Oratory of the Paraclete, accepting an invitation to become the abbot of the monastery of Saint Gildas in wild and pirate-infested western Brittany.

ABELARD AS ABBOT OF SAINT GILDAS

The monastery of Saint Gildas mirrored its wild habitat: the monks there were undisciplined and unruly; they did not live a communal celibate life as demanded by the Benedictine Rule, but instead openly supported concubines, fathered children, and neglected to protect the monastery's property from the predations of an aggressive local magnate. No doubt monastic discipline had broken down long before Abelard arrived, and the monks were determined to maintain the status quo. Abelard struggled against the disorderly monks for ten years, apparently placing himself at risk of physical attack from the recalcitrant monks. In his *Historia,* he writes that by trying to reform the obstinate monks, he feared that he would not escape with his life; yet, if he ignored their undisciplined conduct, so obviously at odds with their vows of poverty, chastity, and obedience, he feared for his eternal soul. Indeed, the monks of Saint Gildas tried to murder their reform-minded abbot by poisoning the sacramental wine, and Abelard had to resort to threats of excommunication, which would compel the worst offenders to leave the monastery. He forced the worst of them to swear to leave the monastery, but when they tried to flout their oath, Abelard enforced it with the support of a council composed of the count Conan III, a papal legate, and bishops. Nonetheless, corruption in the monastery ran deep, troublemakers remained, and eventually Abelard was forced to live outside the monastery.

Abelard's abbacy at Saint Gildas must have ranked among the one of the lowest points in his life. His enemies had seriously undermined his passion for the study of logic and theology, his pursuit of Heloise had disastrously ended in castration, and he found himself the target of hostile monks far from the intellectual center of France. Yet, while he was at Saint Gildas, Abelard's life once again intersected with Heloise's. At Argenteuil, Heloise's considerable abilities had been directed toward the administration of the religious community as its prioress, and her reputation had grown as a result. In a bid to expand his own monastery's holdings and secure a point of access to the Seine, Abelard's formidable enemy, Abbot Suger of Saint Denis, aggressively attempted to oust the nuns from Argenteuil. In 1129, Suger produced a forged charter purporting that King Louis the Pious, the son of Charlemagne, had given Argenteuil to Saint Denis some 300 years earlier. He also claimed that the nuns at Argenteuil were engaging in immoral sexual activity. Heloise and her nuns were expelled, and their convent was taken over by the monastery of Saint Denis (ironically, the monastery where Abelard first took monastic vows). Since no provisions were made for them, Abelard offered to the displaced nuns the Oratory at the Paraclete, where they established a new religious house with Heloise as the abbess. Pope Innocent II confirmed the donation in 1131.

THE LETTERS OF HELOISE AND ABELARD

After his flight from Saint Gildas, Abelard wrote *Historia calamitatum*. About this time, the two former lovers began a correspondence, although around 15 years had passed since they were separated. Heloise initiated a correspondence with Abelard, likely after she had read his autobiography, which is written in the form of a letter addressed to an unnamed friend, although likely this was simply a stylistic choice on Abelard's part. Heloise wrote to Abelard not to revive their past love, which she remembered in every detail, but she implored him to give her the small comfort that he owed her by establishing this minimal contact. Thus her first letter begins by chastising him for his silence in the years since the attack—because, in fact, she reminds him, they are still married. Although she complied with Abelard's wish that she become a nun, from this correspondence with Abelard we know that she had been reluctant to do so. She writes that she "changed her habit"; that is, she took the veil and became a nun only to demonstrate that Abelard possessed her body and her mind. Yet, her transformation to religious life was superficial; her habit and religious life did not mask her enduring love, which she would not sublimate. In her correspondence with Abelard, although about 15 years had passed since Abelard's castration, she still writes of her love for him in the present tense and by obeying his will (that she become a nun), she writes that "now [that I am a nun], even more I am yours." For Heloise, Abelard's inability to make love to her as he once did is of no difference. She writes that he is obligated to her by a debt that even transcends the sacrament of marriage because of the depth of her love that knows no bounds. She closes the letter by referring to him as her only love.

Lost and Found Letters?

Sometime around 1470, in the monastery of Clairvaux, a monk named Jehan de Vepria copied a collection of love letters from the twelfth century. The art of letter writing, or in Latin ars dictaminis, *was a subfield of the discipline of rhetoric, one of the subjects studied in the trivium, and it was an important and valued skill honed by educated persons after years of practice. Letters were a means of communication across long distances, a way to preserve essential information, and a type of literary convention, bound by very particular rules of composition and structure. To master the complicated art of epistolary rhetoric, theoretical treatises and model letter collections were produced for purposes of instruction based on imitating various forms, parts, and language of letters. Formularies were collections of model documents, either public or private, somewhat akin to the modern form letter.*

The text copied by Jehan de Vepria was given the name Epistolae duorum amantium (The Letters of the Two Lovers) *in 1974 by its modern
editor Ewald Könsgen. Könsgen suggested that the letters in fact may have
been written by Heloise and Abelard during their affair. Since Könsgen
first raised the issue, other historians, especially Constant J. Mews, have
attempted to demonstrate that in fact the correspondence is that of the two
famous lovers, although not all historians agree with Mews's assertion.
These are not the well-known letters that have been attributed to the pair,
which were written between about 1133 and 1138, long after the tragic
events in Paris. (There has also been some debate about the authenticity
of these letters, although most historians agree that they are authentic.)
That letter collection consists of eight letters that most historians attribute
to Heloise and Abelard; they were probably collected at the Paraclete and
first appear in the early 1280s in Jean de Meun's version of the* Romance
of the Rose. *The* Epistolae duorum amantium, *if indeed they were
authored by Heloise and Abelard, were probably composed over a period of
about one year, between late 1115 and some time in 1117. Although the
text of the letters lack firm references in which to place their context, some
of the letters may have been composed before Abelard took up residence
in Fulbert's house, and they seem to end as the relationship breaks down,
perhaps when Abelard learns of Heloise's pregnancy.*

*Because the letters cannot be positively attributed to Heloise and Abe-
lard by virtue of their content, historians have tried to rely on similarities in vocabulary and style between the love letters and works known to
have been written by Abelard and Heloise. Although the controversy over
authorship continues, these letters are nonetheless especially valuable for
gaining insights into attitudes toward love, a blossoming topic among
twelfth-century educated men and women.*

In the twelfth century, love was emerging as an important theme in secular
and religious literature. Today, we take for granted that love is an acceptable
motif in literature; we have literally centuries of writers who have approached
the subject in their works. However, in Heloise's day, love—its emotions and
consequences—was a theme that was being newly explored in Latin and vernacular literature. Although romantic love certainly was a favored theme of
troubadour poets who wrote and performed their works in courts across
southern France, the love founded in friendship and the comradeship among
men who had chosen a religious life was an emerging theme in twelfth-century
writing as well. Heloise's frank description of her love for Abelard in her letters,
especially in her early letters, should be viewed within this context of expanding awareness and description of human emotion. Nonetheless, Abelard's
reply to her letter does not invite romantic images of love. He opens the letter

as an abbot (he was still the abbot of Saint Gildas) addressing an abbess and is coolly detached. Heloise possessed a clever and sophisticated intellect; she could not have mistaken his tone, yet in her next letter to Abelard, she continues to write of her love, describing her sexual frustration, putting her situation in unmistakable terms. She became a nun because she loved Abelard, not God, and it was impossible for her to be truly dedicated to religious life because she loved only him. Her profession is insincere in the extreme, she writes, and those who admire her religiosity see only her outward behavior—privately, she is driven not by love of God, but by love for Abelard, and she feels the hypocrisy deeply. She knows God cannot forgive her, because her denial of God is deliberate and intentional; she asks only that Abelard forgive her.

Her deliberate tone must have shocked Abelard into a more meaningful response; in his second letter to her, he speaks more directly to her personal despair, but his tenor likely was not what Heloise had hoped from him. Abelard apparently had limited appetite for Heloise's nostalgia, and he rejects her attempt to relive the past. For Abelard, love of Christ, not physical love, should be the object of their desires. He reproaches her for what he calls her "perpetual complaint against God" and tells her that God's punishment—or his mercy—has freed them from the bonds of physical desire and opened to them boundless promise of divine love. Their earlier behavior, their lovemaking during Lenten season in the refectory of Argenteuil, and their disguising Heloise as a nun when she traveled to Brittany had mocked God, yet in his mercy he had not punished them but freed them. Abelard downplays their former love and his mutilation. He maintains that their love was really lust, which led them to sin; divine love would lead them to love Christ, who had truly suffered, as Abelard had not. Therefore, he urged her to discover her own beauty as the bride of Christ, which her religious life now gave to her. By alluding to Heloise as a bride of Christ, Abelard was drawing on a familiar image from the Middle Ages, which linked the union of the bride and her husband to the religious joy of the union between the soul and God, Christ to his church. This was not carnal human love between men and women, but the pure ideal divinely inspired love. When she became a nun and took her vows, Heloise did become the bride of Christ, and Abelard reminds her that this is indeed her refuge. As Heloise had passionately expressed her love for Abelard in her letters, his reply could not have been welcome. He basically claims that he never truly loved her, and that his desire for her was rooted in sexual lust, and therefore was a sin against God.

Bride and Bridegroom

Imagery of the bride and bridegroom in religious writing may seem startling, but in fact, it is a very old image, one that finds its source in scripture. The imagery intends to evoke not the physical union between the sexes, but sustained spiritual union on a plane that could not be experienced in the conventional physical sense. The Old Testament book the Song of Songs (also known as the Song of Solomon and Canticles) is a collection of eight erotic love poems that provided the language for Christian medieval writers to describe spiritual love of Christ for his church. Bernard of Clairvaux, Abelard's harsh critic, famously wrote a work titled A Sermon on the Song of Songs, *which was a commentary on the Song of Songs, in which he reveals the soul as the bride of Christ. Humankind, he wrote, was created in God's likeness, and therefore the soul's love for God was mirrored in the loving bride giving herself to the Divine Bridegroom. Another source for the image of bride and bridegroom in religious writing, one that was often cited in tandem with the Song of Songs, was from the Apocalypse or the Revelation of Saint John the Divine, which is an account of the end of the world as a fulfillment of God's plan. The description offers an image of new creation of heaven and earth following the destruction of the world, in which a new Jerusalem descends from God in heaven like a bride adorned for her husband. Thus, the metaphorical language of the union of the husband and bride represented the realization of religion.*

In the subsequent letters, Heloise states her resignation to their fate, and her recognition that they now must live as brother and sister, as Abelard wrote they must. Their correspondence thereafter concerns matters of faith and the administration of the Paraclete, rather than, as Heloise initially had encouraged, their passionate love for each other. No doubt the abbess realized that if their correspondence was to continue, she had to approach it on Abelard's terms. Abelard served as spiritual director for the women at the Paraclete, and the correspondence between Heloise and Abelard reflects her questions on the best way to oversee the religious house of which she was now abbess. As their benefactor, Abelard preached to raise money for the nuns and even visited the Paraclete on occasion, prompting further malicious rumors from the controversial monk's expanding list of enemies. Surely, Abelard now saw Heloise only as a sister in Christ, and he writes that his castration ensured that the former lovers' contacts related to issues regarding the proper administration of the Paraclete. Eventually, Heloise poses a series of questions to Abelard concerning the place of women in religion, the will of God, the nature of sin, and the source of right and wrong. In his fourth letter to Heloise, Abelard lays out a rule by which the nuns should live, since the standard monastic rule, the Rule of Saint Benedict, was written as a guide to the communal lives of monks and often was imperfectly suited to regulation of a convent.

The Authenticity of the Eight Letters

The eight letters of Heloise and Abelard have figured prominently in their enduring fame because they reveal with startling intimacy the private emotions and inner thoughts of the famous couple. Most historians hold that Abelard wrote Historia calamitatum *(usually regarded as the first letter) and that the subsequent correspondence between Heloise and Abelard was composed by the party to whom the letters are ascribed—which is to say, Heloise wrote letters to Abelard and he wrote letters to Heloise. Medieval letter writers often kept copies of the letters they wrote and, in some instances, edited them for circulation as an epistolary collection. In the decades following Heloise's death in 1163, an unknown person made a copy of the letters, which were probably left in a manuscript in the library of the Paraclete, and a copy came into the hands of the poet Jean de Meun. In the 1270s, he translated them into French and inserted the story of Heloise and Abelard into his poem* Roman de la Rose (Romance of the Rose). *Therefore, the earliest attestation of the letters cannot be dated before the late thirteenth century, some 150 years after the letters were written. Perhaps for this reason, some historians have raised concerns about the authenticity of the letters.*

A few historians, although not the majority of them, assert that the letters are literary fiction composed solely by Abelard himself. In other words, Abelard wrote all eight letters himself, perhaps based on an actual correspondence between the former lovers that has not survived, writing first as himself, then adopting the voice of Heloise in the response that he wrote, thereby creating a fictitious exchange and a work of literature. Those who hold this view contend that Heloise never would have expressed the irreligious opinions contained in her letters. In fact, that any woman of the Middle Ages, much less an abbess of Heloise's renown and dedication, could have given written expression to the unconventional opinions, sensual longings, and self-reflections contained in the letters seems highly unlikely to these historians. Indeed, writers in the Middle Ages generally did not write of their personal emotions, and for a woman to have done so is quite extraordinary.

Furthermore, assigning authorship of all letters to Abelard strips Heloise of the intellectual vigor that is apparent in her letters. Contemporaries of Heloise such as Peter the Venerable, Hugo Mettelus, William Godel, and Hugh Matel spoke of her learning. William Godel attributes to Heloise expert knowledge of Greek and Hebrew letters, an accomplishment that was almost unknown in her day by men or women. Moreover, Abelard himself, the greatest master of the age, writes that she stood supreme in the extent of her learning. Although it cannot be determined with certainty, it seems likely that Heloise did not lack the erudition to have composed the letters attributed to her.

Others have suggested that neither party wrote the letters at all, that in fact the letters are an imaginative product written after—perhaps more than a century after—the deaths of Heloise and Abelard. Most scholars reject this hypothesis. Based on meticulous investigation of details within

*Abelard's letters, they have shown that likely no forger could have imi-
tated Abelard's writing so thoroughly.*

*Barring a heretofore-undiscovered twelfth-century manuscript that con-
tains or refers to the letters, the controversy over their authorship will never
be resolved. Indeed, the discussion over the authenticity of the letters figures prominently in how we view Heloise and Abelard themselves. Was
Heloise an inferior intellect to Abelard's brilliance, incapable of original
thought? Does the correspondence demonstrate the exceptional qualities—
philosophical, religious, and literary—of the fateful couple? How one
answers these and other questions points to whether one accepts the
authenticity of the letters themselves.*

ABELARD'S RETURN TO TEACHING AT SAINT GENEVIÈVE

Even as Abelard was assisting Heloise with the Paraclete, his life was changing yet again; after more than five years as abbot, he left the unruly monks at
Saint Gildas and once again returned to teaching in Paris. Well-known twelfth-
century intellectual John of Salisbury writes that he heard Abelard's lectures at
Saint Geneviève in 1136, although it seems likely that Abelard had returned to
Paris a few years before then, perhaps around 1133. Saint Geneviève was outside the actual city limits of Paris, and, therefore, Abelard as master was beyond the jurisdictional reach of the bishop of Paris. Abelard's return to Paris at
this time was probably precipitated by the return once again to royal favor—
this time as chancellor—of his patron and protector, Stephen of Garlande in
late 1132. The school was located on land that belonged to the abbey of which
Stephen of Garlande was dean, which perhaps gave Abelard the confidence to
take up the role of schoolmaster once again. Abelard had not been a master
in Paris for about 15 years, and in the intervening period, the city had become
a beacon of learning for masters and students alike. John of Salisbury writes
that students were drawn to Abelard as the most exciting and accomplished
teacher—that he was famous and admired by all. Abelard's return to Paris
marks likely his longest period of uninterrupted teaching. From about 1133
to about 1140, he was probably teaching logic and theology, and this time,
although his students were as enthusiastic about their charismatic master as
ever, Abelard's rival teachers, while probably not in accord with many of his
ideas—he was refining his ideas on the Trinity—did not attack him as Alberic
had in 1121. This time, the attacks on Abelard would come not from the masters of the schools but from William of Saint Thierry, Thomas of Morigny, and
Bernard, the powerful abbot of the Cistercian monastery of Clairvaux.

THE COUNCIL OF SENS AND ABELARD'S DEATH

Bernard's hostility toward Abelard went back at least to his days at the Paraclete, when, during a visit to the convent in 1138, Bernard had corrected

Heloise and her nuns on the version of the Lord's Prayer that they were reciting. The correction was a minor one, centered on whether one followed the version of the Lord's Prayer from the gospel of Saint Matthew or that of Saint Luke; Bernard preferred the latter. Rather than letting the criticism pass, Abelard took issue with Bernard over this relatively insignificant matter, and he wrote to the great abbot disputing the recommendation and impertinently pointing out that Bernard's own monastery had committed at least six such minor deviations from orthodox practices. It was certainly an impolitic confrontation, but Abelard's life was replete with ill-considered brashness. Bernard's animosity toward Abelard stemmed from more than an argument over this minor irritation; the two men differed fundamentally over the proper approach to religion. The clash between Abelard and Bernard grew from a fundamental disagreement over their approach to theology. Abelard held that rationality was the foundation of theology, while Bernard insisted that only through faith, founded not in rational intellectual processes but on an unreasoned spiritual leap, could humankind know God and his will. For Bernard, it seemed that Abelard's reliance on logic might attack the great mystery of faith.

The movement to silence Abelard began in the Lenten period of 1140. William of Saint Thierry, who had been present when Abelard first had been condemned at the Council of Soissons in 1121, wrote to Bernard accusing Abelard of general evils and specific heresies relating to Abelard's interpretation of the Trinity and the concept of sin and redemption. Abelard's ideas on the nature of the three persons of the Trinity had led to his condemnation at Soissons, and it seems that in the intervening years he had been reworking the condemned book. His interest in the question of sin goes back to his early days in Paris with Heloise, when the two lovers engaged in philosophical dialogues. We should remember that Abelard held that words themselves were not necessarily an accurate guide to truth: that they could distort the reality rather than define it, producing empty meanings. In a similar vein, Abelard's philosophy of intention, or intentionalism, asserted that right or wrong actions were predicated on the intentions of the person committing the acts, not on the actual results of those acts. The only true guide to morality was the intention of the soul, because sometimes an outward act of wickedness might produce a good result, and likewise an act of goodness might result in an evil outcome. Therefore, only interior motives, which can only be identified by the soul and cannot be falsified, can determine the moral value of an action. There is no consensus among historians as to whether Abelard's ideas were heretical or contrary to church orthodoxy of his day, but most agree that Abelard's views were not anti-religion or anti-clerical. However, around this time, he suffered a kind of guiltiness by association, as one of his students from Paris, Arnold of Brescia, was overtly subversive, advocating radical ideas like the abolition of church property.

A few months later, in mid-Lent 1140, Thomas of Morigny also attacked Abelard's ideas as heretical, citing many of the same sources William of Saint Thierry had cited. Bernard was keenly aware that Abelard had built his reputation by defeating his opponents in public disputation, and he was anxious to avoid a public confrontation with the feisty logician. On the other hand, Bernard was at his strongest in one-on-one encounters, drawing on his immense gravitas and authority. Bernard's prominence depended on reprimanding Abelard in such a way that confirmed the great abbot's prestige and demonstrated that Abelard was subject to his judgment, and so he met privately with Abelard. According to Bernard's biographer Geoffrey of Auxerre, Abelard agreed to accept Bernard's corrections, although other sources disagree with this statement. Whatever the truth of the matter, shortly after the meeting with Bernard, Abelard requested of Henry the archbishop of Sens that either the matter should be determined at the upcoming large church council or Bernard should withdraw his accusations. For his part, Bernard now took actions to garner support, preaching against Abelard to students in Paris and denouncing Abelard to Pope Innocent II in Rome, urging him to move against the heretic.

The Council of Sens that was convened on June 2, 1140, was a large affair. Although he did not play a role in the proceedings, King Louis VII of France attended. Louis's father had died about three years earlier, resulting in the final fall from grace of Stephen of Garlande, who was no longer chancellor, although his replacement was an ally. Others in attendance included Henry the archbishop of Sens; Hugh the bishop of Auxerre, Bernard's relative and biographer; Geoffrey the bishop of Chartres, who had spoken in Abelard's favor at the Council of Soissons; and Thibauld the count of Champagne, Abelard's supporter but also a patron of Bernard's monastery at Clairvaux. The auspicious occasion, attended by so many of the luminaries of the day, was held not simply to address the charges levied by Bernard against Abelard, although the dispute between the powerful and influential abbot and the famous master must have loomed large in the minds of many in attendance. In 1140, a formal judicial procedure to try heretics had not yet been established under canon law, so technically the council was not a trial, although it certainly has that flavor. The chief prosecutor, essentially, was Bernard of Clairvaux.

Bernard must have recognized that defeating Abelard in a disputation before the council would be difficult, so instead he turned to a strategy that drew on his personal dignity and authority. The night before the council convened, Bernard assembled a private meeting of almost all of the bishops in attendance plus the archbishops of Sens and Reims. The men met in an informal atmosphere that Bernard dominated by reading out the 19 propositions or supposed heretical teachings of Abelard one at a time and then inviting the assembled bishops to condemn the charges. Although Hyacinth Boboni, an official from the papal court who would be elevated to the papal throne as Pope Celestine III in 1191, opposed Bernard, the impressive abbot prevailed in securing the support of most of the bishops; the bishops agreed to condemn the 19 heretical propositions.

The following day at the council, Bernard gave a striking presentation (described by Henry the archbishop of Sens). He held up a copy of Abelard's *Theologia Christiana* before the assembled and declared that he would expose all the charges as either absurd or heretical. Then Bernard began to enumerate the questionable propositions, which the bishops had agreed to condemn the night before. The propositions were essentially identical to those in the letter from William of Saint Thierry to Bernard of the previous year. Abelard was given three options: deny them, defend them, or correct them. Abelard instead chose to bring the proceedings to a halt by appealing to the judgment of the pope, and he and his supporters departed the council. Writing of events after the fact, Geoffrey of Auxerre describes Abelard as confused; his reason had left him. It is impossible to know whether Abelard was indeed confused by events or whether, perhaps, he was ill. However, it is just as likely that he saw the papal appeal as a way to avoid Bernard's trap and sidestep the condemnation that he recognized was the inevitable outcome of the council.

Pope Innocent II and Abelard had met when Innocent had approved the transfer of the Paraclete to Heloise at the dedication of the abbey church of Morigny in 1131. Yet the situation with Innocent was complicated. As a cardinal, he had worked with William of Champeaux, Abelard's former master and rival, to negotiate the Concordat of Worms in 1122, which ended the protracted controversy between the German emperor and the papacy, a classic conflict between the proper roles of church and state. During the papal election in 1130, because of a split among the cardinals, one faction elected Pope Innocent II and the other elected Pope Anacletus II, thereby creating what was termed a dual election. The party supporting Anacletus took control of Rome, forcing Innocent to flee the city and take refuge in France. Bernard of Clairvaux and Geoffrey the bishop of Chartres supported Innocent over Anacletus, and their prestige and influence drew the support of the French bishops and King Louis VI. Anacletus died in 1138, and the Second Lateran Council in 1139 asserted that Innocent was the rightful pope, ending the dual election. Therefore, Pope Innocent II was deeply in debt to Bernard for his support of the contested papal throne.

Abelard had appealed to the pope, although no condemnation had been actually pronounced by the council, an irregularity to be sure. Abelard, now in his sixties, set off for Rome. After he departed, the council indeed condemned Abelard's allegedly heretical writings. Yet Bernard was not pleased with the outcome; he, the archbishop of Reims, and the French bishops moved preemptively to influence the pope by writing to him, linking Abelard with the rebellious Arnold of Brescia and cautioning the pope and other cardinals not to be swayed by Abelard. To supplement the epistolary campaign, Bernard sent his secretary, Nicholas of Clairvaux, to deliver the letters to Innocent and his curia.

Although he was determined to pursue his appeal in Rome, on his way there Abelard stopped off, probably to rest, at the great Benedictine monastery of Cluny in Burgundy. The abbot of Cluny, Peter the Venerable (ca. 1092–1156), took in the troubled Abelard and tried to assure him that papal justice would not fail. Around 1128, Peter the Venerable had engaged in a dispute with Bernard of Clairvaux over the virtues of the Cluniac monasteries over Cistercian ones. Cluny had been founded in 910 as a reformed monastery; its founding charter explicitly placed it under the authority of the pope, thereby limiting lay influence in the affairs of the abbey. Dedicated to independence from lay control and emphasizing performance of the liturgy, Cluny inspired dozens of daughter houses across Europe; these subsidiary houses were a kind of federation that answered to the abbot of Cluny. The Cistercians, on the other hand, were of a much more recent foundation in Abelard's day. Emblematic of twelfth-century religious piety, the Cistercian order sought to return to the religious life laid out in the Rule of Saint Benedict, rejecting the developments monasteries such as Cluny had undergone over the centuries. As such, the Cistercians tended to emphasize an austerity that Bernard of Clairvaux asserted the Cluniacs lacked. Bernard had rebuked Peter the Venerable for Cluny's laxity.

Meanwhile, within six weeks of the Council of Sens, Pope Innocent II in consultation with bishops and cardinals had ruled against Abelard's appeal, condemning him for his malicious doctrines and teachings that were contrary to the Catholic faith. A sentence of perpetual silence was imposed on the heretic, and his defenders and followers were excommunicated. Furthermore, Abelard and Arnold of Brescia—although there is no evidence that Abelard was in communication with Arnold at this time, it seems that the seed that had been planted by Bernard had taken root—were to be confined to separate religious houses and their books burnt. Despite the condemnation, Peter the Venerable wrote to Innocent describing how he and Abbot Rainard of Cîteaux of the founding Cistercian monastery had guided a reconciliation between Abelard and Bernard at Clairvaux after advising Abelard that he should take correction from the abbot of Clairvaux if he had written or said anything that deviated from orthodoxy. Furthermore, Peter wrote that Abelard wished to make Cluny his home and to refrain from teaching. Mentioning his age and weakness, the abbot of Cluny wrote that he hoped Abelard would not be forced out of the monastery, rather that he be allowed to spend his remaining days in the shelter of the great monastery in Burgundy.

Abelard was surely ill at this time, perhaps suffering from cancer. He was allowed to remain at Cluny, although, out of consideration for Abelard's declining health, Peter the Venerable moved him to the small priory of Saint Marcel near Chalon-sur-Saône, not far from Cluny and still in Burgundy, but where the climate was more moderate.

Although this was to be Abelard's final journey, he remained intellectually active until his death. He wrote to Heloise a final letter, his so-called confession of faith, which he begins by naming her as his sister in Christ who had once been dear to him in the world, a reminder that his love for her was spiritual, not carnal. He affirms his Trinitarian orthodoxy and his confidence in faith as his refuge: "The storm may rage but I am unshaken, though the winds may blow they leave me unmoved; for the rock of my foundation stands firm." Peter the Venerable informed Heloise of Abelard's death in 1142 in a letter that is remarkable for its kindness and affection. He tells Heloise that her husband, he "who was yours, he who is often and ever named and honored as the servant and true philosopher of Christ" was active until the end, reading and engaging in philosophical discussions. To comfort Heloise in her loss, Peter wrote, "And so Master Peter ended his days. He who was known all over the world for his unique mastery of knowledge. God cherishes him in his bosom, and keeps him there to be restored to you through his grace at the coming of the Lord." Abelard had requested that his body be sent to the Paraclete, a request that was honored, although at the time of his death he was a monk of Cluny and should, therefore, have been buried there.

HELOISE'S LATER LIFE

Peter the Venerable continued to correspond with Heloise and visited the Paraclete on at least one occasion, probably when he brought Abelard's body for reburial. Heloise wrote to him in thanks and reminded him that he had agreed to send a document of absolution to be placed over Abelard's tomb, which he did. He also wrote an epitaph, praising Abelard as "our Aristotle, prince of scholars." Peter also offered to find a prebend in a great church for "your Astralabe," presumably the son of Heloise and Abelard, who would have been in his twenties. There is no definitive record of what became of Astralabe, although there are tantalizing but inconclusive clues as to what may have been his fate. The name was uncommon, and so any mention of an Astralabe stands out in the records. Astralabe was the name of a cathedral canon at Nantes in 1150, and of an abbot at the Cistercian monastery of Hauterive in Fribourg from 1162 to 1165, where the necrology lists "Peter Astralabe son of our Master Peter," although it is not possible to know irrefutably whether these mentions refer to the son of Heloise and Abelard.

Peter the Venerable never read the eight letters exchanged between Heloise and Abelard, and he assumed that she had set aside her desire for the physical love of her husband in favor of her new life as a nun. Had he read their letters, he would have realized that Heloise had not surrendered her yearning for physical closeness and refrained from writing about it only out of obedience to Abelard. She acknowledged in her second letter to Abelard that her inner life, her soul, in which her intention dwelled, had not embraced the religious life, and so before God she deserved no praise. Heloise lived another 22 years after Abelard's death, until about 1164. During this final third of her life, she further demonstrated her considerable abilities as the abbess of the Paraclete. When she died, the convent had given life to six daughter houses and owned considerable properties in the valley of the Ardusson, the small stream on which the Paraclete was situated. In all, Abelard had provided the nuns with a rule that established a uniform liturgy between Paraclete and her daughter houses, a hymnal (Heloise had complained to Abelard that there were no hymns to honor women who were neither virgins nor saints), and a series of six *planctus*, or laments on biblical themes.

THE FINAL RESTING PLACES OF ABELARD AND HELOISE

Heloise was buried next to Abelard in the abbey church at the Paraclete, the small oratory that had been built by Abelard's students in the early years after his arrival there. Beginning soon after her death, their remains contributed significantly to their enduring fame. In 1204, an anonymous poet wrote that when the tomb was opened to receive Heloise's body, Abelard raised his arms and clasped her in an embrace. A new oratory was built, and the bones were moved from the dampness of the original tomb (caused by the proximity of the Ardusson stream) to positions on either side of the high altar. By 1621, a more impressive monument was constructed for the famous couple, below an altar that was atop a stone with a carving depicting the Three Persons of the Trinity that Abelard had supposedly commissioned. As with so much else in France, the Revolution changed the circumstances of the dead lovers. Their bodies had been moved twice before then, in 1701 and 1780, each time to a more prestigious location in the Paraclete, but in 1791, the Paraclete was dissolved, the building abandoned, and the buildings sold and eventually demolished. Heloise and Abelard were moved to the church of Saint Laurent in nearby Nogent-sur-Seine, where they reportedly attracted visitors, although revolutionaries had vandalized their tomb in 1794. By 1800, the couple was on the move again, this time to Paris. Alexandre Lenoir had been instructed by the Assemblée Nationale to preserve artifacts from religious institutions that had been destroyed in the Revolution. Therefore, the remains of Heloise and Abelard were moved to the Musée des Monuments Français, where they stayed from 1800 to 1817.

In 1817, the remains were moved for the final time, to Père Lachaise Cemetery, originally called Mont Louis, in an effort to raise the prestige of the 10-year-old cemetery, which had struggled to attract the attention of well-heeled Parisians because it was considered too far east of the city. The bodies, still in what Lenoir believed was Abelard's original tomb, were installed under a large Gothic Revival canopy. Père Lachaise today is a cemetery to the famous, the final resting place of notables like Oscar Wilde, Jim Morrison, Honoré de Balzac, Sarah Bernhardt, Georges Bizet, Maria Callas, Frédéric Chopin, Jacques-Louis David, Molière, Édith Piaf, and Richard Wright. Today, the tomb of Heloise and Abelard attracts many visitors; most Parisian travel guides recommend a visit and often mention the tomb of the famous couple. On most days, flowers are found surrounding the full-sized effigies, left by admiring moderns who feel they know the celebrated couple through their extraordinary letters. What is actually in the tomb is uncertain. The last abbess of the Paraclete reported in 1792 that Abelard's body had been completely reduced to dust except for the skull, which she described as unusually large.

THE ENDURING LEGACY

Why have Heloise and Abelard captured the public imagination for nearly 900 years? Although any single explanation is certainly insufficient, a likely reason is that their story is so amenable to differing interpretations. At least from the time that the anonymous poet wrote of Abelard reaching out in death to embrace his beloved as she was interred next to him, only about four decades after Heloise's death, poets have been preoccupied by their tragic yet enduring love. The great medieval poet Jean de Meun was so taken with the letters of Heloise and Abelard that he translated them from Latin into French and inserted them into his continuation of the *Romance of the Rose*. In 1717, the English poet Alexander Pope published a poem titled "Eloisa to Abelard." Written as a letter from Heloise to Abelard after his castration and their separation, Pope's intent was to give voice to Heloise's torment over her love for Abelard that could no longer be expressed. Her dreams of their lost love haunt her, and in her anguish, she pleads not for forgiveness but to forget.

Lines 207–10 of Pope's "Eloisa to Abelard" are quoted in the 2004 film *The Eternal Sunshine of the Spotless Mind*, from a screenplay by Charlie Kaufman, and the title itself comes from line 209. In 1999, Kaufman had also borrowed Pope's poem for the film *Being John Malkovich*, this time as a puppet show featuring the two lovers. Other film adaptations from literature include *Stealing Heaven* (1988), based on Marion Meade's book of the same title. Directed by Clive Donner, the film is clearly produced for modern sensibilities: it is packed with erotic scenes. It is no surprise that the film is largely devoted to Abelard's first Parisian period, when he met and seduced Heloise. The book also served as a model for the 2002 opera by Stephen Paulus, with a libretto by Frank Corsaro, that was commissioned by the Juilliard School in New York.

The tragic love story of Heloise and Abelard has also made the transition from novels to stage play. Irish scholar Helen Waddell's novel *Peter Abelard* (1933) was used as the basis for Ronald Millar's play *Heloise and Abelard* (1970). The book enjoyed considerable success and brought a balanced presentation of the lovers' story to a general audience. The play based on the book was produced first in a small London staging in 1969, starring Diana Rigg and Keith Mitchell, and then on Broadway in 1971 in a larger production.

On the operatic stage, the New York Opera Repertory Theatre put on a 1984 production of an opera titled *Abelard and Heloise*, scored by Robert Ward and with a libretto by Jan Hartman. Enrico Garzilli's *Rage of the Heart* is a musical play based on the Heloise-Abelard love story, with a symphonic score and lyrical songs (copyrighted 1971–95). It was produced in 1997 in Providence, Rhode Island, and, according to the official website (http://www.rageoftheheart.com/index.php), a new production is being planned in Germany. An 11-track CD is available, and the lyrics are given on the website.

Incidental cultural references to Heloise and Abelard are far too numerous to relate here, but they range from Mark Twain, Robertson Davies, Henry Miller, J. D. Salinger, and Leonard Cohen to a 2004 episode of the TV series *The Sopranos* ("A Sentimental Education"). The endless fascination with the lovers stems in part from their tragic love, yet the full story is more complex than the merely sensational. On the eve of the emergence of medieval universities, their lives intersected with some of the towering figures of their day: the indomitable Bernard of Clairvaux; Peter the Venerable, abbot of the influential monastery of Cluny; scholar and diplomat John of Salisbury. Furthermore, Abelard's innovative philosophical ideas on universals, the application of dialectic to the study of theology, his willingness to use propositions to sort out contradictions, and his conviction that language was the chief concern of logic were startling in their originality. With Heloise, he articulated an ethical system that placed the moral value of actions on the intention of the individual, rather than on the outcome. Heloise was renowned for her learning, and her knowledge of languages and letters is demonstrated in her correspondence. Therefore, to reduce the lives of Heloise and Abelard simply to their love affair may trivialize their contributions as mirrors of the twelfth-century renaissance, but it remains central to the fascination that they have produced over the centuries in the popular imagination.

FURTHER READING

Abailard, Peter. *Sic et non: A Critical Edition*. Ed. Blanche Boyer and Richard McKeon. Chicago: University of Chicago Press, 1976.

Abelard, Peter. *Ethical Writings: "Ethics" and "Dialogue between a Philosopher, a Jew, and a Christian*. Trans. Paul Vincent Spade. Introd. Marilyn McCord Adams. Indianapolis: Hackett, 1995.

Abelard, Peter. *Collationes*. Ed. and trans. John Marenbon and Giovanni Orlandi. Oxford Medieval Texts. Oxford: Clarendon Press, 2001.

Brower, Jeffrey E., and Kevin Guilfoy, eds. *The Cambridge Companion to Abelard*. Cambridge: Cambridge University Press, 2004.

Burge, James. *Heloise & Abelard: A New Biography*. [San Francisco]: Harper San Francisco, 2003.

Clanchy, Michael T. *Abelard: A Medieval Life*. Oxford: Blackwell, 1997.

Dronke, Peter. *A History of Twelfth-Century Western Philosophy*. Cambridge: Cambridge University Press, 1988.

Levitan, William. *Abelard & Heloise: The Letters and Other Writings*. Indianapolis: Hackett, 2007.

Luscombe, David E. *Peter Abelard*. 2nd ed. Burford, Oxfordshire: Davenant Press, 2001.

Marenbon, John. *The Philosophy of Peter Abelard*. Cambridge: Cambridge University Press, 1997.

McLaughlin, Mary Martin, with Bonnie Wheeler, eds. and trans. *The Letters of Heloise and Abelard: A Translation of Their Collected Correspondence and Related Writings*. New York: Palgrave Macmillan, 2009.

Mews, C. J. *Abelard and Heloise*. New York: Oxford University Press, 2005.

Mews, Constant J. *The Lost Letters of Heloise and Abelard: Perceptions of Dialogue in Twelfth-Century France*. The New Middle Ages. With translations by Neville Chiavaroli and Constant J. Mews. New York: St. Martin's Press, 1999.

Newman, Barbara. *From Virile Woman to Woman Christ: Studies in Medieval Religion and Literature*. Philadelphia: University of Pennsylvania Press, 1995.

Radice, Betty, trans. *The Letters of Abelard and Heloise*. Rev. ed. Introd. and annot. M. T. Clanchy. Penguin Classics. London: Penguin Books, 2004.

Wheeler, Bonnie. *Listening to Heloise: The Voice of a Twelfth-Century Woman*. New York: St. Martin's Press, 2000.

Ziolkowski, Jan M., trans. *Letters of Peter Abelard: Beyond the Personal*. Washington, DC: Catholic University of America Press, 2008.

Merlin tutoring Arthur, from the *Roman du Roy Meliadus de Leon-noys*, about 1352. (British Library/Art Resource, NY)

King Arthur and Merlin

Stephen T. Knight

INTRODUCTION

The story of Arthur, exploring the possibilities and the fragilities of secular power, is vigorously alive after a thousand years. It originates in early Welsh mythic story and has long been disseminated in richly varied ways in transnational cultures. It is not a basis of a historical or biographical tradition: the idea of a "real King Arthur" derives from modern obsessions with identity—personal and national—and will be discussed in the context of other modern realizations of the myth.

Medieval Arthur stories have two major formations. In Arthurian romance, Arthur is a largely offstage overlord, dispensing chivalric honor to the individual knights who are focal to each story; in Arthurian saga, he is himself central as the emergent, triumphant, and finally tragic, though always mythic, king. The Round Table is a linking mechanism, the base for the separate knights of romance, the guarantor of their values, and the domain of their glory; then its fall is the marker of Arthurian tragedy. Merlin has no real role in the single-hero stories, but in the Arthur-focused tragedies his knowledge both helps establish the king and foresees worse days to come. Guinevere tends only to be part of the honorific context for the romances, with an exceptional role as Lancelot's beloved in his own romance: this double role also makes her central to the tragic saga as love and duty, both honorable in different ways, come into inevitable conflict.

THE EARLIEST TEXTS

The two earliest Arthurian texts exemplify the two forms of romance and saga. In *Culhwch and Olwen,* a Welsh prose story dating in large part from about 1000, Arthur is a tribal lord, chief of the princes of the island of Britain—never a king: Wales did not then, and scarcely does now, envisage such centralization—who assists his nephew Culhwch to win the beautiful daughter of the terrible Ysbaddaden, chief giant of the island of Britain. Interweaving folklore, comedy, and myth (a wise salmon, a teasing wedding-preparation test, and a ferocious giant boar who was once a wicked prince), this archetypal pattern of single-hero story was later sophisticated, and also simplified, into French feudal romance.

Another Welshman, Geoffrey of Monmouth, produced the original Arthurian saga in about 1136. The idea that he was a Breton draws merely on his criticism of the Welsh and his praise of the Bretons, a judgment naively unfamiliar with the incisive attitudes of writers, notably Celtic ones: the clerics who wrote the early Welsh saints' lives at times ridicule Arthur to aggrandize their church. Geoffrey's *History of the Kings of Britain* offers in fine Latin prose an origin-legend for Celtic Britain, founded by the Trojan exile Brutus, and rich in elaborated narrative and royal shenanigans. Arthur's glory is the focal moment before the British are swamped by the Saxons: as a result the

Norman conquest of Arthur's enemies is implied by Geoffrey to be a justified anti-English vengeance. Like any Norman king, Arthur boldly leads heavy cavalry against the whole of Europe, builds castles and cathedrals to confirm and ratify his triumph, and in equally Norman fashion suffers the treason of his family members.

For Geoffrey of Monmouth, Merlin is behind Arthur, if at some distance. Under this name are combined the Welsh Myrddin, a sixth-century forest exile and visionary (quite possibly a historical prince of Celtic Cumbria, remembered in Wales), and the late fifth-century myth of Ambrosius, a wonderful sub-Roman boy. As the archetype of knowledge in service of, and so inherently opposed to, power, Geoffrey's Merlin outwits the pro-Saxon Vortigern and his doltish advisers, and then skillfully serves Uther, Arthur's father, building Stonehenge as a war memorial to the British dead in the anti-Saxon wars. He also prophesies the Celtic *reconquista* of Britain, long awaited in Wales, but though he arranges Arthur's conception, he never actually encounters the mythic king.

Arthur succeeds Uther when young, seizes his kingdom, defeats France, builds a great capital at Caerleon, and responds to insults from Rome by humiliating it in war. In this hubristic process, future figures of romance like Gawain and Kay lead Arthur's columns in ferocious fighting, described in the Latin tradition of martial writing. But as Arthur is to seize Rome like his Celtic ancestor Brennus, he hears that Mordred (here just his nephew) has seized his own capital and queen. He hurries back, fights his usurper and—the first appearance of a crucial part of the myth—may or may not have died.

ROBERT WACE AND CHRÉTIEN DE TROYES

Geoffrey's story was amazingly popular, surviving in some two hundred Latin manuscripts and translated across the European languages. The crucial transmission was into French verse, in about 1155, by the Channel Islander Robert Wace. The saga he transmitted interacted with orally transmitted Celtic hero stories—Breton as well as Welsh, like those transmitted in the mostly non-Arthurian lais of Marie de France—as Chrétien de Troyes created his Arthurian romances by the 1170s, assuming the existence of the saga structure and richly elaborating it by exploring with suggestive genius the genre of single-hero adventure. Unlike the essentially communal and tribal epic lord, the romance hero rides and fights alone, testing his own inner resources and gaining love. Not just any amorous individual, he is the son of a great lord or king, and he will enjoy not only the beauty of the lady he loves but also the kingdom she happens to inherit.

Chrétien's poems are lucid, deeply imaginative, and subtly varied. *Yvain*— alias "The Knight with the Lion"—is the archetype, as a king's son gains, loses, and through his suffering (and with the help of a lion) regains his lady— and so his land. *Cligès,* the first, is a more classically oriented story of love lost and found, while the powerful, enigmatic *Lancelot*—also de-individualized as "The Knight of the Cart"—both realizes and idealizes the hero's love for Guinevere. *Erec and Enide* reverses the hero-alone story, showing a husband becoming too uxorious for honor, but finally he, and indeed she, will regain a contemporary balance of gender and power, in which the male is officially in charge. In the unfinished, and so presumably last of Chrétien's extraordinary repertoire, *Perceval,* deheroized as "The Story of the Grail," a naive knight from North Wales learns a deeply moral rather than blandly chivalric lesson in the context of a "grail," an object that seems clearly, if also obscurely, Christian in its thematic connections.

These potent stories would reverberate for centuries. They symbolically project the concerns of the newly peaceful, newly rich medieval world that also created superb cathedrals and manuscripts. Women like Chrétien's sponsor Marie countess of Champagne now played major cultural roles, and *fin amor* recognizes their power, if from a male viewpoint, just as Morgan la Fée represents their threat to masculinity. The lonely knight, winning Arthur's praise and a land outside royal power, seems to represent the dukes and counts of France, powerful vis-à-vis the weak but still glorious central king: even more materially it has been suggested the heroes are also fantasy figures for the landless warriors who were in substantial numbers generated by the new practice of restricting inheritance to the eldest son.

Many writers followed Chrétien in the single-hero romance, in many languages, if without his genius, and new story-threads were attracted to this sprawling world of Arthurian narrative. The story of Tristan and Isolde came into French from Celtic (Drwst is quite probably a Pictish prince, and Cornwall has a memorial stone that appears to honor him): their fated tragic love inspired a great German poem by Gottfried von Strassburg and would interweave with the Arthurian story and be the source for the royal adultery of Guinevere and Lancelot. Another major implant was the story of the Holy Grail. Chrétien's tenuous symbol of a knight's need for charitable morality soon becomes a chalice secreting the blood of Christ, and the intense popularity of this idea appears to respond to the Western loss of the Holy Land after the catastrophic battle of Hattin in 1187: it appears that Chrétien's supple and mysterious narrative, which can hardly post-date that event, provided a matrix to displace the spiritual trauma. The Grail story asserts that something was indeed saved from the ruin. It is here, somewhere in the West, but we can find it only through our own perfection, and by implication our regular attendance at Mass.

Chrétien's continuators of *Perceval* made the Grail more mainstream Christian, but the key event was when in about 1200 Robert de Boron generated a back story for the Grail, in which the chalice arrives from the Holy Land with the crucifixion witness Joseph of Arimathea. Robert also wrote a *Merlin* that linked this Christian continuity to the arrival of Arthur and gave his vizier the capacity to foresee Christian teleology. Though Wolfram von Eschenbach's German *Parzifal* (ca. 1205) drew grandly on Robert de Boron, in the French developments both Merlin as the devil's-son-turned-Grail-prophet and Perceval as the holy-fool-turned-Grail-achiever were to be replaced with the perfect knight Galahad as by about 1220 the story was reshaped in more austerely Christian mode as the *Queste del Saint Graal*.

THE VULGATE

More fully within the Arthur story was the development of Chrétien's *Lancelot* into a massive prose epic. French and Breton, never British, in setting as well as in courtly and chivalrous themes, this story joined the Grail and the *Mort Artu*, the final tragedy, as the major elements of the Vulgate or *Lancelot-Grail*, in which the separate hero stories, now massively expanded, were by about 1225 consolidated into a great Arthurian saga that embraces the French feudal efflorescence of single-hero romances in the new medium of secular demotic prose narrative, an Arthurian parallel to the originary narratives of the new European nations, and a validating gift of the new administrative clerical class to their lordly secular employers.

First in this massive Vulgate collection comes the *History of the Holy Grail*, reworking Robert's Grail prequel; then his *Merlin* was both expanded and made more secular. No Grail prophet now, Merlin helps Arthur develop and defend his kingdom until he himself disappears through the power of Vivian, both an image of the new authority of the courtly lady, like Chrétien's own countess, and also a sign of the lord-pleasing idea of the inherent vulnerability of knowledge on its own. Then follows a massive set of Lancelot's honorific adventures in war and love; next the *Quest of the Holy Grail* shows through Galahad's perfection how chivalry makes sinners of the knights, especially Lancelot; and finally the *Mort Artu* reveals how the tragedy is linked to the sins that have been exposed in the heavily moralized Christian Grail story.

There is no one authoritative version of the Vulgate, just a mass of manuscripts with overlapping texts. Some scholars argue there was a full revised "Post-Vulgate," but in fact this has no textual entity other than a version of the *Merlin* notable for its darker tone, in keeping with the *Queste*—and probably just a rewriting in the light of that saintly intervention. Here Balin and Balan figure fraternal violence, Merlin is a sex-pest whom Vivian disposes of fiercely, all ends bleakly, and the Arthurian tragedy to come is regarded with some complacency. Though rare in manuscripts, this version is well-known in the English tradition, simply because Malory chose it as the source for his opening sequence, but the concept of a complete "Post-Vulgate" is a modern scholarly invention, remarkably unchallenged. It relies on nothing more than the revised *Merlin* and two stray Spanish and Portuguese texts that develop the role of Merlin as a from-the-grave prophet after his entombment by Vivian.

The Vulgate's massively influential combination of single-hero romance and Arthurian saga was much transmitted and translated, often in reduced and locally varied form. An example is the English *Arthur and Merlin*, a poem of about 1300 that cuts back the France-focused action of the Vulgate and simplifies the British history to suit an English viewpoint: Arthur eventually fights not the Saxons, the actual and in this nation-building context embarrassingly British-hostile ancestors of the English, but very remarkably—and still in Britain—the Saracens.

THE ARTHURIAN LEGEND IN ENGLAND

This re-politicizing, and re-nationalizing, of Arthur meshes with other important English versions. Two massive alliterative sagas in English drew intimately and independently on Geoffrey of Monmouth, if through Wace: Lawman's *Brut* from about 1200 and the anonymous late fourteenth-century alliterative *Morte Arthur* are epic celebrations that appropriate Arthur from his originary Celtic Britain to be a king of an imagined and racially united English kingdom. Lawman has the boldness, or perhaps the effrontery, to assert finally that Arthur might return after his mysterious passing "to help the English"—not what the Celtic "chief of the princes of this island" would have had in mind.

In the late medieval period Arthur had a specific political role in Britain, appearing in many chronicles, often with Merlin's support, as an archetype of British, and often just English, kingship. He also had Europe-wide status, being enlisted as one of the three Christian worthies, ranking with Charlemagne, who was the founder of the Holy Roman Empire, and Godfrey of Bouillon, who conquered Jerusalem on the First Crusade. That grandeur led to Arthur's being used as a mythic validator for English kings—Edward I appears to have built a real Round Table; Edward III installed Arthurian culture at court; Henry VII, claiming a Welsh right to the throne, named his eldest son Arthur, though Renaissance scholarship also nudged the name toward the classically named star Arcturus, and the Tudor affiliation to Arthurian glory has been overstated by some scholars.

SIR THOMAS MALORY'S *MORTE DARTHUR*

Linking medieval and modern Arthurian traditions stands Sir Thomas Malory. Varied medieval literary traditions are gathered in his *Morte Darthur* (1485), drawing on French and English work, and once more combining many romance narratives inside the saga frame. He starts by condensing the post-Vulgate *Merlin* but follows it, as no French source does, with the story of Arthur's war on Rome taken from the English alliterative *Morte*, without its tragic ending. Then he fills the massive middle of his book with a very short Lancelot romance out of the huge French prose *Lancelot*, apparently invents a Gareth romance, and then drifts into the Tristram story. After many pages he abandons this to start a powerful final sequence. The Grail story asserts the Christian virtues as in its source, the *Queste* (perhaps linking with, even explaining, Malory's choice of the highly Christian post-Vulgate *Merlin* to begin), but it also elevates Lancelot who, though a moral failure, is still "the best earthly knight." The last two sequences are the "Lancelot and Guinevere," a skillfully assembled and invented sequence that shows the steady darkening of events around the lovers, though also maintaining their inherent nobility, then "The Death of Arthur" retells the familiar story with some fine new speeches in which characters reflect on their situation. The whole culminates in a calm—and so highly memorable—account of the mysterious passing of Arthur and, staying with Lancelot to the end, shows how he and Guinevere atone for their sins.

Both a very late manuscript and a very early printed book, with a driving coordinate narrative style that can also pause for subordinated subtlety, especially in the late speeches that Malory adds, his hugely influential Arthuriad is not a single unity, nor is it simply didactic in its meanings. Its creative multiplicity has given it enormous impact over time, though there was a fallow period as Malory, like Arthur, became somewhat recessive from the time that the Renaissance scholar Polydore Vergil rejected the historical claims of Geoffrey of Monmouth and the Puritan Roger Ascham found Malory contained "bold bawdry and open manslaughter."

KING ARTHUR IN THE RENAISSANCE AND POST-RENAISSANCE

There were some Renaissance reformations of Arthur, like Spenser's moralized Prince Arthur in *The Faerie Queene* (1590–96), who represents the "Magnanimous Man," the sum of all the allegorical virtues that the knights represented, but he is basically outside the narrative, replaced as warrior and romantic hero by his equal, Arthegal, and as glorious monarch by Gloriana—or Elizabeth—herself. Neither Thomas Hughes's Senecan tragedy *The Misfortunes of Arthur* (1587) nor Michael Drayton's Arthurian topographic myths in *Poly-Olbion* (1612) had real impact: Jonson, Milton, and Dryden all considered an Arthurian epic but saw the error of such non-classical thoughts, though Dryden did produce the fine early opera *King Arthur the British Worthy* (1691), with even finer music by Henry Purcell. This stimulated Richard Blackmore, a literary-minded doctor memorably described by Pope as "the everlasting Blackmore," to produce in 1695 and 1697 two pro-Whig epics, *Prince Arthur* and *King Arthur,* which turgidly validate the new Protestant king, William of Orange, who knighted him. A Tory response was the comedy of Fielding's *Tom Thumb* (1730), in which the tiny hero comes to the court of Arthur and his queen, Dollalolla, and all ends in burlesque massacre. Eliza Haywood turned it into a musical comedy in which Merlin rescues Tom Thumb when the cow who swallowed him succumbs to the wizard's emetic magic.

KING ARTHUR IN THE NINETEENTH CENTURY

Even after these embarrassments, neither Arthur nor Merlin was quite forgotten, especially on the stage, and by the end of the eighteenth century scholars like Thomas Warton and Joseph Ritson and anthologists like Thomas Percy, Thomas Evans, and George Ellis had transmitted the materials of the tradition to a reviving interest: three reprints of Malory appeared in 1816–17. But the English Romantics saw little value in a medieval tradition that was not based in personal moral authenticity: an interesting effort to rewrite Malory in verse like Reginald Heber's *Morte D'Arthur* (ca. 1810) was uncompleted, while Wordsworth in *The Bridal of Triermain* (1813) and Scott in *The Lady of the Lake* (1810) made Arthurian characters, especially Merlin, the enemies of morality. But Arthur did have some positive role in the period. Cornish, Welsh, and Scottish writers found him and Merlin useful to validate a separate identity, and some little-remembered English texts offered Arthurian adventure in the far north—including the Arctic and the Northwest Passage. John Dee had drawn this idea from Arthur's Norman-Viking adventures in Geoffrey of Monmouth to justify Elizabethan claims, and the Arctic Arthur thrived in Richard Hole's *Arthur, or the Northern Enchantment* (1789), John Thelwall's *The Fairy of the Lake* (1801), Charles Milman's *Samor, Lord of the Bright City* (1818), and, grandest and most Northwest Passage–connected of all, Bulwer Lytton's stanzaic epic *King Arthur* (1848).

Interesting as these activities are, it was Tennyson who brought Arthur back to vigorous life. His scholarship and his feeling for the death of Arthur Hallam led to the "Morte Darthur" in 1833, and he long planned the discontinuous epic that started with four poems in 1859, to be completed as the 12 *Idylls of the King* in 1885, ending with the still Hallam-connected "The Passing of Arthur." As he began the great work, Tennyson drew on the Vulgate for "Merlin and Vivien" and the Welsh Mabinogion romances for what would be "The Marriage of Geraint" and "Geraint and Enid" (originally one long idyll), but his major source was Malory, selecting episodes to explore aspirations and, mostly, failures. Arthur is a moral monarch with no real enemies except human weakness: most of his supporters are derailed by temptation, whether sexual (as with Merlin, Pelleas, and Tristram), mystical (as with Galahad), or simply the attractions of indiscipline (as with Gawain, Pelleas, Balin, and Balan). But for male weakness in general, the ultimate blame is sheeted home to women like Vivien, Ettare, and Isolt, and the central errant figure of Guinevere, whose infidelity is made, in Arthur's own and almost completely unforgiving voice, the main cause for tragedy.

Tennyson reestablished the Arthurian theme in terms of a masculinist, moralist, and royalist myth that had failed in the face of modern fallibility and sensuality, but the poem's text and imagery richly creates the sensual world that it sees as the bane of all goodness. Many conservative writers in Britain and the United States reworked these themes, usually clumsily, especially in verse plays around 1900: poets such as T. S. Eliot and David Jones were to see both Tennyson and Arthur as old-world and used the myth only in referential ways, but, through working in the modernist fragmentary mode, their treatment was also potent. The strongest anti-Tennysonian voice was Mark Twain in *A Connecticut Yankee at King Arthur's Court* (1889). In *Yankee,* Arthur is at first a cruel fool, and Twain's illustrator, Dan Beard (1850–1941), depicted the mean-minded Merlin as Tennyson himself. But Twain also projected his satire of medieval and modern England into a critique of the United States. The final battle is a Civil War version of Camlan, as the Yankee, rich in both technology and self-confidence, slaughters the whole chivalry of England and Arthur is finally seen not as a feudal bully, but as a valid human spirit, a royal individual.

KING ARTHUR IN THE MODERN AGE

Arthur the man, trying to be a good ruler in time of conflict, is central to twentieth-century versions of the myth, and his efforts and struggles dominate the thematic action as never before. Crucial to this is Merlin as the humanist educator of this modern human king. The idea of an educative Merlin had been around for some time, especially as a containment of the bearded druid-bard that non-English Romantics, from Wieland to Emerson, saw as Merlin. Yet it is learning, not magic, that empowers Arthur's education: a key development is the long poem *Merlin* (1917), by the American Edwin Arlington Robinson, in which Merlin is a highly intelligent person, not a seer or magician, who leaves his beloved and equally human Vivien to watch helplessly as the world of the Arthur he has mentored falls tragically apart. Robinson was well aware of the context as the United States set itself to send men to face the brutalities of modern war. This kind of Arthurian tragedy was more fully realized through Malory's narrative by T. H. White, writing between 1936 and 1941. In White's prequel *The Sword in the Stone* (1938), Merlin trains Arthur in natural knowledge, and so he grows up to know that Might should not be Right—but fails to achieve his dream of an educated liberal order as the tragic events slowly build up in three books based on Malory and with their own nobility of tone. White, writing like Robinson in the darkness of war, confronted the problems in his final volume *The Book of Merlyn,* which argues fractiously about human limitations and, like White himself, places more faith in the world of nature. Antihumanist and prophetic of ecology, an avatar of Orwell's contemporary dark fantasies, this last book was not published until 1977 and still haunts Arthurian writing as a version of the tragedy without the consolation of either Christianity or literary elegance.

Both the imaginative charm of White's first book and the sweep of the full Malorian series of *The Once and Future King* (1958) stimulated many stories, often for juveniles, most retaining faith in Arthurian values. Authors like Catherine Christian, Victor Canning, and Mary Stewart continued the combination of single adventures in a saga frame, often published in series form. These reworkings can be highly original, like Susan Cooper's *The Dark Is*

Rising series (1965–77); they can involve fantasy and time-travel, mix in elements of Celtic magic, bring Americans to Arthurian Europe, or even relocate the story to America. So they continue the tradition of Hawthorne and Twain in reshaping European myth to have modern meaning in the United States, and often showing a greater precision in history, geography, and especially names than the more casual British writers feel the need to offer.

Arthurian film has been less rich than fiction. *A Connecticut Yankee* was often adapted, usually for children, with notable successes starring Will Rogers and Bing Crosby, but adult Arthurian films are relatively few, and his name in the title is even rarer: kings seem to appeal less in the United States than England, and the story is locked into an unappealingly dark ending. Some Arthurian films acquire positive endings: *The Knights of the Round Table* (1954) leaves Perceval to carry on in the light of the Grail; in *First Knight* (1995) Lancelot and Guinevere simply inherit the kingship and the future; the 1999 television series *Merlin* makes Arthur's death a secondary event as the magician acquires final happiness with a rejuvenated Nimue. Tragedy was avowed in Robert Bresson's French *Lancelot du Lac* (1974), but its brutal ending was one of the many Arthurian sonorities mocked in *Monty Python and the Holy Grail* (1975).

Another strand in Arthurian modernity has been the idea, or fantasy, of the historicity of Arthur. Though some scholars had, since Gibbon, long suspected some truth behind the ninth-century *Historia Brittonum*'s account of Arthur's battles with the Saxons, it was R. G. Collingwood in 1935 who first argued forcefully that Arthur was a Roman-British leader who held up the Saxon advance for some time, and so made Britain neither fully Germanic nor fully Celtic (and also conveniently linked the British Empire back to Rome). The appeal of an un-Teutonic Britain was especially evident after the Nazi period, and fiction developed the Collingwood concept vigorously. John Masefield offers in *Badon Parchments* (1947) a strictly archival account, while Rosemary Sutcliff's *Sword at Sunset* (1963) is a highly effective novel treatment of this modern English ideology in which Arthur has supplanted as a national founder the genuinely heroic, but apparently inappropriately Germanic, King Alfred.

A tide of Dark Age quasi-historicist novels, weaving romance, Celticism, and mysticism into military and sometimes sadomasochistic detail, have flowed recently from male authors like Parke Godwin, Bernard Cornwell, and Stephen Lawhead. Variation of this masculinization started with Marion Zimmer Bradley's long and scholarly feminist rewriting in *The Mists of Avalon* (1981): that produced various spinoffs, and Sharan Newman and Persia Woolley have also feminized the tradition. The most recent visual versions seem to accept as now canonical a mix of history, myth, women, and children. The 2009 British television series *Merlin* not only makes the lead figure a wise juvenile—not a bearded ancient—but blends in medievalism, Celticity, and helpful children of both genders and several ethnicities.

Similarly, while the film *King Arthur* (2004) asserted Arthur and his warriors were Sarmatians from southwestern Russia (but with the traditional names), its narrative mixed the Romano-British concept, a wise woodland Merlin, and a glamorous young warrior Guinevere. As the film ends with Arthur's marriage and rise to rule, it is able, with no sign of a *Morte*, to deploy his name in the title.

If many modern versions prefer the simplicities of romance to the scope and sonority of Arthurian saga, there is also the recurrent chatter of the "real King Arthur" industry. A personalized version of Arthurian historicism remains an ineluctable interest of television and print journalism, offering topography, maps, dates, and speculative statements from scholars and non-scholars in a quest for the real, historical Arthur. But King Arthur has been in the underworld before. The early Celtic saints' lives belittle his merely secular powers; early modern English ideologues made him a mere validator of dubious incomer kings, fighting cardboard Saracens across his former land; from Milton to Wordsworth, Arthur and Merlin were lay figures of a distastefully royal and Catholic past. But like all great mythic heroes, he has the power of return, in a new form, with new meanings for new contexts, and it seems rational to expect many substantial returns for Arthur. He remains the king of an enormously rich literary tradition that is itself in truth the reality of this dynamic, changing, and deeply revealing myth.

FURTHER READING

Archibald, Elizabeth, and Ad Putter, eds. *The Cambridge Companion to the Arthurian Legend*. Cambridge: Cambridge University Press, 2009.

Barron, W.R.J., ed. *The Arthur of the English*. Cardiff: University of Wales Press, 1999.

Bromwich, Rachel, A.O.H. Jarman, and Brynley F. Roberts, eds. *The Arthur of the Welsh*. Cardiff: University of Wales Press, 1991.

Burgess, Glyn S., and Karen Pratt, eds. *The Arthur of the French*. Cardiff: University of Wales Press, 2006.

Fulton, Helen, ed. *A Companion to Arthurian Literature*. Oxford: Blackwell-Wiley, 2009.

Jackson, W. H., and S. A. Ranawake, eds. *The Arthur of the Germans*. Cardiff: University of Wales Press, 2000.

Knight, Stephen. *Merlin: Knowledge and Power Through the Ages*. Ithaca, NY: Cornell University Press, 2009.

Krueger, Roberta L., ed. *The Cambridge Companion to Medieval Romance*. Cambridge: Cambridge University Press, 2000.

Lacy, Norris J. *The New Arthurian Encyclopedia*. New York: Garland, 1991.

Lupack, Alan. *The Oxford Guide to Arthurian Literature and Legend*. New York: Oxford University Press, 2005.

Moll, Richard J. *Before Malory: Reading Arthur in Later Medieval England*. Toronto: University of Toronto Press, 2003.

APPENDIX: WILLIAM CAXTON'S PREFACE TO HIS EDITION
OF SIR THOMAS MALORY'S *MORTE DARTHUR*

Lister M. Matheson

William Caxton's preface to his edition of Malory's *Morte Darthur* (Westminster, 1485) offers a fascinating glimpse into how late-medieval and later reading and listening audiences approached the story of King Arthur.

Caxton relates how (unnamed) "noble and divers gentlemen" have come to him to demand why he hasn't printed the stories of the Grail and King Arthur. The printer sets himself up as a straw man for one of the gentlemen to knock down when he remarks that various people do not believe that Arthur ever existed; the gentleman offers proof after proof that Arthur had indeed been real, and the printer has to concede the case. That Caxton is simply playing devil's advocate is suggested strongly by the fact that he had printed the full history of Arthur in his published *Chronicles of England* (1480 and 1482) and John Trevisa's translation of the *Polychronicon* (1482). Caxton's copy-text of the latter work had omitted a vigorous defense of Arthur's historicity that appears in other copies of the work; he seems to be making restitution here in his preface for that earlier omission, which occurs in one of the chapters of the *Polychronicon* to which he makes direct reference.

The kinds of proof that the gentleman adduces are interesting: some are references to written sources, which could, of course, be false or fictitious, while others are to physical objects, which could, of course, be fakes or forgeries. (Ah! the difficulties of establishing true facts in pre-Internet days!)

Caxton's comments on the themes and emotions in Malory's *Morte Darthur* constitute the best short summary ever written of the work's range and scope. His coy remark that we are at liberty to believe what we will in the work is disingenuous in the context of the previous arguments.

The following text constitutes the bulk of Caxton's preface, with modernized spelling and punctuation. A few Middle English words that do not have direct modern descendants are printed in italics; these, and some archaic words or usages, have following glosses in brackets.

> After that I had accomplished and finished divers [various] histories, as well of contemplation as of other *hystoryal* [historical] and worldly acts of great conquerors and princes, and also certain books of examples and doctrine, many noble and divers gentlemen of this realm of England came and demanded [asked] me many and oft-times wherefore that I have not do made and imprinted [caused to have made and printed] the noble history of the Saint Greal [Holy Grail] and of the most renowned Christian king, first and chief of the three best Christian and worthy, King Arthur, which [who] ought most to be remembered among us English men before all other Christian kings.

For it is *notoyrly* [famously] known through the universal world that there are nine worthy, and the best that ever were, that is to wit [know] three paynims [pagans], three Jews, and three Christian men.

As for the paynims, they were before the Incarnation of Christ, which were named, the first, Hector of Troy, of whom the history is come [has come down] both in ballad and in prose; the second, Alexander the Great; and the third, Julius Caesar, Emperor of Rome, of whom the histories are well known and had.

And as for the three Jews, which also were before the Incarnation of Our Lord, of whom the first was Duke Joshua, which brought the children of Israel into the land of behest [promised land]; the second, David, king of Jerusalem; and the third, Judas Maccabaeus—of these three the Bible rehearseth all their noble histories and acts.

And sith [since] the said Incarnation have been three noble Christian men *stalled* [installed] and admitted through the universal world into the number of the nine best and worthy, of whom was first the noble Arthur, whose noble acts I purpose to write in this present book here following. The second was Charlemagne, or Charles the Great, of whome the history is had [available] in many places, bothe in French and English, and the third and last was Godfrey of Boulogne, of whose acts and life I made a book unto [for] the excellent prince and king of noble memory, King Edward the fourth.

The said noble gentlemen instantly required me to imprint the history of the said noble king and conqueror King Arthur and of his knights, with the history of the Saint Greal, and of the death and ending of the said Arthur, affirming that I ought rather to imprint his acts and noble feats than of Godfrey of Boulogne or any of the other eight, considering that he was a man born within this realm and king and emperor of the same, and that there are in French divers and many noble volumes of his acts, and also of his knights.

To whom I answered that divers men hold opinion that there was no such Arthur and that all such books as are made of [about] him are feigned, and fables, because that some chronicles make of him no mention nor remember him no thing [not at all, nothing], nor of his knights. Whereto they answered, and one in special [especially] said that in him that should say or think that there was never such a king called Arthur might well be *aretted* [attributed] great folly and blindness. For he said that there were many evidences of the contrary.

First, ye may see his sepulture in the monastery of Glastonbury, and also in *Polycronicon* [a work by Ranulph Higden, translated into English by John Trevisa and printed by Caxton in 1482], in the fifth book, the sixth chapter, and in the seventh book, the twenty-third chapter, where his body was buried and after [later] found and translated into the said monastery. Ye shall see also in the history of [by] Boccaccio, in his book *De casu principum* [*Of the Fall of Princes*], part of his noble acts and also of his fall. Also Galfridus [Geoffrey of Monmouth] in his British book recounteth his life.

And in divers places of England many remembrances are [exist] yet of him—and shall remain perpetually—and also of his knights. First, in the abbey of Westminster at Saint Edward's shrine remaineth the print [survives the imprint] of his seal in red wax, closed [enclosed] in beryl, in which is written "Patricius Arthurus, Britannie, Gallie, Germanie, Dacie Imperator" ["Noble Arthur, emperor of Britain, Gaul, Germany, Denmark"]. Item, in the castle of Dover ye may see Gawain's skull and Cradok's mantle, at Winchester the Round Table, in other places Lancelot's sword and many other things. Then, all these thynges considered, there can no man reasonably gainsay [deny] but there was a king of this land named Arthur.

For in all places, Christian and heathen, he is reputed and taken for one of the nine worthy, and the first of the three Christian men. And, also, he is more spoken of beyond the sea—more books made of his noble acts than there be in England, as well in Dutch, Italian, Spanish, and Greek as in French.

And yet of record remain in witness of him in Wales, in the town of Camelot, the great stones and marvellous works of iron lying under the ground and regal vaults which divers now living hath seen. Wherefore, it is a marvel why he is no more renowned in his own country, save only [except] it accordeth to [agrees with] the word of God which saith that no man is accepted for [as] a prophet in his own country.

Then, all these things foresaid alleged [declared, adduced], I could not well deny but that there was such a noble king named Arthur, and reputed one of the nine worthy and first and chief of the Christian men.

And many noble volumes are made of [about] him and of his noble knights in French, which I have seen and read beyond the sea, which are not had [available] in our maternal tongue—but in Welsh are many, and also in French, and some in English, but no where nigh [nearly] all.

Wherefore, such as have late [recently] been drawn out briefly into English I have, after the simple cunning [knowledge, ability] that God hath sent to me, under the favor and correction of all noble lords and gentlemen, *enprysed* [undertaken, enterprised] to imprint a book of the noble histories of the said King Arthur and of certain of his knights after [according to] a copy unto me delivered, which copy Sir Thomas Malory did take out of certain books of French and reduced [summarized] it into English.

And I, according to my copy, have done [have caused to] set it in imprint, to the intent that noble men may see and learn the noble acts of chivalry, the gentle and virtuous deeds that some knights used in those days, by which they came to honor, and how they that were vicious were punished and often put to shame and rebuke.

Humbly beseeching all noble lords and ladies, with all other estates (of what estate or degree they are of) that shall see and read in this said book and work, that they take the good and honest acts in their remembrance—and to follow the same. Wherein they shall find many joyous and pleasant histories and noble and renowned acts of humanity, gentleness, and chivalries [chivalrous deeds]. For herein may be seen noble chivalry, courtesy, humanity, friendliness, hardiness, love, friendship, cowardice, murder, hate, virtue, and sin. Do after [according to] the good and leave the evil, and it shall bring you to good fame and renown.

And for to pass the time, this book shall be pleasant to read in—but for to give faith and belief that all is true that is contained herein, ye are at your liberty. But all is written for our doctrine [teaching] and for to beware that we fall not to vice nor sin, but to exercise and follow virtue, by which we may come and attain to good fame and renown in this life, and, after this short and transitory life to come unto everlasting bliss in heaven, the which he grant [may he grant] us that reigneth in heaven— the blessed Trinity. Amen.

Then, to proceed forth in this said book, which I direct unto all noble princes, lords and ladies, gentlemen or gentlewomen, that desire to read or hear read of the noble and joyous history of the great conquerour and excellent king, King Arthur, sometime king of this noble realm (then called Britain), I, William Caxton, simple person, present this book following, which I have *enprysed* [undertaken, enterprised] to imprint. And [it] treateth of the noble actes, feats of arms, of chivalry, prowess, hardiness, humanity, love, courtesy, and *veray* [true] gentleness, with many wonderful histories and adventures.

[Caxton goes on to describe the division of the volume into 21 books, containing 507 chapters, and the contents of each book.]

Illustrated page from the early fourteenth-century *Chronicle of England* by Peter of Langtoft, showing King Henry II arguing with St. Thomas Becket. Henry touches his left hand with his right forefinger as if admonishing Archbishop Becket, who stands holding a staff with a cross, and gestures back. Becket was murdered by Henry's men in 1170. (The British Library/StockphotoPro)

Thomas Becket (1118/1120–1170)

Emily Z. Tabuteau

INTRODUCTION

Thomas, usually called Thomas Becket, rose from relatively humble beginnings to the archbishopric of Canterbury, an office he held from 1162 until his murder in 1170. Although he had risen in part through the patronage and friendship of King Henry II of England, who appointed him to the archbishopric, Thomas is famous largely for his quarrel with Henry over the proper relations of archbishop and king, of church and state. This "Becket controversy" vexed not only England but all of western Europe for most of a decade and has figured in discussions about the proper relations between religious institutions and governments ever since. The murder was such a cause celèbre that Thomas was canonized just two years after his death.

BECKET'S FAMILY BACKGROUND

Thomas's father, Gilbert Becket, was a London merchant and landowner of sufficient standing to entertain middle-level lords, one of whom, Richer de l'Aigle, became an early patron to his son. Gilbert was born in Normandy, perhaps in Rouen, the capital, but more probably in a small settlement called Thierville (because he once chatted with Archbishop Theobald—his son's predecessor at Canterbury—about their common place of origin, and Theobald was certainly from Thierville). Gilbert's social status was not particularly high, though he was not a peasant. In England he would have counted as part of the ruling class merely by virtue of being French-speaking and of French origin. His wife was also from Normandy. She was known both as Matilda and as Roheise, in an example of a sort of double-naming of women not unusual among Norman families in the eleventh and twelfth centuries.

The Name "Becket"

In the twelfth century, it was common to have only one name (e.g., Thomas), and most last names were little more than nicknames. "Becket," usually spelled "Beket" in the twelfth century, seems to have been the nickname of Thomas's father Gilbert. The name undoubtedly comes from the French bec, *which might be the nickname for a man with a beak-like nose (*becquet *in Norman French could mean a small bird) or refer to a small stream (*bec *in Norman French. Thomas himself never used the name. While he was in Archbishop Theobald's household, he was called Thomas of London; in the writs of Henry II between 1154 and 1162, he appears as Thomas the Chancellor; and when he became archbishop, he was known as Thomas of Canterbury. According to one of the early accounts of his* *murder, one of his murderers entered the cathedral demanding to know "Where is Thomas Becket, traitor to the king?" but this is the only time the nickname is used for Thomas in any twelfth-century source. That it comes from (or was put into) the mouth of a murderer suggests that, in the eyes of his enemies, the nickname denoted Thomas's relatively lowly origins.*

Some of Thomas's relatives, however, did use the name. His sister Agnes, for example, was known as Agnes Becket even after she married. This, in turn, suggests that "Becket" was recognized as the archbishop's family name and that it is, therefore, not inappropriate to use it for him despite the lack of contemporary usage. The form "à Becket," however, is an affectation dating from the sixteenth century and should not be used.

Gilbert was well established in London by the time of his son's birth, and the family lived in a large house in Cheapside, then a fashionable area for merchant families. Exactly what trade or trades he followed is not known, but he became prominent and prosperous enough to serve as one of the sheriffs of London for a while, perhaps in the 1130s. He lived into the 1140s, at least, but may have lost much of his wealth in his later years because of fires that destroyed his property. Matilda died before her husband, probably about 1140.

The Legend of Thomas's Saracen Mother

There is no warrant for the late, romantic story that Thomas Becket's mother was a Saracen princess whom Gilbert met on Crusade: he was supposedly her father's prisoner, whom she helped to escape. Knowing only two English words, "Gilbert" and "London," she then followed him back to England, where they were married. The tale first occurs in a manuscript compiled about a century after Thomas's death. The story provides a major element of the plot of Thomas Costain's 1945 novel, The Black Rose, *which became a 1950 movie of the same name. In the introduction to the novel, Costain says, "The story itself grows out of a legend, a most beguiling and romantic legend which is found in a very few old English histories. . . . [I]t concerns an English crusader, who later became the father of Thomas à Becket, and an Eastern girl who knew just two words of English. It is pure legend, of course, but it has always seemed to me too engaging a tale to be buried away between the covers of forgotten histories; and so I have borrowed it and adapted it to my needs."*

BIRTH, SIBLINGS, AND EARLY LIFE

Thomas appears to have been Gilbert and Matilda's only surviving son. They also had at least three daughters who survived into adulthood. Two of those daughters, Agnes and Roheise, married, though their husbands' names are not certain, and both had children. In the 1160s, they and their husbands and children suffered greatly at the hands of Henry II because of his anger at Thomas. The third daughter, Mary, entered a nunnery; in 1173, King Henry II appointed her abbess of Barking Abbey. It is possible that there was a fourth daughter who was the mother of Agnes's eventual heir, Theobald of Helles (or Hulles), because Theobald called himself Saint Thomas's nephew but did not refer to Agnes as his mother. All told, Gilbert Becket had at least seven grandsons, two of whom became priests, and two great-grandsons.

Thomas was born on December 21, probably in either 1118 or 1120. December 21 was the feast day of Saint Thomas the Apostle, after whom the future archbishop was probably named. Indeed, it is likely that it was the fame of Saint Thomas of Canterbury that popularized the name Thomas among the English, for the name was not common in England or Normandy before the late twelfth century. Little is known about Thomas's early life. His biographers, even the earliest ones, are interested primarily in his career as archbishop and tell us little about anything before 1162, and medieval sources about the lives of children, even the children of monarchs, are usually sparse and uninformative. There are a few stories, typical of the lives of saints, about his mother's dreams of his future greatness and about events in his early childhood that prefigured it.

EDUCATION IN ENGLAND AND PARIS

Given his later career, Thomas must have received a relatively good education. Even if he had been intended to follow his father's career, he would have needed to read and write—at least French and probably Latin—and calculate figures in Roman numerals, no mean task. In fact, he seems to have been destined for a clerical career from relatively early on, and to advance through the ranks of the clergy he would need not only Latin but training in theology and law. In his adolescence Thomas lived and studied at the priory of Merton for a while and also attended one or more grammar schools in London. He would have learned aristocratic manners—and he became notorious for his aristocratic demeanor—from Richer de l'Aigle, who used the Beckets' home as his London residence. The story was later told that Thomas once nearly drowned when he fell into a millrace while out hawking with his patron.

Probably when he was in his early twenties, Thomas spent time in Paris, whose schools, just then developing into a university, were the center of theological study in twelfth-century Europe. It seems to have been a brief period, however, and Thomas certainly did not complete the course that would have entitled him to call himself *magister* ("master"), a title that conveyed that its holder was adept in Latin, theology, and Roman law. How well- or ill-educated Thomas was became a matter of controversy once he had been elevated to the archbishopric, and the debate has never ceased: his supporters portray him as fully capable of reading and writing the best Latin and of holding his own in theological and legal debate; his detractors portray him as struggling in all these matters, as dependent on his loyal clerical staff for the production of the sort of elegant, rhetorical Latin documents his position demanded, even as overly influenced by some of his supporters because he was not educated enough to fully understand some of the underlying issues in his quarrel with the king. Similarly, his supporters portray his departure from Paris as due to changing circumstances at home: his mother's death, his father's difficulties, the need for him to begin a career. His detractors, in contrast, portray him as never having intended to study seriously: Paris was, at most, a sort of finishing school intended to give him the polish he needed to make a career in the world, and he soon got bored with study. Certainly, some aspects of Thomas's later career suggest that he knew that he was somewhat deficient in the niceties of written and spoken Latin.

EARLY CAREER

Once he had returned to London, Thomas entered the household of a merchant named Osbert Huitdeniers ("Eight-pence"). Osbert and Thomas were related, perhaps through Thomas's mother. Thomas kept Osbert's accounts for over two years. If, as his name suggests, Osbert was a moneylender, the years Thomas spent in his service must have provided him with practical expertise of great value to employers in the developing economy of the twelfth century. Life in London in the early 1140s would also have provided an education in national politics because this period saw the height of the rivalry for the throne between King Stephen (r. 1135–54), nephew of King Henry I (d. 1135), and Henry's daughter Matilda, "the Empress." London was in the thick of events, and an intelligent, ambitious young man would have learned much by observing the ins and outs of the struggle for the throne.

In the middle 1140s, certainly by 1146, Thomas left Osbert's household and entered that of Theobald, archbishop of Canterbury. The archbishop of Canterbury was the highest church official in the kingdom of England: the only other archbishop was at York, but York was in the north, was relatively poor, and had only one suffragan (that is, subordinate) bishop, whereas Canterbury was located close to the center of power, was extremely wealthy, and had nearly 20 suffragans in England and Wales. Moreover, while all bishops were among the great lords of the land, Canterbury, by virtue of his leadership of the church and his wealth, was the most prominent of them. Like all great lords, he expected to be consulted by the king on important matters, he regularly attended the royal court, and the king expected his loyal support of royal policies. In the conflicted politics of the 1140s, a successful archbishop needed to be a consummate politician. Theobald was.

An active archbishop required a large staff, some of them based in the ca-thedral church of Canterbury but many of them traveling with him as he moved about the country. Like all great landowners and lords at this time, the archbishop and much of his household were itinerant rather than resid-ing primarily in one place. When he joined Theobald's household, Thomas became a member of an elite group of highly able functionaries in one of the major centers of power, secular as well as religious, in England. It is no accident that, of the members of Theobald's household, four later became archbishops and another six became bishops. Thomas initially was one of the second tier of the archbishop's officials, but he rose rapidly. Theobald al-lowed him to study law at Bologna and Auxerre for a while. He accompanied Theobald to the Council of Reims in 1148 and represented the archbishop at the papal curia several times. In late 1154, Theobald made him archdeacon of Canterbury. All over Europe, the twelfth century saw the rapid advance of administrative techniques, and this was as true for the church as for secular governments—or even truer. As bishops developed the administration of their dioceses, the archdeacon emerged as the most important official engaged in the day-to-day management of affairs. To be archdeacon of Canterbury was, therefore, to be in some sense the second in command to the most important person in the kingdom after the king himself. Because Thomas had neither important family connections nor important patrons promoting his career, his rise must be credited to his administrative skills and, no doubt, his ability to ingratiate himself with his superiors.

ROYAL SERVICE AS CHANCELLOR

The next step in Thomas's advance made him the second in command to the king himself. The long struggle for the throne that had sputtered on through most of the years since the death of King Henry I finally came to an end in 1153–54 through, first, King Stephen's designation of his rival Matilda's eldest son, Henry, as his heir and then, conveniently, Stephen's death in the next year. Thus, in 1154, King Henry II ascended the throne at the age of 21. By this time, Henry had been functioning as duke of Normandy (his mother's ances-tral land) for five years or so. He had inherited his father's county of Anjou in 1151. In 1152, he had become duke of Aquitaine, a province that constituted approximately a quarter of the area of the kingdom of France, by virtue of his marriage to Eleanor duchess of Aquitaine, the divorced wife of King Louis VII of France (see the chapter on her). Because control of Normandy brought with it hegemony over Brittany, by the time he became king of England Henry was the ruler of most of western France, an area substantially larger than that belonging directly to the man from whom he held all these territories, the king of France. From his late teens on, Henry had taken over leadership

of the effort to oust Stephen from England and restore the direct line tracing from his grandfather, Henry I, through his mother to himself. He had led
several inconclusive military campaigns in England, but he had relatively little
experience of the kingdom. The civil war and Stephen's ineffectual government of the kingdom had weakened governmental institutions put in place by
Henry I and his predecessors and had created what felt to contemporaries like
chaos (though England was actually, by comparison with most areas of the
Continent, relatively peaceful and well governed even during Stephen's reign).
Henry came to the throne determined, as he often said, to restore conditions in
England to their state "on the day when my grandfather was alive and dead."
To do so, however, he needed help from men familiar with English institutions
and practices. A few of his grandfather's officials were still alive, and several
of them reentered royal service under Henry, but they were not enough. To
help out, Theobald made the king a gift: only three months after promoting
him to the archdeaconry, he gave Thomas to Henry to be his chancellor.

The Chancery

The chancery of England had developed out of the writing office of the late
Anglo-Saxon kings, which produced many of the documents issued by those
monarchs. Under William the Conqueror (r. 1066–87) and his sons, William II (r. 1087–1100) and Henry I (r. 1100–35), as more and more acts of
government came to be written, the chancery and its head, the chancellor,
became increasingly important in the government of England. Most especially,
the Norman kings of England and their chancellors developed the writ—a
terse written directive from the king usually addressed to a subordinate official and instructing him to perform some action—into a major means of
communicating orders from the center to the localities. Modern judicial writs
such as habeas corpus, certiorari, and mandamus are the descendants of these
instruments; but from the twelfth century through the end of the Middle Ages
writs served much wider functions than just moving judicial cases through
the courts. Like most other aspects of government, chancery had deteriorated
during Stephen's reign, but even at the end of the reign it was producing writs
as well as the more formal documents of government. Thomas therefore took
over a going concern, though one that needed modernization and the restoration of its efficiency.

The Chancellor

While the chancery was, by 1154, an indispensable element of English government, the chancellor was not necessarily the most important official in
England next to the king. Under Henry I, an official called the chief justiciar
had developed as the king's second-in-command. That position had vanished

under Stephen, but it was revived by Henry II, and for much of his reign the chief justiciar functioned as what one modern scholar has called the king's alter ego. The twelfth century was, however, an age when the person was more important than the office; and while Thomas was chancellor few would have doubted that he was the single most important adviser and companion of the king. Not only did he restore the chancery to efficient functioning, but he took on responsibilities that did not necessarily have anything to do with writing the king's documents. He often accompanied the king on his journeys around the country and to the Continent. He hunted with him. He went on diplomatic missions for him. Thomas's embassy to King Louis VII of France in 1158 was famous in its day for the magnificence of the ambassador's equipage and the imperiousness of his approach to his mission. Indeed, though he was in clerical orders, he even accompanied the king on several military campaigns—and allegedly even fought in them.

FRIENDSHIP WITH THE KING

Henry and Thomas rapidly became fast friends. Henry may have seen in his chancellor a surrogate father. Thomas was 13–15 years older than Henry, about the same age as Henry's own father, Geoffrey Plantagenet count of Anjou, who had died three years before Henry became king. Thomas certainly threw himself wholeheartedly into the role of adviser and companion to the king, to such an extent that his critics have sometimes accused him of betraying Archbishop Theobald just as, in their eyes, he later betrayed the king. The reason for this accusation is that it is sensible to assume that Theobald had more in mind than the restoration of good government in England when he sent Thomas off to become Henry's chancellor. He probably hoped that Thomas would be a spokesman for the interests of the church in the heart of the king's household. If so, he must have been disappointed because, at those points where the king's interests did not seem to run directly with those of the church, Thomas supported Henry without apparent qualm, sometimes even taking the lead in measures that the church saw as against its interests. Thomas's defenders see these actions as attempts to maintain a balance between the interests of the church and the interests of the state.

Younger Husbands and Older Wives

Most royal and aristocratic marriages in the Middle Ages were arranged to advance the interests of the families of the spouses. Love, compatibility, and even age were not important considerations. Both Henry II's father and Henry himself married women who were considerably older than they were.

Geoffrey count of Anjou (Henry II's father) and Matilda were married in 1128, when Geoffrey was only 15 years old. Matilda, who was then 26, was already a widow: in 1114, when only 12 herself, she had become the second wife of Emperor Henry V, but she bore him no children. After Henry V died in 1125, Matilda's father, Henry I, king of England and duke of Normandy, arranged for her to marry the young count of Anjou in order to forge an alliance with the ruler of this area that had long been a competitor and enemy of the duchy of Normandy.

Before he ascended to the throne of England, Henry of Anjou married Eleanor duchess of Aquitaine in 1152, when he was 19 and she was about 30. Eleanor had been married to Louis VII of France since 1137 and had given him two daughters. Louis, however, wanted sons, and he and Eleanor did not get along at all. With permission of the pope, the marriage was annulled in 1152 on grounds of consanguinity—that is, that Louis and Eleanor were too closely related to have married in the first place. Consanguinity was an often-used excuse for dissolving marriages in an era when the church believed strongly that marriage was for life. That, however, left Eleanor in a predicament. As duchess of Aquitaine she was the greatest prize on the twelfth-century marriage market. Any enterprising man who could kidnap her and force her into marriage would thereby come into control of a significant portion of the kingdom of France. Indeed, the tale is told that, on her progress back from Paris to the capital of Aquitaine, Bordeaux, at least two French lords attempted the feat. For this reason among others, Eleanor had prearranged with Henry, whom she had probably met only once, to marry him as soon as she was free of her first marriage. Although they were at least as closely related as Eleanor and her first husband, they were married a bare eight weeks after Eleanor's first marriage was annulled.

Though Geoffrey and Matilda had three sons in three and a half years, and Henry and Eleanor had at least five sons and three daughters, both marriages were, perhaps not surprisingly, famously unhappy. After the birth of their third son, Geoffrey and Matilda spent very little time together. Eleanor went so far as to support the revolt of her sons against their father in 1173–74. As a result, Henry threw her into prison and kept her there until his death in 1189. The play The Lion in Winter, *by James Goldman, produced on Broadway in 1966 and made into a movie in 1968 and a television film in 2003, depicts, in somewhat heightened form, the relations among Henry, Eleanor, their sons, and the young King Philip II of France in the aftermath of the sons' revolt against Henry. Matilda survived Geoffrey by 15 years, and Eleanor survived Henry by an equal period.*

ARCHBISHOP OF CANTERBURY

Theobald had been made archbishop in 1139. He had managed to protect the interests of the church quite well both against deliberate encroachments by the warring Stephen and Matilda and against depredations traceable to the relative absence of effective royal government during the "anarchy" of Stephen's reign. Although Theobald welcomed Henry's accession with great hopes, having a strong monarch on the throne, while it made defense against depredations by private parties easier than under Stephen, only increased the possibility of royal encroachments on what the church saw as its rights and privileges. Still, on balance, Henry and Theobald got along relatively well. Indeed, in light of the dramatic events to come, a certain amount of nostalgia for what in retrospect looked like the minimal church-state quarrels of Theobald's archiepiscopate is not surprising in some of the surviving sources of the twelfth century.

Theobald died in April 1161, giving Henry the opportunity to name a new archbishop of Canterbury. At this point, Henry made what is usually counted the greatest mistake of his life. He decided that Thomas should be the new prelate and ensured that the monks of the cathedral chapter, who were the formal electors of archbishops of Canterbury, would choose him. The "election" occurred in May 1162. At the time, it undoubtedly seemed to Henry like a brilliant stroke. This was a man whom he knew, trusted, and probably even loved, who had spent more than seven years faithfully carrying out royal policies, who could be expected to carry into his new position a sympathetic understanding of what the king needed and wanted from the church in his kingdom.

Appointment of Bishops in the Twelfth Century

In the earlier Middle Ages, important church officials such as bishops and abbots were often appointed by kings and other local secular rulers. From the middle of the eleventh century, the so-called Investiture Controversy raged over the attempts of several successive popes to challenge these practices. The English side of the controversy, in which Archbishop Anselm was pitted against Henry I, was resolved in 1107 by the establishment of a set of rules to which, usually, only lip service was paid. The initial demand made by papal reformers was that bishops and abbots (and abbesses) be elected in the manner envisioned by the earliest generations of church leaders—that is, bishops by the faithful of their dioceses and abbots and abbesses by the monks or nuns of their convents. This rule was observed to some extent in the case of abbots and abbesses, though in elections to head an important institution the monks or nuns often came under a good deal of pressure to elect a specific person. In the case of bishops, the letter of the rule may have been observed but the spirit was certainly violated. In practice, to speak of England specifically, the king appointed every bishop in the kingdom: having decided whom he wanted in the see, he would send a writ to the cathedral chapter, the monks or canons who served as the clergy of the cathedral, ordering them to elect that person.

The faithful of the diocese had no say in the matter at all, and any cathedral chapter that flouted the king's command was in for serious, prolonged trouble. In the most dramatic example, in 1205 a majority of the members of the chapter of Canterbury refused to elect King John's nominee, leading to—among other things—eight years of increasingly oppressive attempts by the king to force them to accept his candidate, Pope Innocent III's placement of an interdict on England, the pope's excommunication of the king, and a plot against the king's life on the grounds that, as an excommunicate, he was not owed allegiance from anyone. The quarrel was resolved in 1213, when the king again promised free elections, a promise repeated in the first clause of Magna Carta when John was forced to agree to it in 1215. Nevertheless, for as long as the church in England remained subordinate to the church in Rome, it was effectively the king who named bishops, subject only to the veto of the pope, which he rarely exercised. When in the 1530s King Henry VIII wrenched the Church of England out of its allegiance to Rome, even this vestige of outside control disappeared. Bishops of the Church of England are to this day still, in form, appointed by the monarch.

Thomas was certainly, at the time of his appointment, less acceptable to the church as archbishop than he was to the king. Though he would have taken the minor clerical orders at the latest when he entered Theobald's household and Theobald consecrated him a deacon before appointing him archdeacon of Canterbury, Thomas was not a priest. None of the offices he had held had required him to be able to exercise the "cure of souls"—that is, to minister to the faithful, so he had never celebrated the Mass, never heard a confession, never administered any other sacrament. Unlike every other archbishop since the Conquest, he was not a monk, which displeased the monks of the chapter of the cathedral church of Canterbury because the archbishop was automatically their abbot. He was, moreover, by no means the most obviously qualified candidate for archbishop. Many, perhaps all, of the English bishops probably thought they were more qualified. Conspicuously, this was true of Gilbert Foliot the bishop of London, who had probably been expecting the promotion to Canterbury for years. Gilbert subsequently became, in part at least out of disappointment, one of the leaders of Thomas's opponents among the English clergy.

Even Thomas, it is said, advised Henry that appointing him was a bad idea, but Henry would not take no for an answer. Consequently, Thomas repaired to Canterbury, where he was ordained a priest on June 2, 1162, and consecrated archbishop the next day. He celebrated the Mass for the first time in his life immediately after his ascent to the highest clerical office in the land. In August, he received from the pope the *pallium,* the stole of office bestowed on archbishops to symbolize the delegation of papal jurisdiction to them.

FRICTION AND CONFRONTATION
BETWEEN BECKET AND KING HENRY

Henry's hopes for a compliant archbishop were bitterly disappointed, for Thomas began, almost immediately after his appointment, to oppose the king on a wide variety of matters. At some point early in his archiepiscopate, he ceased to function as chancellor. Some sources report that he formally resigned after he received the pallium, sending the great seal of England to Henry, who was in France and who was incensed when he received it. Then Thomas turned his attention to the estates of the archbishopric, many of which had been granted out on unusually favorable leases to the king's men and to men of local importance in Kent. Some lessees had been in place for so long that there was a danger that their families would come to consider the estates their hereditary property. Thomas revoked all these agreements and took the estates back into his direct control. He also demanded from the king custody of three castles—Rochester, Hythe, and Saltwood, the last of which was to become the base of operations of his opponents during his exile and his murderers in the days before and after the murder—and lordship over a man named William de Ros, who owed the service of seven knights. These actions not only irritated the king but turned many of the great families of Kent against the archbishop.

Thomas was not entirely successful in securing control of these estates. In 1163, the constable of England, Henry of Essex, who had fled from a battle in 1159, was tried on charges of cowardice and convicted; among the estates Henry seized as a result was the castle of Saltwood, which Henry of Essex held from the archbishop. The king appointed Ranulf de Broc its custodian, and de Broc and his brothers quickly emerged as the most determined of Thomas's opponents in Kent. Later the same year, the royal court found that Roger de Clare held Tonbridge directly from the king, not from the archbishop, and also that William de Ros was the king's direct vassal. King and archbishop also quarreled about Thomas's appointment of a priest to the church of Eynsford. When the lay lord of the estate, William of Eynsford, who claimed to be a direct vassal of the king, objected, Thomas excommunicated him. He then refused for quite a while Henry's order to absolve William; by the time he gave in, Henry was angrier than ever.

Thomas also opposed Henry in matters having little or nothing to do with Canterbury or his religious duties. Most notably, at a council in July 1163, Henry proposed that he collect directly an age-old levy known as the sheriff's aid rather than continuing to allow it to be paid to the sheriffs themselves. Thomas opposed him and declared that no such payment would be made by his estates or any church lands. Henry backed down, but he was furious.

To Henry, and to those who, through the ages, have supported him, Thomas was needlessly confrontational about matters that were of little importance until he made them so. From the point of view of Thomas and his supporters, the underlying issues in these matters would have made it necessary for any man of principle in Thomas's position to take the stands he took. In the reform atmosphere of the mid-twelfth century, it was inappropriate for a prelate to remain the servant of the king, so Thomas *had* to surrender the chancellorship if he was to be able to present himself as a reforming archbishop. He needed to be a good steward of his church in its material as well as its spiritual dimension and therefore could not allow its lands to remain in the hands of inappropriate men, men who either had no right to what they held or were trying to convert Canterbury's estates to their own permanent control. Even in the matter of the sheriff's aid, Thomas was opposing the conversion of a customary but free-will offering to the local authorities into a national tax. One of Thomas's modern adherents notes that, on this last point, "it is likely that he was voicing the opinion of every baron in England." If so, it was a rare instance in which Thomas's actions were widely popular.

Why wouldn't or couldn't Thomas be the kind of archbishop the king hoped for? This is the central conundrum of the whole affair, for there is nothing surprising about Henry's reaction to his archbishop's opposition or, indeed, about Thomas's actions once he had so angered the king that he had put his own life in danger. Thomas's critics then and now have often cited careerism as the explanation for his changes of allegiance, noting that he changed sides not once but twice. As Theobald's servant, he had supported the church against the state, but when he became Henry's chancellor, he supported the king against the church. Then, once he had attained the archbishopric, he adopted the position of radical support of the church against the king. The argument goes that his chief purpose was to advance his own interests and that, to do that, he needed to ingratiate himself with his superiors. The problem with this explanation is obvious: while the first two allegiances he adopted did serve to advance his career, the third, taken to the extreme to which he took it, was self-evidently counterproductive. It is hard to imagine that a man whose principal purpose was to rise to great importance and, presumably, wealth, would so rapidly paint himself into a corner from which the only escape was exile, poverty, or death. A more sympathetic interpretation argues that Thomas had to conceal his real view of the relationship of church and state while he was Henry's chancellor but that, once he had become archbishop, he was free to act on his real sentiments: having risen to the highest office to which he could rationally aspire—the only higher office in the church was pope, and that would have been an unrealistic ambition—he had no reason to conceal his true beliefs. Moreover, in an age when almost everyone was brought up to believe that God expected them to perform loyal service to their superiors, there would be nothing shameful in adapting one's attitudes to fit one's circumstances. The simplest explanation of all is that Thomas, as he claimed and as many of his biographers report, underwent a religious conversion once he was appointed archbishop.

There must also have been other psychological factors in the developing quarrel. It is likely that Thomas, having reluctantly agreed to accept the position of archbishop, was well aware of how his appointment would look to many: that he would appear to be an unqualified, time-serving lackey of the king, the purpose of whose appointment was to make sure that the church would do the king's bidding without protest. To demonstrate that this was not the case, he would need to show, as soon as possible and as spectacularly as he could, that he was independent of his former patron and capable of confronting him. Therefore, he would need to seize on whatever issues came to hand, even if they were not the most cogent ones for his purpose. On Henry's side, the disappointment must have been colossal. A man whom he thought of as a close friend and trusted adviser was suddenly and inexplicably opposing him on all fronts. He felt betrayed. And Henry was not a man to suffer frustration patiently.

In the aftermath of the meeting in July 1163, Henry apparently decided to bring the confrontation to a head and lay down the rules once and for all. He had been brought up to believe—however unrealistically—that during the reign of Henry I, England had been an entirely peaceful and easily governable place. When he came to the throne, he declared his intent of restoring conditions in England to their state "on the day when my grandfather was alive and dead." He had been relatively successful on the secular side: England was a marvel of good government by comparison with its Continental and Celtic neighbors. Now the time had come to bring the church into line. He began to demand that the leaders of the church recognize that he was entitled to all the ecclesiastical rights that he alleged his grandfather had had.

Several major developments over the last quarter century made this demand difficult for the church to accept. Internally, in England the church had largely gone its own way for much of Stephen's reign, and its leaders were reluctant to give up the autonomy that, to many of them, was the norm under which they had grown up as churchmen. Externally, in the Western church in general, the claims of the papacy for its own powers and for the independence of the church from lay interference in its affairs, which had been developing since the mid-eleventh century, had continued apace through the years when England was involved in civil war. Moreover, in that period canon law, the law of the church, had grown by leaps and bounds. Most especially, an Italian monk named Gratian had produced the first great book of canon law; it had rapidly become an easily available, well-organized textbook for those who needed to make legal arguments about church matters. English churchmen, therefore, were both unaccustomed to regular, strong royal interference in the affairs of the English church and armed with new tools for resisting royal demands they thought inappropriate.

At a council at Westminster in October 1163, Henry secured from the bishops, led by Thomas, an agreement in principle that he was entitled to his grandfather's rights over the church, though they added the proviso "saving our order," which undercut the significance of their concession. Henry retaliated by removing his eldest son, also named Henry, from Thomas's control and depriving Thomas of all the lands he had received in his capacity as chancellor. Nonetheless, had Henry been content with the bishops' vague agreement, there might never have been a "Becket controversy." Unfortunately for the peace of the kingdom, however, Henry decided that he wanted the bishops' agreement to this principle recorded in writing—and with specifics. He therefore summoned the bishops to join him at Clarendon, one of his favorite hunting lodges, in late January 1164. Quite a few of the great lords of England who could be expected to support the king's efforts to put pressure on the church were also summoned to attend. Once everyone had arrived, Henry presented the bishops with a document, known as the Constitutions of Clarendon, listing 16 particular rules he claimed had existed in his grandfather's day. He demanded that the bishops set their seals to the document in recognition that these rules still applied.

THE CONSTITUTIONS OF CLARENDON

The bishops were, to put it mildly, rocked back on their heels by what they read. Many of the statements of the Constitutions of Clarendon violated their understanding of the proper relations of church and state. It should be noted, however, that not all of the provisions were controversial. Even Thomas found a few innocuous: in 1166 at Vézelay when he formally declared the whole document quashed, he explicitly condemned only half of its provisions. When, in 1165, he presented the document to Pope Alexander III for his condemnation, the pope declared that some of the provisions were bearable. Later he specified six clauses that could be tolerated.

The clauses of the Constitutions of Clarendon can be grouped under a number of rubrics. Two clauses concern communications between the church in England and the church as a whole, specifically, with the pope. Clause 4 forbids archbishops, bishops, and priests from leaving the kingdom without the king's permission and provides that the king can require them to give sureties that their travels would in no way result in harm to the king or the kingdom. Clause 8 provides that cases in church courts may be appealed from the archdeacon's court to the bishop's court and thence to the archbishop's court but can not go any further—that is, can not be appealed to the pope; instead, such cases should be sent to the king for him to settle. From Henry's point of view, it was only sensible to maintain oversight over contacts between churchmen in England and the wider church, especially the pope. To members of the clergy, however, these restrictions were a gross interference with the freedom of the church to manage its own affairs and with the ability of the church in England to participate in the governance of the larger institution. It is no wonder that the pope was perhaps even more offended by these two clauses than Thomas was.

A second set of clauses concerned areas of law in which the question was whether a case should be tried in a church court or the king's court. Under the Anglo-Saxons, both ecclesiastical cases and lay cases had been heard in the same courts. When a lay case was before a court, laymen presided and decided the outcome. When the matter was ecclesiastical, a bishop presided.

By the later eleventh century, such a situation seemed wrongheaded to the reforming papacy and its supporters. It was one of the reasons that Pope Alexander II supported William of Normandy's attempt to conquer England. In recompense for that support, shortly after 1066 William issued an order separating church courts from lay courts. As a result, by the mid-1160s, despite or perhaps because of nearly a century of attempting to work out where the line should be drawn, questions involving which kinds of cases should be tried by church courts and which by lay courts were often very hard to answer. William I had insisted that all cases involving land be tried in lay courts, even if both parties were clerics; and he and later kings recognized certain issues as belonging to the church courts, not only allegations of sins but such matters as the validity of marriages and the legitimacy of children. Nonetheless, a large gray area remained, and several clauses of the Constitutions of Clarendon attempt to address them.

Clause 11 baldly states the rule established by William the Conqueror: ecclesiastics who hold land directly from the king hold their lands as baronies, and disputes about those lands are to be decided in the king's court. Moreover, the great men of the church are to take part with the lay barons in judgments of the king's court unless a judgment involves execution or mutilation as a punishment. This was one of the clauses to which the pope did not object. Equally categorically, clause 15 maintains that all cases involving debt belong in the king's court. To the laity, debt was a matter of property. Because debts were normally secured by oaths, however, and oaths were promises to God, the church regarded violations of such oaths, like all oaths, as matters of sin, justiciable in church courts. Thomas specifically condemned both these clauses at Vézelay.

In contrast, clause 9 modifies William's rule in one particular respect. It assumes that, if a case arises about land held by a member of the clergy by the typical clerical tenure, known as free alms because it required no secular services, the case should be tried in the church court rather than a lay court. The clause explicitly contemplates the situation in which the suit is between a layperson and a member of the clergy and the layperson alleges that the land is held not in free alms but by one of the types of tenure characteristic of laypeople ("lay fee"). In those circumstances, the court that is to try the case cannot be determined until the question of the type of tenure is settled. What clause 9 says is that, if such a dispute arises, the sheriff is to empanel a jury, put its members on oath, and ask them whether (*utrum* in Latin) the land was held in lay fee or free alms. The jury's verdict would determine which court tried the case. This "assize utrum" is generally recognized as the earliest known of the four "petty assizes" in existence by the end of Henry II's reign—and the creation of the petty assizes is one of the reasons why Henry II is often accorded the honor of inventing the common law of England. In this instance, of course, if the Constitutions of Clarendon are right in what they claim—that the practices they describe were in fact the practices of Henry I's reign—the honor for creating the "assize utrum" belongs to Henry I or an even earlier king.

Clause 1 provides that cases involving patronage ("advowson") over churches should be tried in the king's court even if both parties to the dispute were clergymen. In the eyes of the king and other laypersons, advowson was a valuable property right like any other income-producing aspect of owning land, and cases about it properly belonged in the same court that tried other cases involving property. To the church, however, advowson was a spiritual matter. It included the right to nominate the priest of the church, subject to the bishop's approval, and the priest exercised the cure of souls and ministered to the needs of parishioners. Therefore, to churchmen, disputes about advowson should be adjudicated in the same court that tried other spiritual cases. This is one of the clauses Thomas specifically condemned at Vézelay.

Clauses 13 and 14 require the two jurisdictions to help and not to interfere with each other. Clause 13 provides that the king will punish any lay magnate who interferes with a prelate's ability to administer justice and requires the prelates to assist the king against anyone who tries to prevent the king from administering justice. Clause 14 forbids the practice whereby people whose goods had been forfeited to the king prevented them from being seized by moving them to a church or churchyard. Pope Alexander III found both these clauses tolerable, and Thomas did not specifically mention either one at Vézelay.

A third set of clauses of the Constitutions concerned instances in which the church might be seen as interfering between the king and his vassals. Clause 2 provides that churches on lands held directly from the king could not be permanently granted away without the king's permission. It was common practice in the twelfth century for a layperson who controlled a church on his or her estate to give the church to a neighboring abbey as a pious act, a practice the church encouraged because it both enriched the church and solved the problem of laypersons interfering in church affairs by exercising control over individual churches. Any such grant permanently diminished the value of the estate, however, since the lord or lady who had given away the church no longer enjoyed lucrative rights over it. Henry did not want his tenants impoverishing themselves in this way, at least not without his permission. Alexander III found this clause acceptable, and Thomas did not specifically mention it at Vézelay.

The other clauses that concern relations between the king and his vassals concern excommunication and interdict. Excommunication was the church's power to exclude misbehaving individuals from the community—to put them out of communion with good Christians—as a method of pressuring them into conforming to the strictures of the church. No good Christian was to have anything to do with an excommunicated person: he or she was literally to be shunned. Moreover, the excommunicate could not attend Mass or receive any other sacrament or be buried in consecrated ground. Interdict was a method the church used to put pressure on a recalcitrant person by depriving everyone living on that person's lands of most of the consolations of the church: church bells were not be rung; no processions could be held; only minimal church services could be performed; no burials could be performed in consecrated ground. Clause 7 provides that no major tenant of the king should be excommunicated, nor should his or her land be interdicted, without the king's or the chief justiciar's permission. Clause 10 allows minor tenants of the king, residents of towns and peasants on his manors, to be put under interdict without permission but requires the permission of the king's agent in the town or manor before such persons could be excommunicated. It continues that, if the king's agent fails to act, the king will punish him and the bishop may use all ecclesiastical methods of coercion against the original miscreant. Clause 5 provides that in order to receive absolution and thereby be restored to the fold, an excommunicate should only have to provide surety that he or she would abide by the judgment of the church, not take an oath or provide surety covering all his or her actions for the rest of time. Thomas specifically condemned the first two of these clauses at Vézelay but did not mention the last.

In addition, the Constitutions included a few miscellaneous but not unimportant items. Thus, clause 16 requires that any serf who wishes to become a member of the clergy get his lord's permission to do so. This was necessary because all members of the clergy were, by definition, free men, and entering the church was, therefore, a way for ambitious and able, or simply rebellious, young serfs to escape their inherited condition. Neither the pope nor Thomas objected to this requirement. Clause 6 concerns accusations against laymen in the courts of archdeacons: to ensure that false accusations are not brought there, the clause requires that the accusations be supported either by the testimony of reliable witnesses or, if witnesses are too scared of the potential accused to bear witness, by oath of 12 reliable men empaneled as a jury by the sheriff. This clause is, incidentally, one of the earliest pieces of evidence from England of an institution like the grand jury that Henry was to introduce into English criminal procedure two years later. Thomas specifically condemned it at Vézelay, but Alexander III declared it unobjectionable.

To Thomas, the two most offensive clauses undoubtedly were clauses 3 and 12. Clause 12 addressed the basic issue that had roiled relations between church and state over the preceding century—namely, how important churchmen were to be selected for their offices. It provided that when a prelate—archbishop, bishop, abbot, or prior—died and his office thereby became vacant, the king was to take the estates into his own hands and thereby acquire all the revenues of the position. He was then to assemble the "greater persons" of the church and hold an election for the new prelate in his own chapel, in his presence and the presence of all the "greater persons" of the church. Not only that, but the newly elected prelate was to do homage and fealty to the king for the estates of the church before he was consecrated as bishop or abbot or prior. This set of provisions benefited the king in two ways. First, while the church was vacant he collected its revenues, and the bishoprics and abbeys of England were richly endowed with estates. Their revenues could greatly swell the king's coffers. Second, these rules, while paying lip service to the idea that prelates should be elected by the clergy, gave the king a great deal of control over who became a bishop, abbot, or prior in England. He would be present on his own ground for the election and could, at least when the king at issue was Henry II, expect to be able to overawe the assembled clergy into choosing the person he wanted. Not only that, but the new prelate was expected to swear his fidelity and subordinate himself to the king by homage before he was consecrated: by implication, if the king refused to accept the fealty and homage, the elect could not be consecrated. This last provision had been the subject of a fierce dispute between Henry's grandfather and Saint Anselm, archbishop of Canterbury, which was settled in 1107 when Henry I agreed that he would require only fealty (an oath of loyalty), not homage, which could be seen as demeaning because it was a recognition of subordination, and also that he would not require that fealty be sworn before the elect was consecrated into his position. Henry II was now choosing to regard his grandfather's concessions as merely personal and not binding on his successors.

"CRIMINOUS CLERGY"

In Thomas's eyes, clause 3 of the Constitutions of Clarendon was the most inflammatory. It concerned "criminous clergy"—that is, members of the clergy who committed crimes. Even in the modern age, when entering the ministry is a voluntary act of adults, members of the clergy have been known to commit crimes. In the Middle Ages, a significant percentage of the population—it has been estimated as 2 percent—consisted of members of the clergy, and many of these men had taken clerical orders for reasons that had little to do with vocation or virtue. As noted, entry into the church was a way for serfs to escape a life of drudgery. The church was also used to place children for whom aristocratic parents had no other use. Sons were often put into monasteries when they were too young to have any say in the matter (as were daughters into nunneries) or were sent off to train to be priests when they were still young. All formal schools were church institutions, and all students in them were considered to be in minor clerical orders. Schooling was a way for ambitious parents to ensure that their sons would be able to make good careers in administration, church or lay, and in business. For all these and other reasons, the church was full of people who were no less likely to misbehave than the general population.

Yet the church's rules about how to deal with members of the clergy who committed crimes were widely seen as inadequate, both as to proof and as to punishment. As to proof, the church used compurgation, which meant that an accused man was allowed to prove his innocence by swearing that he had not done the act and bringing with him a specified number of "oath-helpers" who also swore that he had not done it—that is, that they believed him when he swore. This was an age-old method of proof. It had been the principal method used by the Anglo-Saxons and had persisted, though it was supplemented after the Norman Conquest by the judicial duel, also known as trial by battle. Members of the clergy, however, could not be asked to fight to prove their innocence, so compurgation remained for them the chief method of proof. By the middle of the twelfth century, however, all the old-style methods of proof, whether compurgation, trial by battle, or trial by ordeal, were coming into disrepute. In an age when philosophers were busy reviving advanced human thought, the idea that the only way to prove something in court was to rely on God to point to culpability or right seemed outmoded. Moreover, in England there had recently been several scandals in which clerics alleged to have committed crimes, including murder and rape, had been acquitted by the old procedures even though "everyone knew" that they were guilty.

The other aspect of the treatment of criminous clergy that was objectionable to many by the middle of the twelfth century concerned punishment. The church was not supposed to shed blood, and members of the clergy were not supposed to be subject to corporal punishments, which made the use of the usual punishment for crimes—execution—impossible. Members of the clergy who were convicted of crimes were, therefore, usually imprisoned by their bishops, a punishment that seemed utterly inadequate to many laypersons of the time. Given how many clerics there were in society in the mid-twelfth century, it is not surprising that disputes about jurisdiction over their crimes were common. In 1163 alone, three separate cases aggravated the deteriorating relations between the king and the archbishop.

The third clause of the Constitutions of Clarendon attempts to deal with at least the problem of punishment. Its language is, probably deliberately, murky. Here are two translations of the clause:

> Clergymen charged and accused of anything shall, on being summoned by a justice of the king, come into his court, to be responsible there for whatever it may seem to the king's court they should there be responsible for; and [to be responsible] in the ecclesiastical court [for what] it may seem they should there be responsible for—so that the king's justice shall send into the court of Holy Church to see on what grounds matters are there to be treated. And if the clergyman is convicted or [if he] confesses, the Church should no longer protect him. (Stephenson and Marcham, no. 30)
>
> Clerks cited and accused of any matter shall, when summoned by the king's justice, come before the king's court to answer there concerning matters which shall seem to the king's court to be answerable there, and before the ecclesiastical court for what shall seem to be answerable there, but in such a way that the justice of the king shall send to the court of holy Church to see how the case is there tried. And if the clerk

be convicted or shall confess, the Church ought no longer to protect him. (Douglas and Greenaway, no. 128)

What was Henry demanding here? If the language of the clause is deliberate, then it appears that the king's court could determine which "matters" were "answerable" in which court. Moreover, if the case was to be tried in the church court, agents of the king would observe the trial in order to ensure that procedures were properly carried out. Although Henry does not seem to be requiring that some novel form of proof be used, the mere presence of lay overseers in a church court was an affront to the independence of the clergy. Even more outrageous in Thomas's eyes was the last provision: that, if the accused was found guilty, he was to be turned over to the lay authorities to be punished as though he were a layman, which meant, in practice, to be executed. In the eyes of the clergy, priestly status could not be undone. A misbehaving priest might be "defrocked"—that is, ordered not to exercise his powers as a priest or to wear the clothing that denoted clerical status—but he was a priest nonetheless. The anointing of priests was as indelible as that of kings; indeed, it was the model for the anointing of kings. By extension, all clerical status was considered to be permanent, though those in lesser orders could be released from their status by higher clerical authorities. In the eyes of Thomas and his supporters, in short, no member of the clergy could be demoted to lay status—much less at the demand of a secular authority.

Clerical Orders

In the medieval Western church, there were seven levels of clerical orders. The four minor orders were porter, lector, exorcist, and acolyte (subdeacon). These orders could be conferred very early in life. For example, all students in schools at higher levels than the village were considered, during the course of their study, to be clerics in minor orders. Only receipt of the first of the major orders, deacon, committed the recipient to continue to live as a cleric for life. The two higher major orders were priest and bishop. Only these last two orders could exercise the cure of souls.

For whatever reasons, and they are mysterious, in all his arguments against the Constitutions Thomas chose to make his stand primarily on the issue of criminous clergy. He argued that expulsion from the ranks of the clergy was sufficient punishment for a cleric convicted of a crime, that to add on any additional punishment was to punish twice for the same crime, and, citing various biblical texts, that such double punishment was forbidden. Some of his arguments suggested that even a defrocked cleric could not be subjected to a corporal punishment. At other times he seemed to admit that once a man had been expelled from the clergy, he could, for a second or later offense, be treated as a layman.

ROYAL JUSTIFICATIONS, EPISCOPAL CAPITULATION, AND A CHANGE OF MIND

More broadly, the question can be raised whether Henry's claim is correct that the 16 practices described in the Constitutions were in fact the practices of his grandfather's reign. Two clauses state—and to some extent amplify—rules known to have been established by William the Conqueror, namely, clause 4, forbidding English clerics to travel outside the kingdom without the king's permission, and clause 11, stating that ecclesiastical tenants of the king are members of his court and cases concerning their lands are justiciable in his court. Clause 12, in contrast, appears to go back to practices Henry I had abandoned in 1107. There is, however, no doubt that the earlier Henry had been able to place the men he wanted into positions of power in the church, so the degree to which the Constitutions misrepresent the actual practice of Henry I's day is a moot question. Otherwise, it is difficult to determine what the practices of Henry I's day were. Sources for twelfth-century England are relatively abundant, but for the first half of the twelfth century they do not address most of the issues raised in the Constitutions, so that avenue of evaluation is not available. All that can be said is that, in the whole long dispute about the Constitutions, their opponents, Thomas's supporters, never alleged that Henry II had invented the rules he attributed to Henry I.

At Clarendon, however, there scarcely was time for reasoned arguments, whether from history or from theology. Instead, the bishops were subject to strong political pressure and even threats of violence if they did not accede to the king's wishes. The rage of any twelfth-century king of England was a fearful thing: kings used the threat or actuality of their anger as a technique of government, and Henry was a master at the art of pressuring people into doing what he wanted. He was assisted at Clarendon by some of the lay lords. Gilbert Foliot, supporter of the king though he later was, described the bishops as "all enclosed in one chamber" for three days and menaced by "all the princes and nobles of the realm" who "blazed up in the greatest anger, roaring and brawling" and threatening them with bodily harm if they did not agree to the king's demands. Nevertheless, the bishops held out in unison, though some of them probably already were on the king's side and others were clearly very frightened, fearing that the king might go so far as to accuse them of treason, exile them, and confiscate their estates. Then, suddenly, Thomas announced that he would accept the Constitutions, though he managed to get the king to agree that he could postpone setting his seal to them. The bishops were nonplussed but followed their leader in his capitulation to the king.

Satisfied for the moment, Henry allowed Thomas and the other bishops to depart from Clarendon. Scarcely had he left, however, than Thomas announced that he had been wrong to give in to the king's threats, no matter what the physical dangers of the moment. He declared that the Constitutions were a grave violation of the liberties of the church, that he was withdrawing his agreement to them, and that all his fellow bishops were to do the same.

To signify the gravity of the sin he felt he had committed in agreeing to the Constitutions, he donned sackcloth and ashes, the traditional garb of the penitent sinner seeking absolution for serious sins. The bishops understandably felt betrayed and abandoned by their leader. Despite their qualms and fears, they had held out against the king's threats until Thomas caved. Now he had changed his mind yet again, and he expected them to brave the king's anger by reversing their stance, too.

ACCUSATIONS AGAINST BECKET AT NORTHAMPTON

Henry's fury was titanic. From then on it was war, almost literally to the death, on Thomas and anyone who supported him. It took the king a while to organize his stroke against the archbishop, which became public at a council held at Northampton in October 1164. Once again, Henry summoned Thomas, the other bishops, and the great lords of England to meet him. His specific purpose was to prefer a hodgepodge of charges against Thomas, from the petty to ones so grave that they might carry a sentence of death. Among other things, Thomas was accused of having lined his own pockets while he was chancellor—even though he had had the foresight, when Henry appointed him archbishop, to secure a pardon for any acts he might have committed while chancellor. Initially, Thomas tried to secure a postponement of his trial on the grounds that he had not been advised of the charges in time to prepare his defense. Again, however, as at Clarendon, the king and the lay lords resorted to pressure and threats against Thomas and the bishops in an attempt to secure a favorable outcome. Perhaps what Henry wanted was for Thomas to resign and retire into a monastery or overseas, leaving the way clear for him to appoint a more accommodating prelate. What he got, however, was Thomas's defiance.

The council's deliberations, which were little more than a trial of Thomas, began on October 8, a Thursday. The climax was reached the following Tuesday. By this time, it had become clear to Thomas that Henry intended to destroy him. He began the day with a meeting with his suffragan bishops in which he complained of their failure to support him, appealed to the pope against a possible criminal verdict against him, and ordered the bishops to excommunicate anyone who laid violent hands on him. He then celebrated a Mass whose introit was "Princes did sit and speak against me," after which he proceeded to the castle dressed in his most formal archiepiscopal vestments and carrying his own archiepiscopal cross. Normally, when an archbishop made a formal procession, a member of his staff carried his cross before him. For Thomas to carry the cross himself was apparently the equivalent of throwing down the gauntlet. The action caused outrage not only among the laymen present but even among at least some of the bishops. Gilbert Foliot muttered, but not so low that others could not hear, "He always was a fool." Details of what happened thereafter are unclear, because none of the writers on whom we depend was present and all had to rely on the confused recollections of those who were. Thomas apparently spent the day in an antechamber to the room where the king was meeting with the lay barons and most of the bishops, while various emissaries attempted to negotiate some solution to the issues. Tempers flared on all sides and eventually, when confronted by the justiciar and several other barons, Thomas declared that the proceedings were illegitimate and, to shouts of "traitor" and "perjurer," stomped out.

There was one last attempt later in the day to find a solution by which the king and the archbishop could be reconciled, a proposal by the bishops of London and Chichester for Thomas to pledge two of the Canterbury manors as surety for payment of the fines assessed against him; but Thomas indignantly rejected this. Early the next morning, Thomas left Northampton and made for the coast in stealth and disguise. His flight was probably arranged in advance, though he may have hoped that he would not have to resort to so drastic an action. Three weeks later, on November 2, with a few companions, he boarded a small boat at the port of Sandwich and sailed for the Continent, landing on the beach at Oye in Flanders. In leaving England without the king's permission, of course, he violated clause 4 of the Constitutions of Clarendon. He also began six years of exile on the Continent. When he finally returned to England, he would live only about a month.

BECKET IN EXILE

Thomas was joined in exile by many of his staff, some of whom had actually preceded him in fleeing. Probably the most important to the unfolding of events were Herbert of Bosham and, arriving somewhat later, John of Salisbury. John was one of the great political theorists of the twelfth century, author of the *Policraticus* (1159). He and Thomas had worked together in Archbishop Theobald's household, and this work was dedicated to Thomas. The *Policraticus* actually argues that a tyrannical ruler may be assassinated, hardly a common idea in a period when the usual teaching was that God placed rulers in their positions and the faithful were required to suffer in patience even their most high-handed actions. Despite this, John often tried to tone down the heat of Thomas's actions and statements in the course of the quarrel with Henry. Herbert of Bosham was another university-trained theologian and writer. Of all Thomas's companions, he was perhaps the most adamant in insisting on the complete independence of the church from interference by secular authorities. He clearly wrote some of Thomas's most important letters as the archbishop pursued his quarrel with Henry over the six years of exile and may have been especially responsible for Thomas's most vociferous pronouncements and dramatic actions.

By appealing to the pope and fleeing to France, Thomas became a player, sometimes little more than a pawn, in a diplomatic game that had been going on at least since Henry became king of England in 1154. The major parties were Henry, King Louis VII of France, who was Henry's overlord for his

French domains (as well as his wife's former husband), Pope Alexander III, and Frederick Barbarossa the Holy Roman Emperor, whose quarrels with Alexander had led him, by 1164, to advocate the right to the papal throne of an "antipope." Indeed, in the course of the years of Thomas's exile, Frederick supported no less than three men in sequence as pope instead of Alexander. In the very complicated diplomacy of these years, Louis and Henry, as overlord and overly powerful vassal, formed one axis of tension, and Alexander and Frederick formed the other. Because Alexander needed the support of other monarchs against Frederick's attempts to oust him from the papacy, Henry had a strong card to play: if Alexander supported Thomas wholeheartedly, Henry would side with Frederick and recognize the antipope as the rightful pope. Louis, however, found Thomas very useful: by supporting Thomas against Henry he could blacken his vassal's reputation by publicizing his maltreatment of a man of the cloth. Louis also offered Alexander refuge from Frederick, who, in 1164, was in military control of most of the Italian peninsula, including the city of Rome itself. Indeed, in 1164 the pope was residing in the French town of Sens. In the crosscurrents of diplomacy as it came to be structured from the moment of Thomas's flight on, the usual alliance was Louis and Thomas against Henry, with Alexander supporting them as passively as he could and Frederick hovering in the background hoping to detach Henry from Alexander if the pope went too far in his support of the archbishop.

Emperors, Popes, and Antipopes

In the early Middle Ages, popes were elected by the clergy and people of Rome, often with much interference from outsiders. From time to time, disputes meant that two men at a time claimed to have been chosen. The title used for the ones who, in the long run, failed to vindicate their claims is "antipope." In 1059, the power to choose the next pope was given to the College of Cardinals, but this hardly ended the phenomenon of antipopes. Indeed, the heyday of antipopes coincides with the period of the greatest conflict between popes and emperors over control of the church, of Rome, and of Italy. Between 1058 and 1138, there was an antipope more than half the time. Later, the Emperor Frederick Barbarossa supported four men successively against Alexander III (pope 1159–81): antipopes who called themselves Victor IV, Pascal III, Callistus III, and Innocent III. Thereafter, the phenomenon of antipopes disappears until the fourteenth century.

Naturally, therefore, once in France Thomas went first to the court of King Louis. With his departure from England, he passed in one moment from being one of the richest men in western Europe to being so poor that it was often a question how he was to support those who had accompanied him or pay for even the most basic necessities of life, his food, lodging, and travel. Louis was quite generous despite the fact that he himself was none too rich and had many calls on his purse. Thomas then traveled to Sens, where the pope had already entertained an embassy from Henry, whose members had been disappointed by Alexander's failure to grant what they wanted. Thomas may have offered to resign his office into the pope's hand, but, if he did, the pope restored him. He certainly presented Alexander with a copy of the Constitutions of Clarendon, which both he and the king's main supporter in the papal curia, William the cardinal of Pavia, then expounded. At the end of the day, the pope ruled that, while none of the constitutions was ideal, some were tolerable. Neither now nor at any time later, however, did the pope issue a written ruling against the intolerable customs.

After his visit to the pope, Thomas and a few companions took up residence at the Cistercian abbey of Pontigny, in Burgundy, which was not part of the domain of either king. He did not become a monk, although he adopted monastic garb while he was living at Pontigny. He lived in the abbey for about two years, until threats by Henry against the Cistercian order in England made it prudent for him to leave. Thereafter, Thomas and his small household made their base an abbey just outside of Sens, although they moved around a good deal. Throughout the years of exile, many of Thomas's supporters had to be accommodated elsewhere in France and Flanders.

KING HENRY'S ANGER

Back in England, Henry, thwarted of his revenge against Thomas, took his anger out against Thomas's family members and his supporters and tenants on the estates of Canterbury. He confiscated all of Thomas's possessions as well as the possessions of all the clerics who had followed him into exile and declared that Thomas had forfeited the archbishopric, whose possessions were entrusted to Ranulf de Broc, already one of Thomas's principal opponents in Kent and at the king's court. Ranulf, in turn, entrusted the actual administration of the archdiocese to his brother Robert, a member of the clergy. It was decreed that no one was to help the archbishop in any way, not even by prayers. At the same time, Thomas's relatives, the members of his household who had not fled the country, and their relatives as well as the relatives of Thomas's companions in exile were arrested. A few bought their way back into the king's favor, but most—probably several hundred persons—were forced out of the country and had to be sheltered at Pontigny or elsewhere.

DIPLOMATIC MANEUVERINGS, PERSONAL MEETINGS, AND RECONCILIATION

The diplomatic negotiations of the years from 1165 through late 1170 were conducted primarily by means of letters, a remarkable number of which survive or can be reconstructed from the details given in surviving replies. Thomas and his supporters kept up a barrage of correspondence intended to prevent Louis, Alexander, or any other Continental authority from abandoning or decreasing their support for him. He wrote repeatedly to the bishops who remained in England—conspicuously, none of them followed him into exile—to urge them to remain steadfast in his support and not to let Henry run roughshod over the church in his absence. He also tried as best he could to keep in touch with supporters in England and prevent them from giving in to despair or to Henry. Henry's chancery poured out equally voluminous amounts of material intended to encourage Louis, Alexander, and others to accept his case against Thomas and abandon him. After Thomas excommunicated several of his opponents in 1166 and 1169 and they appealed to the pope against his sentences, dealings with the papal court about the validity of these sentences added substantially to the volume of correspondence. The ins and outs of all this correspondence and the diplomacy it represents are too complicated for us to follow here.

Gilbert Foliot's Indictment of Thomas

The most famous contemporary denunciation of Thomas occurs in a long letter to him from Gilbert Foliot written in 1166. It describes the origins of the quarrel from the point of view of a bishop who sided with the king throughout. Its principal point is that the matters at issue were relatively unimportant: "[T]here is no dispute between us regarding faith, nor regarding the sacraments, nor morals. . . . The entire dispute with the king . . . is about certain customs which he claims were observed, and enjoyed by his predecessors, and he wishes and expects to enjoy. . . . As very many people say, and the whole history of the realm testifies, he did not himself set up these customs: this is how he found them." The quarrel needed never have become serious and would not have if the personality and actions of the archbishop had not exacerbated the situation beyond the king's bearing. "For what cure is useful that heals one wound, and inflicts one far greater, far more dangerous?" In the most famous passage in the letter, concerning the capitulation at Clarendon, Foliot exclaims, "Who fled? Who turned tail? Who was broken in spirit? . . . Let [God] judge on what account we could not be turned by the threats of princes; let him judge who fled, who was a deserter in the battle. . . . [T]he leader of the army turned tail, the commander of the battlefield ran away, the archbishop of Canterbury departed from the common counsel and association of his brothers." Foliot also expresses his—and other bishops'—sense that Thomas had put them in an impossible position: "You bent the knee at Clarendon, took to flight at Northampton, changed your dress and hid for a time, and secretly left the king's lands, and what did you achieve? What did you gain in doing this, except to evade studiously that death which no one had deigned to threaten? . . . The sword which you have thrown away hangs over us."

The major moments in the attempts to resolve the dispute were those when meetings between Henry and Thomas were arranged. All the parties professed—despite all evidence to the contrary—that the quarrel could most easily be solved if the two protagonists could just get together and talk out their differences. Repeatedly, therefore, meetings were attempted. The first was scheduled to take place at Angers on Easter 1166, but it did not come off, though Henry met with John of Salisbury, Herbert of Bosham, and another of the archbishop's clerks. In November 1167, papal legates moved back and forth between Henry in Normandy and Thomas just beyond the border, but nothing notable came of this attempt. Again in July 1168, a proposed meeting between Henry and Thomas at La Ferté-Bernard failed to occur. At Montmirail in early January 1169, Henry and Thomas actually met but wound up quarreling even worse than before, to the disgust of the French king and the papal legates in attendance. A month later, Thomas was nearby while Henry and Louis tried but failed to work out a compromise. An elaborate round of negotiations throughout much of the rest of the year resulted in a near meeting at Montmartre, outside Paris: the two principals were in adjoining spaces while their emissaries worked out a compromise, but their efforts came to nothing because Thomas demanded that Henry exchange the kiss of peace with him, as a guarantee of his sincerity, and Henry refused to give it. He alleged that his only reason was that he had once sworn never to exchange the kiss with Thomas and he would not break an oath. He offered to have his eldest son kiss Thomas instead, but Thomas found this insufficient. Predictably, an attempt in early 1170 to arrange another conference failed yet again.

Finally, however, a second meeting actually came off. On July 22, 1170, in a meadow near Fréteval, the king and the archbishop faced each other. By this time, Thomas was more alarmed that his exile was harming the interests of the church of Canterbury than he had ever been. In the spring of that year, Henry had decided to crown his eldest son, also named Henry (afterward known as "the Young King"), during his own lifetime. The kings of France had been using this practice for nearly two centuries as a method of ensuring an undisputed succession to the throne. It had occasionally been used by Anglo-Saxon kings of England but had never become a regular part of English practice and had not been used in England since long before the Norman Conquest. Henry may have decided to adopt the practice largely in order to put pressure on Thomas, for one of the prerogatives of the archbishops of Canterbury had long been to crown the kings of England, yet Henry had the act performed by Roger of Pont l'Evêque archbishop of York, assisted by perhaps as many as 10 of Henry's supporters among the bishops of England and Normandy, including Gilbert Foliot of London and Joscelin of Salisbury.

To see York exercise a right that properly belonged to Canterbury must have alarmed Thomas greatly. Perhaps for this reason, he was much less confrontational at Fréteval than he had been in previous negotiations. Henry, too, may have felt that the time had finally come for all this exhausting drama to come to an end. The two men met, alone, for most of the day, which led, later on, to a good deal of dispute as to exactly what they had agreed upon. Nonetheless, they came to an apparent resolution: Henry would allow Thomas to return to Canterbury. The king would rectify the matter of the Young King's coronation, probably by allowing Thomas to re-crown young Henry and to punish the bishops who had participated in the first ceremony. The king restored both the archbishop and his servants, including Herbert of Bosham and John of Salisbury, to his peace, though without the kiss of peace; and Thomas blessed the king, though he refused to issue immediate pardons to those who had supported the king throughout the quarrel. It is noteworthy that few of the underlying causes of the quarrel were addressed. The Constitutions of Clarendon were apparently not even mentioned.

Henry II and His Sons

Henry and Eleanor had four sons who survived at least into young adulthood. The eldest was also named Henry; by 1170 he was probably 16 and was married to Margaret, daughter of King Louis VII of France. As chancellor, Thomas had gone on a famous embassy to the court of the king of France to arrange this marriage. The "Young King," whose coronation in 1170 played a role in motivating the attempt to end the controversy between Henry II and Thomas and whose unsympathetic treatment of Thomas in the month after his return to Canterbury is described in several sources, led a revolt against his father in 1173 and 1174. He died in 1183, before his father, and never became king in his own right. The other three boys were too young in the 1160s to play any role in the famous controversy. As they grew up, however, how their father was going to divide his domains among his sons became one of the major causes of conflict in the reign. As events played out, two of Henry's sons succeeded in turn to an undivided inheritance. When Henry II died in 1189, he was succeeded by his second son, Richard I, famous as Richard the Lionhearted. When Richard died in 1199, he was succeeded by the youngest of the brothers, John, the king who granted Magna Carta in 1215. The fourth brother, Geoffrey, third in order of birth, had been married to the heiress of the county of Brittany, but he died in 1186. His only son, Arthur, did try to raise a claim to the succession in 1199, only to be captured by his uncle John in 1204, after which he disappeared; he was probably murdered.

Thomas then returned to Sens to wind up his affairs there and rejoined the king in September. Relations were decidedly cool: indeed, when the two attended Mass, Henry ensured that he would not have to exchange a kiss with Thomas by arranging to have the mass for the dead celebrated instead of the usual service. The two met on and off throughout much of the fall, quarreling and making up. Eventually, it was agreed that Thomas should return to England and his see in November. Henry gave Thomas a letter of safe conduct and letters addressed to his son the new king and the king's men at Canterbury ordering them to allow the archbishop back into the country, his see, and his possessions. He may have intended to accompany Thomas back across the Channel and attend his reinstallation. If he had, things might have turned out very differently, but Henry fell ill—or feigned illness—and Thomas traveled without a royal escort. Allegedly, on parting from Henry he predicted that the two would not meet again in this life.

BECKET'S RETURN TO ENGLAND

Thomas arrived at the English port of Sandwich on the first of December and proceeded from there to Canterbury the next day. He was, so his biographers report, greeted by huge, cheering throngs all along his route and in the city itself. It is clear, however, that not everyone was happy to see him return. Most conspicuously, the men to whom Henry had entrusted the archbishop's estates were not pleased at the prospect of losing these lucrative properties.

Once he arrived at Canterbury, Thomas took up residence in the archbishop's palace and recommenced his archiepiscopal duties while he attempted to recover the properties of his see from their intruded occupants. After about a week at Canterbury, he began traveling, showing himself throughout his diocese, visiting London, and attempting to secure an audience with the Young King, who was at Winchester. Instead, however, emissaries from the young Henry ordered him back to Canterbury and told him to stay there. He was back in his cathedral by December 20.

Unfortunately, even before he left France Thomas had decided that he needed to take action against the most prominent of the bishops who had supported Henry against him during the preceding six years. He had long had in his possession a letter from Pope Alexander authorizing him to excommunicate his opponents when and if he thought he needed to do so, reinforced by a second letter from Alexander that he received in November, and the king had agreed that he could punish his opponents among the bishops. Therefore, before he even embarked for England, Thomas excommunicated the three bishops who had most conspicuously opposed him: Roger of Pont l'Evêque of York, Gilbert Foliot of London, and Jocelin de Bohun of Salisbury. He thereby precipitated the events that led to his death.

The three bishops were understandably upset when they heard the news of their excommunication—Thomas's messenger delivered it at great personal danger—and they immediately appealed to the pope and hastily set off for France, where they found the king in Normandy just before Christmas. When Henry heard the news, he delegated several of the senior members of his entourage to go to Canterbury and deal with the archbishop, perhaps by arresting him. Unfortunately, at some point, perhaps on Christmas Day itself, while he was in a rage, he also uttered the fateful words that led to Thomas's death. They are variously reported, but he exclaimed something like, "Will no one rid me of this meddlesome priest?" Or maybe he said "turbulent"—or even "lowborn." Whatever exactly he said, four knights of his household decided to take him at his word and rode off to rid him of the archbishop.

THE MURDER OF BECKET

The four knights made remarkable speed, leaving the king on December 26 and arriving in England on the 28th, several days before the official delegation. They were William de Tracy, Reginald FitzUrse, Hugh de Morville, and Richard le Bret (or Brito). All were of middling status and middling wealth in the aristocracy. Le Bret was somewhat less important than the others, but all had places at the royal court and all but Le Bret had apparently been Thomas's vassals when he was chancellor. They may all have had connections with King Stephen, the previous king, whose reign Henry II regarded as illegitimate; if they did, that may have made them even more eager than the average courtier to prove themselves loyal to Henry. It may have been the reason why they responded with alacrity to whatever demand they perceived the king to have thrown at his entourage. What demand did they think the king had given? From their reported actions when they arrived at Canterbury and confronted the archbishop, it would seem that the knights themselves were not entirely sure what they were going to do with or to him. Force him to resign? Kidnap him and deliver him to the king? Kill him? The last is what ultimately happened, but it is quite possible that it was done on the spur of the moment rather than as a premeditated act.

Once they had landed in England, the four repaired to Saltwood Castle, one of the archbishop's estates, which had been in the hands of the de Broc brothers since Henry confiscated them. The de Brocs had been among Thomas's local enemies almost from the moment that he was appointed archbishop. They were the logical persons to whom the knights would turn for shelter and support. They provided the knights with a sizable military force, perhaps two dozen men, when they set out for Canterbury on December 29. Having arrived at Canterbury about 3:00 p.m., which, only eight days after the winter solstice, was the late afternoon, this hostile force first tried to recruit townsmen to their active support. When this failed, they ordered the townsfolk to stay in their houses and out of the way and surrounded the cathedral precincts to prevent anyone from coming to Thomas's aid.

Accounts of what happened next differ somewhat. None of the knights left an account of his side of the story, at least not one that has survived the ages. On the archbishop's side, five eyewitnesses to at least part of the drama—John of Salisbury and William FitzStephen, two of Thomas's clerks; Benedict of

Peterborough and William of Canterbury, both visiting monks; and Edward Grim, a visiting cleric—left narratives of what happened. Many of Thomas's companions had not yet, of course, arrived back in Canterbury by December 29. Grim was present by happenstance: he had been priest of Saltwood but had been expelled shortly after the de Brocs took control of the castle, perhaps in 1164, and was in Canterbury to pursue his claim to be restored to that church. Of the five, it was probably only Grim who was present throughout the confrontation. All the others vanished at some point in fear of their lives: John of Salisbury, for example, saw the beginning of the final confrontation but then hid behind an altar. Grim, moreover, was badly wounded attempting to defend Thomas, which undoubtedly interfered with his understanding of the last moments of the attack. For all the witnesses, moreover, the noise, the confusion, the deepening darkness, and their own fear must have made it difficult to know exactly what was going on.

The knights' first interview with the archbishop was peaceful in the sense that they divested themselves of their arms before coming into his chamber, where Thomas was consulting with his close confidants and some of the monks of the abbey. The meeting rapidly degenerated into a shouting match, however, and the two sides separated, the knights withdrawing to arm themselves. When they attempted to return, they found that the monks' servants had managed to bar the doors, so they had to break in through a disused door in the archbishop's palace and make their way toward the church itself. By this time it was probably about four o'clock, rapidly darkening, and the archbishop—in his full vestments and with his cross carried before him—was heading for the church, where the monks were celebrating Vespers. Both the monks and Thomas's staff tried to persuade him that, in the circumstances, he could either forgo the ceremony or order the doors to the church locked. Thomas, however, insisted that God's church could not be barred to the faithful and, therefore, the doors could not be locked.

What Was Thomas Wearing When He Died?

When he died, Thomas was wearing what seems to a modern person like a remarkable amount of clothing. It was, after all, wintertime in a period when heat was provided only by fires, and a huge church like Canterbury cathedral must have been frigid. Here, drawn mostly from the account given by a contemporary biographer named Guernes of Pont-Sainte-Maxence, is Frank Barlow's list of what he had on: "Next to his skin was his long hair shirt, the unusual breeches hidden by white underpants. . . . Thomas had put this garment on shortly after he was ordained priest and retained it all his life. On top of this . . . came . . . a linen shirt followed by a cowl. . . . [A]bove it came two ample but short soft pelisses, both of lambskins. Finally, he wore the supposed habit of a canon regular: another pelisse of lambskins, a fine white surplice or tunic . . . and, to cover it all, a black mantle without a fringe, lined with white lambskins, and with a black tassel for fastening it up." He also wore a cap on his head, which one of the murderers knocked off early in the final confrontation, and "heavy shoes." Several of these layers of garments took on great significance as the body was prepared for burial.

The discovery that Thomas was wearing a hair shirt did much to persuade the monks of the cathedral—many of whom had, until then, regarded him as an exceptionally interfering intruder—that he was a holy man after all, as did the linen shirt and cowl, which were taken to be monastic garb. Before burial, the outer layers of clothing were removed, and Thomas was dressed instead in garments he had long had set aside for this purpose, again a remarkable number of layers: "the alb in which he had been consecrated priest, a simple superhumeral or amice, a stole and maniple and, on his head, the chrismal cloth from his baptism and a mitre. Finally, . . . his archiepiscopal vestments, his tunic, dalmatic, chasuble and pallium with its pins."

Thomas and the knights confronted one another in a small vestibule leading into the church itself. First the knights tried to arrest the archbishop and laid hands upon him. Reginald FitzUrse may have tried to hoist him onto the back of William de Tracy. If so, Thomas broke away, and it seems to be at this point that one of the knights struck the first blow. At approximately the same moment, Thomas seems to have resigned himself to his fate, for the accounts say that he knelt and prayed, putting up no further resistance. Edward Grim tried to protect him—the only person to do so—but the first blow, struck by either FitzUrse or de Tracy, cut through the arm he had thrust forward to protect the archbishop and partially severed the crown of Thomas's head. The second blow drove Thomas to the floor. The third, from Richard Le Bret, was so forceful that it not only completed the severing of Thomas's crown but broke off the tip of the sword, which was later retrieved by the monks and eventually displayed in a shrine of its own at the site of the murder. By this time Thomas must have been dead, but a hanger-on of the knights, a disgraced cleric named Hugh of Horsea, with his sword pushed some of the archbishop's brains out of his skull and smeared them on the floor.

The knights left the church, stopping on the way to loot the archbishop's palace of all the documents they could find, which they turned over to the king, and of valuables later estimated to be worth two thousand marks, a huge sum in that day, which they kept for themselves. Then they retired to Saltwood. Later they holed up in a royal castle in northern England, Knaresborough, of which Hugh de Morville was custodian, where they remained for about a year. Various stories are told about what eventually happened to them. If they thought that their actions would bring them advancement at the court of Henry II, they must soon have recognized how grave a miscalculation that was. The horror and sacrilege of the crime were too great. Indeed, it seems that the knights themselves were soon overcome with guilt. The few contemporary sources that discuss their fate concur that they had penances imposed on them by the pope that required them to go on pilgrimage to Jerusalem and that all of them died there within a few years of the murder and were buried there. Some modern scholars have suggested that, instead, they lived on and eventually worked their ways back into the king's good graces and resumed their estates and their lives as minor barons. The most recent investigation, however, concludes that the contemporary version is correct: all four made significant donations to religious institutions beginning almost immediately after the murder; the estates of all four passed to female relatives or cousins, excluding their direct male heirs, in such a way as to suggest that the king had confiscated them and retained part for himself; and it is likely that they were, indeed, all buried in Jerusalem. The de Broc brothers, however, apparently suffered no serious consequences for their support of the murderers.

THE AFTERMATH OF BECKET'S MURDER

In the cathedral, the frightened monks, clerics, servants, and other bystanders—there probably were townspeople who had come into the church to attend the evening service—gradually crept out of their hiding places and regarded the spectacle of an archbishop dead on the floor. His body was placed on a bier, which was deposited before the high altar of the cathedral. A few dipped handkerchiefs into the blood on the floor, and some attempt was made to gather up the blood and brains as relics. The next day the body was hastily buried in the crypt of the cathedral when Robert de Broc returned with armed men and threatened to carry off the body and dump it in a drain unless it was buried in an obscure place.

It is likely that, in the first few days after the murder, the monks and Thomas's staff were so dazed and so fearful of what might still happen that they did not immediately contemplate airing a grievance about what had happened or promoting the idea that Thomas was a martyr. Nonetheless, as rumors of what had happened spread within and then beyond Canterbury, stories began to accumulate that he was performing miracles. Soon pilgrims were attempting to visit the site. As the site of an act of violence, the church was regarded as polluted and in need of reconsecration. It was not even reopened to the public until Easter 1171, and it was not reconsecrated until the feast of Saint Thomas the Apostle on December 21, which was Thomas of Canterbury's birthday. For a while the de Brocs did their best to deter pilgrims, but on Pentecost 1171, their own brother, William, was cured at Thomas's tomb, after which they ceased to oppose the development of the cult.

Murdered Politicians as Popular Saints

It was quite common in the high Middle Ages for prominent persons to be regarded as saints after they died, at least by the populace if not by the institutional church, especially if they had died by violence in the course of political quarrels. King Olaf II of Norway became Saint Olaf after his death in battle in 1030. Charles "the Good" count of Flanders was treated as a saint by the people of Flanders after he was murdered in the church of Bruges in 1127. In England, the remains of Simon de Montfort, the great opponent of King Henry III, were buried inconspicuously, allegedly under a tree, after his death at the battle of Evesham in 1265, probably to prevent a cult from developing around it. Nonetheless, people made pilgrimages to the site in the abbey of Evesham where parts of his body had briefly been buried and collections were made of the stories of miracles performed there. There were pilgrimages to the tombs both of King Edward II, murdered after his abdication in 1327, and of his great opponent, Thomas of Lancaster, who was killed at Edward's order in 1322; King Richard II at the end of the fourteenth century made an effort to secure the formal recognition of Edward II's sanctity. King Henry VI, who was murdered in 1471 and who had lived a notably religious life, was acclaimed a saint: his canonization was pursued by King Henry VII. These are only some of the most prominent examples. Public reaction to the death of Princess Diana in 1997 might be cited as a modern parallel.

News of Thomas's death spread very rapidly. Henry learned of it three days after it happened. The news reached the pope early in 1171, and he was soon bombarded by emissaries and letters from Thomas's supporters demanding action and from Henry and his supporters asking that nothing be done in haste. The question to which everyone wanted an answer—and to which we still today would like an answer—is, did the murderers act on an instruction from Henry? Henry adamantly insisted that the four knights acted entirely on their own and that he was devastated by Thomas's death. He certainly seemed to demonstrate genuine grief at the loss of a man who had, after all, once been his best friend. It does, however, have to be recognized that, on December 25, 1170, it may have seemed to the king that there was no way out of the quarrel so long as he and Thomas were both alive. Indeed, some historians of the affair have suggested that, by December 29, Thomas had come to the same conclusion and that, in effect, he voluntarily sacrificed himself in the interest of peace.

March 25 was the traditional date on which the pope anathematized enemies of the church. By promising that Henry would submit himself entirely to the pope's judgment, Henry's envoys managed to ensure that, on March 25, 1171, only those directly involved in the murder and those who had helped them were condemned. Henry's person and his Continental lands, but not England, were put under interdict, but the king was not excommunicated. Henry spent much of 1171 and early 1172 in Ireland, attempting to conquer it, ironically on the basis of a papal bull from 1155 authorizing him to do so. In the meantime, his representatives negotiated quite a lenient settlement with the pope. In the same period, Thomas's excommunications and suspensions from office of the three bishops were gradually lifted and they were restored to control of their sees. In the spring of 1172, Henry met with papal legates in France, and on Sunday, May 21, at Avranches in Normandy, he was reconciled with the church after he publicly admitted responsibility for Thomas's death, took an oath that he had not intended the murder, and agreed to terms, of which two were most important. First, he would permit free appeals to the pope in ecclesiastical matters, though he could require that the appellant provide security that he was seeking nothing harmful to the king or the kingdom. Second, more vaguely, he would not require the church to observe any bad customs that had been introduced in his time. He also promised to restore all of Canterbury's possessions, to receive all his recent opponents back into his peace, to maintain two hundred knights in defense of the kingdom of Jerusalem, and to go on crusade himself by the following summer.

It is notable that, while Henry did surrender what he had claimed in the eighth clause of the Constitutions of Clarendon, and appeals flowed from England to the pope for nearly four centuries, until they were outlawed in 1533, his broader promise about customs pertaining to the church at least theoretically did not require him to abandon any of the other claims he had made in the Constitutions of Clarendon because he alleged that all of those were the customs of his grandfather's day, not his own. It is possible that at a council held at Caen at the end of May he did release the bishops of England from the promise they had made back in 1164 to observe the customs listed in the Constitutions. However, he also sent a letter to various dignitaries in England announcing the settlement at Avranches in which he "reckoned" that the customs he had been forced to renounce were "few or none." It is also notable that Henry changed little about his treatment of major offices in the church. In attempting to secure support for his rebellion against his father in 1173 and 1174, the Young King quoted the writ in which his father had ordered the clergy of Winchester to hold a free election to fill the vacant bishopric: he nonetheless ordered that they "elect no one but my clerk, Richard of Ilchester," who did indeed become bishop. The monarch of England's control over choice of the bishops of the church in England, and later of the Church of England, was not seriously affected by the settlement of the "Becket Controversy."

HENRY'S PENANCE AND PUNISHMENTS

Henry visited Thomas's tomb in the crypt of Canterbury cathedral in July 1174 and, once again, confessed to inadvertently causing his death. He underwent public penance that included flagellation and a full day and night of fasting, as well as making lavish presents to the church. Then, in 1176, in a further series of definitions of the rights of the king and the church that were arrived at by the king in discussion with a papal legate, Henry conceded the following: First, he would not keep churches vacant for more than a year except for great necessity, another concession that made little difference as it was the king who determined when there was necessity to keep a church vacant for more than a year. Second, he would allow the church to discipline members of the clergy when they committed crimes. There was a significant exception: clergy accused of forest offenses were to be treated like anyone else. Nonetheless, Henry's concession on the matter of criminous clergy created a special privilege for clerics, known as "benefit of clergy," which survived until the early nineteenth century. For a few decades, indeed, it looked as though the whole church might adopt the principle that members of the clergy who were accused of crimes could be tried and punished only in church courts, not by lay courts, but that did not turn out to be the case.

The Later History of Benefit of Clergy

As benefit of clergy functioned at first, if a man (the privilege did not apply to the only women who could be considered clergy—that is, nuns) who was brought into court on criminal charges claimed to be a cleric, the authorities would send a message to the bishop of his diocese, asking if his claim was true. If the bishop recognized the accused as a cleric, he would be turned over to the bishop for trial and, if convicted, punishment. The punishment would include defrocking, so that for any second offense the accused could be treated as a layman. This procedure proved cumbersome, however, and relatively soon a quicker method of deciding whether someone was a cleric was devised: namely, asking the accused to read. This worked because in the Middle Ages almost the only persons who could read (especially in Latin) were members of the clergy. One verse of the Bible, the beginning of Psalm 51 ("Have mercy on me, O God, according to your steadfast love; according to your abundant mercy blot out my transgressions"), was chosen so often that it became known as the "neck verse" because if an accused man read it successfully— including, presumably, one who memorized it beforehand rather than actually being able to read—he saved his neck. Moreover, it became the habit of the courts to release anyone who successfully read what was put before him, rather than actually shipping the alleged cleric off to a bishop for trial. Benefit of clergy therefore functioned as a first offender's privilege: it could be claimed only once, and, at least from the sixteenth century on, anyone who successfully claimed it was branded on the thumb so that he could not claim it a second time. Letting first offenders off with a warning made quite a lot of sense in a period when the punishment for all but the most minor offenses was execution and the confiscation of all property.

Basing the determination of clerical status on a man's ability to read had complicated implications as more and more people became literate in later centuries. To cope with the ramifications of this, the most serious crimes were eventually excluded by statute from the privilege, first treason and later murder, rape, arson, witchcraft, and so on. There was, in effect, a tripartite division of crimes: non-clergiable felonies (those for which one could not claim clergy) were the most serious; in the middle were clergiable felonies, and the least serious infractions were mere misdemeanors. By a statute in 1547, the privilege was extended to illiterate members of the House of Lords. In 1575, a statute provided that the benefit should be pled after conviction rather than at the start of the trial and that the convict could be imprisoned for a year even if he successfully pled clergy. A statute of 1624 extended the privilege to women, and a statute of 1706 abolished the reading test, which made the privilege available to everyone, literate or not. In 1770, John Adams, counsel for the defendants in the Boston Massacre case, pled the clergy of the two soldiers who were convicted, thereby saving them from execution. By then, however, changes in the criminal law had made the privilege obsolescent. Benefit of clergy was one of the first medieval oddities to go when modernization of the Common Law began: a statute of 1827 abolished it, six and a half centuries after Henry II first granted it.

All in all, therefore, and with the exception of appeals to the pope and benefit of clergy, the years of conflict between Henry II and Thomas of Canterbury made very little difference to church-state relations in England. The monarchs of England retained and, indeed, retain to this day, at least on paper, a great deal of control over the church. Throughout the rest of the Middle Ages and for centuries beyond, great churchmen were figures of importance in secular government as well as in the church itself, and appointing them gave the monarchs the control they needed over their servants as well as a great source of patronage with which to assuage the cravings of the great families of England for wealth and power.

THOMAS'S LEGACY

In so far as Thomas left a great legacy, it was as a saint rather than as a politician. By the time that Henry performed his penance at Thomas's tomb, Thomas had officially been recognized martyr for the faith. After some investigation of claims that Thomas was performing miracles, Pope Alexander III formally canonized him on February 21, 1173, less than 26 months after his death, a remarkably short interval for a canonization. The veneration of the new martyr spread with notable rapidity around Europe. No earlier medieval saint's cult spread anything like as fast, and only Saint Francis of Assisi compares among later saints. Thomas's cult remained a major one for centuries, celebrated in architecture, art, music, the liturgy, and plays. In Scotland, the abbey of Arbroath, founded by King William the Lion in 1175, was dedicated to Thomas. The spread of veneration for him on the Continent was undoubtedly helped by the marriages of three of Henry II's daughters to rulers of foreign lands: Joan married first in Sicily and then in southern France, Matilda in Germany, and Eleanor in Spain. Thus, possibly the earliest known representation in art of Saint Thomas of Canterbury is a mosaic in the church of Monreale in Sicily, which may have been done as early as sometime between 1174 and 1182, probably after Joan of England's marriage to William of Sicily in 1177. By about 1190, a stained-glass window in Sens cathedral depicted scenes from Thomas's life; from about 1206 comes a window in Chartres cathedral, to which John of Salisbury, as bishop of Chartres between 1176 and his death in 1180, had given two vials of Saint Thomas's blood. Relics of Saint Thomas were distributed very widely, and, for most of the thirteenth century, the great French center of enamelware at Limoges turned out small chests, most of them intended as reliquaries, depicting the scene of the murder, often accompanied by the scene of the saint's burial. More of these chests survive of Thomas than of any other saint. From Scandinavia to Iceland to Spain to Rome to the Holy Land, churches and chapels were dedicated to Saint Thomas.

At least 184 sermons on him survive from between the 1170s and about 1400; the preachers whose nationalities are known were English, French, Italian, Portuguese, German, Austrian, and Polish. Thomas became the patron saint of the London Company of Brewers and the Venetian wine coopers. By the early sixteenth century, if not earlier, the tale of Saint Thomas was the subject of popular plays: a pageant was performed annually at Canterbury from 1504 until the suppression of Thomas's cult and revived under Queen Mary; in 1519 Becket's life was the subject of a pageant in the London midsummer show. These are only a few of the examples of the ways in which Saint Thomas of Canterbury became one of the most famous saints in all of Europe.

CANTERBURY CATHEDRAL AND SAINT THOMAS'S SHRINE

The great center of the cult of Saint Thomas was, of course, Canterbury itself. Chaucer's pilgrims in the *Canterbury Tales* were off to see "the holy blissful martyr." Indeed, Canterbury became certainly the most popular pilgrimage site in England and perhaps the fourth most popular site for all Europeans, after Jerusalem, Rome, and Saint James of Compostella. As was usual with a canonization, the monks of Canterbury Cathedral were ordered to translate—that is, move—the new saint's body to a place of honor in the church. Unfortunately, there was a major fire in the cathedral on September 5, 1174. While it did not damage either the site of the murder or the tomb of the saint, which was then in the crypt, rebuilding took so long that the formal translation of Saint Thomas's remains to the elegant shrine in the Trinity Chapel behind the main altar of the cathedral—where they would stay for more than three centuries—did not take place until 1220, the fiftieth anniversary of his martyrdom. The ceremony was conducted, of course, by the archbishop of Canterbury of the day, Stephen Langton, and attended by King Henry III. That shrine was magnificent. Its most notable feature was a great ruby, known as the Régale of France, which King Louis VII had presented to the cathedral on a visit on 1179, allegedly to pray for the welfare of his son and heir. There was also a shrine enclosing the sword point that had broken off in the course of the attack on the archbishop, and visitors to the cathedral were also shown a separate relic alleged to be the piece of the saint's skull that was struck off in his murder. Trinity Chapel was adorned with a magnificent series of stained-glass windows depicting the miracles the saint had performed.

The Shrine of Saint Thomas

No particularly good depictions of the shrine survive, but from the extant evidence John Butler has derived this description of the monument: "The shrine . . . was raised up on steps and fronted by an altar and consisted of three parts: a stone plinth with an open arcaded base, the richly gilded and decorated wooden casket in which the feretrum [reliquary] containing the relics of the saint was laid, and a painted wooden canopy, suspended from the roof by a series of pulleys that enabled it to be raised or lowered to reveal or cover the casket itself. The casket was covered in gold plate and decorated with fine golden trellis-work. Affixed to the gold plate were innumerable jewels, pearls, sapphires, diamonds, rubies and emeralds, together with rings and cameos of sculptured agates, cornelians and onyx stones. Also attached to the casket was the great Régale of France." Writing of his visit to the cathedral in about 1512, the great humanist Desiderius Erasmus said of the shrine that "every part glistened, shone, and sparkled with rare and very large jewels, some of them larger than a goose's egg."

The Trinity Chapel is raised above the level of the main body of the cathedral by flanking flights of steps. "After making their way [up one of these flights of stairs] from the site of the martyrdom and the crypt, many of [the pilgrims] crawling on their hands and knees and prostrating themselves before the shrine, the climactic moment came for the canopy to be raised on its pulleys and the glistening casket revealed." According to Erasmus's narrative, "silver bells tinkled and one of the officers of the priory came forward with a white wand, touching the many jewels with it, indicating their quality and value, and naming their donors. After prayers and intercessions had been offered and gifts surrendered, the canopy descended and the pilgrims withdrew . . . down the opposite flight of steps from that by which they had ascended."

It was apparently not possible for anyone actually to see the portions of the saint's body that were enclosed in the feretrum. Most of the relics of Saint Thomas that were separately housed at Canterbury and elsewhere were either cloth soaked in the blood he shed when he was murdered or items he had used, or at least touched, while alive. Archbishop Langton, however, was reported to have retained some small bones when Thomas's body was laid in the feretrum in 1220 so that they could be distributed elsewhere, and the part of Thomas's skull that was struck off at the time of his murder was kept in a separate shrine. By the sixteenth century, the monks were apparently claiming that this was the whole of the saint's skull: Erasmus described this item as the "perforated skull of the martyr . . . covered in silver, but the forehead is left bare for people to kiss." Other contemporary descriptions agree. As Butler says, "With the removal [in 1538] of Becket's bones from the shrine, skull and all, the abuse became openly known."

SAINT THOMAS AND THE REFORMATION

And so things remained until 1538. By then, the king of England was Henry VIII, and he was engaged in separating the Church of England from the Roman Catholic Church. Both to Henry and to his opponents, Saint Thomas was the preeminent symbol of denial of the new regime. The powerful influence of this martyr had to be destroyed if Henry was to succeed. In September 1538, the Royal Commissioners for the Destruction of Shrines, having already dealt with many prominent saints, came to Canterbury to deal with Saint Thomas. Henry VIII's chief henchman, Thomas Cromwell, was an active participant in what followed, and the king himself was close by. The shrine was dismantled, its jewels and precious metals were seized for the king and transported to the Tower of London, and the saint's body was removed from the reliquary at the center of the shrine. What became of it? By October 1538, the story was beginning to spread on the Continent that the body had been burned in Cromwell's presence and the ashes had been scattered to the winds, dumped in the River Stour, or even shot out of a cannon at Cromwell's order, depending on who was telling the story. Whether some version of this tale is true or, if not, what happened to Thomas's mortal remains provides a minor but interesting mystery to this day.

What Happened to Thomas's Bones?

In a thorough and well-argued, but ultimately inconclusive, book, The Quest for Becket's Bones: The Mystery of the Relics of St. Thomas Becket of Canterbury *(1995), John Butler explores the evidence for and against the story that the saint's bones were burned in 1538 and considers the many hypotheses as to what may have happened to them if, in fact, they were not burned. Butler sums up many of questions about possible resting places thus:*

> *Whose remains rest in the two unmarked graves in the north aisle of the eastern crypt [of the cathedral]? Who, if anyone, lies beneath the irregular and unidentified ledger slab near the altar of St. Mary Magdalene in the north transept of the crypt—a slab that is embossed with the cross of Canterbury and is almost identical to the one covering the tomb of Archbishop Stephen Langton . . . ? Does the disturbed pavement immediately to the south of this slab, in the Chapel of St. Nicholas, conceal a grave, and if so, whose? Why is the lamp that burns above the altar of St. Mary Magdalene red, the colour of a martyr? Is there a grave behind the altar of Our Lady in the Undercroft, and if so, whose? And is there a parish church somewhere in east Kent that, as one popular legend has it, unknowingly harbours the bones of the saint . . . ? Of all the many speculations, none has aroused greater interest . . . [than] that which sprang dramatically to life on 23 January 1888, when workmen excavating part of the crypt of the Cathedral uncovered a hitherto unknown collection of bones.*

Ultimately, however, Butler concludes that those bones cannot be Becket's, though they may, nonetheless, have something to do with what happened to his body. He leaves it up to the reader to decide among five possible solutions to the mystery.

Shortly after the destruction of the shrine and the disposal, one way or another, of the saint's body, on November 16, 1538, the king issued a proclamation declaring that, because "Thomas Becket, sometime archbishop of Canterbury, stubbornly [opposed] the wholesome laws established against the enormities of the clergy by the king's highness' most noble progenitor, King Henry the second," and because "his canonization was made only by the bishop of Rome because he [Thomas] had been a champion to maintain his [the pope's] usurped authority and a bearer of the iniquity of the clergy," the king now "has thought it expedient to declare . . . that . . . there appears nothing in his life and exterior conversation whereby he should be called a saint, but rather esteemed to be a rebel and traitor to his prince." Therefore, the king ordered that "from henceforth the said Thomas Becket shall not be esteemed, named, reputed, nor called a saint . . . and that his images and pictures through the whole realm shall be put down and avoided out of all churches, chapels, and other places and that . . . the days used to be festival in his name shall not be observed, nor the service . . . and prayers in his name read, but razed and put out of all the books." In many surviving manuscripts, images that once depicted the life, death, and miracles of Saint Thomas of Canterbury have been cut out, scraped off, or otherwise mutilated, and many of the reliquaries and other precious objects that had commemorated Thomas must have been destroyed. The archbishop of Canterbury removed the image of Saint Thomas from his seal, as in 1539 did the city of London along with the motto on the seal, which had read, "Thomas, do not cease to protect me, who gave you birth."

In England for centuries Thomas remained a pro-Catholic, anti-Protestant symbol and a symbol of church claims for what supporters defined as independence of lay control and opponents defined as ecclesiastical supremacy over lay government. When, between 1553 and 1558, Queen Mary I tried to restore Catholicism in England, attacks on newly installed images of Saint Thomas of Canterbury were one way of expressing opposition to the queen's policy, for example. In the seventeenth century, some English Catholics sported medallions with Thomas of Canterbury on one side and Thomas More on the other—two men named Thomas who opposed kings named Henry in support of the Catholic Church and were executed at the king's command, a parallelism that had been noted in print in several sixteenth-century English works of history. Almost without fail, Catholic historians of the Middle Ages and biographers of Thomas of Canterbury and Henry II supported Thomas's cause; Protestants supported Henry. Only in the twentieth century did the ideal of the dispassionate historian begin to prevail, leading scholars to attempt to evaluate the ins and outs of Thomas's story with as little polemical input as possible.

BECKET IN THE MODERN AGE

In the nineteenth and twentieth centuries, the story of Thomas Becket attracted the notice of quite a few playwrights, no doubt because of the inherently dramatic quality of the subject. In 1840 George Darley published *Thomas À Becket: A Dramatic Chronicle in Five Acts*. In 1863, an American, Alexander Hamilton (not, needless to say, the founding father), published *Thomas A'Becket: A Tragedy, in Five Acts*. Much better known than either of these is the play *Becket,* which the poet laureate of Great Britain, Alfred Lord Tennyson, finished in 1879, but did not publish until 1884. First produced by Sir Henry Irving in 1891, it became the most successful of Tennyson's plays. Shakespearean in form and, no doubt, in aspiration, in five acts and a mixture of iambic pentameter and prose, with a number of songs, longer than the uncut *Hamlet,* it covers the period from just before Becket's appointment as archbishop to his death. A fairly even-handed exposition of the matters at issue between Henry and Becket and the events that ensued is muddled up (as in the plays of Darley and Hamilton) with a subplot about Henry's famous mistress Rosamund Clifford, whom Becket protects against the jealousy of Eleanor of Aquitaine. Becket is aware of the possibility of martyrdom from the very beginning of his archiepiscopate. The four knights stomp through the whole of the story, rather than appearing only at its end, especially FitzUrse, portrayed as Eleanor's loyal agent. It is Eleanor's taunting that drives Henry to his infamous outburst, here rendered, "Will no man free me from this pestilent priest?" Rosamund actually witnesses the murder and is left alone with Becket's body at the end of the play. This play was made into a silent film in 1923. (There had been an earlier silent short, also called *Becket,* in 1910.)

In 1935, the poet Thomas Stearns Eliot published the play *Murder in the Cathedral,* which concentrates on the last month of Thomas's life and whose central theme concerns the temptations of martyrdom. Henry does not even appear in the play: the main characters are the archbishop; a chorus of women of Canterbury, who are full of foreboding and want nothing more than to be left in peace, even if they are less than fully happy; three priests, who are much more welcoming to the archbishop on his return than is the chorus; and four men who are "tempters" in the first act and the murderers in the second. As literature, *Murder in the Cathedral* is undoubtedly the best of the modern works on Becket. It remains a standard of performance and criticism. It was made into a movie in 1952. Eliot's play also forms the basis of the libretto of the opera *Assassinio nella cattedrale* by the Italian composer Ildebrando Pizzetti, which was first performed at La Scala in Milan in 1958.

In 1959, the French playwright Jean Anouilh published *Becket ou l'honneur de Dieu* ("Becket or the Honor of God"), which was translated into English simply as *Becket* and produced on Broadway in 1960. It was made into a movie starring Richard Burton as Becket and Peter O'Toole as Henry in 1964. This play attempts to depict the whole course of the relationship between Thomas and Henry, from their days as the best of friends to the aftermath of the murder; as the subtitle of the French original suggests, the main theme is Becket's choice between serving the honor of the king and the honor of God. The play tells the story in gripping fashion, but two significant elements of the plot are factual errors: Anouilh's Becket is of Saxon rather than Norman origin, and he shares a mistress with the king, while not even his enemies challenged the chastity of the historical Becket.

Two more recent plays have received less attention. The English playwright Christopher Fry wrote *Curtmantle* for the Royal Shakespeare Company, though the first performance, in 1961, was in the Netherlands and in Dutch. "Curtmantle" ("short cloak") was a nickname for Henry II, and the play is actually about the Henry's life "from 'the proud years when all events were Henry' to the King's final, ignominious defeat at the hands of his own sons and the son of his old enemy. Louis VII of France," as the playwright told *Time* magazine in a March 1961 interview. "[H]is character covers a vast field of human nature," says Fry in his foreword to the play. "It is difficult to think of any facet of man which at some time he didn't demonstrate, except chastity and sloth." Becket figures as a central character in the first and second of the three acts. He dies offstage at the end of the second act: what is actually portrayed, unusually, is Henry's appalled reaction, first to the news that the four knights have set off and then to the news that his attempt to recall them in time has been unsuccessful. The third act begins with Henry's penance. The treatment of the controversy between the two men is quite even-handed: summing it up, Becket is made to say, "There is a true and living/Dialectic between the Church and the state/Which has to be argued for ever in good part. / It can't be broken off or turned/Into a clear issue to be lost or won."

Most recently, Paul Corcoran wrote *Four Knights in Knaresborough* (1999) about the year during which Thomas's murderers holed up in that Yorkshire castle. The author describes the play as a comedy about "the worst career move in history," as he makes Hugh de Morville call it, and the *Daily Telegraph* reviewer opined that the play is "full of nervous laughter, sudden violence and expletive-laden dialogue that is often outrageously funny," but it is a dark comedy at best. The first scene of the play is the murder of the archbishop: Becket is present, of course, but speaks not a word. In the second scene, the knights turn to the audience and try to explain why they did what they did: Morville sums up, "An extraordinary man had to die—because he opposed the work of a great one!" The rest of the play—entirely invented, because, as Corcoran says in his brief preface, "[f]ortunately nothing is known about the year the killers spent in Knaresborough"—visits the knights on four nights during that year, as they quarrel, make up, worry, and muse about what they did. It emerges that possibly the murder was not provoked by Henry at all but was a plot that Reginald FitzUrse concocted to avoid having to repay a great deal of money that he owed Becket and that the archbishop would have been able to collect if he had been reconciled to the king. By the time this possibility emerges in the last scene, the other knights are so demoralized that they barely blink.

Thomas has also appeared in a good deal of literature aimed at the more popular market. Two novels have Thomas as their central character: Shelley Mydans's *Thomas* (1965) and Margaret Butler's *The Lion of Christ* (1977), whose British title is *This Turbulent Priest*. The archbishop is also a character in novels about Henry II and the Plantagenet family, such as Jean Plaidy's *The Plantagenet Prelude* (1980) and *Time and Chance* (2002), the middle volume of Sharon Kay Penman's "Plantagenet Trilogy," which follows the life of Henry II from start to finish. Ken Follett's *Pillars of the Earth* (1989) includes the scene of the murder. And in 2004 a television documentary considered the question of "Who Killed Thomas Becket?"

In some quarters, Thomas still stands forth as a champion of the separation of church and state. Thus, for example, the Becket Fund for Religious Liberty describes itself on its website as "a Washington, D.C.-based public interest law firm protecting the free expression of all religious traditions. We are nonprofit, nonpartisan, and interfaith."

CONCLUSIONS

If a tragedy is a conflict in which both sides are right, then the conflict between Archbishop Thomas and King Henry was undoubtedly a tragedy, for each side could make a good case, based on both history and policy, for its interpretation of the proper relationship between church and state. The tragedy, however, mutates into melodrama when we consider the behavior of the two protagonists, as there can be little doubt that both men behaved very badly and thereby made the conflict much worse than it need have been. It is almost impossible to attempt to evaluate Thomas of Canterbury without citing the definition by Saint Augustine that it is the cause, not the suffering, that makes the martyr. Undoubtedly, Thomas suffered. But whether his cause was his own advancement, the liberty of the church, clerical tyranny over lay society, or something else is in the eye of the beholder. Whether the methods he used to fight for his cause were appropriate or inflammatory is also an irresolvable dispute. The one thing on which scholars largely agree, now that some of the sectarian fires that overheated previous generations' discussions have died down, is that the "Becket Controversy" made relatively little difference to the evolution of church-state relations. Nonetheless, the most famous of all murders of a bishop in his cathedral is an unforgettable story that became and remains a subject of endless fascination.

FURTHER READING

Barlow, Frank. *Thomas Becket*. Berkeley: University of California Press, 1986.

Borenius, Tancred. *St. Thomas Becket in Art*. London: Methuen, 1932.

Butler, John A. *The Quest for Becket's Bones: The Mystery of the Relics of St. Thomas Becket of Canterbury*. New Haven, CT: Yale University Press, 1995.

Constitutions of Clarendon, Translation. Available at http://www.constitution.org/sech/sech_.htm.

Douglas, David C., and George W. Greenaway, eds. *English Historical Documents*. Vol. II: *1042–1189*. London: Eyre and Spottiswoode, 1953.

Duggan, Anne. *Thomas Becket*. Oxford: Oxford University Press, 2004.

Duggan, Anne, ed. *The Correspondence of Thomas Becket, Archbishop of Canterbury, 1162–1170*. 2 vols. Oxford: Oxford University Press, 2000.

Gameson, Richard. "The Early Imagery of Thomas Becket." In *Pilgrimage: The English Experience from Becket to Bunyan*, edited by Colin Morris and Peter Roberts, 46–89. Cambridge: Cambridge University Press, 2002.

Knowles, David. *The Episcopal Colleagues of Archbishop Thomas Becket*. Cambridge: Cambridge University Press, 1951.

Morey, A., and C.N.L. Brooke, eds. *The Letters and Charters of Gilbert Foliot*. London: Cambridge University Press, 1967.

Robertson, J. C., and J. B. Sheppard. *Materials for the History of Thomas Becket, Archbishop of Canterbury*. 7 vols. Rolls Series. London: Longmans, 1875–1885.

Slocum, Kay Brainerd. *Liturgies in Honour of Thomas Becket*. Toronto: University of Toronto Press, 2004.

Southern, R. W. *The Monks of Canterbury and the Murder of Archbishop Becket.* Canterbury: Friends of Canterbury Cathedral, 1985.

Staunton, Michael. *Thomas Becket and His Biographers.* Woodbridge, Suffolk: Boydell Press, 2006.

Staunton, Michael, ed. and trans. *The Lives of Thomas Becket.* Manchester: Manchester University Press, 2001.

Stephenson, Carl, and Frederic George Marcham, eds. *Sources of English Constitutional History.* New York: Harper and Row, 1937 (reprinted New York, 1972, and Holmes Beach, FL, 1997).

Vincent, Nicholas. "The Murderers of Thomas Becket." In *Bischofsmord im Mittelalter/Murder of Bishops,* edited by Natalie Fryde and Dirk Reitz, 211–72. Göttingen: Vandenhoek and Ruprecht, 2003.

Warren, W. L. *Henry II.* Berkeley: University of California Press, 1973.

Eighteenth-century engraving of Robert the Bruce, king of the Scots from 1306 to 1329 (*left*). (Library of Congress) Portrait of Sir William Wallace, painted about 1870, Scottish (*right*). (Smith Art Gallery and Museum, Stirling, Scotland/The Bridgeman Art Library)

Robert the Bruce (1274–1329) and William Wallace (ca. 1272–1305)

Alexander L. Kaufman

INTRODUCTION

Robert the Bruce and William Wallace are two symbols of Scottish national-ism and independence. As near contemporaries, both men fought in a series of battles in the late thirteenth and early fourteenth centuries against an oppressive, some even would argue tyrannical, English government. While Robert the Bruce (King Robert I of Scots 1306–29) is today often overshadowed by the heroic outlaw figure of William Wallace, the Scottish king's history remains central to Scotland's aim for a nation separate from England. The Bruce's history is also grounded on a far more level field of facts than Wallace's own record. What we know of Wallace is based on a degree of historical truth but mingled with legend, folkloric accounts, works of fiction and historical literature, and rumor. Perhaps this is why Wallace is such a more fascinating figure to modern audiences: the truth, many times, is not nearly as interesting as the story told in a big-budget Hollywood action film (1995's *Braveheart*). Yet each of these two icons has been celebrated in chronicle accounts, quasi-historical verse narratives, songs, poetry, historical novels, film, and other cultural artifacts.

HISTORICAL FACT: ROBERT THE BRUCE

Robert the Bruce was born on July 11, 1274, most likely at Turnberry Castle in Ayrshire, Scotland. His father was Robert de Brus (d. 1304), sixth Lord of Annandale. His mother was Marjorie countess of Carrick. The Bruce's lineage was aristocratic nobility of Scotland's highest order. His mother had been married first to Adam of Kilconquhar; he died on crusade in 1271 in Acre while accompanying the future King Edward I of England (1239–1307, r. 1272–1307). She met Robert de Brus, an erstwhile comrade of her late husband, and the two were married around 1272.

Robert the Bruce became earl of Carrick after his mother's death in 1292 and made a claim to the Scottish throne though his mother's side, but it was rejected and the crown given to John de Baliol (ca. 1249–1314), who was, though his mother's side, the great-great-great-grandson of King David I (1085–1153). Baliol's service to the English king created much discord among the Scottish nobility, however. In 1295–96 the Scottish lords staged a coup and initiated an alliance with France and its king, Philippe IV. On July 10, 1296, Baliol abdicated the Scottish throne. The Scottish wars did not please Edward I, yet it appears as if the Bruce and his father were at first loyal to their English monarch.

This fealty to Edward I changed, and suddenly. Edward had invaded Scotland and turned it into an occupied country garrisoned by English troops—essentially an English colony—and the Bruce decided to fight this English aggression. William Wallace's insurrection began in May 1297, and for the next several years the Bruce participated in the rebellion. In 1298, the Bruce burned down the castle of Ayr so that the English would not seize it as a base for military operations. By 1298, the Bruce was made a guardian of Scotland, a post that he gave up in 1300. John Comyn of Badenoch was also made a guardian; he and the Bruce had a tumultuous rivalry. By 1302, the Bruce's stance toward the English softened, and he was once again loyal to Edward I. At times, under the command of Edward, he hunted the Scottish rebels William Wallace and Simon Fraser.

In 1304, the Bruce made a secret agreement with Bishop William Lamberton of Saint Andrews to help one another in times of peril and to show no loyalty to Edward I. Stirling Castle surrendered to Edward and his army on July 20, 1304, and the Scottish lords, including the Bruce, were obliged to make their peace with the English king. Soon thereafter, however, the Bruce began a serious campaign to gain the throne of Scotland. On February 10, 1306, the Bruce and many of his allies met John Comyn, his main rival, in the Franciscan church in Dumfries in southern Scotland. A fight broke out, and in the end Comyn and his uncle were dead. Word was sent to England that the Bruce would soon become the next Scottish king, and he was crowned on March 25, 1306, at Scone. Celebrations were short-lived. Edward regarded the Bruce's coronation as treachery; he again invaded Scotland, and the Bruce was defeated on June 19, 1306, at Methven, after which he, with a small band of followers, became a fugitive. The Bruce's second wife and queen, Elizabeth, his daughter Marjorie, his sisters Christina and Mary, and Isabella MacDuff countess of Buchan were eventually captured by the English and sent into harsh imprisonment, which included Mary and Isabella being hung in a cage on the walls of Roxburgh and Berwick castles respectively for about four years, while the Bruce's brother Niall (or Nigel) was executed.

Nevertheless, the Bruce's popularity among his people only grew. Moreover, his guerrilla army began to defeat the English. The battle of Loudoun Hill around May 10, 1307, was a small but significant Scottish victory. The greatest boon to the Bruce's increasing military success against the English before the battle of Bannockburn was certainly the death of Edward I on July 7, 1307. Still, the Bruce had to deal with internal divisiveness, as a number of mostly northern Scots were aligned against him. The Bruce's first parliament was held at Saint Andrews in March 1309. French envoys were sent, and their king, Philippe IV, recognized Robert the Bruce as King of Scots. Over the next few years, the Bruce's forces consolidated their power and regained strongholds that had been captured and manned by English garrisons, except for Stirling Castle.

The event that has forever marked Robert the Bruce's life is his army's victory against the English under King Edward II at the battle of Bannockburn, the main action of which occurred on Monday, June 24, 1314, the Feast of Saint John the Baptist. The Scottish army had between 8,000 and 9,000 men, while the English force numbered some 16,000. The Scots fought mainly on foot in *schiltrons* (closely knit formations, armed primarily with long pikes, that could operate both defensively and offensively)—"They had axes at their sides and lances in their hands. They advanced like a thick-set hedge and such a phalanx could not easily be broken," as one contemporary English chronicler described the Scots. The English lines were broken, and they suffered heavy casualties. Edward II escaped to Dunbar and then took a ship to England. The victory did not gain for Scotland English recognition of its independence; however, it did establish the Bruce as the rightful (and popular) king of Scotland. For the English, the loss at Bannockburn was "a stain on their character, a defeat they took very much to heart."[1]

Robert the Bruce decided next to turn his attention to Ireland. His sole surviving brother, Edward, was declared to be the High King of Ireland in May 1315. In January 1317, the Bruce took a large force to the island and proceeded, with his brother, south to Dublin. Their aim was to rid Ireland of the English; in doing so, the Scots would of course take their place. But poor weather and widespread disease forced the Scots to retreat. The Bruce's brother remained in Ireland until his death on October 14, 1318, near Dundalk.

King Edward II of England was deposed in 1327. His successor, Edward III (1312–1377), was only a teenager, and so in the early years of his rule his mother, Queen Isabella, and her lover, Roger Mortimer, ran the government. The young king was almost captured in battle against the Scots, near Stanhope Park in 1327. As a result, the Treaty of Edinburgh-Northampton was drafted on March 17, 1328, and ratified by the English parliament at Northampton on May 4. Scotland was now recognized by England as a free and independent realm with its own monarch.

On June 7, 1329, at his home in Cardross, near Dumbarton, King Robert the Bruce died. He had been ill for a number of years, and it would seem the primary cause of his death was leprosy. Modern-day physicians who have examined casts of his skull support this conclusion. Because the Bruce had never taken part in a Crusade as he had wished, after embalming, his heart was removed and placed in a silver casket; thus Sir James Douglas carried it to fight against the Moors in Granada. Meanwhile the Bruce was buried in Dunfermline Abbey. After Douglas died in battle at Tebas de Ardales on March 25, 1330, the casket containing the Bruce's heart was found next to Douglas's body; Sir William Keith of Galston and Sir Symon Locard returned both Douglas and the casket to Scotland, where the heart was buried at Melrose Abbey.[2]

HISTORICAL FACT: WILLIAM WALLACE

The origins of the Scottish outlaw are almost completely shrouded in myth and uncertainty. We do not know the exact year of his birth. Indeed, for several centuries, it was believed that he was a descendant of a Ricardus Wallensis ("Richard Wallace" [i.e., "Welshman"]) who traveled to Scotland sometime in the mid-twelfth century. Richard's great-grandson, Malcolm, has been identified as William Wallace's father; this was first described by the poet Blind Hary. However, a recent discovery has called Wallace's genealogy into question:

"In 1297, after the battle of Stirling Bridge, the victorious Wallace and his wounded dying colleague, Andrew Murray, sent a letter to the mayor and communes of the German towns of Lübeck and Hamburg," and the inscription on the seal of the letter states "[Wilelm]vs Filius Alani Walais"; in other words, "William, son of Alan Wallace."[3] This discovery "demolishes the names given by literary sources for William's father; he was, we can be sure, Alan Wallace."[4]

Much of what we know of Wallace's early years is from Blind Hary's book *Wallace*. Hary describes Wallace as being 18 years old when he killed the son of Selby, who was the English constable of Dundee, and this event took place in either 1291 or 1292.[5] What information we have on Wallace that is grounded in historical evidence and not based on Hary's literary work all points to the year 1297 as a true starting point for his career. In May of that year, Wallace killed William Heselrig, who was the English sheriff of Lanark. Hary describes this murder as retaliation for the sheriff's having murdered Wallace's love, Marion Braidfute. Further exploits and successful raids on English garrisons boosted Wallace's fame, and he soon gained the support of a large section of the Scottish populace.

In early August 1297, Wallace laid siege to Dundee; the English responded by sending a considerable army northward from Berwick. The battle of Stirling Bridge was fought on September 11, 1297. The English were led by John de Warenne earl of Surrey, and the Scots were commanded by Wallace and Andrew Murray. The Scots fighters were almost all footmen, while the English and Welsh had archers and horsemen. The English were outmaneuvered, and dissension grew in their ranks. Hugh Cressingham, the arrogant treasurer of Scotland under Edward I, took an active role in commanding the English troops but did so unconvincingly; at one point he refused reinforcements. The English were forced to cross the narrow bridge, and the Scots attacked from the high ground. The bridge was so narrow that the English could neither retreat from it nor have reinforcements brought in to aid the soldiers. All told, the English defeat was sizable: "A hundred knights and many infantry, perhaps as many as five thousand, died, either killed or drowned."[6] Warenne survived, but Cressingham was killed by a spear. The Scotsmen then "flayed his obese body. Strips of skin were sent throughout Scotland to proclaim the victory at Stirling. Other strips were used to make saddle girths. Tradition tells us that Wallace himself had a belt made for his sword from what was left of Cressingham's skin."[7]

Soon after the battle, Wallace had a series of successes: Dundee Castle surrendered, and Berwick and Edinburgh were taken. Under Wallace's influence, William Lamberton was elected as the bishop of Saint Andrews on November 3, 1297. Wallace and his forces were by then in English territory, and there are widespread accounts of Scottish brutality inflicted on the English population, both soldiers and civilians alike. Bad weather ended this invasion, and Wallace returned to Scotland to await the inevitable English counteroffensive. At some point between his return in November 1297 and the upcoming campaign in 1298, Wallace was knighted and was named "guardian" of Scotland.

On Tuesday, July 22, 1298 (the feast day of Saint Mary Magdalene), the battle of Falkirk took place. Wallace's forces were outnumbered, and the English army had a large number of heavily armored artillery men and cavalry. Even though the Scottish *schiltrons* were successful against the English cavalry, a large portion of the Scots army fled (out of either fear or treachery). In the end, the Scottish losses were sizable. Wallace escaped and fled to France by November 1299, having relinquished his title of guardian of Scotland. While in France, Wallace managed to befriend King Philippe IV (after an initially hostile reception), and the French king seems to have facilitated Wallace's participation in a mission to Rome.

It is unclear when exactly Wallace returned to Scotland. In March 1304, he was officially outlawed by the parliament at Saint Andrews; however, there were reports that he was in Scotland as early as 1303. On August 3, 1305, servants of Sir John Menteith of Ruskie, the Scottish keeper of Dumbarton Castle, captured Wallace in or near Glasgow. Wallace was taken to Dumbarton Castle and subsequently handed over to the English knight John de Segrave. On August 22, Wallace was brought to London in a procession that caused much excitement in the city. The following day, in Westminster Hall, he was tried for treason (a charge he denied) and was summarily and publicly executed at Smithfield by hanging, drawing (disembowelment), and quartering. Sir John de Segrave, who had brought Wallace to London, personally distributed the outlaw's severed limbs to the towns of Newcastle, Berwick, Stirling, and Perth.

ROBERT THE BRUCE AND WILLIAM WALLACE
IN THE CHRONICLE OF PETER OF LANGTOFT

Peter Langtoft was an Augustinian canon of Bridlington and wrote in the late thirteenth and early fourteenth centuries. His French verse chronicle spans the years from Brutus, the Trojan-descended founder of Britain, to 1307 and is written in three parts. Antonia Gransden has commented how Langtoft's chronicle belongs to the "romance" tradition of historical writing, for he "wrote in chivalric terms and in places vividly reflects the courtly cult of King Arthur," and that he "ascribes chivalric virtues to King Edward [I]."[8] Indeed, like many historical writers of the Middle Ages, Langtoft relied on his own personal observations as well as hearsay and rumor for his sources of information. His attitude toward the Scots is not at all flattering, and he is downright nasty in some of his remarks. Gransden believes that Langtoft wrote "for recitation, to amuse men and stir their bellicosity against the Scots."[9] Langtoft's representations of William Wallace and Robert the Bruce are decidedly negative. Regarding Wallace, Langtoft views him as nothing but an outlaw who lives in the forest and robs:

Our subject compels us to return to the history,
To treating with the Scots for peace without molestation,

To William Wallace who lives in the forest.
At Dunfermline, after the holy festival
Of Christmas, through friends he has made request to the king,
That he may submit to his honest peace,
Without surrendering into his hands body or head;
But that the king grant him, of his gift, not a loan,
An honorable allowance of woods and cattle,
And by his writing the seizure and investment
For him and for his heirs in purchased land.
The king, angered at this demand, breaks into a rage,
Commends him to the devil, and all that grows on him,
Promises three hundred marks to the man who makes him headless.
Wallace makes ready to seek concealment by flight
Into moors and mountains, he lives by robbery.[10]

Langtoft's chronicle (like the slightly later one of Walter of Guisborough) contains a gruesome description of Wallace's execution and death. For Langtoft, it seems as if Wallace's death is wholly justified and reasonable; after all, in Langtoft's words, he was "the master of thieves":

In the first place to the gallows he was drawn for treasons,
Hanged for robberies and slaughters;
And because he had annihilated by burnings,
Towns and churches and monasteries,
He is taken down from the gallows, his belly opened,
His heart and his bowels burnt to cinders,
And his head cut off for such treasons as follow:
Because he had by his assumptions of authority
Maintained the war, given protections,
Seized into his subjection the lordship
Of another's kingdom by his usurpations.
His body was cut into four parts;
Each one hangs by itself, in memory of his name,
In place of his banner these are his gonfanons . . .
By the death of Wallace may one bear in mind
What reward belongs to traitor and to thief,
And what divers wages to divers trespasses.[11]

The English chronicler Matthew of Paris, in his *Flores Historiarum* in the early fourteenth century, describes an equally brutal death:

He was hung in a noose, and afterwards let down half-living; next his genitals were cut off and his bowels torn out and burned in a fire; then and not till then his head was cut off and his trunk cut into four pieces.[12]

For these medieval English chroniclers, the death of this icon was one to be remembered in the most specific of ways. Future generations who would have read these chronicles would remember the ill deeds of Wallace and his men, and these readers would also recall the grisly end of the outlaw. Public executions in the Middle Ages sought to deter more violent crimes; likewise, the recording of these spectacles of death in historical literature served to warn others of the dangers associated with traitorous acts. R. James Goldstein has commented that Langtoft insists that "the execution reminds us that the authority Wallace dared to transgress against was not King Robert I or the Scottish baronial class he represented, but the sovereign of England, Ireland, and Wales."[13] However, one could also read the description of Wallace's death (and similar descriptions of others executed in similar ways in the Middle Ages) as a memorial to the dead. While Langtoft and Matthew of Paris did not seek to make a martyr out of Wallace, one can not help but feel sorry for the outlaw, especially after one reads how he was tortured and yet did not cry out for leniency or mercy.

Robert the Bruce is also derided in Langtoft's chronicle. The Scottish king's sanity is called into question, and Langtoft pointedly calls him insane:

> King Robin has drunk of the drink of dan* Warin,   *dan:* sir (*cf. Spanish* Don)
> Who lost cities and towns by the shield,
> Afterwards in the forest, mad and naked,
> He fed with the cattle on the raw grass.[14]

The Bruce is here compared to the outlaw of the Welsh Marches, Fouke fitz Waryn (ca. 1167–ca. 1258). That the English chronicler compares the Bruce to this outlaw figure is rather intriguing, for there is no record that the Bruce tried to emulate Fouke's outlaw tactics that he used against King John (1167–1216). Nevertheless, Langtoft's association of the two underscores that chronicler's animosity toward the Bruce and solidifies the Bruce's reputation among the medieval English as that of an enemy of the state.

ROBERT THE BRUCE AND WILLIAM WALLACE IN POLITICAL SONGS OF THE MIDDLE AGES

The Scottish wars and their iconographic heroes were the focus of several popular political songs in England. The majority of these verses were, like Langtoft's chronicle, highly critical of the Scots, especially William Wallace. The Latin "Song of the Scottish Wars" survives in several medieval manuscripts, although the earliest would seem to have been composed in 1298, soon after the battle of Falkirk.[15] Throughout this poem, there is a strong anti-Scottish sentiment; the anonymous poet seems to delight in the murder of the Scots and sees them as base animals:

> The kilted people, numerous and savage, who are accustomed to detract
> from the Englishmen, fell at Dunbar, and now stink like a dog; thus do

fools, who are tormented by vain glory.—Vain glory made the deceitful people deny the true lord of Scotland. . . . William Wallace is the leader of these savages; the rejoicings of fools breed increase to griefs.—To increase the wickedness which they had hitherto perpetrated, these wicked men deliver Alnwick to the flames; they run about on every side like madmen.[16]

Not all English political poems, though, celebrate the death of Scots. "The Battle of Bannockburn" was written soon after the battle; in Latin, it describes the defeat of the English and the death of the earl of Gloucester. The mood in the poem is somber, and the writer "laments the humiliation to which his country had been reduced" and also suggests that the defeat was caused by pride, evil counsels, and traitorous acts on the battlefield.[17] Robert the Bruce is not directly named in the poem, and this omission is purposeful and significant. The anonymous poet certainly did not wish to ascribe the reason for the Scottish victory on the Bruce's superior army on that given day; to do so would have almost been treasonous and heretical. Those English who were killed "deserved to suffer judgment of decapitation, since voluntarily they have betrayed such a soldiery."[18]

JOHN BARBOUR'S *BRUCE*

John Barbour's date of birth is uncertain, but it is believed to be around 1325; he died on March 13, 1395. He was a member of the clergy in Scotland and became archdeacon of Aberdeen, presumably in 1355, and served as an auditor as well. His poem, which comprises some 14,000 lines in the language of Early Scots, was composed sometime between 1375 and 1377, a period in which the poet was "only in his diocese and not called thence on the king's business."[19] The poem survives in two manuscripts: Cambridge, Saint John's College Library, MS G.23, which dates to 1487, and Edinburgh, National Library of Scotland, Advocates MS 19.2.2., which dates to 1489. Barbour was connected to the Scottish royalty; he first served Robert II when he ascended to the throne on March 26, 1371.[20] His demanding position at Aberdeen allowed Barbour to come into close contact with many of the royal family, yet it is difficult to determine if he had patrons for his poetry.[21]

Barbour's poem focuses on the Bruce's life from 1286 to 1322; it does not include any details on the life and times of William Wallace. The genre is a mixture of chivalric romance and verse chronicle. The battle of Bannockburn is the highlight of the poem. Here, the violence of the day is described in rich detail, and the English defeat becomes one of the poem's central moments. Barbour's words on the concept of freedom are poignant, romantic, idyllic, and influential. Scottish patriotism is stressed throughout the work, and the Bruce, being its symbol, shines. The complicated (some might argue duplicitous) nature of the Bruce's figure is represented by the compelling, bold, courteous, and chivalric hero. While there are a number of historical inaccuracies, the poet's "themes of freedom and leadership are effectively stated and illustrated, effectively enough for the epic nature of his subject to be felt."[22]

BLIND HARY'S *WALLACE*

The single greatest source for the life and times of William Wallace is Blind Hary's (or Hary the Minstrel's) long poem *Wallace*. The poem comprises 8,877 lines and is written in decasyllabic couplets.[23] Editors have organized the poem into 12 books. Matthew McDiarmid dates the poem, which is written in Middle Scots, to 1476–78.[24] The poem survives in a single manuscript that also contains a version of Barbour's *Bruce*: Edinburgh, National Library of Scotland, Advocates MS 19.2.2. The *Wallace* section of the manuscript dates to 1488. John Major was the first to claim that Hary was blind from birth (see the next section), yet McDiarmid has determined that Hary lost his eyesight after he had finished writing *Wallace*.[25] Hary's realistic descriptions of warfare led McDiarmid to suggest that the poet perhaps had his own experiences at war in France.[26] The poet was born around 1440 at Linlithgow to a "locally respected family variously named Hary or Henry," and his education in that neighborhood or at Dundee allowed him to learn Latin, French, and Middle English.[27] He died sometime between 1492 and 1495.[28]

Almost certainly, Hary composed *Wallace* between 1476 and 1478, and his motivation for doing so was multifaceted: "the literary one of surpassing Barbour's achievement, a patriotic enthusiasm for Scottish prowess in the endless war with England, a similarly inspired dislike of the English connection then being cultivated by his king, and a wish to please his influential friends."[29] Hary certainly threw all of his literary and historical knowledge into the poem, as it is a work that cannot be pigeonholed into a single genre. Walter Scheps has called *Wallace* a combination of "epic, romance, and *débat*,"[30] while Goldstein adds "chronicle, saint's life, and complaint."[31] McDiarmid, likewise, presents a dizzying array of sources that Hary used for his poem: vernacular, Latin, and French histories; the chronicles of Barbour, Wyntoun, Bower, and Froissart; didactic and philosophical works, such as Boethius's *The Consolation of Philosophy*; *The Travels of Sir John Mandeville*; saints' legends; astrological treatises; the major and minor poems of Chaucer, including *Troilus and Criseyde* and the *Canterbury Tales*; the romances of Charlemagne, King Arthur, and Alexander the Great; and possibly John Lydgate's *Troy Book*.[32]

Hary's *Wallace* is a celebration of the Scottish hero and a vilification of the English people and especially their government. Hary's description of the outlaw is a wonderful blend of fantasy and realism: "Ix quartaris large he was in lenth indeid" (that is to say, he was "nine quarters"—a fraction under seven feet—tall).[33] Wallace is also described as large and muscular, careful in his speech, and having scars all over his body. "Off Ryches he kepyt no propyr thing, / Gaiff as he won, lik Alexander the king" ("Of wealth he kept none for himself, but gave away that which he won, like King Alexander").[34]

The activities in which Wallace takes part in the poem showcase not only Hary's indebtedness to other literary genres and works, but also, and indeed more so, the poet's innate literary ability to craft a vivid and exciting narrative. Wallace's life as an outlaw and his adventures throughout Scotland, England, and France read just like an action film. Yet Hary was also deliberate in his description of Wallace as a thoughtful and religious man: "A psalter buk Wallace had on him euir, / Fra his childeid fra it wald nocht deseuir" ("A psalter Wallace had on him always, and from his childhood he would not part with it").[35]

Hary's description of Wallace's execution is a politicized event; for Hary, Wallace becomes a martyr for the Scottish cause and he does not delve into the details of his death. While the poem is certainly about Wallace, it is also about Scotland. As Richard Moll has argued, Hary's *Wallace* "demonstrates that a unified Scotland, bound by common descent and political ideals, is necessary to protect the realm from the aggressions of the 'auld enemy,' [i.e., England] both in Wallace's day and in the late fifteenth century."[36]

WILLIAM WALLACE IN JOHN MAJOR'S *HISTORIA MAJORIS BRITANNIAE*

The medieval British chronicle tradition remains a corpus of writing that, as a whole, presents readers with a decidedly subjective point of view of medieval history and culture. John Major's *Historia Majoris Britanniae* (*History of Greater Britain*, although one could also translate the title as *Major's History of Britain*) was written toward the tail end of the fifteenth century and published in 1521, most likely in Paris.[37] Major (whose name is sometimes spelled "Maior" or "Mair") lived from 1467 to 1550; he was a logician, a biblical commentator, and a theologian.

In the preface to his English translation of Major's Latin chronicle, Archibald Constable states that he would like to "say something about the singular fairness, the anxious impartiality, of Major's judgment of the English nation, the cordiality of his appreciation of English customs."[38] Summarizing Major's contribution as a humanist writer, Constable remarks that the chronicler "showed the insight of a philosophic statesman," which makes him "unique among Scottish writers."[39] But as with most medieval historiographers, Major was not subtle when it came to identifying those whom he disliked. The English printer, translator, and editor William Caxton (ca. 1422–1491) was perhaps Major's most notable target, for the Scottish chronicler, in Constable's words, "heartily abhorred" the notable editor and translator for his inability to foster a sense of "national amity" in his *Chronicles of England* (published at Westminster in 1480 and 1482).[40] Major, it can be said, sought to unify the English and Scottish people under their shared sense of religion and humanity. However, this unification of peoples meant that certain histories needed some degree of reinterpretation and refashioning, and Major set to work.

First, Major describes how "the Scots chose for their king a certain William Wallace, up to this point a man with nothing illustrious in his origin."[41] True to his training as a humanist, Major decidedly revises Caxton's original text and rebukes Caxton, not so much for his unfavorable portrait of the Scottish outlaw as for his inability to craft a true and objective version. For Major, Caxton's narrative contains a "mass of incoherencies" and "silly fabrications."[42] Major then proceeds to "place the history of the Scots in its true light."[43] Major's version of Wallace's birth, breeding, and valor is somewhat awe-inspiring. It is full of vivid details of Wallace's upbringing, his physical and social characteristics, his martial abilities, and how he was "hailed as regent by most of the Scots, with the universal acclamation of the common people."[44] At one point, Major compares Wallace's ability to draw up an army and lead it successfully on the field of battle to some the heroes of classical antiquity: "Hannibal, Ulysses, and Telamonian Ajax."[45] In another work of Major's, his *In Quartum Sententiarum*, the chronicler compares Achilles's penchant for eating the muscles from oxen and not fowl with Wallace's similar dietary predilections.[46] And while Major concurs that Robert the Bruce flourished at a later date, nonetheless he argues that Wallace "had no other instructions in warfare than experience and his own genius."[47] Major does not dwell upon the various English atrocities that were carried out during Wallace's tenure as rebel leader. Instead of underscoring the hatred that so many Scots felt toward Edward I (as well as toward many of the Scottish nobility who surrendered to Edward, such as John de Baliol), Major dispenses with this overheated political rhetoric and chooses instead to elevate Wallace to mythical status. The English are not represented as bloodthirsty animals; instead, they are weak, clueless, and confused, unable to match Wallace's abilities: "[T]wo or even three Englishmen were scare able to make stand against him,—such was his bodily strength, such also the quickness of his understanding, and his indomitable courage."[48]

Major does indeed humanize Wallace, and he also makes him into more of a character out of literature. Perhaps he was influenced by Blind Hary's narrative, for Major is the first to mention the supposed author of the Middle Scots poem. Near the end of Major's own history of Wallace, he describes how, "in the time of [his] childhood," the blind author "fabricated a whole book about William Wallace. . . . I however can give but a partial credence to such writings as these."[49] While Hary the Minstrel's long verse narrative does include a sizable number of literary embellishments (moments of fantasy, comedic interplay, elements of romance), his overall portrait of Wallace as a fierce leader who commands respect is very similar to Major's outline of the hero.

WILLIAM WALLACE AND ROBERT THE BRUCE IN ROMANTIC LITERATURE

The Romantic movement of the eighteenth and nineteenth centuries saw a reaction against the formal rules and the predominance of reason that marked

the Neoclassical period. Some of the characteristics that we most often associate with romanticism are a love of nature, an intense interest in the past
(particularly things medieval), individualism, a sense of primitivism, and mysticism. The figure of William Wallace was one in which several romantic writers took a keen interest. After all, in the person of Wallace we see an individual
spirit from the Middle Ages who, as a fighter for the nationalist cause of
Scotland, was still very much alive in writers' imagination. The wild, untamed
nature of Wallace, and that of Scotland itself, were directly and indirectly celebrated by a host of romantic writers.

William Wordsworth (1770–1850) is one of the best-known romantic
poets. Along with Samuel Taylor Coleridge (1772–1834), he published *Lyrical
Ballads* in 1798, thus ushering in the Romantic Age. Wordsworth's autobiographical poem *The Prelude* is one of the poet's great works. Written in blank
verse, it is deeply philosophical and just as sophisticated as John Milton's epic
Paradise Lost. In book I, Wordsworth recalls William Wallace's exploits and
speaks of them in the context of the revolutionary ideals of romanticism:

> How Wallace fought for Scotland; left the name
> Of Wallace to be found, like a wild flower,
> All over his dear Country; left the deeds
> Of Wallace, like a family of Ghosts
> To people the steep rocks and river banks,
> Her natural sanctuaries, with a local soul
> Of independence and stern liberty.[50]

The Wordsworths visited the various Scottish locales where Wallace and his
men fought and hid. The turbulent life and times of Wallace, it seemed, had
some impact upon Wordsworth; his sister Dorothy mentions how in 1803
they visited two caves reputed to have been hideouts of Wallace's.[51]

Robert Burns (1759–1796) is perhaps the only Scottish figure who could
(in his day or today) eclipse either Wallace or Bruce. Burns's poem *Scots wha
hae,* which is also known as *March to Bannockburn* (1793–94), is set to the
melody of the old Scottish song "Hey, Tuttie Tatti." As William Everett comments, the song was "quite probably heard at the Bannockburn victory which
Burns's words celebrate. Scottish archers took the tune to France, and it was
played when Joan of Arc entered Orleans. The song exemplifies Scottishness
on both levels discussed above: the independent Scotland of the Middle Ages,
immortalized in a distant time, and the romanticization of the Jacobite ideology, recreated in nostalgic and benign terms."[52] As one can see from Burns's
poem, which is printed below, the author places the reader squarely in the
nationalistic past. However, the poem also addresses the future of Scotland
and proposes that the heroes of the past (Bruce and Wallace) should serve as
symbols of yet-unattained political and social freedom. As Everett observes,
Burns's use of the future-tense "shall" signals a look into the future in which
there exists the liberation of the sons of Scotland.[53] Burns's poem was one

that could be sung to a specific tune; however, it works perfectly fine on its own literary and linguistic merits as it captures the author's own Scottish pronunciation.

> Scots, wha hae wi' Wallace bled,
> Scots, wham Bruce has aften led,
> Welcome to your gory bed,
> Or to Victorie!
> Now's the day, and now's the hour;
> See the front o' battle lour;
> See approach proud Edward's power—
> Chains and Slaverie!
> Wha will be a traitor knave?
> Wha can fill a coward's grave?
> Wha sae base as be a Slave?
> Let him turn and flee!
> Wha, for Scotland's King and Law,
> Freedom's sword will strongly draw,
> Free-man stand, or Free-man fa',
> Let him on wi' me!
> By Oppression's woes and pains!
> By your Sons in servile chains!
> We will drain our dearest veins,
> But they shall be free!
> Lay the proud Usurpers low!
> Tyrants fall in every foe!
> Liberty's in every blow!—
> Let us Do or Die![54]

One of Scotland's most prolific writers was Sir William Scott (1771–1832), and he is primarily known for his lengthy historical novels that depict a highly romanticized notion of Scottish history, its people, and its geography. *Waverley* (1814), *Rob Roy* (1817), and *Ivanhoe* (1819) are in many ways the novels of Scott that best represent his romanticized notions of the Scottish and English past. Like a number of writers in the romantic period, Scott was very familiar with medieval literature and history. He was acquainted with a number of important medieval manuscripts (for instance, the Auchinleck Manuscript, which contains many well-known and significant medieval romances) and with the scholars who edited these texts (such as Joseph Ritson, George Ellis, and Henry Weber).[55] According to Jerome Mitchell, Barbour's *Bruce* was one of the texts that Scott knew quite well and cited often in his own works; indeed, it is referred to in two of Scott's letters: one to George Ellis in 1805 and another to Jacob Grimm in 1814, and in the latter Scott is critical of John Pinkerton's 1790 edition.[56] As John Sutherland notes, Scott was wholly consumed with his homeland, particularly during the first two decades of the nineteenth century when he was writing the poems *The Vision of Don Roderick* (1811) and *Rokeby* (1813), for Scott was "wild about Scottish gallantry at this period. Even his new terrier (who sat on his lap while he wrote *The Vision*) was called 'Wallace.'"[57] While Scott's 1814 novel *Waverley* is set during the 1745 Jacobite Rising, the novel really addresses the unstable national and social relationship between England and Scotland. One of the characters of *Waverley*, the Baron of Bardwardine, is "the perfect example of a sympathetic portrayal of a sentimental Scottish Jacobite who reluctantly, but perhaps with relief, accepts the Hanoverian reality of Great Britain."[58] In a nuanced reading of the Baron's middle name, which is Comyne, Julian Meldon D'Arcy points out the dubious nature of this name, for it is associated with duplicitous figures in Scottish history, such as Sir John Comyn (Robert the Bruce's rival) and the earls of Menteith (originally from the Comyn family), one of whom was the elder brother of the "false Menteith" who betrayed William Wallace to Edward I in 1304.[59]

Scott's *The Lord of the Isles* (1815) is a poem in six cantos whose narrative and characters are right out of medieval romance. In fact, the primary source for the poem is Barbour's *Bruce*. In Scott's romantic verse, the character of Edith is set to marry Ronald, Lord of the Isles, at Artonish Castle, but she is unsure of his love. Three strangers sail to the castle: the brothers Robert and Edward Bruce as well as their sister, Isabel. A fight ensues, for God is on the side of King Edward I of England. The bride meanwhile disappears, and we learn that the groom has feelings for Isabel. Ronald and Robert venture to Skye, rescue a young, mute, male page (who really is Edith in disguise), and are rejoined by Robert's brother Edward. Robert discusses Ronald's feelings with his sister, and she agrees to consider his hand if he ends his relationship with Edith. Isabel, meanwhile, realizes that the young mute is really Edith in disguise. However, Edith is captured by Clifford, an English leader. She refuses to reveal her identity to her captors and is to be executed, whereupon Bruce and his army rescue her and defeat the enemy. The final canto describes the battle of Bannockburn, wherein Edith (who is still disguised as the mute male page) commands the Scottish onlookers to join in the fight. The bystanders are convinced that, since a mute has spoken, a miracle has occurred. They join in the fight, the English are defeated, Ronald and Edith marry, and Isabel (in an unusual twist) takes her holy vows so as to enter into a convent. Appended to the poem are a substantial number of Scott's own textual and historical notes, the majority of which are drawn from Pinkerton's three-volume edition (1790) of Barbour's *Bruce*. Jerome Mitchell states that the poem "owes a lot to medieval literature, not only to Barbour's *Bruce* for its historical content but to Chaucer and medieval romance for other content, general atmosphere, and matters of style and structure."[60]

Scott's own *History of Scotland* (1830) is a curious mixture of history, myth, and legend. In this work, as in his novels, there exists, as Murray G. H. Pittock has observed, a "strange dual loyalty" to "Scotland's past and Britain's present (Bruce and Wallace on the one hand, England and Empire on the other)."[61] Scott's historical prose writings are highly descriptive and detailed, and he seems to have prided himself on the sheer amount of specific, factual information that he included in his histories. In the preface to his *History of Scotland*, Scott writes:

> Our limits oblige us to treat this interesting subject more concisely than we could wish; and we are of course under the necessity of rejecting many details which engage the attention and fascinate the imagination. We will endeavour, notwithstanding, to leave nothing untold which may be necessary to trace a clear idea of the general course of events.[62]

In his descriptions of Wallace, the Bruce, Edward I, and the Scottish wars, Scott displays an even temper, one that the humanist John Major would have admired. The divisiveness of the early medieval historians is wholly absent; rather, Scott attempts to highlight the positive qualities of the principal figures:

> Edward, on his return from the Low Countries, found himself at the head of a gallant muster of all the English chivalry, forming by far the most superb army that had ever entered Scotland. Wallace acted with great sagacity, and, according to a plan which often before and after proved successful in Scottish warfare, laid waste the intermediate country between Stirling and the frontiers, and withdrew towards the centre of the kingdom to receive the English attack, when their army should be exhausted by privation.
>
> Edward pressed on with characteristic hardihood and resolution. Tower and town fell before him: but his advance was not without such inconvenience and danger as a less determined monarch would have esteemed a good apology for retreat.[63]

Scott does not divulge the gory details of Wallace's death, but he does conclude with some moving words on the place of the Scottish outlaw in the country's history:

> Thus died this courageous patriot, leaving a remembrance which will be immortal in the hearts of his countrymen. This steady champion of independence having been removed, and a bloody example held out to all who should venture to tread in his footsteps, Edward proceeded to form a species of constitution for the country, which, at the cost of so much labor, policy, and bloodshed, he had at length, as he conceived, united for ever with the English crown.[64]

This populist reading of historical events was almost certainly written for the general reading public. Scott himself was a rather self-assured individual and, like Mark Twain, a great spokesman for his literary output. He was also rather honest about the limitations of his *History of Scotland*: "I have not the least doubt that I will make a popular book, for I trust it will be both interesting and useful; but I never intended to engage in any proper historical labor, for which I have neither time, talent, nor inclination."[65] Scott also saw the importance of his history books for adolescent readers, and so a series called *Tales of a Grandfather* was soon created that would make Scott's historical novels more appropriate for a younger reading audience. As the editor of *Tales of a Grandfather: Being the History of Scotland* (1831), Edwin Ginn states that the "present work has been slightly abridged by the omission of detailed descriptions of some of the more barbarous cruelties of those times and other important matter."[66] What Scott does add to his children's book to make it livelier than his adult version is a heavy dose of dialogue, which, at times, reads right out of a modern comic book or an action movie:

> "Go back to Warenne," said Wallace, "and tell him we value not the pardon of the King Of England. We are not here for the purpose of treating of peace, but for abiding battle, and of restoring freedom to our country. Let the English come on;—we defy them to their very beards!"[67]

Schoolchildren who read this account of Wallace and Scott's later chapter on Robert the Bruce would have been impressed (and understandably so) by the exploits and characters of both figures. Scott's narrative of the Bruce's (possibly legendary) encounter with a spider became a central moment in the hero's biographical narrative. The story is as follows: In 1306 the Bruce was a discouraged fugitive, apparently unable to gain the throne. He happened to observe a spider that was trying to attach its web to a beam; after several attempts, the spider succeeded.[68] This determination on the spider's part encouraged Bruce to try harder for the throne and for the freedom of his country. The moralizing and didactic nature of this episode must have been prime fodder for schoolteachers and children alike.

The early nineteenth century also saw a handful of literary reinterpretations of the Wallace figure and legend. In 1802, John Finlay's *Wallace; or the Vale of Ellerslie* was first published in Glasgow, and the text went through three revised and expanded editions; in 1809, Margaret Holford published *Wallace, or the Battle of Falkirk*; in 1810, Jane Porter's commercially successful romance novel *The Scottish Chiefs* appeared;[69] and, in 1813, R. P. Gillies had his *Wallace; a fragment* published.[70]

In 1819, the literary journal *Blackwood's* announced a contest for the best work in verse or prose on William Wallace. The top three submissions came from Felicia Hemans (who won first prize and £25), James Hogg, and Joanna Baillie. As Nancy Moore Goslee has noted, these three poems, and the aim of the competition, "show how subtle and complex such reinterpretations" of a pan-British narrative of a heroic nature can be, and that in these three poems "the medieval struggle for Scottish independence against England comes to stand for the modern struggle for British liberty against Napoleonic tyranny," and in a post-Waterloo environment they can also represent a struggle for "individual civil liberties."[71]

Wallace and Bruce continued to be the focus of other forms of art, both high and popular. In the nineteenth and twentieth centuries, the icons became the centerpieces of musical compositions, paintings, and films.

WILLIAM WALLACE AND ROBERT THE BRUCE AS SCOTTISH POLITICAL SYMBOLS

Both William Wallace and Robert the Bruce have had a long-standing role in the formation of Scottish political organizations and of the dissemination of their ideologies. Some cultural critics and political scientists have viewed this appropriation of their native Scottish men as a prime example of political propaganda. While the images and historical narratives of the two were obviously exploited for political gains, the vast majority of Scots (and especially the politicians) during the nineteenth and early twentieth centuries sought to cool the heated political rhetoric that had existed for centuries between England and its northern neighbor.

Between 1852 and 1856, the National Association for the Vindication of Scottish Rights (NAVSR), which was formed by two brothers, James and John Grant, "used their literary skills to produce a myriad of pamphlets, petitions and newspaper contributions to make their case that Scotland's right as a nation, not a region of Britain, should be recognized in complete equality with England in matters of taxation, expenditure and parliamentary time."[72] As Graeme Morton has observed, the NAVSR focused on the Union of 1707, when Scottish rights were established as being equal with English rights; now, the political party spoke of the union of British and English heroes as a link between England and Scotland: "We glory in the triumph of a Marlborough, a Nelson and a Wellington, but might we not look with pride to the achievements of a Wallace and a Bruce?"[73]

Formed in 1886, the Scottish Home Rule Association (SHRA) was active in the distribution of its literature much like the NAVSR, and it members were very much Unionists who now "argued for federalism" through the Liberal Party.[74] In the wake of deep involvement in Ireland's cause for home rule, in 1896 the publication *Scottish Highlander* printed an article in which the SHRA's Theodore Napier used Wallace and the Bruce to refocus and energize the organization's members:

> [Scottish people nowadays] are more interested in a football or golf match than in the political welfare and freedom of their country. Was it for this our great hero-patriot Wallace struggled for so long and lost his life? Was it not for the object of delivering Scotland from English aggression and predominance? Do we not hail Bruce as the successful champion of our independence from English thralldom? And yet we have

basely surrendered our political freedom to England. For a country that does not govern itself cannot be regarded as free.[75]

Throughout the rest of 1896, various publications such as the *Scottish Highlander* and the *Montrose Review* carried inspirational poetry that celebrated Wallace and the Bruce as patriotic Scots. It was also in this year that the SHRA marked the anniversary of Bannockburn and the Bruce's victory with a seven-verse poem that was read on the battlefield at Bannockburn. In a keen political move, the poem celebrates both Wallace's victory and the Bruce's victory in 1314, even though Wallace was executed in 1305. As Morton has commented, this poem and its performance marked "the now orthodox view that it was Bruce who avenged the death of Wallace, and completed his work."[76]

The Scottish National Party (SNP) was formed in 1934. In an inflammatory nationalistic speech in 1943, the party's leader, Professor Douglas Young, invoked Wallace to object to the conscription of Scotsmen into the British army:

Wallace was against union with England, not merely because England was a feudal state (that is, a state run by the police and the bureaucracy in the interests of the landlords and the financiers), but because the English are a different nation. Wallace suffered martyrdom, in the most bestial way which the King of England could contrive, because he refused to stop doing the job that the Scots had committed to him, namely, to defend the freedom of the Scots nation in arms. . . .

Wallace died for Scottish nationhood, the greatest tribute and honour he could pay. The degenerate posterity of 1707 abandoned the cause of Scotland, Wallace's cause, for a share of the proceeds of London's overseas financial exploitation. . . .

William Wallace would never have believed that a day could come when Scotsmen would be hauled off like sheep to defend far-flung tracts of the London profiteer's empire, while the defense of the Scottish homeland was committed to the polyglot and heterogeneous influx of Poles, Czechs, Anglo-Saxons, Negroes and other species. Incidentally, conscription furth of Scotland is unconstitutional under the Scots-English Treaty of 1707, which instituted a lamentable affair called Great Britain.[77]

Following World War II, however, neither Wallace nor the Bruce was frequently referenced by Scottish politicians, and not until Mel Gibson's film *Braveheart* were these icons again seen as symbols of Scottish political power.

WILLIAM WALLACE AND ROBERT THE BRUCE IN CLASSICAL MUSIC

As we have seen in Burns's poem, Wallace and the Bruce were often the inspiration behind literary works that contained an element of song. Indeed, in the early twentieth century, two composers were themselves so much influenced by the pair that they created extended pieces of music that focused on the individuals' character.

William Wallace (1860–1940) hailed from Greenock, Scotland, and, after qualifying as an ophthalmic surgeon, turned to music and studied at the Royal Academy of Music in London. The year 1905 marked the 600th anniversary of the death of William Wallace, and his musical namesake seized upon the opportunity to create an orchestral work that combined elements from the classical tradition—Wallace the composer was influenced by Richard Wagner and Franz Liszt—as well as Scottish folk songs. The work that Wallace created was titled *Sir William Wallace: Scottish Hero, freedom-fighter; beheaded and dismembered by the English (Symphonic Poem No. 5)*. Its premiere was September 19, 1905, at a Queen's Hall Promenade Concert under the direction of Sir Henry Wood.[78] The music is forceful at times, because it is in many ways a celebration of the outlaw hero's power, might, and courage. The main theme of the work is derived from "Scots wha hae" in which it fully emerges "in a blaze of glory."[79] As Everett notes, the celebration at the end of Wallace's symphonic poem does not address his namesake's torture and execution, but instead the close of the piece is a celebration of "Britishness in the spirit of Burns and Scott and does not dwell on the Scottish-English conflict which resulted in Wallace's execution."[80] In 1996, the well-respected classical label Hyperion released on CD two newly recorded performances of works by Wallace, one of which, *William Wallace: Symphonic Poems,* performed by the Glasgow BBC Scottish Symphony Orchestra conducted by Martyn Brabbins, contains the piece *Sir William Wallace*.[81]

Frederick James Simpson (1856–?) was a contemporary of the composer William Wallace. He was brought up in Portobello, Scotland, and educated at Edinburgh Academy and later in England, Switzerland, and Germany. After Simpson returned from Germany, he entered the National Training School, which later became the Royal College of Music.[82] Simpson's symphony *Robert the Bruce* was performed but apparently never published. It received its premiere at the Crystal Palace Concerts on November 2, 1889, and it too included the tune of "Scots wha hae" as its principal musical theme.[83] Simpson's works that were published, such as *Coronach from the Lady of the Lake* (1891) and *Old English Songs Arranged for Three Voices* (1894), also show his interest in medieval culture.

WILLIAM WALLACE AND ROBERT THE BRUCE IN ART

The various paintings that depict William Wallace and Robert the Bruce are in many ways the most iconographic references that we have. One of the oldest and most significant surviving portraits of Wallace is a pencil sketch by David Steuart Erskine, the eleventh earl of Buchan (1742–1829). It is supposedly based on a medieval original, and Wallace "takes the form of a bearded warrior with a dragon on top of his helmet."[84] The piece is housed in the Scottish National Portrait Gallery in Edinburgh.

The scene in Sir William Allan's *Heroism and Humanity: An Incident in the Life of Robert the Bruce* (1840; Kelvingrove Art Gallery and Museum, Glasgow) depicts the king with his right hand raised to heaven in denunciation of those who have abandoned a woman who has just given birth. The topic is apparently based not on any historical moment but on an incident in Scott's *Tales of a Grandfather: Being the History of Scotland*. According to Scott, while the Bruce was in Ireland on campaign, he was forced to retreat; however, he discovered that a laundress who was with his force had just given birth, and so instead of leaving her behind and at the mercy of the English army, the Bruce rallied his troops to fight. John Morrison comments that this work displays the Bruce as the "embodiment of nobility and, as the title indicates, humanity. It was these qualities, Allan suggests, that motivated the heroes of the Wars of Independence and allowed Scotland to emerge unconquered to take an honourable place alongside England, rather than subject to it."[85] Phillip's *Bruce About to Receive the Sacrament on the Morning Previous to the Battle of Bannockburn* (1843; The Mechanics' Institute, Brechin, Angus, Scotland) stresses the Bruce's "saintly character," and the presentation aligns him within the British heroic tradition rather than a "singularly Scottish one."[86] In the twentieth century, Stewart Carmichael (1867–1950) captured the mystical elements of the Bruce. His 1943 oil *Robert the Bruce Receiving the Wallace Sword from the Sprit of Scotland* (sold at Christie's, London, November 25, 2004, to the Stirling Smith Art Gallery and Museum, Stirling, Scotland) depicts the king kneeling and receiving the sword from a "Lady of the Lake"-type figure.

ROBERT THE BRUCE AND WILLIAM WALLACE
IN THE NOVELS OF NIGEL TRANTER

Nigel Tranter (1909–2000) was an author of a variety of types of written work, from histories, to children's works, to historical fiction, to Westerns. He was born in Glasgow, and a number of his best-known books focus on Scotland—its land, people, and architecture.

In 1969, Tranter published the first of three books that would become *The Bruce Trilogy*. *Robert the Bruce: The Steps to the Empty Throne* was soon followed in 1970 by *Robert the Bruce: The Path of the Hero King*. The third and final installment, *Robert the Bruce: The Price of the King's Peace*, was published in 1971. All three books sold extremely well, but the reviews were mixed. Robert the Bruce was and remains a national hero in Scotland. Tranter, as he did with a number of his protagonists, wrote the Bruce and "all his heroes largely out of his own experience, posing the question, 'What would *I* have done?'"[87] As a work of historical fiction, *The Bruce Trilogy* largely succeeds in its presentation of the Bruce as a complex figure.

Tranter went on to write about the exploits of William Wallace. In *The Wallace,* published in 1975, he was able to give a larger stage to a figure who was given a limited role in *The Bruce Trilogy.* Tranter believed that Wallace was a greater hero than the Bruce, for while the latter fought for "a throne, Wallace fought for a nobler cause, for liberty and the idea of nationhood."[88] Wallace's capture, his procession to and through London, and his torture and eventual death are, in the hands of Tranter, moments of real tension, despair, and pathos.

MEL GIBSON'S *BRAVEHEART* (1995)

No recent cultural artifact has had a greater influence upon the public's perception of both William Wallace and Robert the Bruce than Mel Gibson's 1995 film *Braveheart,* scripted by Randall Wallace. The film was nominated for 10 Academy Awards and won 5 of them. John Toll won the Oscar for Best Cinematography, Gibson won Best Director, and the film took home Best Picture. While the film could not really be considered a blockbuster (it earned around $75.5 million at the box office in the United States and $133.4 million internationally), it seems to be in constant rotation on cable channels in the United States.[89] And even though its running time of 177 minutes may be a tad too long for those audiences whose ability to remain focused and attentive is lacking or limited, Gibson's film has enough action, romance, gore, and shouting to capture viewers' attention.

Even today, it is not hard to see why the film was so popular among critics as well as audiences. First and foremost, we have Gibson as Wallace himself. As a leading Hollywood star for the better part of the 1990s, Gibson was and remains firmly entrenched within Western popular culture (though in recent years he has become more notorious for his behavior and disparaging comments about homosexuals, women, African Americans, and Jews). Early in his career, he had starred in a handful of critically well-received films, such as *Gallipoli* (1981) and *The Year of Living Dangerously* (1982). The *Mad Max* and the *Lethal Weapon* films, however, propelled him into the spotlight as a box-office draw and a leading man who equaled in many ways Harrison Ford's popularity of the 1980s and 1990s. *Braveheart* was the film that gave Gibson both critical and commercial success. And because *Braveheart* is so firmly ingrained within our popular culture, it is difficult for many to see Gibson as anything other than the fighter/lover that he created in his character of William Wallace.

Like Blind Hary's *Wallace,* Gibson's *Braveheart* is an interesting mixture of fantasy, history, folklore, legend, romance, and artistic bravado, though much of the history in the film is seriously flawed.[90] Moreover, as a film, Gibson tried to do far too much with the life and times of Wallace, even with the film's almost three-hour running time.

The film begins with an interesting back story of the murder of Wallace's father and brother at the hands of the English. As a result, young William is sent to live with his learned uncle. Some 20 years later, Wallace returns to his native village; he is now fluent in a handful of foreign languages (which comes in handy when trying to court his childhood crush), and he knows of the arts of war and government (which comes in handy when he decides to fight the English and join forces with Robert the Bruce). The turning point in the film occurs early. Wallace's love Murron (played by Catherine McCormack) is publicly executed for her assault on one of the king's soldiers who attempted to rape her. It seems that there was a conscious effort by the filmmakers not to name her "Marion," as Hary does in his poem; after all, Robin Hood's love interest is Maid Marion/Marian, and confusion might have set in. Wallace revenges this act by killing the English garrison commander who had executed Murron, and thus begins a series of well-orchestrated battles both large and small.

The clean-shaven, blue-eyed Wallace of Gibson's film is a stark visual contrast to his enemies and even his supporters, and the outlaw's exterior is almost certainly one of the many ahistorical elements of the film. Wallace's fellow Scottish nationals are almost all bearded, and the Irish force presents a rugged appearance. Gibson's exterior, including his two-toned painted face at the battle of Stirling Bridge, allows his face to stand out as the hero of the narrative's. In contrast, of course, is Edward I, "Longshanks," as portrayed in menacing style by Patrick McGoohan, who is complete with fierce eyes, severe countenance, and an almost pathological personality.

Gibson's choice to portray the blood and nastiness of warfare in a number of the battles but to eschew the gore of Wallace's execution was an interesting move. The scene had been filmed in graphic detail, but test audience reaction was negative. Thus, in the final version for cinema release, while we do see Wallace on the rack and witness one of the torturers wield the hook that will disembowel the hero, the camera focuses on faces: those of Wallace, the crowd (which at first delights in the torture), Wallace's cloaked supporters in the square, the executioner, a gravely ill Longshanks, and the loves of the hero: Princess Isabelle (played by Sophie Marceau) and the ghost/hallucination of Murron. Gibson's Wallace shows no weakness whatsoever in the film; even in death, he is strong and heroic. The death of Wallace in Gibson's film is in many ways Christ-like. Indeed, many of the shots and framings that the filmmaker used in the execution scenes were again used in the torture and crucifixion scenes in his later movie *The Passion of the Christ* (2004). The possible conflation of these two filmic interpretations of historical figures is inherently problematic.

The story of Robert the Bruce in *Braveheart* is pushed to the backburner (behind Wallace's military exploits and the two romantic subplots), even though this is a film that is ostensibly about Scotland's freedom from English governance and oppression. The Bruce is played by Scotland's own Angus MacFadyen. The voiceover that begins the film is the voice of the Bruce; however, the audience does not yet know this. In this narration, the character of Robert the Bruce addresses the issues of historical truth, though not convincingly: "Historians of England will say I am a liar. History is written by those who have hanged heroes." Some, like Władysław Witalisz, have interpreted this voiceover as a means for filmmakers, much like medieval historical writers, to give themselves open license to interpret and represent history as they see fit: "From the beginning of the film, when the narrator assumes his critical stance toward written history," the audience participates in or listens to "an official, private story. The character of the hero is thus made more real and tangible, unlike the hypostatized figures of epic and heroic discourse."[91] Perhaps the character of Robert the Bruce can be interpreted by audiences as more "realistic" than Wallace; however, we are still working within the medium of film, in which representation and interpretation are highly subjective.

That Gibson's film begins with Robert the Bruce's narration and ends with his first charge at the battle of Bannockburn is a fine example of film unity and cohesion. In the final scene, the Bruce is shown caressing Wallace's love token, which he has hidden inside his armor. This is the same embroidered kerchief that Murron gave to Wallace and which he let fall the instant the axe came down on his neck. Apparently, the Wallace's supporters were able to smuggle it out. It is a rather odd moment, and it is one of many ahistorical details that appear to be added for the sake of sentimentality, romance, and nostalgia. The final scene of the film is, in many ways, an open door for a possible sequel. After all, the real success story of Scottish independence is not Wallace's but rather that of Robert the Bruce. The Bruce's story, apparently, does not present the fodder for an appealing Hollywood story: he was not as much an underdog as Wallace was, his historical personage is at times duplicitous and sinister, and there are far too many concrete details of his life (as opposed to Wallace's life and times, which is itself based mainly on legend and historical literature).

Upon the film's release, it was met with cheers and jeers from a variety of political and social movements that saw something uplifting or offensive in the film and its characters. Michael Sharp has noted that the Scottish National Party (SNP) seized upon the emotional and rational argument for Scottish independence but that in the United States the Gay and Lesbian Alliance Against Defamation (GLAAD) staged numerous protests in which the organization objected to the depiction of Edward II, which was seen as homophobic.[92] Sharp argues, indeed convincingly so, that Gibson plays Wallace and the Scots as natural in their sexuality, while the English are a collection of closeted gays, rapists, men who are keen on incest, and misogynists. According to Sharp, the film uses women "to mark Wallace as fair, honest, and enlightened, and to mark the English as abusive and duplicitous."[93] The union of Wallace and Isabelle in the film is one that suggests how Scotland may indeed persevere and overcome England. In a remarkable turn, Isabelle informs Longshanks on his deathbed that the child whom she is carrying is perhaps Wallace's, since apparently the prince could not impregnate her. Thus, Wallace and the Scots can beat England externally on the field of battle and also biologically through an apparently half-Scottish illegitimate heir to the throne of England.[94]

In the end, *Braveheart* is one more repository of semi- and non-historical evidence for the lives of William Wallace and Robert the Bruce. The outlawed Wallace and his guerrilla army are portrayed is such a favorable light that audience members often delight in the savagery on the field of battle that is inflicted upon the English. The iconic image of Gibson's two-toned face, sword in hand, may in fact become the dominant image that comes to be associated with the Scottish outlaw. Gibson's film did indeed bring the figure back into the public consciousness. Just as there are few who wish to read the adventures of Robin Hood in Middle English, there are perhaps fewer still who wish (or can) read Wallace's acts and deeds in Middle Scots. In many respects, the dissemination of the narratives of the two Scottish national heroes in *Braveheart* has made the icons more accessible and available to a far wider audience than any previous medium was able to do. Part of the popularity of the icons today (and especially Wallace) can be attributed to the power of film and its ability to connect with a global audience.

THE BRUCE (1996)

The year after the release of *Braveheart* appeared a rather different sort of film, *The Bruce,* that was based on the story of Robert the Bruce. This full-length feature film was produced by Cromwell Productions, an independent filmmaking company known primarily for documentary videos on historical topics, and released on VHS. *The Bruce* was made on a shoestring budget of approximately $500,000 (*Braveheart*'s was approximately $53 million), partially raised by guaranteeing small investors from the general public parts as extras in the battle scenes. The film was directed by Bob Carruthers and David McWhinnie and featured Sandy Welch, a minor Scottish actor (mainly on TV), as Robert the Bruce. Oliver Reed as Bishop "Wisharton"[95] and Brian Blessed as a booming King Edward I added some name recognition to the cast. Despite the best intentions, *The Bruce* cannot be judged a success. The script is often melodramatic; the acting is generally poor, as are the sound quality, continuity, and other production values; the battle scenes are not as impressive as the filmmakers claimed; and unnecessary liberties are taken with historical facts and events. Nevertheless, *The Bruce* remains interesting as a cheap, almost homemade foil to the expensive, Hollywood *Braveheart*.

GRAVE DIGGER AND THE ICONS

In the years following Gibson's film, other forms of media have revisited the Scottish icons but have done so mainly through the lens of *Braveheart*. Rather than start anew, filmmakers, television writers and producers, and musicians have gone to *Braveheart* for inspiration on the Scottish outlaw. One of the more interesting products of this reductive method of creativity, in which the source for Wallace and the Bruce is not the primary documents but rather a filmic representation that is itself far removed from pure history (and is in many cases ahistorical), is the concept album *Tunes of War* (1996) from the German heavy-metal band Grave Digger. The album is a retelling of the Scottish fight for independence and the early history of Scotland. With song titles such as "Scotland United," "The Bruce," and "Cry for Freedom (James VI)," it is obvious that the band has put its ideology squarely behind Scotland's right.

The music on this album, as on most of Grave Digger's efforts, is characterized by intense guitar riffs and rapid drumming interspersed with introspective, dramatic, and cathartic moments. A synthesized bagpipe sound even makes an appearance. The heavy-handedness of the material is, perhaps, understandable; after all, this is heavy metal and not chamber music. What is interesting, though, is that this is a German band and not a Scottish one. Much like King Arthur and even Robin Hood, the Scottish icons have become a global phenomenon.

BRAVEHEART AND THE AMERICAN SOUTH

After the release of *Braveheart*, the Southern Poverty Law Center (SPLC), a nonprofit organization based in Montgomery, Alabama, that tracks hate groups in the United States and prosecutes them, identified the film as being extremely popular among certain white supremacist groups and neo-Confederates. One such fan of the film is Louis Beam, a former Ku Klux Klan leader from Texas.[96] Beam predicted that the film "may well become a movement piece de resistance for Christian Patriots."[97] Euan Hague has noted that right-wing organizations in the southern United States have also attempted to link Gibson's Wallace with the founder of the Klan: "In 1996, Clyde Wilson, a director of the right wing secessionist neo-Confederate organization the League of the South, told delegates at his political movement's annual conference to 'Imagine the film of our *Braveheart*: The Life of General Nathan Bedford Forrest.'"[98] In an analysis of neo-Confederate behavior and attitudes in the South, the SPLC identifies certain Celtic traits that many white supremacists and neo-Confederates would like to appropriate. They see Gibson's film as a perfect source:

> Popular films like *Braveheart* have been interpreted by neo-Confederates as mirror images of their own struggles and proponents of the Celtic South thesis simplistically conflate Confederate with Celtic. Within this interpretation, Celtic culture is assumed to be genetic and evidence of supposedly Celtic behavior (fighting, drinking, emotional reactions, clannishness, disdain for authority, etc.) is taken as proof of Celtic ancestry. In turn, Celtic ancestry legitimates these supposedly Celtic behaviors, practices that are typically understood to be unchanged since the Bronze

Age. This Celtic culture and ethnicity is understood by neo-Confederates to be under attack from a mainstream U.S. policy that favors non-white ethnicities over others. Proponents maintain that malevolent actors are deliberately committing "cultural genocide" against the "Anglo-Celtic" white southern population. Invoking the language of multiculturalism and self-determination, neo-Confederates demand the right to pursue and preserve their own culture in their own communities. When coupled with neo-Confederate beliefs about the ideal unit of self-governance, the result is an intellectualized argument for racially homogeneous and ethnically segregated self-sufficient communities.

One of the most troubling aspects of neo-Confederacy is how proponents understand the relationship between culture and ethnicity. What is lauded in the "Anglo-Celtic" population (e.g. violent masculinity) is derided in other ethnic groups, particularly those of African descent. Neo-Confederacy proposes the antiquated position that cultures do not change over time. The behaviors of "Celtic" peoples in the seventeenth and eighteenth century British Isles are understood to have been transmitted intact to the southern states of the U.S.A.[99]

Colin McArthur is quick to remind us that not all of those living within the southern United States share this hatred and that reports such as the one above "have a tendency to over-dramatize the American appropriation of *Braveheart* by concentrating on its being embraced by the most extreme of the Southern groups. . . . What tends to be elided is the diversity of the 'real' South."[100] However, Mark Potok, director of the SPLC, states that the Klan is not the only hate group in the United States that has used the film for nefarious means. Militia groups have also grown attached to the film: "That film is on the shelf of every white supremacist in America. . . . The Christian Identity and Klan groups have always believed the Celts are the most racially pure, but the neo-Nazis, by definition not Christian, really got into Scotland after *Braveheart*. Now it's often a focal point for discussions."[101]

THE NATIONAL WALLACE MONUMENT

In 1859, a competition was held in Scotland for architects to submit plans for the creation of a national monument that sought to honor and commemorate the battle of Stirling Bridge. John Thomas Rochead (1814–1878) was chosen winner among 76 entrants, and the monument was completed in 1869 at a cost of £18,000 on the Abbey Craig near Stirling.[102] The monument is 220 feet tall and made of sandstone, and from the top of the observation area one can view the field of Stirling where Edward I's forces were said to have organized. James Coleman has argued that, from the inception of the monument, the site has become a place where Wallace's role in Scottish nationalism has been misinterpreted. Coleman argues that we should "shrug off this post-*Braveheart* image of William Wallace and its associations with modern Scottish nationalism" and reexamine the monument in light of its original political context in the nineteenth century, where it marked "the patriot-hero's achievement of independence for Scotland and to commemorate what he had done for the Union and the Empire."[103] Coleman's point is duly taken; however, the popularity and staying power of Gibson's film makes the scholar's argument (though valid) less likely to be actualized.

In 1996, Tom Church, a stonemason, sculpted a 13-foot, 12-ton statue of Wallace that was directly based on Gibson's character, and this was placed in the monument's parking lot at the foot of Abbey Craig. Most visitors, critics, and Scots apparently disliked the piece. On the figure's shield is the word "Braveheart," and his mouth is open as if shouting a battle cry, in a way that definitely recalls Gibson's Wallace. Andrew Ross has alluded to the commercialization of the monument in recent years, noting that the "Disney touch is evident in an audiovisual 'talking head' display that dramatizes dialogues between Wallace and his antagonists."[104] The National Monument also has a "Legends Coffee House/Gift Shop," where one can relax, have a cappuccino, and take in the view of the (now cleaned-up) battlefield. The creation of this eatery forced the removal of Church's statue in 2008; it went back to the artist's residence after he put it up for auction and received no bids.[105]

CONSUMING THE ICONS

In the very strange collision of postmodernism, iconography, fetishism, and our consumer culture, one can now ingest a little bit of both Wallace and the Bruce—well, in theory at least. The robust nature of these two icons has even made its way into the beverage industry. The Bridge of Allan Brewery, Ltd., in Scotland brews a year-round Scottish ale simply called "William Wallace." Other beers in the company's line include more (of course!) Scottish ales: "Bannockburn," "Stirling Brig 1297," and "Sheriffmuir" (named after the battle in the Jacobite Rising of 1715). These can be purchased at the gift shop at the National Monument. Maclay Inns, Ltd., in Alloa, Scotland, brews an India pale ale (IPA) simply called "Wallace"; that this is an IPA, an ale that was originally brewed in England for export to the British in India during the eighteenth and nineteenth centuries, is interesting when one considers the history of English "colonialism" in Scotland. The Three Floyds Brewery in Munster, Indiana, has a decidedly strong reputation among lovers of quality beer. Their award-winning "Robert the Bruce Scottish Ale" is a mahogany-colored, malty ale with hints of chocolate and caramel; it is also available in a very limited barrel-aged version that has a significantly higher alcohol content by volume. The illustration of the Bruce on the label is less stern and warlike than the Wallace-themed images on other bottles and is more comical: bearded, in armor and with a crown on his head, sporting a big and somewhat mischievous grin, the Bruce is raising his foaming tankard in one hand while holding a small hatchet in the other. Duncans, an erstwhile chocolate company in Scotland (now owned by an English firm and relocated to the north of England), once made a chocolate bar in honor of Wallace: "Independence."[106] Of course we will never know what the Bruce and Wallace would have thought of all of this; indeed, neither one had access to chocolate in their lifetimes. Many replica versions of Wallace's *Braveheart* sword are available for purchase; had *Braveheart* not received an "R" rating, perhaps the movie would have spawned a line of toys.

CONCLUSION

The Scottish chronicler Andrew of Wyntoun, an Augustinian canon of Saint Serfs Inch on an island in Loch Leven, wrote around 1420 of Wallace in such a manner that is still very much the image of the outlaw today:

> In all Ingland þare wes nocht þan
> As William Wallace a lelare man.
> That he did agane þe nation,
> Thai maid him prouocation;
> Na to þaim oblist neuer wes he
> Off faith, fallowschip, na lawte;
> For in his tyme, as I herd say,
> That fals and fekill þai were of fay.[107]

> [In all England there was not then a more loyal man than William Wallace. That which he did against the nation [i.e., England], they gave him provocation; not to them did he ever make a pledge of faith, fellowship, nor loyalty; for in his time, as I heard say, that they were false and fickle of their faithfulness.]

Both Robert the Bruce and William Wallace continue to inspire, and both icons it seems are forever embedded in the conscious (or unconscious) mind of those who strive for an independent voice. Whether that voice is for Scottish independence or for the re-secession of the Southern states from the United States of America, it does not matter. Popular culture has been rather kind to Wallace and, considering the Bruce's many shortcomings, he too has benefitted from a rather rosy reappraisal in popular fiction and film. In the United States in particular, whose citizens almost unanimously prefer the underdog, both men, but especially the outlaw Wallace, still resonate with readers and viewers. Like Robin Hood, each generation has a slightly different Wallace and the Bruce. It will be interesting to see whether Gibson's film will be the final popular statement on both icons or whether other filmmakers and writers will craft new versions of these icons that will inspire future generations.

NOTES

1. David Cornell, *Bannockburn: The Triumph of Robert the Bruce* (New Haven and London: Yale University Press, 2009), 253.

2. G.W.S. Barrow, *Robert Bruce and the Community of the Realm of Scotland* (Edinburgh: Edinburgh University Press, 1988), 323–24. The heart was discovered in 1920, but the site of its reburial was not marked. In 1996, a casket containing a human heart was unearthed during construction work at the abbey. It was reburied in Melrose Abbey in 1998.

3. Andrew Fisher, *William Wallace* (Edinburgh: Birlinn, 2007), 14.

4. A.A.M. Duncan, "William, Son of Alan Wallace: The Documents," in *The Wallace Book*, ed. Edward J. Cowan (Edinburgh: John Donald, 2007), 42–63 at 50.

5. *Hary's Wallace (Vita Nobilissimi Defensoris Scotie Wilelmi Wallace Militis)*, ed. Matthew P. McDiarmid, 2 vols., Scottish Text Society, Fourth Series, 4, 5 (Edinburgh and London: William Blackwood and Sons, 1968–69), 1:1–16.

6. Fisher, *Wallace*, 106.

7. Ibid.

8. Antonia Gransden, *Historical Writing in England I: c. 550 to c. 1307* (Ithaca: Cornell University Press, 1974; repr. London: Routledge, 1996), 480.

9. Ibid.

10. *The Chronicle of Peter Langtoft*, ed. and trans. Thomas Wright, 2 vols., Rolls Series 47 (London: Longmans, 1866–68), 2:253.

11. Ibid., 2: 263, 265. A "gonfanon" was a small flag that was attached to the steel head of a knight's lance.

12. Translation quoted in D. J. Gray, *William Wallace: The King's Enemy* (New York: Barnes and Noble, 1991), 152.

13. R. James Goldstein, *The Matter of Scotland: Historical Narrative in Medieval Scotland* (Lincoln: University of Nebraska Press, 1993), 270.

14. *Chronicle of Peter Langtoft*, ed. Wright, 2: 373.

15. *The Political Songs of England, from the Reign of John to that of Edward II*, ed. and trans. Thomas Wright, Camden Society, OS 6 (London: J. B. Nichols and Son, 1839), 159–79.

16. Ibid., 166–67, 173.

17. Ibid., 261; the text of the poem is on 262–67.

18. Ibid., 265.

19. *Barbour's Bruce: A Fredome is a Noble Thing!* ed. Matthew P. McDiarmid and James A. C. Stevenson, 3 vols., The Scottish Text Society, 4th Series, 12, 13, 15 (Edinburgh: Blackwood, Pillans, and Wilson, 1980–85), 1:3.

20. Ibid., 1:7.

21. Ibid., 1:9–10.

22. Ibid., 1:50.

23. Walter Scheps, introd. and trans., "From the Acts and Deeds of William Wallace," in *Medieval Outlaws: Twelve Tales in Modern English Translation, Revised and Expanded Edition*, ed. Thomas H. Ohlgren (West Lafayette, IN: Parlor Press, 2005), 420–69 at 423.

24. McDiarmid, *Hary's Wallace*, 1: xvi.

25. Ibid., 1: xxiv–xxxviii.

26. Ibid., 1: xxxviii–xlvi.

27. Ibid., 1: lviii.

28. Ibid., 1: xxxiii.

29. Ibid., 1: lix.

30. Walter Scheps, "The Literary Nature of Blind Harry's *Wallace*" (PhD diss., University of Oregon, 1966), 135.

31. Goldstein, *Matter,* 250.

32. McDiarmid, *Hary's Wallace,* 1: xxxvii–xxxviii.

33. Ibid., 2: 38, line 1225. Hary's measurement is reckoned as nine-quarters of the Scots ell of 37 inches.

34. Ibid., 2: 39, lines 1241–42.

35. Ibid., 2: 120, lines 1393–94.

36. Richard J. Moll, "'Off quhat nacion art thow?' National Identity in Blind Hary's *Wallace*," in *History, Literature, and Music in Scotland, 700–1560,* ed. R. Andrew McDonald (Toronto: University of Toronto Press, 2002), 120–43 at 138.

37. John Major, *Historia Majoris Britanniae* (Paris: Josse Badius, 1521).

38. John Major, *A History of Greater Britain as well England as Scotland*, trans. and ed. Archibald Constable, Publications of the Scottish History Society 10 (Edinburgh: University Press, 1892), xxi.

39. Ibid., xxii.

40. Ibid., xxiv.

41. Ibid., 193.

42. Ibid., 194.

43. Ibid.

44. Ibid., 196.

45. Ibid.

46. Ibid., 195 n. 1.

47. Ibid., 195.

48. Ibid., 196.

49. Ibid., 205.

50. William Wordsworth, *The Prelude: The Four Texts (1798, 1799, 1805, 1850)*, ed. Jonathan Wordsworth (London: Penguin Books, 1995), 49, lines 214–20.

51. Dorothy Wordsworth, *Journals of Dorothy Wordsworth*, ed. E. de Selincourt. 2 vols. (London: Macmillan, 1952), 1: 228.

52. William A. Everett, "National Themes in Scottish Art Music, ca. 1880–1990," *International Review of the Aesthetics and Sociology of Music* 30, no. 2 (1999): 151–71 at 159. See also Anne Dhu Shapiro, "Sounds of Scotland," *American Music* 8, no. 1 (1990): 71–83.

53. Carol McGuirk, "Jacobite History to National Song: Robert Burns and Carolina Oliphant (Baroness Nairne)," *The Eighteenth Century* 47, no. 2/3 (2006): 253–87 at 261.

54. Robert Burns, *The Poems and Songs of Robert Burns* (London: J. M. Dent), 457–58.

55. Jerome Mitchell, *Scott, Chaucer, and Medieval Romance: A Study in Sir Walter Scott's Indebtedness to the Literature of the Middle Ages* (Lexington: University of Kentucky Press, 1987), 1–10.

56. Ibid., 14.

57. John Sutherland, *The Life of Walter Scott: A Critical Biography* (London: Blackwell, 1997), 159.

---

58. Julian Meldon D'Arcy, *Subversive Scott: The Waverley Novels and Scottish Nationalism* (Reykjavík: University of Iceland Press, 2005), 66.

59. Ibid., 67.

60. Mitchell, *Scott, Chaucer, and Medieval Romance*, 79.

61. Murray G. H. Pittock, *The Invention of Scotland: The Stuart Myth and the Scottish Identity* (London: Routledge, 1991), 54.

62. Walter Scott, *The History of Scotland*, 2 vols. (London: Longman, 1830), 1:1.

63. Ibid., 1:74.

64. Ibid., 1:80.

65. John Constable, *John Constable's Correspondence*, ed. Ronald Brymer Beckett, 6 vols. (London: H. M. Stationary Office, 1962–68), 3:93.

66. Walter Scott, *Tales of a Grandfather: Being the History of Scotland*, ed. Edwin Ginn (Boston: Ginn, 1981), iii.

67. Ibid., 66.

68. Versions differ as to the location of the episode, either within a house or in a cave on Rathlin Island off the northeastern coast of Ireland.

69. The numerous editions of Porter's novel were hugely successful in both Britain and the United States, and it remains readily available in the secondhand market, in a print-on-demand version, and as a free e-book.

70. Ibid., 41–42.

71. Nancy Moore Goslee, "Contesting Liberty: The Figure of William Wallace in Poems by Hemans, Hogg, and Baillie," *Keats-Shelley Journal* 50 (2001): 35–63 at 36.

72. Graeme Morton, *William Wallace: Man and Myth* (Stroud, Gloucestershire: Sutton, 2001), 114.

73. Ibid., 114–15.

74. Ibid., 117–18.

75. Ibid., 119–20.

76. Ibid., 121.

77. Douglas Young, *William Wallace and This War (Speech at the Elderslie Commemoration, 1943)* (Glasgow: Royal Exchange Press, 1943).

78. Everett, "National Themes in Scottish Art Music," 163.

79. Ibid.

80. Ibid.

81. William Wallace, *William Wallace: Symphonic Poems*, conducted by Martyn Brabbins, CD, Hyperion Records, CDA 66848, 1995.

82. Kenny M. Sheppard, "Selected Choral Works of Learmont Drysdale, Scotland's Forgotten Composer" (PhD diss., Texas Tech University, 1987), 25.

83. Everett, "National Themes in Scottish Art Music," 163.

84. Elspeth King, "The Material Culture of William Wallace," in *The Wallace Book*, ed. Cowan, 117–35 at 126.

85. John Morrison, *Painting the Nation: Identity and Nationalism in Scottish Painting, 1800–1920* (Edinburgh: Edinburgh University Press, 2003), 120–21.

86. Ibid., 121–22.

87. Ray Bradfield, *Nigel Tranter: Scotland's Storyteller* (Edinburgh: B&W Publishing, 1999), 222.

88. Ibid., 225.

89. The Numbers: Box Office Data, Movie Starts, Idle Speculation, "Braveheart," http://www.the-numbers.com/movies/1995/0BRVH.php.

90. Gibson has admitted that the film is heavily fictitious, noting that changes were made for dramatic purposes. For example, in truth King Edward II did not marry Princess Isabella (born ca. 1295) until 1308, soon after her first-ever arrival in England; Wallace died in 1305 and Edward I died in 1307; the future Edward III was not born until 1312. In truth Wallace was not a commoner; in Wallace's time blue body paint had not been used in battle by Scottish/Celtic warriors for roughly eight centuries, standardized patterns of tartan had not been invented yet, and English soldiers had no set uniform. In the film, no bridge plays a part in the battle of Stirling Bridge. In truth Robert the Bruce was not present at the battle of Falkirk, on the English side (as in the film) or otherwise. Wallace was actually captured near Glasgow, not at Edinburgh Castle.

91. Władysław Witalisz, "Blind Hary's *The Wallace* and Mel Gibson's *Braveheart*: What Do Medieval Romance and Hollywood Film Have in Common?" in *Medievalisms: The Poetics of Literary Re-Reading*, ed. Liliana Sikorska with Joanna Maciulewicz (Frankfurt am Main: Peter Lang, 2008), 221–29 at 226.

92. Michael D. Sharp, "Remaking Medieval Heroism: Nationalism and Sexuality in *Braveheart*," *Florilegium* 15 (1998): 251–66.

93. Ibid., 263.

94. The film's proposition that Edward II was homosexual is not new; nonetheless, it is historically spurious, and it is a narrative thread that is linked not to Scottish historians but to English ones. For an examination of Edward II's sexuality, see John Boswell, *Christianity, Social Tolerance, and Homosexuality* (Chicago: University of Chicago Press, 1980), 298–302; Pierre Chaplais argues against the claim of homosexuality in his study *Piers Gaveston: Edward II's Adoptive Brother* (Oxford: Clarendon Press, 1994), 109.

95. Presumably a combination of the historical William Lamberton bishop of Saint Andrews and Robert Wishart bishop of Glasgow—both of whom were, in varying degrees, supporters of William Wallace and Robert the Bruce—with, perhaps, a trace of William Wishart, elected bishop of Glasgow but translated to Saint Andrews before his consecration. Lamberton and Wishart presided at the coronation of King Robert in 1306. Neither bishop was present at the battle of Bannockburn nor did either belong to a military religious order (perhaps the legendary Scottish combined Order of Saint John and the Temple?), as portrayed in the film.

96. The Southern Poverty Law Center, "The Clan Overseas: They're not just in the U.S. Anymore," *Intelligence Report* no. 89 (1998); available online at http://www.splcenter.org/get-informed/intelligence-report/browse-all-issues/1998/winter/the-klan-overseas. The SPLC has termed Beam "[a]n iconic figure of the radical right."

97. Kirsty Scott, "The Fatal Attraction," *The Herald*, August 6, 1997, 12.

98. Euan Hague, "Representations of Race and Romance: The Portrayal of People of Scottish Descent in North America by British Newspapers, 1997–1999," *Scottish Affairs* 57 (2006): 39–69 at 53.

99. Euan Hague, "Essay: The Neo-Confederate Movement," The Southern Poverty Law Center, http://www.splcenter.org/get-informed/intelligence-files/ideology/neo-confederate/the-neo-confederate-movement.

100. Colin McArthur, *Brigadoon, Braveheart and the Scots: Distortions of Scotland in Hollywood Cinema* (London: I. B. Tauris, 2003), 201.

101. Gerard Seenan, "Klansmen Take Their Lead from Scots," *The Guardian (London)*, January 30, 1999, 12.

102. Dictionary of Scottish Architects, DSA Building and Design Report, "Wallace Monument," http://www.scottisharchitects.org.uk/building_full.php?id=207377.

103. James Coleman, "Unionist-Nationalism in Stone? The National Wallace Monument and the Hazards of Commemoration in Victorian Scotland," in *The Wallace Book*, ed. Cowan, 151–68 at 151.

104. Andrew Ross, "Wallace's Monument and the Resumption of Scotland," *Social Text* 18, no. 4 (2000): 83–107 at 101.

105. BBC News UK, "Wallace Statue Back with Sculptor," http://news.bbc.co.uk/2/hi/uk_news/scotland/tayside_and_central/8310614.stm; Kevin Hurley, "They Make Take Our Lives but They Won't Take Freedom," Scotland on Sunday, http://scotlandonsunday.scotsman.com/williamwallace/They-may-take-our-lives.2565370.jp.

106. Morton, *William Wallace*, 148.

107. Andrew of Wyntoun, *The Original Chronicle of Andrew of Wyntoun Printed on Parallel Pages from the Cottonian and Wemyss MSS, with Variants of Other Texts*, ed. F. J. Amours, 6 vols., Scottish Text Society (Edinburgh: William Blackwood and Sons, 1903–14), 5:370, lines 2761–68.

FURTHER READING

Editions and Translations of Primary Texts

Duncan, A.A.M., ed. and trans. *The Bruce*. Edinburgh: Canongate, 1997.

Major, John. *A History of Greater Britain as well England as Scotland*. Edited and translated by Archibald Constable. Publications of the Scottish History Society 10. Edinburgh: University Press, 1892.

McDiarmid, Matthew P., ed. *Hary's Wallace (Vita Nobilissimi Defensoris Scotie Wilelmi Wallace Militis)*. 2 vols. Scottish Text Society, Fourth Series, 4, 5. Edinburgh: William Blackwood and Sons, 1968–69.

McDiarmid, Matthew P., and James A. C. Stevenson, eds. *Barbour's Bruce: A Fredome Is a Noble Thing!* 3 vols. The Scottish Text Society, 4th Series, 12, 13, 15. Edinburgh: Blackwood, Pillans, and Wilson, 1980–85.

McKim, Anne, ed. *The Wallace: Selections*. TEAMS Middle English Texts. Kalamazoo, MI: Medieval Institute Publications, 2003.

Scheps, Walter, introd. and trans. "From the Acts and Deeds of William Wallace." In *Medieval Outlaws: Twelve Tales in Modern English Translation, Revised and Expanded Edition*, edited by Thomas H. Ohlgren, 420–69. West Lafayette, IN: Parlor Press, 2005.

Wright, Thomas, ed. and trans. *The Political Songs of England, from the Reign of John to that of Edward II*. Camden Society, OS 6. London: J. B. Nichols and Son, 1839.

Secondary Readings

Barrow, G.W.S. *Robert Bruce and the Community of the Realm of Scotland*. Edinburgh: Edinburgh University Press, 1988.

Cornell, David. *Bannockburn: The Triumph of Robert the Bruce*. New Haven, CT: Yale University Press, 2009.

Cowan, Edward J., ed. *The Wallace Book*. Edinburgh: John Donald, 2007.

Fisher, Andrew. *William Wallace*. Edinburgh: Birlinn, 2007.

Goldstein, R. James. *The Matter of Scotland: Historical Narrative in Medieval Scotland*. Lincoln: University of Nebraska Press, 1993.

Gransden, Antonia. *Historical Writing in England I: c. 550 to c. 1307*. Ithaca, NY: Cornell University Press, 1974; repr. London: Routledge, 1996.

Gray, D. J. *William Wallace: The King's Enemy*. New York: Barnes and Noble, 1991.

McArthur, Colin. *Brigadoon, Braveheart and the Scots: Distortions of Scotland in Hollywood Cinema*. London: I. B. Tauris, 2003.

Morrison, John. *Painting the Nation: Identity and Nationalism in Scottish painting, 1800–1920*. Edinburgh: Edinburgh University Press, 2003.

Morton, Graeme. *William Wallace: Man and Myth*. Stroud, Gloucestershire: Sutton, 2001.

Pittock, Murray G. H. *The Invention of Scotland: The Stuart Myth and the Scottish Identity*. London: Routledge, 1991.

Equestrian statue of Charlemagne (ca. 742–814), bronze, French. (Louvre, Paris, France/Giraudon/The Bridgeman Art Library)

Charlemagne (ca. 742–814)

Dominique T. Hoche

INTRODUCTION

Charlemagne is one of those icons of the Middle Ages whose name is familiar to many people, some of whom might be able to estimate roughly when he lived, but the majority know no more than that. The connection between the name of Charlemagne and the term "Carolingian" is not immediately or automatically obvious, much less to imagine that the man is considered to be the "Father of Europe" and is responsible for a renaissance that extinguished the so-called Dark Ages and brought about a revival of art, religion, culture, and economic standards. But he is very important to know about—in fact, if one were going to know of one man between the fall of the Roman Empire and the rise of the Middle Ages, that man should, perhaps, be Charlemagne.

OVERVIEW

Charlemagne's name comes from the Latin *Carolus Magnus*, meaning "Charles the Great." He was the king of the Franks from 768 and emperor of the Romans from 800 until he died in 814. The reason he is called "the Great" is because of what he did to the map of Europe, both in terms of land and in terms of culture. He expanded the small Frankish kingdom into an area larger than France is now, incorporating parts of northern Spain and Italy, western Germany, and a great amount of central Europe. Adding Italy to his lands earned him the gratitude of the pope, who crowned him "Imperator Augustus" on December 25, 800.

He didn't start out that great, though. He was the eldest son of King Pepin the Short and Bertrada of Laon, and his parents were not technically married until after he was born—as a way of making sure Bertrada produced a son, otherwise, why get married? She did produce more children after the wedding—including Charles's brother Carloman, with whom he never got along. After their father's death in 768, following tradition and law, the kingdom of the Franks was divided between the brothers. They soon began to squabble, but Carloman died in 771 before the two could resort to warring. Charlemagne continued in his father's footsteps, protecting the papacy, and settling power struggles in both Italy and Spain. One of his incursions into Spain has become very famous—as his army retreated from his attempts to offer military aid in Barcelona, he was attacked by the Basques at the battle of Roncesvalles in 778—and the battle was memorialized in fiction as the *Song of Roland*. Charlemagne's commitment to Christianity encouraged him to campaign against the Saxons in the northeast, and after a long series of wars he subdued them, converted them, and added them to his realm.

His empire united most of Western Europe for the first time since the Roman Empire, and today he is considered the founding father of both French and German monarchies. He is also the "Father of Europe" because his actions spurred the creation of a common European identity.

DATE AND PLACE OF BIRTH

Charlemagne's life—or much of what is known of it—comes from his biographer, Einhard, who wrote a *Vita Caroli Magni*, the *Life of Charlemagne*. It is commonly believed that Charlemagne was born in 742, but there are some problems with that date—first of all, it's an estimate to begin with, based on his age given at death, rather than evidence from primary sources. Critics consider another date to be possible: April 2, 747, but the second of April of that year was Easter, and the birth of a prince on Easter would have provoked a lot of discussion, yet there are no comments on such an auspicious birth in the chronicles and annals of the year 747. That date, then, might simply be some fiction written by a pious devotee of Charlemagne to honor the emperor.

Other scholars suggest that his birth was one year later, in 748, but at present it is impossible to be certain of the true date of the birth of Charlemagne. Our best guesses are April 1, 747, after April 15, 747, or April 1, 748. We do know he was born in Herstal (the town where his father was born), which is near Liège in Belgium today. When he was about seven, he was sent to live at his father's villa in Jupille, which has caused Jupille to be listed as a possible birthplace in many history books.

Charlemagne was named after his grandfather, Charles Martel, and the birth name of Charles comes from the Germanic word *karlaz* or "free man" and from which we get the German *Kerl,* "man" or "guy," and the English word "churl." His name is first seen in its Latin form as Carolus or Karolus. One sign of how much of an effect Charlemagne had on Europe is how his name has become the very word for "king" in many European languages: Bulgarian: крал, Serbian: краљ, Croatian: *kralj,* Russian: король, Polish: *król,* Czech: *král,* Lithuanian: *karalius,* Latvian: *karalis,* Hungarian: *király,* Turkish: *kral,* Slovak: *král.*

NATIVE LANGUAGE

What was Charlemagne's native language? Most people might answer French, but in the area in which he was born they did not then speak French, as we know it. Scholars believe it was a form of a German idiom, but which one? Some argue it was a Germanic dialect of the Ripuarian Franks, and others say he did not speak Old Frankish at all. Linguists have reconstructed old Frankish today by loanwords in Old French, and from its descendent, Old Low Franconian, a tongue which is the ancestor of the Dutch language and the modern dialects heard in the German area of North Rhineland; these dialects were named Ripuarian by modern linguists. Old Frankish, though, is a mystery today because all we have left of it are phrases and words in the law codes of the main Frankish tribes (the Salian and Ripuarian Franks), which are written in Latin but sprinkled with Germanic phrases. The Franconian language was a form of Lower German, but in some areas it was being replaced with a form of Old High German.

Sound confusing? The problem is that Charlemagne was born in an area of great linguistic diversity. If we went to Liège around the year 750, we would hear Old East Low Franconian in the city, north and northwest; Old Ripuarian Franconian to the east and in Aachen; and Gallo-Romance (the ancestor of the Walloon dialect of Old French) in the south and southwest. The one confirmation that he might have spoken a German dialect comes from the fact that he gave his children Old High German names.

What else did he speak? We have evidence that he spoke Latin fluently and understood Greek—Einhard, his biographer, writes, "Grecam vero melius intellegere quam pronuntiare poterat," or "He understood Greek better than he could pronounce it" (26). It is also possible that he spoke Arabic, for in the fifteenth-century Irish work the *Gabhaltais Shearluis Mhoir* or *Conquests of Charlemagne* from the Book of Lismore, it states, "When Agiolandus heard the Saracen language from Charlemagne he marveled at it greatly. For when Charlemagne was a youth he had been among the Paynims in the city which is called Toletum (Toledo) and he had learnt the language of the Saracens in that city" (Hyde 35).

APPEARANCE

We do not have an exact description of Charlemagne from his lifetime, but we do have one from his biographer Einhard, who wrote in 826:

> His body was large and strong. He was tall, but not unduly so, since his height was seven times the length of his own foot. The top of his head was round, his eyes were large and lively, his nose was a little larger than average, he had fine white hair and a cheerful and attractive face. So, standing or sitting his presence was greatly increased in authority and dignity. His neck seemed short and thick and his stomach seemed to project, but the symmetry of the other parts hid these flaws. His pace was firm and the whole bearing of his body powerful. Indeed his voice was clear but given his size, not as strong as might have been expected. His health was good until four years before he died, when he suffered from constant fevers. Towards the end he would limp on one foot. Even then he trusted his own judgment more than the advice of his doctors, whom he almost hated, since they urged him to stop eating roast meat, which he liked, and to start eating boiled meats. (34)

Einhard's description matches the images we have of him on the coins of the time as well as the eight-inch (20.3 cm) bronze statue prized by the Louvre Museum in Paris. Charlemagne's tomb was opened in 1861 by scientists who reconstructed his skeleton and measured it, finding that it was 74.9 inches (190 cm), and a modern study based on the dimensions of his tibia suggest that his height was 72.44 inches (1.84 m). Since the average male was 66.54 inches (1.69 m), he was probably one of the tallest men of his day.

Charlemagne was supposedly stately, with fair hair and a thick neck. The contemporary paintings and sculpture of the man, however, show an ideal vision of him. The Roman tradition of realistic portraits was out of favor at the time, and so pictures of rulers were made with the view of showing them as perfect beings, which more often made them all look alike. Pictures of Charlemagne the Emperor and God's representative on Earth resemble images of an ideal ruler and often look similar to icons of Christ as Ruler. Even his hair is portrayed incorrectly—Einhard describes Charlemagne as "canitie pulchra" ("with beautiful white hair"), suggesting that the man went prematurely gray, but portraits of him render his hair as blond or yellow.

Einhard describes Charlemagne's clothes to show how the emperor was an unassuming man—he wore the traditional costume of the Frankish people:

> He used to wear his national, that is, Frankish, costume; close to his body he put on a linen shirt and linen underwear, then a tunic fringed with silk and stockings, then he wrapped his thighs and his feet with stockings, and covered his shoulders and chest in winter with a jacket made of otter-skin or ermine and a blue cloak, and he was always armed with his sword, which had a gold or silver hilt and belt. Sometimes he used a jeweled sword, but only at great feast days or when he received foreign ambassadors. He spurned foreign clothes, even the most beautiful, and never wore them except at Rome, when, asked once by Pope Hadrian and then by his successor Leo, he wore a long tunic and a chlamys and put on shoes made in the Roman way. On feast days he would process wearing a robe woven of gold and jeweled leggings and fastened his cloak with a golden brooch, and wore a crown of gold adorned with jewels. But on other days his costume was little different from that of the common people. (35)

Judging from Einhard's reports of his being moderate in food and drink, especially drink, as he hated to see anyone drunk, Charlemagne was comfortable with being seen as—and it seems odd to use this word—*ordinary*.

MARRIAGES

Charlemagne had four wives and six concubines, and the result was 20 children. One might think that he would have had heirs galore, but he ended up with only four legitimate grandsons—the children of his fourth (third legitimate) son, Louis. Bernard of Italy, the only son of Charlemagne's third (second legitimate) son, Pippin of Italy, was born illegitimate but was included in the line of inheritance. The reasons for this slim inheritance situation are very complex and interesting, but first let us take a look at the list of Charlemagne's wives and children:

1. **Himiltrude** was the woman with whom he had his first official relationship. Some scholars call the relationship a legal marriage, but most believe it was concubinage because Charlemagne was able to easily put Himiltrude aside when he had to officially marry Desiderata. Himiltrude had two children by him:
   a. **Amaudru**, a daughter
   b. **Pippin the Hunchback** (ca. 769–811)
2. **Desiderata**, daughter of Desiderius king of the Lombards; they married in 770, but the marriage was quickly annulled in 771.
3. **Hildegard** (757 or 758–783) was Charlemagne's second official wife. They married in 771, and she died in 783. By her, he had nine children:
   a. **Charles the Younger** (ca. 772–December 4, 811), duke of Maine, and crowned king of the Franks on December 25, 800
   b. **Adalhaid** (774), who was born while her parents were on campaign in Italy. She was sent back to Francia, but the infant died before reaching Lyons.
   c. **Rotrude (or Hruodrud)** (775–June 6, 810)
   d. **Carloman**, renamed Pippin (or Pepin) (April 777–July 8, 810), king of Italy
   e. **Louis** (778–June 20, 840), twin of Lothair, king of Aquitaine from 781, crowned Holy Roman Emperor in 813, senior Emperor from 814
   f. **Lothair** (778–February 6, 779/780), twin of Louis, died in infancy
   g. **Bertha** (779–826)
   h. **Gisela** (781–808)
   i. **Hildegarde** (782–783)
4. **Fastrada** was Charlemagne's third wife. They married in 784, and she died in 794. By her he had two children:
   a. **Theodrada** (b. 784), abbess of Argenteuil
   b. **Hiltrude** (b. 787)
5. **Luitgard** was his fourth wife. They married in 794, but she died childless.

CONCUBINES AND ILLEGITIMATE CHILDREN

Charlemagne also had several known concubines, who bore him many illegitimate children. The list of these individuals is as follows:

1. **Gersuinda**, his first known concubine. By her he had:
   a. **Adaltrude** (b. 774)

2. **Madelgard,** his second known concubine. By her he had:
   a. **Ruodhaid** (775–810), abbess of Faremoutiers
3. **Amaltrud** of Vienne, his third known concubine. By her he had:
   a. **Alpaida** (b. 794)
4. **Regina,** his fourth known concubine. By her he had:
   a. **Drogo** (801–855), bishop of Metz from 823 and abbot of Luxeuil Abbey
   b. **Hugh** (802–844), arch-chancellor of the empire
5. **Ethelind,** his fifth known concubine. By her he had:
   a. **Richbod** (805–844), abbot of Saint-Riquier
   b. **Theodoric** (b. 807)

CHARLEMAGNE AND HIS CHILDREN

Taking advantage of the first lengthy peacetime in his rule (780–82), Charlemagne began to appoint his young sons to positions of authority, following the traditions of French kings and mayors of the past. The eldest, Charles, he kept at his own court to learn from his tutors and officials. The two younger sons he had crowned kings by Pope Hadrian in 781, and they were sent away from home to "rule" their subkingdoms.

The elder of these two, Carloman, became king of Italy in a ceremony in which he was renamed Pippin (or Pepin) and took the Iron Crown of Lombardy that his father had first worn in 774. The younger of the two, Louis, became king of Aquitaine. Charlemagne ordered Pippin and Louis to be raised in the customs of their kingdoms, and he gave their regents some control of their subkingdoms, but real power was always in his hands, though he intended his sons to inherit their realms some day. Until that day, it was their job to maintain their father's high profile, and by giving the boys their lands when they were young, Charlemagne hoped to insure the future divisions of his realm against infighting. He made sure, though, that his sons were educated by Alcuin of York at the palace school in Aachen, and as soon as they were old enough he took them on campaigns; by the time they were in their teens they were expected to lead their own troops in battle.

Charlemagne did not tolerate insubordination in his sons: in 792, he banished his eldest son, Pippin the Hunchback, to the monastery of Prüm because the young man had joined a rebellion against him. The rebellion was easily predicted because even though Pippin was considered illegitimate, he was still the emperor's firstborn, and the insult to him of renaming the young Carloman "Pippin" was not easy to bear—it was as if Charlemagne had erased Pippin the Hunchback's very existence. Banishing him to a monastery was the final step to making the young man disappear.

Charles the Younger focused on the Bretons, who shared a border with the Franks and who rose up against him and his father on at least two occasions before they were easily defeated. He was also sent against the Saxons on multiple occasions. In 805 and 806, he was sent into the Böhmerwald, which today is modern Bohemia, to deal with the Slavs living there (today's Czechs). He subjected them to Frankish authority and devastated the valley of the Elbe, forcing a tribute on them. He took his responsibilities seriously, rising to his duty as a king, and was noted to have been very careful to watch for corruption among his people.

Pippin fought the Slavs to his north, but had to hold the Avar and Beneventan borders—making him uniquely poised to fight the Byzantine Empire when conflict arose after Charlemagne's imperial coronation. Pippin's personality was that of a natural-born warrior, so much that his teacher Alcuin nicknamed him "Julius."

Finally, young Louis was in charge of the Spanish March and also went to southern Italy to fight the duke of Benevento. At age 19, he took Barcelona in a great siege in the year 797. Despite his military skill, he was considered to be the scholar of the family and so devout that he would later be nicknamed Louis "the Pious." He was Alcuin's favorite, but the teacher noted that the boy "never showed his white teeth in a smile."

Among the sisters, Rotruda, Bertrada, and Gisla, life was very different. It was culturally expected that as soon as they reached puberty they were to be married off, but Charlemagne decided to keep all his daughters single and at home. Einhard writes that it was because "he could not live without them," but scholars speculate that he did not let them get married because the resulting heirs would make inheritance much more complicated.

Rotruda was at one time betrothed to the Byzantine Emperor, and Bertrada was supposedly going to marry Offa king of Mercia, but no actual alliances ever came about. Instead, the princesses stayed at court, were educated under Alcuin, and were spoiled rotten with the all the luxury and pampering that the court could offer. They were chaperoned—but not closely enough. Rotruda had an affair with Rorgon count of Maine and had a son, Louis. Bertrada, the prettiest and liveliest of the sisters, had a passionate and long-lived affair with Angilbert, one of Charlemagne's closest friends—who was also 30 years her senior! He was an early version of a Renaissance man—a brilliant soldier, scholar, poet, statesman, courtier, and diplomat and ultimately a lay abbot of the monastery of Saint-Riquier. He must have been an amazing man, beloved of Alcuin and the court, and was noted for his zest for living—a fact that must have attracted the princess, for she bore him two sons. One of their sons was named Nithard, who was a loyal servant to the Carolingians (the descendants of Charles Martel) and who became one of the greatest of the early Frankish historians.

Charlemagne tolerated his daughters' relationships, even rewarding their common-law spouses, and adored the illegitimate grandchildren they produced for him. He refused to believe stories of any sort of scandalous behavior from his daughters—scholars believe that Charlemagne knew perfectly well what his girls were doing, but he accepted it as the result of his not letting them marry sacramentally. While Charlemagne lived, the tug-of-war between Christian morals and the libertarian Frankish court life was easily managed because of the balance between earthiness and piety that came from the emperor himself. Indeed, his daughters' bastards had many playmates because of the emperor's own many concubines. After Charlemagne's death, however, the surviving daughters were banished from the court by their brother, the pious Louis, to take up residence in the convents they had been bequeathed by their father.

One of the court poets described the emperor's homecoming with his sons falling over themselves to help him undress and carry his gloves and sword, while his daughters fawned over their father with gifts of flowers and ripe fruit. Charlemagne loved to be surrounded by people at all times and so he had very little want of intimacy. All the stories we have about him tell of a king who was rarely without the company of his family or his scholars, or enjoying the camaraderie of his fellow warriors on campaign or while hunting. Charlemagne loved swimming, and that was one of the reasons why he chose Aachen as his favorite residence—he loved the warm springs and often invited his children, friends, courtiers, and evidently even the royal guards to join him in the water.

Charlemagne's daily routine, when he was at home or at one of his residences, began at dawn when he woke and went to matins. When he returned, he began the business of the day—he was a complete workaholic and kept his scribes, advisors, and messengers busy with a constant flow of letters, legal judgments and instructions, or receiving petitioners. At noon he heard Mass, followed by the main meal of the day, and even during his meal he liked to be read to, hearing morally improving books like Augustine's *City of God*. He enjoyed his food and drink, refusing to fast (it was reported that he thought fasting, like the church's prescriptions regarding sex, did not apply to kings), but he was not excessive. The royal family dined alone, surrounded by well-born retainers, while the rest of the court watched them eat; only when Charlemagne rose from the meal was the rest of the court allowed to dine. Einhard portrays Charlemagne as a man who disliked ceremony, but the records show that the emperor did have small ceremonies in his life that meant very much to him.

EARLY LIFE

As mentioned, Charlemagne was the son of Pepin the Short (714–768) and his wife Bertrada of Laon (720–783), daughter of Caribert of Laon and Bertrada of Cologne. Records name a brother, Carloman, a sister, Gisela, and a short-lived child named Pippin as his younger siblings. One late medieval text suggests that a shadowy Redburga, wife of King Egbert of Wessex, might have been Charlemagne's sister, sister-in-law, or niece, and the legendary material makes him Roland's maternal uncle through a Lady Bertha. Einhard refuses to speculate on the early life of Charlemagne:

> It would be folly, I think, to write a word concerning Charlemagne's birth and infancy, or even his boyhood, for nothing has ever been written on

the subject, and there is no one alive now who can give information on it. Accordingly, I determined to pass that by as unknown, and to proceed at once to treat of his character, his deeds, and such other facts of his life as are worth telling and setting forth, and shall first give an account of his deeds at home and abroad, then of his character and pursuits, and lastly of his administration and death, omitting nothing worth knowing or necessary to know. (21)

We do know that Charlemagne was born out of wedlock, also as mentioned. Pepin declined to marry Bertrada until Charlemagne was a few years old, not on account of loose morals, but because of the need to provide the kingdom a healthy heir at a time when the death rate from infantile diseases and childhood mortality was very high. A king often had a harem of mistresses and would choose which one of them to marry based on her proven ability to bear healthy children, especially sons. Pepin the Short chose well. Bertrada must have been a tall and large woman, because Charlemagne had a commanding stature, suggesting that in terms of his size and looks he took after his mother.

Pepin's father was Charles Martel (ca. 688–741), for whom the Carolingian dynasty is named, a bastard son of Austrasia's mayor of the palace. The mayor of the palace usurped power from the king; the Merovingian-dynasty monarchs, who had ruled since 476, were by this time rulers in name only. Martel was an aggressive man who from a disadvantaged start, by sheer force of personality and military genius, established his authority over his father's heirs (his legitimately born brothers) and put his own Merovingian puppet-king on the throne. When Martel died he divided his empire between his elder sons Pepin and Carloman and their half-brother, Grifio; almost immediately Pepin and Carloman attacked, captured, and locked Grifio away, and Grifio's mother was sent off to a nunnery.

Pepin and Carloman then moved to take over the Frankish empire, dragging their own puppet-king named Childeric III and putting him on the throne so their actions would look legitimate. Pepin and Carloman began to have tensions in their partnership, and soon Carloman was "encouraged" to become a monk with the promise that his son, Drogo, would be Pepin's heir. Because Pepin was unmarried and had no legitimate heirs, it seemed like a good idea, and Carloman soon joined the Benedictines. Within months, however, Pepin showed his hand. He married his concubine Bertrada, legitimized his son, Charles, and began consolidating his power. He had to fight his half-brother Grifio when the man escaped from prison, but fortunately for Pepin, Grifio was killed in battle in 753. Drogo was quickly put under lock and key, and the now unnecessary puppet-king Childeric could return to the monastery from whence he came. Pepin did some fancy negotiating with Pope Zacharias (who knew a powerful ally when he saw one), who in turn authorized Boniface to crown Pepin and his two sons Charles and Carloman in 751 at the tender ages of nine and three, respectively.

The boys were not sent away to school but educated under their father's eyes. In order to found a new dynasty, Pepin knew that he had to make sure that his heirs would follow his thinking and beliefs, that they were protected from being kidnapped and murdered, and that they were taught that any influence other than their father's was the sin of rebellion. Thus they were educated in the art of war along with the sons of Pepin's most trusted followers—as soon as they were able to walk and speak, they began learning how to ride a horse, and their boyhood games were modeled on the military arts. At age six, military training began in earnest and all luxuries ceased. They were taken on campaign and subjected to the hardships of camp life, such as long marches in foul weather; simple, cold meals; sleeping in the open around a campfire; and commands enforced with the flat of a sword.

An education like this did not leave much time for book learning, and even though Charlemagne supposedly knew how to read, he is noted for having great respect for men who knew how to write, as he did not know how. The Frankish warrior caste generally regarded literary pleasures and interests as beneath them, but the brothers were still well educated for their time. In later years, Charlemagne oversaw educational reform for the clergy, rationalization of the law codes, and the growth of written communication and administration to keep his empire together. He had a sharp grasp of theology, and he could dispute with church leaders. So somehow Pepin managed to create a balance in his sons' education between ruling at swordpoint and ruling through effective legal and social administration.

On Pepin's death, Charlemagne, then 23 years old, took the outer parts of the kingdom, bordering on the sea—namely Neustria, western Aquitaine, and the northern parts of Austrasia—while Carloman, 18, retained the inner parts: southern Austrasia, Septimania, eastern Aquitaine, Burgundy, Provence, and Swabia, the lands bordering on Italy. Carloman had a solid block of land made of the central and eastern parts of Francia, and Charlemagne's land was in a semicircle around it from the Pyrenees to the Elbe, but blocked from direct contact with Rome.

JOINT RULE

The first event of the brothers' reign was the uprising of the Aquitainians and Gascons, in 769, in the territory split between the two kings. Charlemagne met Carloman at Vienne to plan for the battle, but they quarreled and Carloman refused to participate and returned to Burgundy. Charlemagne turned his anger on the rebellion and led an army to Bordeaux, where he set up a camp at Fronsac. Duke Chunoald II was forced to flee to the court of Duke Lupus II of Gascony, but Lupus, fearing Charlemagne, turned Chunoald II over in exchange for peace, and Aquitaine was considered to be finally subdued by the Franks.

The brothers maintained lukewarm relations with the assistance of their mother, Bertrada, and the new pope, Stephen III. Carloman's actions soon revealed his scheming to gain political advantage over his brother—even though he was the younger brother, he considered himself Pepin's real heir because he had been legitimate since birth. Charlemagne struck back, signing a treaty in 770 with Duke Tassilo III of Bavaria. He set aside his wife/concubine Himiltrude (who had provided him with a son, Pepin the Hunchback; since the supposedly handsome boy sadly had a deformity, it explains why Charlemagne was in no hurry to marry the boy's mother) and married a Lombard princess (commonly known today as Desiderata, though we do not know her real name), the daughter of King Desiderius.

Charlemagne's aim was to create allies with whom he would surround his brother. Though Pope Stephen III first opposed the marriage with the Lombard princess, he would soon have little to fear from a Frankish-Lombard alliance. Charlemagne had cleverly made an alliance with Bavaria and Lombardy that ringed Carloman's territory—land-wise, Charlemagne now held his brother in a vise. King Desiderius took the opportunity to threaten Carloman if the young king tried to break up the alliance, and Carloman, of course, was incensed and decided to bring his forces into Italy to "influence" the pope. The pope was clear—Carloman was not welcome in Rome while Desiderius was well received. That summer and autumn, the two brothers watched each other carefully. It seemed only a matter of time before a fraternal war would break out. The nobles in Francia carefully settled into their positions, awaiting the worst. Then, on December 4, 771, Carloman suddenly died, at the age of 20. With that event, Charles was free to become Charles the Great.

CONQUEST OF LOMBARDY

Upon his brother's death, Charlemagne repudiated Desiderata (she had produced no children anyway) and sent her back to her father's court—there was no more need for a Lombard alliance, and so there was no more need for a Lombard princess. He quickly remarried to a 13-year-old Swabian named Hildegard; his marriage to her secured the eastern region and strengthened his position. This sort of ruthlessness became Charlemagne's trademark response in times of danger for his lands—that and his determination, a cold rationalization of events and actions, and tireless focus on administration. It was now his time to secure his power and his own dynasty, and that is exactly what he focused on for the next 10 years.

Einhard, his biographer, knew Charlemagne only in the later part of his life, but it seems that his later character shows the reasons for his earlier successes:

Charlemagne was by far the most able and noble-spirited of all those who ruled over the nations in this time. He never withdrew from an enterprise that he had once begun and was determined to see through to the end, simply because of the labor involved; and danger never deterred

him. Having learnt to endure and suffer each particular ineluctable cir-
cumstance, whatever its nature might be, he was never prepared to yield
to adversity; and in times of prosperity he was never to be swayed by the
false blandishments of fortune. (63–64)

Einhard, in sum, attributes Charlemagne's success to his indomitable strength
of will.

Carloman had left two sons, and by law they should have inherited their father's lands, but their mother, Queen Gerberga, did not wait to find out what
Charlemagne's intentions were—she fled to Lombardy and put them under
the protection of Desiderius to save their lives. Meanwhile, Charlemagne
began to bargain with Carloman's supporters: some readily transferred their
allegiance, some had to be bribed, and some had to be made kin, thus his marriage to Hildegard.

His next problem would be what to do with the Lombards and to settle
his affairs with the papacy—but first he had to deal with the Saxon problem.
Francia's ancient enemy, the Saxons, held the lands along his northern border, and there was little to no negotiating with them—they were steadfastly
pagan, they were constantly looking for better farmlands than the cold northern mountains, and they had little respect for negotiation or paying tribute.
The moment the Saxons knew Carloman died and there was a potential for
weakness, they attacked. In 772, Charlemagne hit back by attacking the religious icon of the Irminsul (a vast, ancient tree trunk erected in the open air as
a pillar: it was a shrine, believed to be one of the pillars of the heavens) and
destroying it. In one strike, he wanted to prove that his military might was
superior, and that his Frankish God was also superior.

Now he could focus on ending the three-way conflict in Italy between the
papacy, Lombardy, and Francia. Pope Stephen died and Pope Hadrian I succeeded him in 772, and Hadrian was made of sterner stuff than Stephen. He
demanded the return of certain cities in Lombardy that Desiderius currently
controlled; Desiderius denied the pope's charges and instead took over more
papal cities and began heading toward Rome. Charlemagne crossed the Alps,
and over the winter of 773 he laid siege to Pavia, the Lombard capital—and
it was not until the spring of 774 that the city fell and Desiderius was exiled
to a monastery. While he was waiting for Pavia to succumb, Charlemagne
visited the pope and received a warm welcome, as the king not only was a
firm supporter of the papacy but also was about to remove one of the enemies of the pope himself. Hadrian granted him the title of "patrician," and
Charlemagne confirmed and expanded his father's grants of land, adding to
the list Tuscany, Emilia, Venice, and Corsica. When Pavia fell, Charlemagne
took for himself the Iron Crown of Lombardy (so named because a supposed
nail from the True Cross was worked into the golden circlet), making him
not only king of the Franks but also king of the Lombards—and so in less
than two years his reputation showed he was a hugely successful and new
kind of king.

Charlemagne's relationship with Pope Hadrian I was a warm and respectful one, but it is clear from the chroniclers that a lot of it was window dressing. The king was a dutiful son to his holy father, but beyond that he was going to set his own agenda. Hadrian tried to manipulate Charlemagne into more military work, but Charlemagne refused, saying he had to return to his fight with the Saxons. The balance of spiritual and temporal power was a tricky thing, and the pope realized too late that he had exchanged one kind of master (the Lombards) for another (the Franks). Hadrian protested, and he was perfectly within his rights as he had been given the authority by the papacy to dictate, in the name of God, what kings and emperors should or should not do. Charlemagne operated under the idea of divine sanction, in that as a king he and his heirs were allowed to rule, under God, all the affairs of their subjects, both clergy and laymen. Hadrian had to give way as the king left to go north, and Charlemagne won this round—but it was a contest that would be fought between rulers and popes for centuries.

THE ORIGIN OF THE *SONG OF ROLAND*

The king's worst defeat came next—the massacre of his rear guard at Roncevalles—which ironically became the basis of later legends that sang of Charlemagne and Roland as the most heroic Christian knights since King Arthur.

In 777, Saracen envoys came to Charlemagne to beg him to help their masters, who had been cornered in the Iberian Peninsula by the Emir of Cordoba, Abd ar-Rahman I, and they offered their homage in exchange for military support. Charlemagne saw it as a chance to take advantage of Islamic turmoil and extend his kingdom, and possibly Christendom itself. He must have also seen the Saxons as being conquered (and they were, temporarily), so he agreed and set off for Spain. Putting together an army of Neustrians, Austrasians, Lombards, and Burgundians, Charlemagne went over the Pyrenees in 778 and defeated the already weakened Basque city of Pamplona before going on to Zaragoza. The Basques, who had already had their fill of Muslim invaders, did not appreciate being used as target practice by the Franks, and they plotted revenge.

When he got to Zaragoza, Charlemagne was told that his Muslim allies had broken away from each other. Sulaiman had been assassinated, and the caliph's huge forces were marching straight for Charlemagne's army, sweeping the rebels away with every step. The king was a great warrior, but he was also no fool—he beat a retreat.

It was while he was making his way through the pass of Roncesvalles that the Basques attacked, separating his rear guard and baggage train. They massacred the rear guard, including one of the king's relatives and friends—a man named Hruodland, known today as Roland, the ruler of the Breton March. Whether Roland was actually a relative, an illegitimate son, or merely a friend of Charlemagne is unknown, but the Frankish bards seemed to believe the story would be better if he were a relative. They also made the battle not against the Christian Basques but against the Saracens in order to turn Roland into a Christian martyr, and they painted the king as a glorious King Arthur–like character, with the legendary sword Joyeuse in hand and surrounded by elite (possibly cavalry) bodyguards.

The battle was disastrous for Charlemagne, but only in the short term, as the defeat did not undermine his position in Francia as a great warlord. It also helped that he and his military barons were immediately involved in a new war with the Saxons, and the border remained stable because the Moorish caliphs were too busy killing each other to think about trying to cross into Frankish lands.

THE DIFFICULT 780s

The decade of the 780s was full of upheavals and personal grief for Charlemagne. When he visited Rome in 781 he had Pope Hadrian crown his sons, Carloman (renamed Pippin) and Louis, in order to give his empire harmony and continuity. He also agreed to betroth Rotrudra, his daughter, to the Byzantine Emperor, Constantine VI. Both of these moves ended up encouraging rebellion instead of peace and promoting fear instead of security. Hildegard, the wife Charlemagne seemed to genuinely feel affection for, died in 783, and the king's mother followed in the same year not long after his wife. His trusted chamberlain, Adalgisile, and his constable, Geilo, died in battle in 782. His rebound marriage to Fastrada was unpopular with his court, and internal battles among his supporters were constant in the years that followed. Charlemagne, however, rose above all these trials, and, if anything, they encouraged more and higher ambitions in the man.

At the end of the decade, the king had to settle rebellions in southern Italy and Bavaria, although in Bavaria he never did so successfully. In 787 the Lombard duchy of Benevento covered most of southern Italy, and although it technically belonged to Charlemagne from his defeat of Desiderius, it was far enough away that the duchy operated as an independent state. Duke Arechis, who was a good politician and maintained friendly relations with the Byzantine emperors, ruled it. Arechis might have remained relatively inconspicuous to Charlemagne, but one winter, instead of going home, Charlemagne happened to stay in Rome, making it easy for the king to focus on Arechis's lack of follow-through with his promises of fealty. The duke made his submissions, but as soon as the king of the Franks was safely on the other side of the Alps, promptly broke all his vows and ignored the pope's territorial claims. Arechis's son, Grimoald III, followed his father's political maneuvering, successfully fending off the armies of Charlemagne or his sons many times in future years. Charlemagne, however, never returned to Benevento, and Grimoald never was forced to surrender to Frankish rule.

In 788, Charlemagne was compelled to turn his attention to Bavaria, a dukedom that he, and his father and grandfather before him, claimed to be vassal territory. Its duke, Tassilo III, disagreed, believing his little country was independent—and because Bavaria (like Benevento in Italy) was seen as too far away from Charlemagne's rule for the king to bother with it, Tassilo felt very secure. Tassilo tried to make Charlemagne happy by sending military detachments for the king's armies, but on the other hand Tassilo rarely showed up to attend the Frankish gathering in order to vow fealty publicly. The pope warned Tassilo that he was flirting with disaster, and when Charlemagne decided he needed to control the Danube valley against the Saxons, Avars, and Slavs, Tassilo's behavior became an issue.

From the chronicles it is quite clear that Tassilo offered no threats or provocations, but the king had had enough of the so-called independence and put his fist around the dukedom. He ordered Tassilo to appear and immediately restate the vow the duke had made to the king; the duke was understandably reluctant to put his person at risk, and the war was on. Charlemagne sent three armies against Bavaria: one with the king in person, one with a force of Saxons and East Franks, and another under the leadership of his son, the young Pippin, king of Italy.

Tassilo wisely did not resist, and he yielded up the dukedom without a fight. Although it must have frustrated Charlemagne because it appears he wished to somehow do away with the duke and change the way the region was ruled, Charlemagne was merciful and did not punish Tassilo. Months later, however, Tassilo came under charges of rebellion, and he and his family were removed: either forced to take monastic vows or exiled. Bavaria was divided into Frankish counties, and the dukedom became another part of the Frankish empire.

THE SAXON WARS

From 772 to 785, Charlemagne would start each spring by heading to the north to fight with the Saxons, then he would move south to fight other battles. He would win some battles, baptize the people, demand tribute, and take hostages, but as soon as the winter came and the king went home, the Saxons would renege on their agreement, attack, and regain what they had lost. Basically, thousands of men and women accepted the Christian faith, but as soon as the conflict was over they would abandon the newly built churches and monasteries.

The Germanic Saxons were divided into four subgroups in four regions: Westphalia was the nearest kingdom to Austrasia, Eastphalia was the farthest away, and in between these two kingdoms was Engria. To the north of the Saxon kingdoms, at the base of the Jutland peninsula, was the kingdom of Nordalbingia.

It was in his first campaign in 773 that Charlemagne forced the Engrians to cut down the Irminsul pillar near Paderborn. In 775 he returned to

Westphalia and conquered the Saxon fort of Sigiburg, then marched to Engria. He defeated the Saxons again in Engria and then in Eastphalia, where the Saxon leader Hessi converted to Christianity. Charlemagne returned through Westphalia, leaving permanent troops at what had been the Saxon bastions of Sigiburg and Eresburg. All of Saxony except for the northern kingdom of Nordalbingia was under his control, but Saxon resistance had just begun.

Following yet another campaign in Italy the next year, Charlemagne returned to Saxony in 776 because a rebellion had destroyed the fortress and troops at Eresburg. The Saxons were once again defeated, but Widukind, their chief and most charismatic leader, managed to escape to Denmark. Preparing for another round of fighting, Charlemagne built a new bastion at Karlstadt.

The king called together his dukes at Paderborn in 777 to integrate Saxony fully into the Frankish kingdom, but it was more of a political statement than a mark of how well the Saxons had been incorporated into the growing Frankish Christian empire. The Saxons agreed to Charlemagne's terms, were baptized and feasted, but the moment the king left they went back to their pagan ways and customs, ignoring all of the king's laws and treaties.

Thus Charlemagne had to return and return each summer. For two years only there was peace: in the summer of 779 he again invaded Saxony and yet again conquered Eastphalia, Engria, and Westphalia, dividing the land into missionary districts and assisting personally in several mass baptisms. He then returned to Italy in the fall and, for the first time, there was no immediate Saxon revolt. To encourage this submission, Charlemagne ordered the death penalty for all Saxons who refused to be baptized, who failed to follow Christian festivals, and who cremated their dead. Saxony was peaceful from 780 to 782.

Thinking he had finally subdued the Saxons, Charlemagne returned to Saxony in the summer of 782 and set up a code of law and appointed judges and counts, both of Saxon and Frankish ancestry: good idea, but bad laws. The laws were uncompromising about religion, and while the Saxons may have become theologically Christian, they were still socially and philosophically followers of Germanic polytheism.

This renewed the old conflict: in the autumn of 782 Widukind returned and led a revolt that included several assaults on the church, as the Saxon chiefs would not be torn from their independence, and neither bribery nor conversion worked. In response, Charlemagne (allegedly) ordered the beheading of 4,500 Saxons at Verden in Lower Saxony who had been caught practicing their native paganism after conversion to Christianity. (The chroniclers follow the 4,500 figure, but modern scholars estimate it could not have been more than a thousand men killed.) It was known as the Massacre of Verden ("Verdener Blutgericht"), and it caused three years of bloodthirsty warfare, from 783 to 785, during which the kingdom of the Frisians were also finally subdued and a large part of their fleet burned. Charlemagne had his army rampage through the Saxon lands, killing, burning, and tearing down pagan shrines—creating total devastation. It was only when, in the autumn of 785, Charlemagne managed to appeal to the Saxon leader Widukind—and Widukind agreed to accept baptism—that the fighting eased for seven years.

In 792, the Westphalians again rose against their conqueror, and the Eastphalians and Nordalbingians joined them in 793, but the rebellion did not have enough support from the tired masses of Saxons and was put down by 794. It was the turn of the Engrians to rebel in 796, but the quick military presence of Charlemagne, Christian Saxons, and Slavs crushed them. The last rebellion of the independent Saxons rose in 804, more than 30 years after Charlemagne's first campaign against them: it was the Nordalbingians, who quickly found themselves effectively disempowered from rebellion because the Saxons around them refused support. According to Einhard:

> The war that had lasted so many years was at length ended by their acceding to the terms offered by the King; which were renunciation of their national religious customs and the worship of devils, acceptance of the sacraments of the Christian faith and religion, and union with the Franks to form one people. (24)

After the conquest of Nordalbingia, the Franks were discovered by the peoples of Scandinavia as the pagan Danes, "a race almost unknown to his ancestors, but destined to be only too well known to his sons," as historian Charles Oman described them, began to move outward in expansion (367). While they lived on the Jutland peninsula, they had no doubt heard many stories from Widukind (his wife was Danish) and his allies—the Franks were dangerous, unrelenting, and difficult to defeat, and their Christian religion was spreading like wildfire.

In 808, the king of the Danes, Godfred, built the vast *Danevirke* across the isthmus of Schleswig. The *Danevirke* was at its beginning a 19-mile-long earth and stone rampart that protected Danish land and gave Godfred the opportunity to harass Frisia and Flanders with pirate raids. An excellent commander, he invaded Frisia and joked of visiting Aachen in order to upset Charlemagne, but he was murdered before he could do any more conquering (either by a Frankish assassin or by one of his own men). Godfred was succeeded by his nephew Hemming, who knew better than to go up against the Frankish king and agreed to the Treaty of Heiligen with Charlemagne in late 811.

The Saxons were never met with the generosity in victory that Charlemagne had shown in Italy and Bavaria. He treated their areas as conquered lands, and ones that had cost the Franks a lot of lives and blood, and there was always a chance one of the regional warlords could up and start yet another rebellion. The time and tide had turned, however, as the Saxons began to look to their coasts instead of looking landward for enemies: in the early years of the ninth century the Viking raids were beginning.

THE CONSOLIDATION OF THE EMPIRE

The conquest of Italy brought Charlemagne into renewed contact with the Saracens, who, at the time, controlled the Mediterranean. Pippin, his son, spent years fighting with the Saracens in Italy. To keep the area under control, Charlemagne conquered Corsica and Sardinia in the 790s and the Balearic Islands, which were often attacked by Saracen pirates, in 799. The counts of Genoa and Tuscany, with their large fleets of fighting warships, kept the Saracens at bay until the end of Charlemagne's reign.

Charlemagne's reach extended even to places that would have been considered alien worlds, even for the well-traveled king: he had diplomatic contact with the caliphal court in Baghdad. In 797, the caliph of Baghdad, Harun al-Rashid, presented Charlemagne with an Asian elephant named Abul-Abbas and gave him the additional gift of a clock. The decadence and violence seen in the Christian capitals would have been a sharp contrast to the splendor and sophistication of the Muslim court.

Charlemagne's younger son Louis was in charge of the Spanish border, and in Hispania the struggle against the Moors continued without end. In 785, Louis's men captured Gerona and extended Frankish control into the Catalan littoral for the duration of Charlemagne's reign—much longer, actually, as it remained Frankish until the Treaty of Corbeil in 1258. The Muslim chiefs in the northeast of Hispania were constantly fighting against Córdoban authority, and they often turned to the Franks for help, allowing the Frankish border to slowly extend until 795, when Gerona, Cardona, Ausona, and Urgel were joined into the new Spanish March, contained within the old duchy of Septimania.

Louis had as much difficulty with the Moors as his brother Pepin did with the Saracens in Italy. Barcelona fell to the Franks in 797 when Zeid, its governor, who had rebelled against Córdoba and failed, handed it to the Franks out of spite. The greatest city of the region did not stay in Frankish hands for long—the Umayyad authority recaptured Barcelona in 799—but Louis marched the entire army of his kingdom over the Pyrenees and besieged the city for two years, wintering there from 800 to 801, until it capitulated. Seizing the victory, the Franks continued to press the emir, taking Tarragona in 809 and Tortosa in 811, a conquest that brought them to the mouth of the Ebro and allowed them to raid Valencia, prompting (the now exhausted) Emir al-Hakam I to recognize their conquests in 812.

THE AVAR AND SLAV CAMPAIGNS

When Charlemagne incorporated much of Central Europe, he brought the Frankish state face to face with the Avars and Slavs in the southeast. In 788, a new enemy arrived on Frankish lands: the Avars. They were a pagan Asian horde who had settled in what is today Hungary (Einhard calls them Huns), before invading Friuli and then Bavaria. Charlemagne was highly preoccupied until 790 with other political conquests, but in that year he decided he finally had the time to march down the Danube into Avar territory and ravage it all the way to the river Raab. As a second strike, Charlemagne called up a Lombard army under Pippin to march into the Drava valley and ravage Pannonia. Their forked campaign would have continued if the Saxons had not revolted again in 792, breaking seven years of peace and forcing Charlemagne to focus on the Slavs and the Saxons for the next two years.

Pippin and Duke Eric of Friuli, however, continued to attack the Avars' strongholds. The great Ring of the Avars, their capital fortress (so named because the fort was built in 10 rings of earthworks), was taken twice, and the booty was sent to Charlemagne at his capital, Aachen, and redistributed to all his followers and even to foreign rulers, including King Offa of Mercia. The Avar leaders soon learned that fighting Charlemagne or his sons was a losing battle: they traveled to Aachen personally to offer themselves to Charlemagne as vassals and Christians. Charlemagne accepted, and he sent one native chief (baptized Abraham) back to Avaria with the ancient title of *khagan*. Abraham kept his people in line, but not for long: in 800 the Bulgarians under Khan Krum swept the Avar state away, and a hundred years later the Magyars arrived on the Pannonian plain and began a new threat to Charlemagne's descendants.

To consolidate his empire further, in 789 Charlemagne marched an Austrasian-Saxon army across the Elbe into Abrodite or Slav territory. The pagan Slavs immediately submitted under their leader Witzin, and Charlemagne then accepted the surrender of the Witzes under their leader Dragovit. He did demand many hostages from Dragovit and the permission to send missionaries into the pagan region; once his aims were met, his army marched to the Baltic Sea before turning around and returning to the Frankish heartland with much treasure and no harassment.

The Slavs wisely became loyal allies, even helping Charlemagne fight the Saxons. In 795 the Abrodites and Witzes rose in arms with the French king against the Saxons. Witzin died in battle, and Charlemagne avenged him by attacking the Eastphalians on the Elbe. Thrasuco, Witzin's successor, led his men to conquest over the Nordalbingians and handed their leaders over to Charlemagne. The Abrodites remained loyal until Charlemagne's death and even fought later against the Danes. Charlemagne wanted to bring in the Slavic peoples to the west of the Avar khaganate: the Carantanians and Carniolans. Although these people were overcome by the Lombards and Bavarians and made Frankish tributaries, they were never fully incorporated into the Frankish state.

The most southeasterly Frankish neighbors were Croats, who settled into two duchies: the Pannonian Croatia Duchy and the Littoral Croatian Duchy. While fighting the Avars, the Franks had called for their support, and the Pannonian Croatian duke Vojnomir aided Charlemagne. In turn, Charlemagne offered protection to the Croatians of northern Dalmatia, Slavonia, and Pannonia, but not to the Littoral duchy.

This duchy was soon an item on Charlemagne's list of projected conquests. Eric of Friuli, a Frankish commander, wanted to extend his dominion in Charlemagne's name by conquering the Littoral Croatian Duchy, ruled by Duke Višeslav, one of the first known Croatian dukes. Sadly for the Frankish king, the effort failed. In the battle of Trsat, Eric's forces fled their positions and were totally defeated by Višeslav's army. Eric himself was among the dead, and his defeat was a great setback for the Frankish empire.

EMPEROR CHARLEMAGNE

Despite Charlemagne's protests, it was hardly surprising that Charles king of the Franks was to become Charles emperor of the West. Even uncrowned as emperor, he would still have been known as the greatest of the Carolingian kings, who believed himself to be a divine weapon used to bring order and Christianity to the West. History and the pope had other plans for him, including the protection of the Byzantine Empire from the spread of Islam and paganism and from the Iconoclastic Controversy.

The Controversy was a fight that reflected two sides of a very serious and divisive issue in Christianity. On one side, many devout Christians had a deep emotional attachment to their icons of the saints, Virgin Mary, and bible stories, and monasteries worked hard at preserving ancient artifacts, bones, and personal items of the saints that would attract pilgrims (and their money). Other Christians, however, felt that these icons distracted from the true faith and were too gaudy and showy for a truly ascetic view of Christianity.

On one side, then, were Christians who felt (along with Muslims and Jews) that it was blasphemous to represent the divine in art and who followed the Law of Moses to not make or worship "graven images" because it led to idolatry. On the other side, there were those who felt that the images helped pagan believers convert, and ordinary Christians keep focus, because the visuals directed the thoughts and prayers to heaven. Christianity was a religion that asked its followers to take many doctrines on faith alone, and the images helped followers see that which was invisible and mysterious as concrete and believable.

The Iconoclastic Controversy began during the reign of the Byzantine emperor Leo III (d. 741) when a series (726–29) of edicts was issued against images; in most churches they were removed and destroyed, and the frescoes were whitewashed over. Almost immediately there was a backlash, with riots and revolts that were settled with violence. The Roman popes consistently supported the image-worshippers; not only did they refuse to obey the imperial edicts, but they declared any iconoclast to be a heretic.

Charlemagne and the Frankish clergy regarded image-worshipping as idolatrous and superstitious, as set forth in four tracts composed in 789–91 and issued in his name. Nevertheless, despite such opposition, in 800 Charlemagne allowed himself to be crowned as emperor at Rome by Pope Leo III (elected 795; not to be confused with the earlier Byzantine emperor of the same name and number).

In April 799, Pope Leo III had been attacked by assailants who tried to put out his eyes and tear out his tongue, thus disqualifying him from the papal office. It is not certain what his crime was: some say he was guilty of fornication and perjury, others of the time pointed out that he was simply not the son of one of the city's elite families, and that was crime enough. Leo escaped and fled to Charlemagne at Paderborn, asking him to intervene in Rome and restore him. Charlemagne, advised by Alcuin of York that the church was in a deep crisis, agreed to travel to Rome, doing so in November 800 and holding a council on December 1. On December 23, Leo swore an oath of innocence, and Charlemagne took the pope's side, although it seems he did so mostly in the interest of political stability, not necessarily because he believed the pope was innocent. It seems clear that negotiations had taken place between king and pope at Paderborn, and historians have speculated for centuries on just what might have been reached, as there is no record of their discussions.

On Christmas Day of the year 800, Charlemagne attended the nativity Mass in Saint Peter's Basilica, where he prostrated himself for prayers. When he rose, the pope stepped forward and crowned him as emperor (*Imperator Romanorum,* or "Emperor of the Romans"), and the crowd acclaimed him and knelt along with the pope to pay him homage.

The earliest surviving evidence of what contemporaries thought of that event comes to us from 803. The scribe of the Lorsch Annals set down the basic facts: that the pope was transferring the office of emperor from Constantinople to Charlemagne and thus returning it to Rome. This suggests that the event was well planned out and agreed on by Charlemagne and Pope Leo III at Paderborn, but Einhard argues that Charlemagne was ignorant of the pope's intent and did not want any such coronation:

> At first he disliked this so much that he said that he would not have entered the church that day, even though it was a great feast day, if he had known in advance of the pope's plan. But he bore the animosity that the assumption of this title caused with great patience. (38)

Is it possible that Charlemagne was indeed aware of the planned coronation? The huge, jeweled crown that was waiting for him on the altar must have been quite obvious. Einhard may have wanted to give his hero a sense of Christian humility and modesty and to show that it was not personal ambition, but a desire to give stability to Western Christendom, that led Charlemagne to this crown.

In his official charters, Charlemagne preferred to be called "Karolus serenissimus Augustus a Deo coronatus magnus pacificus imperator Romanum gubernans imperium" ("Charles, most serene Augustus crowned by God, the great, peaceful emperor ruling the Roman Empire") instead of the more direct "Imperator Romanorum" ("Emperor of the Romans"), but the latter title became the norm.

Roger Collins suggests that any chance that "the motivation behind the acceptance of the imperial title was a romantic and antiquarian interest in reviving the Roman Empire is highly unlikely." Neither the Franks nor the Church of Rome would have wanted the Roman Empire to be revived, because they viewed it with distrust—it was old, decadent, and pagan. Pepin II, father of Charles Martel and great-grandfather of Charlemagne, described the old Roman Empire as something the Franks took pride in overthrowing, having "fought against and thrown from their shoulders the heavy yoke of the Romans [and] from the knowledge gained in baptism, clothed in gold and precious stones the bodies of the holy martyrs whom the Romans had killed by fire, by the sword and by wild animals" (Collins 151).

Charlemagne's assumption of the imperial title was not usurpation in the eyes of the Franks or Italians, who found it to be completely to their benefit. The risk of Charlemagne being overcome by his new power and making drastic changes was not considered a potential problem—the new emperor had never behaved this way and had always included the needs and protection of the Frankish peoples as his priority in his administration. In Byzantium, however, it was protested by Empress Irene and her successor Nicephorus I, but neither of them had any great effect in having their protests heard.

The title of emperor stayed in Charlemagne's family for years, but it caused his descendants to fight over who had the supremacy in the Frankish state. The papacy continued to reserve the right to bestow the honor of emperor on whomever the pope wished, and so when the family of Charlemagne no longer had a worthy heir to offer for the throne, the pope was happy to crown whichever Italian warlord was agreeable and could protect him from his local enemies. In 962, however, the title passed out of French and Italian control to the person of Otto the Great—bringing the title into Germany for almost a thousand years, helping it become the Holy Roman Empire.

DEATH

In 806, Charlemagne made plans for the traditional division of the empire on his death: Charles the Younger was to be given Austrasia and Neustria, Saxony, Burgundy, and Thuringia; Pippin got Italy, Bavaria, and Swabia; Louis got Aquitaine, the Spanish March, and Provence. There was no mention of the imperial title for any of the sons, which suggests that Charlemagne may have regarded the title at the time as an honorary personal award that his sons could not inherit.

The inheritance division was never to be tested. Pippin died in 810 and Charles died in 811. The emperor then reconsidered the situation, and in 813 he crowned King Louis "the Pious" of Aquitaine, his only surviving legitimate son, as co-emperor and co-king of the Franks—an action that suggests he changed his mind and now regarded the imperial title as a hereditary title and not a singular gift of the papacy. The only part of the empire that Louis did not receive was Italy, which Charlemagne specifically gave to Pippin's illegitimate son Bernard.

The emperor spent the autumn hunting in the lands around the royal residence at Aachen, returning to the palace on the first of November. In mid-January, however, the great king fell ill with a fever and the symptoms of pleurisy, as his lungs were inflamed. Depressed, according to witnesses, because even at the age of 72 most of his life plans had not been achieved, he had decided to fast, abstaining from food but taking in a little liquid as was his custom to rid himself of fevers. This time, however, he became bedridden on the twenty-first of January and, as Einhard tells it:

> He died January twenty-eighth, the seventh day from the time that he took to his bed, at nine o'clock in the morning, after partaking of the Holy Communion, in the seventy-second year of his age and the forty-seventh of his reign. (39)

He was buried the same day, in Aachen Cathedral, although such a hurried burial would seem unnecessary given the cold weather and the nature of his illness. Einhard explains that there was uncertainty as to what to do with the body, as Charlemagne himself had not made plans for a tomb or a burial site, but his people agreed that the best place for his tomb would be in the cathedral he had loved so much. His inscription supposedly read as follows:

> Under this tomb lies the body of Charles, the Great and Orthodox Emperor, who gloriously increased the kingdom of the Franks and reigned with great success for forty-seven years. He died in his seventies in the year of our Lord 814, in the seventh indiction, on the twenty-eighth day of January. (40)

One of the first post-death tales, narrated by Otho of Lomello, Count of the Palace at Aachen in the time of Otto III, claimed that around the year 1000 he and Emperor Otto had discovered and opened Charlemagne's tomb. The emperor had been buried upright, seated upon a throne and wearing a crown and holding a scepter, his flesh almost entirely natural and undecomposed. In 1165, Frederick I reopened the tomb and placed the emperor in a sarcophagus beneath the floor of the cathedral. Not to be outdone, in 1215 Frederick II re-interred Charlemagne in a casket made of gold and silver.

Charlemagne's death was more than just another king's death. It led to grief being expressed in almost every corner of the empire, some people mourning because they feared what might happen next, and others mourning out of love. It affected most those of the literary and intellectual clique who had surrounded and been protected by him at Aachen. An anonymous monk of the monastery of Bobbio lamented:

> From the rising of the sun to the shores of the sea where it sets all hearts are full of sorrow. Alas! The Franks, the Romans and all the Christian peoples weep, bowed in sorrows. . . . The kingdom of the Franks has suffered many disasters but never has it suffered such great grief as in the moment when the awe-inspiring and eloquent Charlemagne was laid to rest at Aachen. O Christ, welcome the pious Charlemagne into your blessed home among the apostles. (Becher 135)

Louis succeeded Charlemagne as intended, but his empire lasted only another generation. The division of the lands made according to law and custom between Louis's own sons after their father's death laid the foundation for the modern states of Germany and France.

CHARLEMAGNE'S LEGACY

Charlemagne is remembered for being an empire-builder, but he is also remembered for his many reforms of the monetary system, the government, the military, the church, and Frankish culture. His reforms became what today is called the "Carolingian Renaissance."

While there was no chance of the survival of the empire as it was when Charlemagne died—there was no constitution to hold it together, and the tensions within the Carolingian descendants were too great, plus in the outlying areas of the kingdom the tribal loyalties were too strong—what did remain was a common memory of a time when there was a united Western Christendom that had a common goal of expanding culture, education, quality of life, and Christian religious values.

Economic and Monetary Reforms

The peace with Byzantium in the 750s ended Byzantine rule in northern Italy, but it created a financial problem: a shortage of gold. The Franks were forced to give up Venice and Sicily, and that meant the loss of trade routes to Africa and the East. When Charlemagne came to power, he followed his father's reforms, but extended them further in 792 to 794 by ending the monetary system based on the gold *sou* and replacing it with a system based on silver, which was in much more plentiful supply in Frankish lands.

This standardization unified, harmonized, and simplified the hundreds of tribal currencies that had been in place for centuries and began new opportunities for trade and commerce. The new currency was called the *livre carolingienne* (from the Latin *libra,* the modern pound), and based upon a pound of silver. This pound, which was a unit of both money and weight, was worth 20 *sous*—from the Latin *solidus* (which was primarily weight used for accounting and trade and never actually minted) or 240 *deniers* (from the Latin *denarius*, equal to the modern penny). During this period, the *livre* and the *sou* were counting units; only the silver *denier* was a coin of the realm.

Charlemagne instituted principles for administrative structure in several documents; the most significant in terms of the economic control of his kingdom was the *Capitulare de villis* of 802. It lists a series of very specific rules about how the king's estates must be run, and it gives us a wealth of detail about the day-to-day expectations of how his subordinates must meet the king's needs. It has rules about the estate's agricultural, craft, financial, and industrial workings, and how each of these must be run in order to meet the needs of the royal household and the palace.

In addition to this macro-oriented reform of the economy, Charlemagne also initiated a number of microeconomic reforms, such as direct control of prices and levies on certain goods and commodities. He prohibited the lending of money for interest, and then strengthened the laws regarding lending in 814 when he made the *Capitulary for the Jews*, a complete banning of the Jewish practice of money-lending.

Much of the European continent took up Charlemagne's system, because it was not his problem alone that gold was no longer heading north. In England, the Anglo-Saxon King Offa of Mercia voluntarily adopted the standard. After Charlemagne's death, the quality of the silver used for coins began to decrease, forcing those in Europe until about the year 1100 to use the more purely minted English coin.

Laws

One cannot have an empire without a common law, the essential ingredient that binds people together and gives society its structure. The *Lex Romana*, for example, allowed Roman citizens the confidence in knowing that they were protected by the same laws and had the same rights wherever they lived in the Roman Empire. Charlemagne's view of law was not that it should be uniform in his empire: that would have been too difficult, considering the differences of language, territory, and custom. He did insist on a uniform Christianity, however, and he based his legal decisions on the church's canon laws first, and then regional law next. To clarify: Charlemagne believed in law and justice, and he made sure the laws of all the areas of his empire were collected and written down. He also documented and circulated the laws of the church. But in terms of individual areas' laws concerning such things as inheritance, trials and punishments, and age of majority for marriage, he allowed the rule of tribal leaders and local law.

Military

One of the myths surrounding Charlemagne's legacy is the idea that he was able to dominate Europe by his cavalry's use of the stirrup, supposedly introduced by Charles Martel in the 730s. The stirrup, however, was not introduced until the late eighth century and was not widely adopted until the twelfth century, and so it could not have been used as a part of a "shock cavalry charge" with the lances held locked in position and the knights locked on the horse as well by means of stirrups. Charlemagne's military success instead can be attributed to clever use of the siege technologies of the time and to brilliant logistics—he fought very few battles directly in the field, as most of his warfare was based on attacking the enemy's forts and laying siege—and so even if he had the skill of a "shock cavalry" among his knights, he would not have had to use the technique enough for it to become famous.

Church Reforms

Charlemagne may have had problems with his dukes, counts, officials, and other political subordinates, but he was very secure in his relationship with the representatives of the church. Because he saw himself as a partner in a divine mission, the church gave him bishops, abbots, monks, and priests to do the work of conversion wherever Charlemagne conquered—but they also were educated men who acted as his trusted secretaries, intellectual support, and administrators.

Many of these men were wealthy in their own right, and one way that Charlemagne showed his favor was to give grants of ecclesiastical titles and land. The men who swore allegiance to the emperor were given certain immunities and were able to receive tithes from the subjects who lived on their lands. Charlemagne, in turn, had a high level of expectations for his ecclesiastical subjects. When he became king, he discovered that the clergy had taken advantage of their privileged position in society and, instead of evangelizing, had sat back and simply enjoyed their security. Most of the clergy were woefully undereducated, and the result was that preaching was substandard: inadequate in both quality and quantity. If he wanted to create a peaceful Christian society, then he had a long way to go—a realization that he would have as much of a problem with creating a standardized spiritual community where dogmas were understood and obeyed as with creating a Christian empire among the borderlands of Frankish territory.

Charlemagne set out his program for church reform in 789 in the *Admonitio Generalis*. In it, he standardized not only the secular life within the church—law courts, building upkeep, the church calendar, and tithing—but also spiritual matters such as how to teach the mystery of the Trinity. He believed (he had a superstitious side) that there was one right way of saying

Mass, one right way of chanting the psalms, and one perfect and faultless text of scripture, and straying from these forms would displease God (and hence would be unlucky). He asked the pope in 790, for example, for an authorized sacramental liturgy, which he then had copied and sent all over his kingdom with the express intent that it would be the one right text that every clergyman would use. He did the same with the Bible in order to get things perfect and thus not tempt the Almighty into displeasure.

His reforms had to be restated, and pushed, over and over again despite the fact that the clergy were supposedly submitting to the papal rule. Almost every year Charlemagne had orders sent out, even up to his death, and in the letters exchanged between the emperor and Alcuin it seems that Charlemagne was going to be frustrated in his life's goal to create an orderly and universally obeyed realm of church law.

Educational Reforms

The term "Carolingian Renaissance" is most closely connected to the flowering of education, scholarship, literature, art, and architecture that the king enthusiastically encouraged. He had always enjoyed a passion for scholarship and learning, mastering languages (he spoke Latin fluently and mastered diplomatic Greek, and evidence suggests he spoke more than a little Arabic). In the 780s Charlemagne began to make his court a center of religious scholarship, controlling, in effect, the intellectual grounding of his empire, and thus boxing in what people might believe or think.

He sent away to monasteries for manuscripts that might be useful and had many copied and sent on to other schools or centers of learning throughout his empire—attempting to create a standard of education among present and future generations of clerics. They were sent holy scripture, commentaries, patristic works, and as much of the Roman and Greek classical authors as were available at the time. He did increase the libraries of monastic schools and scriptoria (centers for book-copying) in his empire: most of the surviving works that we have today of classical Latin were copied and preserved by Carolingian scholars, and the earliest manuscripts available for many ancient texts are Carolingian. If a text managed to survive to the Carolingian age, chances are that it survives today, thanks to Charlemagne.

Charlemagne brought Frankish culture into contact with the culture and learning of other countries (such as the Visigoths in Spain, the Anglo-Saxons in England, and the caliphal court in Baghdad) due to his vast conquests. In his court, he surrounded himself with men of learning from all over his empire: Alcuin, an Anglo-Saxon from York; Theodulf, a Visigoth from Septimania; the historian Paul the Deacon, a Lombard; Peter, later the bishop of Pisa, and Paulinus of Aquileia, both Italians; and Angilbert, Angilram, Einhard, and Waldo of Reichenau, all Franks. This is only a partial list of his legion of scholars.

This blend, however, promoted the liberal arts at the court, and Charlemagne ordered that his children and grandchildren be well educated in this mix. Even he continued to study. At a time when most warlords were basically illiterate, Charlemagne learned Latin grammar from Paul the Deacon; rhetoric, logic, and astronomy from Alcuin; and arithmetic from Einhard. The king's great failure in scholarship, as Einhard confesses, was his seeming inability to learn how to write. Part of the problem was that Charlemagne attempted to learn only in his later years—practicing the formation of letters (in his bed during his free time) on books and wax tablets that he hid under his pillow—and it calls into question his ability to read. Einhard is notoriously silent about that skill, and no contemporary source supports the idea that Charlemagne could read.

Nevertheless, Charlemagne's success as warrior and administrator can be traced to his admiration for learning. One of the reforms named after him, however, was due not to an intellectual advance, but, ironically, an advance in handwriting. Because all manuscripts had to be hand-copied, the handwriting a monk or scribe was taught to use was very important in terms of being easy to read. The Merovingian handwriting was very difficult to follow, as single letters could be written with different shapes—a "c" could easily be mistaken for an "e," for example—and the Insular Script was beautiful but the ligatures and abbreviations also made copying difficult and slow.

The new minuscule, called Carolingian or Caroline, was developed first in Aachen and later from the influential scriptorium at Tours, where Alcuin retired as an abbot. It combined the Roman half uncial script (and its cursive version) with features from the Insular Scripts that were being used in Irish and English monasteries. Its strength was in its uniformity—rounded shapes, clearly distinguishable letters, clear capital letters, and spaces between words—all norms that we take for granted today.

LATER LEGENDS

The legends around Charlemagne began even before the emperor was dead. Even though the Royal Frankish Annals offer readers the detailed facts of year-by-year events, he was too much a larger-than-life figure for speculation and fiction not to arise.

Einhard joined Charlemagne's court in the 790s and served his son Louis the Pious at both Aachen and the king's estates at Selingenstadt. Einhard had been a pupil of Alcuin of York and was most likely the youngest of the circle of international scholars that the king had collected for his court (see section on Charlemagne's educational reforms). What makes his biography of Charlemagne so interesting is that we are reading the account of an insider to the court and to the royal family, and the evidence in court letters of how others held Einhard in high esteem gives the biography a status that others do not hold. A later biography—the anonymous *Visio Karoli Magni,* written around

865 as a visionary, cautionary tale of Charlemagne meeting with a prophetic specter in a dream—uses facts taken from Einhard and the author's own observations on the decline of the emperor's family after the tumult of the civil war in 840.

The emperor still found his way into epic tales. He was considered one of the Nine Worthies, one of the three model knights of Christendom in that body, and so it seems fitting that one of the great topics of medieval narrative, known as the *Matter of France* or the Charlemagne Cycle, focuses on the deeds of Charlemagne. In it he is called "The Emperor with the Flowing Beard," a title seen in the *Song of Roland,* and Roland and the paladins are made equal to the knights of the Round Table in King Arthur's court. Charlemagne was honored by Dante, who placed the emperor's spirit in the Heaven of Mars, among the other "warriors of the faith."

In 1165 Charlemagne was canonized by Antipope Paschal III to gain the favor of Frederick Barbarossa. The sainthood was never recognized by the church, of course, and all of Paschal's ordinances were annulled at the Third Lateran Council in 1179. Charlemagne was later beatified by Pope Benedict XIV (r. 1740–58); he is venerated on January 28.

CHARLEMAGNE'S ENDURING INFLUENCE

The emperor is credited with being one of the reasons behind the East-West Schism in the Christian church, although he may not have done it intentionally. The disagreement has to do with a very important statement in the Nicene Creed, called the *filioque*. The Visigoths believed the Holy Spirit came from God the Father *and Son* (the Son part is the *Filioque*), and the Franks inherited that tradition. Charlemagne, upon the advice of his religious advisors, thus challenged the Council of Constantinople's proclamation of 381 that the Holy Spirit proceeded from the Father alone.

Pope Leo III rejected Charlemagne's challenge and stubbornly had the Nicene Creed carved into the doors of Old Saint Peter's Basilica without the offending phrase, as if that would make the king's challenge less weighty. The Franks, of course, ignored such a gesture, and their insistence on the *filioque* led to years of poor relations with Rome. The Roman Church was later persuaded by Charlemagne's argument and adopted the phrase in its version of the Creed. This, in turn, contributed to the dispute between Rome and Constantinople.

In honor of Charlemagne, the city of Aachen has, since 1949, awarded an international prize (called the *Karlspreis der Stadt Aachen*) annually to "personages of merit who have promoted the idea of western unity by their political, economic and literary endeavours." Winners include Count Richard Coudenhove-Kalergi, the founder of the pan-European movement; Alcide De Gasperi, a founding father of the European Union; and the British prime minister Winston Churchill.

The most valuable and lasting aspect of Charlemagne's life that we have inherited is the idea of "Europe" as a core concept of geography, history, art, science, politics, and religion. As Derek Wilson puts it:

> Over and over again, throughout all the centuries that followed—during which warrior barons and the leaders of nation-states who succeeded them fought to extend or defend their boundaries—bards, kings, political theorists and artists appealed to Charlemagne to justify their actions and support their ideas. A luxuriant myth grew out of the seed of ninth-century reality, putting out new shoots in every generation. Thousands of stories were added to the Charlemagne corpus. He became for different ages a saint, a crusader, the model of chivalry, a cultural icon, a champion of civilization, an exemplar for absolutist monarchs but also an advocate of democracy, a focus of national pride but also the supreme internationalist. Charlemagne—man, monarch, and myth—cannot be disentangled from the story of Europe. (3–4)

I wrote at the beginning of this chapter that Charlemagne is one of those icons whose name is better known than his accomplishments. Yet his accomplishments are in evidence all around us, because what Charlemagne stood for was essential to the development of our Western civilization. When we think of Western art, politics, culture, economics, and most importantly the Christian faith, we should think of Charlemagne.

FURTHER READING

Barbero, Alessandro. *Charlemagne: Father of a Continent*. Translated by Allan Cameron. Berkeley: University of California Press, 2004.

Becher, Matthias. *Charlemagne*. Translated by David S. Bachrach. New Haven, CT: Yale University Press, 2003.

Collins, Roger. *Charlemagne*. Toronto: University of Toronto Press, 1998.

Dutton, Paul Edward. *Carolingian Civilization: A Reader*. Readings in Medieval Civilizations and Cultures Series, 1. Toronto: University of Toronto Press, 2004.

Einhard. *The Life of Charlemagne*. Translated by David Ganz. New York: Penguin Books, 2008.

Hyde, Douglas. *The Conquests of Charlemagne* from *The Book of Lismore*. Vol. 19. Dublin: Irish Texts Society, 1919.

McKitterick, Rosamund. *Charlemagne: The Formation of a European Identity*. Cambridge: Cambridge University Press, 2008.

Oman, Charles. *The Dark Ages, 476–918*. 6th ed. London: Rivingtons, 1914.

Riché, Pierre. *The Carolingians: A Family Who Forged Europe*. Translated by Michael Idomir Allen. Philadelphia: University of Pennsylvania Press, 1993.

Scholz, Bernhard Walter, with Barbara Rogers. *Carolingian Chronicles: Royal Frankish Annals and Nithard's Histories*. Ann Arbor: University of Michigan Press, 1970. (Comprises the *Annales regni Francorum* and *The History of the Sons of Louis the Pious*.)

Sypeck, Jeff. *Becoming Charlemagne: Europe, Baghdad, and the Empires of A.D. 800.* New York: Ecco/HarperCollins, 2006.
Wilson, Derek. *Charlemagne: The Great Adventure.* London: Hutchinson, 2005.

APPENDIX: THE CAROLINGIAN DYNASTY

Pippinids

Pippin (or Pepin) the Elder (ca. 580–640)
Grimoald (616–656)
Childebert the Adopted (d. 662)

Arnulfings

Arnulf of Metz (582–640)
Chlodulf of Metz (d. 696 or 697)
Ansegisel (ca. 602–before 679)
Pepin II "the Middle" (ca. 635–714)
Grimoald II (d. 714)
Drogo of Champagne (670–708)
Theudoald (d. 714)

Carolingians

Charles Martel (686–741)
Carloman (d. 754)
Pepin the Short (714–768)
Carloman I (751–771)
Charlemagne (ca. 742–814)
Louis the Pious (778–840)

Carolingians after the Treaty of Verdun (843)

Lothair I, Holy Roman Emperor (795–855) (Middle Francia)
Charles the Bald (823–877) (Western Francia)
Louis the German (804–876) (Eastern Francia)

Portrait of Geoffrey Chaucer, from the poem *Regiment of Princes* by Thomas Hoccleve, fifteenth century. (British Library/Stockphoto-Pro)

Geoffrey Chaucer (ca. 1340–1400)

Louise M. Bishop

INTRODUCTION

The major Hollywood movie *A Knight's Tale* (2001, written and directed by Brian Helgeland) follows the adventures of William Turner (played by Heath Ledger), a common page to a recently deceased noble. The peasant Turner, disguised in his late master's armor, seeks the rewards of knighthood, despite the supposed dangers of his impersonation. In addition to Ledger and his motley crew who quest for tournament prizes, the film features a thin, sprightly, big-headed (in more ways than one) Geoffrey Chaucer (played by Paul Bettany). Chaucer introduces himself with "Geoffrey Chaucer's the name, writing's the game." He's a down-and-out writer, addicted to gambling and stuck making his living as a scribe. Poetry plays second fiddle to his other interests like wenches and gambling (he suffers from a modern-flavored addiction, without benefit of a 12-step program), but he nevertheless expects his fame to have preceded him. Having lost his clothes in a card game, and standing naked before Turner, Chaucer attempts to jog Turner's memory: "You've probably read my book?" (Beat) "Book of the Duchess?" Turner just looks on, puzzled. The poet's wit glistens only in comparison to the film's generally insipid dialogue as Chaucer, like Turner, pulls a number of fast ones in his attempts to score with damsels as well as dice.

A Knight's Tale is a pretty uninspired movie, but at least it doesn't try to be more than it is: an entertaining teen flick. It reveals a popular culture that has lost touch with its medieval past as well as the figure of Geoffrey Chaucer, except in the most bowdlerized of forms. The film's opening tournament shows its grandstands rocking to Queen's "We Will Rock You"; the film's villain, Count Adhemar of Anjou (played by Rufus Sewell), loses a polite challenge once Turner and company dance enthusiastically, if not brilliantly, to David Bowie's "The Golden Years." It's clear that Helgeland can't trust an audience to find humor in an *authentic* representation of the Middle Ages.

But what Helgeland's movie reveals is that, in the midst of perhaps the most high-stakes commercial enterprise in the United States—filmmaking—even an audience of teenagers intrigued by things labeled "medieval" will recognize Geoffrey Chaucer as an icon of the Middle Ages. Indeed, a YouTube search for "Chaucer" returns hundreds of hits, primarily videos of high school class projects. There are live-action re-creations, energetic cartoons, and Lego-based narratives. Even the video game *World of Warcraft* has been used to bring a version of Geoffrey Chaucer to the home computer screen. Some of these amateur productions take authenticity more seriously than does *A Knight's Tale,* with occasionally accurate Middle English renditions of one or another of Chaucer's *Canterbury Tales.* As for choice of tale, a tally of a sampling of these videos shows that "The Pardoner's Tale," with its challenging combination of moral lesson and scurrilous character, wins the popularity contest, hands down.

Evidently Americans aged 15 to 24 have enough familiarity with Geoffrey Chaucer for Hollywood's money machine, which squarely targets this demographic, to front a major production that features the poet prominently, if not at the film's center. But what about the real Geoffrey Chaucer and his legacy? What has made him available, some six centuries after his death, as an icon viable for commercial use? Is there more to Chaucer than a simple sound bite or a moniker that says "medieval"? Where does his iconic status come from, and how has it changed? What has kept Geoffrey Chaucer alive?

The following essay will treat Chaucer's biography, the creation of his iconic status, and the ways his icon has inhabited English literary culture for more than six hundred years. Here you will find some reasons for his durability, continued importance in literary circles, and commercial viability. We will see why Chaucer endures.

BIOGRAPHY

Birth and Early Life

As with many medieval persons of common stock, the day and even the year of Chaucer's birth are unknown. He is thought to have been born in London sometime around 1340, and we do know he died in 1400. The year of his death is a matter of public record because, by the time of his death, Chaucer had spent most of his adult life in the orbit of the royal family and its prestigious courts. He wasn't necessarily destined to end up at court, but his family was wealthy and well enough placed, both geographically and socioeconomically, to give him a good start. His father, Thomas Chaucer, was a prosperous wine merchant. London was then a burgeoning commercial hub—arguably the most active in Europe—and its power was great enough to necessitate royalty's accession to the city's wishes: London's mayor rivaled the king in political and economic sway.

Among the ironically lucky events early in Chaucer's lifetime was his father's decision, in 1347, to relocate his family, including the young Geoffrey, outside of the city. Their move fortuitously took them out of London, and harm's way, just before the Black Death—bubonic plague—struck. Contemporary chronicles and modern research put the plague's devastating death toll between one-third and one-half of Britain's population. As for London itself, a 2005 article in the journal *Human Biology* puts the population of London at 100,000 before the first wave of plague (1348–51)and 50,000 after the plague (*Human Biology* 77.3 (2005) 291–303). Although calculations vary, it is clear from many remnants of fourteenth-century material culture, such as manuscript illuminations, tombs, and currently excavated burial grounds, that the plague wreaked havoc on London. But the city's importance as commercial center for Britain and Europe remained, and after the plague the Chaucer family returned to the metropolis to augment their fortunes and play a role in local politics.

Chaucer the Page

Family connections got teenaged Geoffrey preferred to court as page, the first step for a royal servant being educated in the ways of aristocratic life. Chaucer first entered court service during the reign of King Edward III (1312–1377, r. 1327–77), but did not serve immediately at any of that king's domiciles. Instead, Geoffrey was "preferred" to the court of the second of Edward's five sons, Lionel (1338–1368). Chaucer took part in the consolidation of the prince's court with that of his wife, the princess Elizabeth. As Chaucer became more accomplished in the courtly arts, he moved among princely venues, including the magnificent courts of the third of Edward's sons, John of Gaunt (1340–1399), a powerful noble and father to the usurping king Henry IV (1366–1413, reigned 1399–1413). This Henry is the one who attained the throne of England, as William Shakespeare's (1564–1616) second tetrology of history plays dramatizes, after forcing the abdication of Richard II (1367–1399) at the end of the fourteenth century, a year before Chaucer's death. In the course of his work life, Chaucer served, and was recognized with substantial rewards from, all three of these kings: the aged Edward, the young Richard, and the usurping Henry.

Diplomat and Soldier

It did not take long for young Geoffrey to move up in responsibilities at Prince Lionel's court. From page he became yeoman; from yeoman, esquire and that rank's foreign service in international diplomacy. The traveling he did in his diplomatic role—he visited Italy, Spain, and France—immersed him in late medieval urbanity. The poetic sophistication upon which Chaucer's iconic status rests derives in no small part from these travels as a young man on royal business. In his youth he saw the French city of Reims, near which he was captured and ransomed after four months of imprisonment. Such ransoming was a common practice among noble courts in the fourteenth century and, because their captors hoped to attain considerable sums in ransom, prisoners were well treated and not abused. Besides Reims and Paris, the increasingly urbane Geoffrey saw the major Italian cities of Genoa and Florence during the 1360s and traveled to Pavia and Milan in the 1370s. These cities exposed Chaucer to the rich international commerce and diplomacy, not to mention the aesthetic pleasures, the burgeoning Renaissance fostered there.

Poet

Chaucer's success as diplomat paralleled his growth as poet. Influenced by the writings of Dante (1265–1321), Petrarch (1304–1374), and Boccaccio (1313–1375), whose works he could acquire as manuscripts through his travels,

Chaucer also found inspiration in the French poets Guillaume de Machaut (ca. 1300–1377) and Eustache Deschamps (1346–1406), the latter of whom wrote to Chaucer letters that survive to this day. Following the styles of these accomplished men of letters, Chaucer wrote ballads attuned to the devices and conventions of courtly love and short poems touched with courtly pretensions, from love-longing to knightly endeavors. His greatest innovation, while prompted in part by his French and Italian literary influences, made him different from them: he wrote in his native, vernacular English.

Chaucer's choice to write in English parallels Dante's decision to write his major work, *The Divine Comedy*, not in Latin, despite its subject matter, but in his vernacular Tuscan Italian, the reasons for which he presents in his Latin work, *De vulgari eloquentia* ("On the eloquence of the vernacular"). Still, Chaucer's choice of English over French went against tradition in England at that time. The business of England had been conducted in French since the Norman conquest of 1066; although "Saxon" survived, it was not the status language of commerce, the royal court, or even law. But Chaucer was no apologist for Saxon, either. He did not take up models available to him outside the court. English verse had relied on alliteration, rather than end-rhyme, for its meter and rhythm in the Anglo-Saxon period (fifth century–eleventh century), but Chaucer's poetry, from his earlier works to his last, *The Canterbury Tales,* use end-rhyme and the syllabic count that governs poetry composed in the Romance languages. Why did Chaucer write in English? Perhaps he was moved by Dante's arguments in *De vulgari eloquentia*; perhaps, court creature and diplomatic voyager that he was, he wanted to explore national identity produced through language. The reasons for his choice are both obscure and manifold, but the choice of English marks Chaucer's iconic status. The creation and continuity of Chaucer's iconic presence in later centuries depends, as did his initial choice of English, on intersections among monarchic power, national identity, aesthetic judgment, and the pleasures of English poetry.

The sweet courtly poems Chaucer composed—in English, of course—during his residency in the courts of Prince Lionel and John of Gaunt were practice runs for his longer dream visions. The dream-vision form was popularized by French poets, but its roots run deep in classical and biblical culture. Chaucer modeled his dream visions on those of his favorite French writer, Guillaume de Machaut, the previous generation's most courtly exemplar and a favorite of Anglo-Norman nobility. Chaucer's dream-vision poems situate him in the literary mainstream of his courtly circles. Most critics agree that Chaucer's first dream-vision poem—the one that Paul Bettany's Chaucer in *A Knight's Tale* erroneously thinks William Turner will recognize—is *The Book of the Duchess*. Most consider the poem a commission from John of Gaunt to honor his late wife Blanche. Blanche had died in 1369, but Chaucer composed the poem, it is argued, for a later ceremony on the anniversary of her death.

William Turner's ignorance of *The Book of the Duchess* in *A Knight's Tale* may match the present audience's: there are no YouTube *Book of the Duchess* videos. Chaucer's current fame rests on his *Canterbury Tales*: 24 tales stitched together with a "frame narrative" of a pilgrimage and a tale-telling contest, the unfinished last of his poetic works in a career that spanned three decades. But Chaucer's signature poetic traits, the ones current fans recognize in *The Canterbury Tales*, also appear in his earliest work. One feature of his early poetry well-attested in his later work is a spark of what moderns would call "realism" as well as an understanding of human psychology. In *The Book of the Duchess*, the grieving Man in Black is brought around to a confession of what his fulsome praise seemed to deny, that his love is dead; his admission brings a kind of relief. There's an insistent dog leading the dreamer around, and even his nightclothes—actually, his lack thereof—are described in the poem. Although allegory was a preeminent mode in the literature Chaucer read, his own work plays with the tension between the real and the allegorical, making his poetry continually enigmatic but eminently re-readable. In addition, Chaucer's early poetry features one of his literature's most recognized traits: a kind of ironic distance, caught in a web of emotion, yet knowing and self-aware. Even in the midst of the conventions of love's tribulations or Fortune's turning wheel, the narrator in Chaucer's poetry seems to have a tongue poised firmly within his cheek. This attitude on the part of a narrator marks all of Chaucer's poetry; it's the attitude for which today, from college classrooms to YouTube, Chaucer is justly celebrated. Not everyone reads such ironic distance the same way. This quality of Chaucer's poetry—and maybe its positive critical reception by twentieth-century critics in particular—prompted critic Camille Paglia to denounce Chaucer's chumminess of the "wink, wink, nudge, nudge" sort: she detests Chaucer's enjoyment of the "in joke." But there is no end of enjoyment to be taken in analyzing the connection between self and words parallel to the vagaries of court life that Chaucer's poetry places in imaginative landscapes poised between fantasy and dreadful reality. The pleasures of such a stance involve readers today and may have been even more attractive to those embroiled daily in the tumultuous years, the 1370s, of one old king's late reign and his grandson successor's early years.

Service under King Richard II

Edward III had groomed his eldest son, Edward the Black Prince (1330–1376) to succeed him, but the prince predeceased his father following a long illness. Upon Edward III's death in 1377, the Black Prince's son Richard, at the tender age of 10, assumed the throne. Due to his youth it was suggested that Richard be ruled by a regency made up of his uncles, but fear of their power—especially that of the exceedingly wealthy and powerful John of Gaunt (Chaucer's patron since Prince Lionel's death in 1368)—was substantial enough to produce a unique configuration of councils, rather than uncles, exercising consultancy. But the uncles—John of Gaunt, Edmund of York (1341–1402), and Thomas of Woodstock (1355–1397)—still exerted the kind of influence that comes with wealth and position.

Chaucer initially served his new king through these avuncular branches of the powerful Plantagenet family. In 1378 he participated in diplomatic efforts to broker a marriage between England's royal interests and the despotic Visconti family in Milan: the goal was to engage a Visconti daughter, Catarina, to the newly crowned young Richard. It's hard to know how surprised Chaucer might have been when, in 1379, Richard II was affianced to Anne of Bohemia, daughter of the Holy Roman Emperor. A choice marriage, but not one with which Chaucer had been involved: we can only guess at his reaction to the engagement. He was, however, undoubtedly present at Richard and Anne's marriage ceremonies in 1382.

Until his participation in marriage negotiations for the young king— Chaucer had accompanied an embassy to Paris in 1377 to explore marital options there as well as in Italy—his travels had been curtailed since 1374, when he was named controller of the "wool custom" and the "petty custom," posts he held for some 12 years. While Chaucer kept books, per se, for both posts, he was not the actual collector of funds. Rather, he was the crown's agent, assuring reliability, accuracy, and the king's interests. Both customs positions required moral probity as well as commercial cognizance, and Chaucer's designation for the posts demonstrates his utter immersion in the mercantile, political, and international issues of his day. Whether his new duties resulted from the king's—or the king's uncles'—desires to reward prior service or were a way to keep him in town, Chaucer's day job resulted in continued connection to royal administration as courtly and commercial patrons gained their footing in a burgeoning economy. These commercial vagaries as crucible of character capture the poet's attention, adding to his inspired explorations of the real in the allegorical and the allegorical in the real.

The Aldgate Years

To satisfy the needs of his new position as customs officer, Chaucer leased a dwelling above one of London's city gates, called in its time Aldgate (now a London Tube stop). This situation, along with the access his administrative post necessitated, afforded Chaucer a front-row seat for the last events of Edward III's reign and the earliest ones of Richard II's, letting him follow the political machinations that accompanied this troubled succession of a preteen king.

Two more dream vision poems date from these years: *The House of Fame* and *The Parliament of Fowls*. The first allows us another glimpse of Chaucer's constructed persona accosted by an eagle that grips him with its talons and flies away, only to engage the narrator in conversation about poetic fame. The bird-motif continues in the second dream vision, which, mimicking Chaucer's diplomatic efforts, treats marriage and the making of a good union. Perhaps predictably, considering the failure of Chaucer's marriage negotiations with the Visconti, the union of the male eagle and female tercelet, the poem's ostensible goal, is deferred at the tercelet's insistence. Chaucer's marriage-themed dream vision, peopled with creatures, counterpoises the seemingly forced marriages in the final acts of Shakespeare's comedies like *Measure for Measure*. Instead, the *Parliament of Fowls* puts off what had seemed the perfect pairing and ends inconclusively. Undoubtedly a finished work, the *Parliament* anticipates the unfinished nature of some of Chaucer's later work, specifically the *Legend of Good Women* and *The Canterbury Tales*. In those instances Chaucer has left his audience with enduring mysteries, and speculation continues about his motives for writing what he did, how he did. Such inconclusiveness has added to his iconic status, just as indecision has assured Hamlet's fame.

But the Aldgate years also saw the beginning of the poem on which Chaucer thought his legacy would rest. *Troilus and Criseyde* is a long epic poem retelling Boccaccio's *Il Filostrato*, which is itself a treatment of the further adventures of the Trojan War as amplified by late classical and medieval poets' many additional stories. Again we meet Chaucer's created persona, a narrator both inquisitive yet bumbling, much like the narrator of the dream visions but wrapped into a narrative at once historical (the Trojan War), courtly (love achieved and frustrated anchors the plot), and philosophical. Many critics suggest that Chaucer had other reasons for injecting a philosophical strain into *Troilus and Criseyde*. One of his shorter poems suggests that Chaucer was at the time translating the late classical *Consolation of Philosophy*, a bellwether Late Latin text (ca. 521) that was adopted by Christianity for its messages about fortune's seductive blandishments and free will's Christian centrality. A good deal of the *Consolation*'s power derives from its dramatic situation. Its eponymous narrator sits in prison, undeservedly condemned to capital punishment. His capacious vision attempts to answer why bad things happen to good people. Chaucer's translation hasn't earned high marks on its own, but some think he translated the text as part of a drive to educate the young king Richard. Although Chaucer's Boethius translation may not sing, his *Troilus and Criseyde* is a compelling masterpiece written in the stateliest English. Its accomplishments include Chaucer's invention of a rhymed, metered poetic form, the diction of which is at once both English and classical. Chaucer had no English-language models for what he did with *Troilus and Criseyde*. But the poem reveals poetic achievement beyond vernacular linguistic invention. Chaucer imbues the poem with equal measures of insouciance—the narrator retains his admiration for Criseyde almost despite himself—and the gravitas of martial realities. *Troilus and Criseyde* is a poem even undergraduates can't stop reading. Its enigmatic ending—Troilus, betrayed by Criseyde and now perched in the spherical heavens, looks down at the piddling earth and laughs—continues to provoke readers and evoke commentary.

The Rising of 1381

In typical Chaucerian fashion, however—meaning that neither motives nor outcome is unambiguous—Chaucer's Aldgate years are known for a staggering event that makes virtually no appearance in his poetry. In June 1381 an enormous confederacy—variously called "rebels," "lollards," and "peasants"—surrounded the metropolitan city of London to press their claims against royal taxes and decrees that were the result of the Black Death. The taxation the rebels resisted included a poll tax of three pence per head—"poll"—payable to the royal coffers. The decrees, called the Statutes of Laborers, had frozen wages in favor of the nobility, to the detriment of landless peasants selling their ability to work in a market straitened by the enormous manpower losses of the plague.

For one warm summer week, London (pop. 50,000) was besieged by a rebel tumult: 10,000 people surrounded the city and milled about below the gate in which Chaucer lived. The rebels meant business: they executed the archbishop of Canterbury and burned the Savoy palace of Chaucer's patron John of Gaunt. The shockwave of the Rising or, as it was called prior to 1968, the Peasants' Revolt, reverberated in contemporary chronicles, which, to please royal masters, took pains to paint the rebels as dastardly and the nobles as wise. As it happened, the 14-year-old king Richard II rode out to meet the rebel leaders in Smithfield, outside Aldgate, and gave assurances, soon to be rescinded, of meeting the leaders' demands. Once the crowds dispersed, the remaining rebel leaders were taken and executed, and a terrifying week in London's history moved into legend. But, remarkably to modern ears accustomed to the concept of "newsworthy," these events did not move into Chaucer's poetry, with the sole exception of a glance at the perhaps legendary rebel leader Jack Straw, whose raucous voice is named and parodied in "The Nun's Priest's Tale," one of the *Canterbury Tales*. If we see Chaucer as primarily caring for his legacy as a poet, guided by Petrarch, Dante, Machaut, and Deschamps, and understanding literature as different from "the news," then we might appreciate the subtlety he brings to his opinions, couched in his signature ironic distance. Our age of surveillance might suggest that Chaucer avoided "the news" because to engage with headlines posed a danger. But Chaucer's poetic choices were, first and foremost, *poetic* ones, designed to engage his audience on every level, not just the most sensational.

None of this detracts from the simmering politics that animated Chaucer's courts and inhabited London's streets. There were those who attributed to the Rising's rebel leadership an affiliation with a contemporary religious reform movement whose adherents were maligned by the obscure term "Lollard." These social critics followed the reformist Oxford theologian John Wyclif (ca. 1325–1384), a prolific scourge of church leadership, especially the papacy, who voiced his disappointment at what he considered the Christian church's failure to adhere solely to biblical traditions. Wyclif was no wild-eyed reformer: rather, during the heyday of his campaign in the 1370s he earned the protection of none other than John of Gaunt, Richard II's uncle and, we should remember, an important patron of Chaucer's. Gaunt's role in Wyclif's career resulted from the main political rationale of Wyclif's reforms: to limit the role of clergy and church administration in the secular courts' affairs. Canterbury Cathedral's martyr Thomas Becket (ca. 1118–1170) had met his end defending the church's prerogatives against those of the English king

Henry II (r. 1154–1189); the popular pilgrimage to Canterbury that frames Chaucer's *Tales* commemorated this check on royal power (see the chapter on Thomas Becket). Wyclif, two centuries later, concentrated not on the Christian church's triumphs but on its abuses. He targeted not only the papacy but the monasteries, the former looking rather bad in light of multiple popes, the latter evidently rich in land and other wealth that rivaled princely holdings. Although the rebels likely were supporters of Wyclif and familiar with his calls to reform, they burned the London palace of Wyclif's protector Gaunt, probably because Gaunt's wealth made him a target analogous to the rich monastic foundations Wyclif denounced. Gaunt himself was not harmed, but the rebels beheaded the politically powerful and perhaps rivalrous archbishop of Canterbury: the besieged nobles, cravenly but accurately, figured that the archbishop would serve to sate the rebels' demand for a sacrificial victim. Although Gaunt lost his palace, he kept his head, and he remained one of the most powerful nobles in England—a fact not lost on his son Henry who, less than 20 years later, ascended the throne as Henry IV after forcing Richard II to abdicate.

Chaucer and Lollardy

Just as Chaucer's attitudes to court intrigue seem to be—and not to be—written into his poetry, so his relationship to Lollardy's theology and ideology has inspired enormous debate. In *The Canterbury Tales*, the pilgrimage's Host, Harry Bailey, explicitly labels the Parson a Lollard. Critics have traced a fair amount of Lollard attitude in the sermon delivered by the Parson in his tale. But the Parson is no supporter of royal prerogative. The pilgrims in *The Canterbury Tales* travel to the tomb of Thomas Becket, defender of the Christian church's prerogatives against royal administration. A pilgrimage to Canterbury thus memorializes the only check available on runaway kingly power and seems to support the Christian church. Yet the pilgrims with whom the narrator (Chaucer) travels, like the secular Lawyer and the religious Prioress, exemplify paradox and, frequently, irreverence, especially when the narrator lauds their character. We can ask, "Who exactly are the targets of Chaucer's satire?" but then we have to question whether the label of *satire* fits at all. The Parson has the last word of *The Canterbury Tales*: is that also Chaucer's last word, or does the unfinished nature of the *Tales* suggest otherwise? One of Chaucer's patrons was John of Gaunt, both supporter of Wyclif and victim of the Rising's fury. Like the ambivalences surrounding the Rising as far as leadership and rationale go, and the ironic distance Chaucer builds into his poetry, Chaucer's nearly total neglect in his poetry of both the Rising and Lollardy—at least, in an overt fashion—reflects the perspicacity, position, and subtlety with which he, perhaps characterologically, endowed his work. The depth of daily life tinged with ideological controversy and the apparently dangerous nature of what may appear to a modern audience as theological niceties may go a long way to explain Chaucer's decision to create and recreate a bumbling and obtuse caricature of himself as narrator for his dream visions, his epic poem *Troilus and Criseyde*, and his last great work, the *Canterbury Tales*. How interesting, in light of Chaucer's iconic status, is the fact that we identify ironic distance as the signature trait not only of Chaucer but of an English literary mentality.

Chaucer in Kent

Like his father's moving his family out of London just before the Black Plague hit, Chaucer's decision to leave his positions with the wool and petty customs, as well as his rooms above Aldgate, was fortunately timed. Richard II's powerful uncles asserted their power over him between 1386 and 1387, citing Richard's tendency to pick bad favorites and his inability to heed good counsel. They had parliamentary help securing their sway over the king just before Richard achieved his majority at age 21. To hamper the king's power, they dismissed his favorites from office, even executing a number of them. Perhaps through reading Chaucer's translation of *The Consolation of Philosophy,* Richard had learned patience—but not a rejection of the blandishments of worldly power. Richard waited 10 years before taking his revenge and regaining his royal clout. Part of his patient plan included Chaucer. In 1389, Richard II appointed Chaucer clerk of the king's works, a post he held for three years. Whether Chaucer left that post because of Richard's dissatisfaction or because of his own worries about Richard's increasingly autocratic behavior (Richard had a famous row with the City of London in 1392) isn't easy to discern. But leave it he did. After his stint as clerk of the works, Chaucer moved to Kent, most likely to Greenwich, seemingly out of kingly purview and in retirement, although he retained old and obtained new sinecures at the hands of both John of Gaunt and King Richard. These gifts and annuities, monetary and sustaining (one was a yearly tun, or large cask, of wine), seem to have been bestowed to reward Chaucer for his good labors. They also demonstrate that Chaucer remained in the good graces of seemingly rival parties.

Greenwich proved fertile for Chaucer's imagination: it was here that Chaucer composed the poetry that for the twenty-first century, from YouTube to Canterbury animatronics (see "Chaucer and the Twentieth and Twenty-First Centuries," below), replays his fame. Chaucer's *Canterbury Tales* are the poetry on which his modern iconic status rests. Yet *The Canterbury Tales*, like Chaucer's other poetry, remain distant in action and import from the intrigue and revenge that closed the reign of Richard II. Between 1397 and 1399 Richard took his revenge on those who, in 1387, had hampered his power. He swept in to clean house, even imprisoning one of the uncles, Thomas duke of Gloucester, who died in captivity: his death can be laid at Richard's doorstep. When Richard's cousin Henry, son of John of Gaunt, challenged the noble who had imprisoned Gloucester and under whose "protection" Gloucester had been murdered—likely at Richard's behest—the king banished cousin Henry. It seemed a prudent decision: banishment falls short of murder—killing John of Gaunt's son would exact a price—and truncates a potential problem's power. In this case, the banished cousin is the Henry who, at his father Gaunt's death and Richard's seizure of Gaunt's fortune, returned to England despite his sentence of banishment (suddenly made permanent, rather than for a term of years, as Richard had originally decided), to rally disaffected nobles to his side in a bid to claim his father's wealth.

Some historians lament Richard's turn to autocracy—his choice to change a temporary sentence to a permanent one, solely on his say-so—and cite it as reason for his downfall; others note Gaunt's son Henry's only partially concealed aim for the throne. Richard's abilities as monarch were debated in contemporary chronicles; the historians that Shakespeare read used Henry-friendly chronicles for their prose histories, and their opinions shape the playwright's history plays. While these chronicles lament Richard's increasing autocratic behavior and his reliance on poor counselors, Terry Jones of Monty Python fame has come to Richard's defense, citing the powerful Henrician propaganda machine working overtime after the fact to paint Richard's foibles and Henry's nobility. According to Jones, today's historians fall prey to Henry's effective propaganda and continue to portray Richard undeservedly in a negative light. In any case, Richard's fall from power was a cataclysmic event in aristocratic circles that dated their chronicles according to the year of a king's reign.

During these controversies in the 1390s, Chaucer lived in Greenwich, remote from these tribulations as the different factions of Edward III's progeny wrestled for power. But events like Gloucester's arrest and death, the passing of John of Gaunt, and his son's attempt to reclaim his inheritance swirled ever closer and with increasing political challenge as the decade wore on.

Return to London

Chaucer moved back to London in 1398 and formulated a long-term lease the following year for a residence within the precincts of Westminster Abbey. Terry Jones, Alan Fletcher, Robert Yeager, Juliette Dor, and Terry Dolan make much of this move to the abbey in their book *Who Murdered Chaucer?* (2004). They detect in this relocation Chaucer's anxieties about the machinations of the resurgent Lancasters and Henry's henchmen. Chaucer had been identified with Richard II, and the new Lancastrian monarch demanded fealty to Henry's dynastic cause, despite the ambiguous grounds—other than force—he used for taking the crown. Chaucer's move to London and then to church precincts at the height of these troubles indicates his desire for sanctuary in light of his former faithful service to Richard. As it happened, after Chaucer's death in 1400, Richard II continued to plague Henry IV. Richard's death was announced in 1400, but the ex-king's "unquiet body," as the Chaucerian scholar Paul Strohm calls it, served as a rallying point for anti-Henry, anti-Lancastrian forces. Only when Henry IV's son Henry V (1386–1422, r. 1413–22) ascended the throne and, in the first year of his reign, ostentatiously put Richard's body into a magnificent newly built tomb did rumors of Richard's continuing existence evaporate.

CHAUCER AND LANCASTRIAN AND YORKIST PROPAGANDA

This story of Richard's unquiet body indicates the difficulties the new Lancastrian dynasty had solidifying its position. Interestingly enough, the new court pressed into service Chaucer's legacy following the poet's death (possibly murder). The Lancasters needed strategies to legitimate their rule. Perhaps Chaucer's prior royal connections made him the right choice for the Lancastrian court's desire for connection with its predecessor; perhaps personalizing an English poetic sensibility in terms of progeny—"Father Chaucer"—could by analogy solidify the progeny of Lancastrian succession; perhaps the first two scions of the usurping Lancastrian line, Henry IV and Henry V, presciently figured that national poetic identity could soothe rebellious spirits or combat them with an ideological effectiveness newly suitable for written vernacular English's growing promulgation. Fifteenth-century followers of Chaucer, Lancastrian apologists to the core, proclaimed Chaucer's preeminence as England's poet. It is not at all surprising that the poets who took up Chaucer's mantle were Lancastrian supporters, allied to a political power structure, albeit an embattled one.

Thomas Hoccleve

The first of these Chaucerian disciples, Thomas Hoccleve (1368–1426), who was personally acquainted with Chaucer, began to frame the elder poet's work, if not with tropes of overt English nationalism, then with covert national sentiment woven in his praise of Chaucer's English writing. He calls Chaucer "England's treasure and riches," but more importantly he deems Chaucer his poetic father. He chose the metaphor of poetic paternity for his relationship to Chaucer's work because paternity and legitimacy shaped every aspect of Lancastrian rule and propaganda. Chaucer's Englishness, forged in linguistic, geographical, and genealogical terms, remains to this day the foundation of his iconic status.

Chaucer may have considered *Troilus and Criseyde* his poetic genius's greatest accomplishment, yet even the manuscript record—copies of Chaucer's works that predate the emergence of the printing press in the late fifteenth century—provide some 80 copies of *Canterbury Tales* but only some 20 of *Troilus and Criseyde*, whole or part. In the Ellesmere manuscript, the most deluxe of fifteenth-century manuscripts of *The Canterbury Tales*, we find a portrait of Chaucer affixed in the margin of the tale the pilgrim Chaucer tells—the prose *Tale of Melibee*. Although we know that the portrait was produced after Chaucer's death, it does include seemingly identifying features—forked beard, slight pudginess, hooded eyes. These same features also appear in another manuscript portrait of Chaucer from the early fifteenth century. London, British Library, Harley MS 4866, folio 88, includes an image of Chaucer very much like the Ellesmere's—some have argued for tracing and copying work between the two manuscripts. But the Harley manuscript's text is not by Chaucer: it is Thomas Hoccleve's *Regiment of Princes*, wherein Hoccleve notes Chaucer's paternity of Hoccleve's poetic vocation. The torso portrait points at lines about this "fresh likeness," calling it a copy of Chaucer's image in Hoccleve's mind. It is reproduced on the page, the lines aver, as a way for readers to find Chaucer in their own "thoughts and mind." These two images in two fifteenth-century manuscripts, one of Chaucer's work and one of the work of one of his fans, are our initial literal "icons" of Chaucer. Surprisingly, his portraiture remained remarkably consistent through the centuries in beard, eyes, and size—until we come to *A Knight's Tale,* with its rangy blond Chaucer. Hoccleve's own desire for preferment may have added to his adoration of Chaucer, whose courtly successes far outweighed Hoccleve's own. But, more importantly, we detect a will to make Chaucer into England's poetic icon within scant years of his death.

John Lydgate

Another of Chaucer's Lancastrian promoters, John Lydgate (ca. 1370–ca. 1451), provides no portrait, but his paeans to Chaucer as "flower of English poetry" sound much like Hoccleve's and reverberate throughout Lydgate's voluminous corpus. Lydgate was a monk, but one who was supported by, and given to pleasing, noble patrons. Unstinting in his praise of Chaucer, he accords him the title "master" and reckons as immeasurable his debt to Chaucer as England's poet. He considers Chaucer "peerless," lauding his ability to made rude English beautiful: this judgment continued to be expressed throughout the fifteenth and sixteenth centuries. Lydgate was a friend to Chaucer's son Thomas (ca. 1367–1434), and the monk's poetic ambitions perhaps got a boost from Thomas's court and political connections: Thomas Chaucer served as chief butler of England and also Speaker of the House. Geoffrey Chaucer, like William Turner, could never claim nobility, but his son Thomas certainly rose up the food chain. Nor did the Chaucer family's ascent stop there: Thomas's daughter Alice (1404–1475) married William de la Pole, first duke of Suffolk.

  Here, then, are the beginnings of Chaucer's iconic status. Hoccleve and Lydgate recognize him for his stately poetry as well as his political connections—connections upon which Lydgate, for one, traded. Their invocation of their poetic father and master demonstrates the almost instant nature of Chaucer's celebrity and the inextricable intertwining of his poetry with politics. Chaucer as icon served a legitimating purpose for a power structure newly cognizant of English literature's nation-building potential—the poet's inscrutability and irony notwithstanding.

Lydgate and Hoccleve's praise of their master-father Chaucer and their shared English identity boosted Lancastrian egos and intertwined politics and poetry. But conflict and threat to Lancastrian hegemony followed the death of Henry V. Chaucer was used as icon not only by Lancastrian sympathizers but by the opposing Yorkist side in the bloody Wars of the Roses, England's internecine conflict between the supporters of Lancastrian claims to the throne and those who supported the claims of the duke of York, one of John of Gaunt's rival brothers, whose progeny contested the legitimacy of the original Lancastrian Henry. The divided loyalties that followed for aristocratic families well intermarried between Yorks and Lancasters, whose political alliances shifted with time and advantage, are not limited to polite arm-twisting. It has been estimated that, by the end of the fifteenth century, half of England's male nobility had succumbed to battle, duel, or judicial execution. The end of the Wars of the Roses also saw the end of Chaucer's literal progeny. Great-granddaughter Alice's son John de la Pole, second duke of Suffolk (1442–1492) married the sister of Richard III (1452–1485, r. 1483–85), making Alice's son brother-in-law to the eventual king. But John had been earlier affianced, as a child, to Margaret Beaufort (1443–1509). That arrangement was annulled in 1453, but Margaret went on to marry Edmund Tudor and gave birth, after Edmund's death (ending a very brief marriage), to Henry Tudor, eventually King Henry VII (1457–1509, r. 1485–1509), scion of the regnant Tudors following Richard III's defeat at the battle of Bosworth field. Ironically, John de la Pole, Chaucer's great-great-grandson, had been named heir to the ill-fated Richard III. Neither Richard III nor John de la Pole ended up having children; Chaucer's bloodline ran out at the same time that the new Tudor dynasty, with Henry VII as its progenitor, was minted. Richard III, like his distant relative Richard II, has been the subject of revisionist history to rehabilitate his reputation and kingly success (see the chapter on Richard III). But, in light of the vagaries of royal power-grabs epitomized by the Wars of the Roses and Chaucer's iconic role in these conflicts, Sir John Harington's epigraph seems as apt today as it was when printed in 1615:

Treason never prospers: what's the reason?
If treason prosper, none dare call it treason.

CHAUCER AND TUDOR PROPAGANDA

Of course, in order to call something patriotic or someone a traitor, the past must be made to fit, and its characters—its icons—pressed into service. The reputation of Geoffrey Chaucer as master English writer who brought rhetorical eloquence to the English language (this is the opinion of George Ashby, ca. 1470) prevailed through the tumult of the fifteenth century and trumped any Yorkist stain sullying his literal progeny's reputation. At the demise of Richard III, Henry VII and the Tudor propaganda machine he invented took hold of Chaucer's English-identified legacy. Not only had Chaucer's iconic reputation survived, but the Tudor monarchy, much in need of good press, took advantage of a new method to promulgate Tudor Chaucer's icon in Britain. The printing press made its debut at the same time that Henry VII, first Tudor king and initial Tudor apologist, defeated Richard III at Bosworth. This coincidence augmented the royal treatment Chaucer's icon received as England's national poet. The press's arrival happily coincided with, and abetted, the spectacular growth of royal administration: courts had grown since the royal functionary Thomas Hoccleve invoked Chaucer's fatherhood of English poetry. Thus the politics and iconic status of Chaucer were shaped to coincide with newly active imperial attitudes and the grandiose visions of the English Tudor monarchy, culminating in the grand success of Elizabeth I (1533–1603, r. 1558–1603).

CHAUCER'S WORKS IN PRINT

The first of Chaucer's works to be printed appeared from the press of England's first printer, William Caxton, who published *The Canterbury Tales* circa 1478. It was, according to some bibliographers, the first book that Caxton printed in England after his return from Bruges in 1476. He reprinted *The Canterbury Tales* in 1483 and also printed, at about the same time, Chaucer's translation of Boethius's *Consolation of Philosophy* (1478), *Troilus and Criseyde*, and Chaucer's dream vision *House of Fame* (both 1483). Caxton's successor, Wynken de Worde, a younger man whom Caxton brought to England from Bruges to help him with his press, also printed the *Tales*, as did, it seems, rival printer Richard Pynson. De Worde's 1517 edition, "newly corrected," became the property of Pynson, who after de Worde's death virtually simultaneously (circa 1526) printed the *Tales, House of Fame*, and *Troilus and Criseyde*. The printer John Rastell published the *Tales* simultaneously with Pynson. Is this evidence of a Chaucer industry? Maybe. Rastell had gotten caught up through marriage (he was married to Sir Thomas More's sister) and public prominence in debates about the "Great Matter" of King Henry VIII (1491–1547, r. 1509–47). From Henry's first attempts (1525) to divorce Catherine of Aragon, his wife of 16 years, claiming that the marriage was incestuous (she was his brother Henry's widow), to Henry's final severance of church ties to Rome (1533), a public and private debate raged, the victims of which were not only Catherine and her daughter Mary, declared illegitimate once Henry married Anne Boleyn, mother of Elizabeth I, but also Sir Thomas More, who, like Becket before him, was martyred on the altar of church prerogative. Perhaps Rastell, concerned with the chill his association with More might bring, thought Chaucer's work and status as national icon could salvage his reputation. But in the greater scheme of things, these editions of Chaucer were a drop in the bucket. Early English printers published many, many titles (de Worde's output is estimated at 400 titles in 800 editions), and the best seller to roll off the presses, in de Worde's case, wasn't Chaucer but a Latin grammar. Still, the rapidity and consistency with which these printers produced early editions of his poetry testify to Chaucer's continuing iconic status.

Pynson's edition of *The Canterbury Tales* provides a nice example of Chaucer as icon for sixteenth-century readers. Woodcut illustrations grace the title pages for various *Tales*—his pilgrims have also become icons—and his "proheme," instructing a reader how to understand and appreciate Chaucer, touts the felicity of *The Canterbury Tales*:

> Great thanks, laud, and honor ought to be given unto the clerk, poets, and historiographers that have written many noble books of wisdom of the lives, passions, and miracles of holy saints and histories of noble and famous acts and faits [deeds] and of the chronicles since the beginning of the creation of the world unto this present time by which we are daily informed and have knowledge of many things of whom we should not have known if that had not left to us their monuments written. Among whom and in especial tofore [before] all other[s] we ought to give a singular laud unto the noble and great philosopher Geffrey Chaucer, the which for his ornate writing in our tongue may well have the name of a laureate poet, for tofore that he by his labor embellished, ornated and made fair our English in this realm was had rude speech and incongruous as yet it appeareth by old books, which at this day ought not to have place nor be compared among, nor to his beauteous volumes and ornate writings, of whom he made diverse books and treatises of many a noble history, as well in meter as in rhyme and prose. And them so craftily made that he comprehended his matters in short, quick, and high sentences, eschewing prolixity, casting away the chaff of superfluity, and showing the picked grain of sentence uttered by crafty and sugared eloquence. Of whom among all other of his books I purpose to imprint by the grace of Jesus the book of the tales of Canterbury in which I find many a noble history of every state and degree.

Chaucer's identity with the English language and England, with poetry, with nobility, with philosophy, as well as with the "old," uses the frame that fifteenth-century poets and their noble patrons had already provided for Father Chaucer. But perhaps the most noteworthy feature, in this cascade of clauses, is Chaucer's reputation for "eschewing prolixity" and "eschewing the chaff of superfluity." These factors remain the centerpiece of English's best prose style. The value of direct and unaffected prose continues to ring in the modern political sphere's reliance on simplicity—to a fault, perhaps.

Notice that it is not Chaucer's ambiguous persona that Pynson lauds: an appreciation for indeterminacy is a trademark of twentieth-century literary studies.

Following the resolution of the Great Matter, the 1530s mark Chaucer's remarkable entry, in a manner of speaking, into the coffee-table book market of the Tudor court. Beginning with William Thynne's edition in 1532, printers produced large and expensive black-letter folio editions of Chaucer's complete works. The handsome and heavy volumes, with illustrations, leather binding, high-quality paper, and voluminous dedications, put together in one book all of Chaucer's works. Chaucer would have been pleased that a movement begun a bit earlier in Italy to preserve the corpus of famous poets like Dante, whose civic and national identity provided a model, had spread west and caught the English poet in its fashionable hold.

Like Chaucer's earlier proponents and printers, folio producer William Thynne (d. 1546), the first in a series of Renaissance collectors and publishers presenting a Chaucerian oeuvre, had royal connections. He was educated at Oxford and attained a prominent position, clerk of the kitchen, in Henry VIII's court. In his Chaucer folio's dedication to Henry VIII, Thynne frames his activities on Chaucer's behalf with the same kind of nationalistic fervor as did Pynson. But his identification of King Henry's brilliance as poet and historian allies antique Chaucer with Tudor royalty. Again publishers deploy Chaucer's fatherhood of English poetry to recertify English nationalism. The point isn't Chaucer's political leanings; rather, the import is Chaucer's embodiment of a burgeoning national consciousness that needs its king to be lettered as much as it needs its venerable poet's Englishness. The folio editions begin their sequential march through the sixteenth century at the same time that Henry, successful in his break with Rome, begins to tangle with challenges from Martin Luther and a diverse Protestant critique, as well as his own problems concerning progeny, legitimacy, inheritance, the crown, and authority. One could suggest that Chaucer's iconic status as England's poet is pressed into the service of Henry's severely challenged court, the survival of which depends on ever more authoritarian methods of retaining control over recalcitrant subjects.

The question of authority, for better or worse, and even to this day, is wrapped up with the presence—or absence—of authors and authenticity. Chaucer's iconic status served to expand his authority. The strength of Thynne's attributions allowed his canon of Chaucer's works to be reproduced in every Chaucer edition for two centuries. But modern scholarship contests some of Thynne's attribution to Chaucer of a number of the folio's poems. On the face of it, a larger canon—a weightier canon—suggests a more prolific poet. Moreover, the idea of collecting an author's works in one large volume imitates the burgeoning idea of "bigger is better" in the first flush of colonial expansionism. Thus Thynne's folio edition includes a number of poems not previously printed under Chaucer's name to augment Chaucer's status, while his gravitational pull as national poet drew recognizably antique texts into his orbit. Piling works on Chaucer's shoulders augmented his reputation, honored his unique status, and affirmed his iconic position.

Thynne's successors reprinted his edition during the short reign of Edward VI (1537–1553, r. 1547–53), Henry's sickly youngest child. Once on the throne, Edward's youth made him an easy mark for the more rabid Protestant counselors kept under wraps during Henry's reign. At Edward's precipitous death, his Catholic sister Mary (1516–1558, r. 1553–58), Henry VIII's eldest daughter, assumed the throne, despite some last-minute efforts to name the Protestant Lady Jane Gray (1536–1554), great-great-niece of Henry VIII, as queen. Queen Mary's successor after her short reign was Henry's second child, Elizabeth I, daughter of Anne Boleyn, who eventually proved an extraordinarily adroit and gifted leader. In the reigns of all three of Henry VIII's Tudor progeny, folio editions of Chaucer's works were printed and reprinted. Chaucer continued to be lauded as England's primordial poet. Ironically, however, because of language shifts in the sixteenth century, Chaucer's poetry, though lionized, had become difficult to read. Moreover, the appearance of the poetry itself became iconic: while for "modern" texts the book trade began to use roman typefaces, Chaucer was kept in recognizably antique black letter.

More than Chaucer's words added to his iconic reputation. In the heat of Queen Mary's Catholic resurgence, Nicholas Brigham erected a canopied tomb for Chaucer's remains. The tomb, founded in 1556, became the cornerstone of Westminster Abbey's eventual "Poet's Corner." This tomb both represents, and solidifies, quite literally, Chaucer's iconic status. The tomb includes a portrait much like that found in the Hoccleve manuscript—could it have been copied?—and verses pertaining to Chaucer's origination of English poetry. Its position in London's parliamentary abbey and its laureation of Chaucer as England's poet parallels the religious iconography affixed in Catholic times to saints and prelates: could it have been an answer to resurgent Catholicism? The similarity of the likeness the tomb displays to those of the Hoccleve and Ellesmere manuscripts demonstrates the durability of Chaucer's iconic image begun with those fifteenth-century manuscript portraits. By the late sixteenth century, portraits of Chaucer were hanging in noble houses, and this practice continued well into the late seventeenth century. Chaucer's aspirations to noble status find their reward in these iconographic renderings, his image occupying both secular and sacred spaces, the cultural weight of which was changing in response to modernity's ascendancy.

Chaucer's next editor, John Stow (ca. 1525–1605), produced not only a fat folio Chaucer edition (1561, over 600 pages) but also a series of history books compiled from his extensive personal collection and exhaustive labors in private archives. Finding unused archives and reestablishing them for antiquarian research were new pastimes for writers and publishers engaged in the process of modernization, which also meant putting the past in its place. After his Chaucer edition, Stow published a *Summarie of Englyshe Chronicles* (1565, over 1200 pages), *Chronicles from Brute to unto the present year* (1560; later *Annales,* 1592, over 1300 pages), and a comprehensive and best-selling *Survey of London* (1598, about 500 pages) that continued to be printed, used, and revised by others into the eighteenth century. In its attachment to English history and archival research, Stow's work exemplifies antiquarian re-creation of "Englishness," verifying its pedigree in a remote, classical (not medieval) past identified with Troy and, later, Rome, while simultaneously creating its English moment as "new." One anonymous 1518 history, printed by Richard Pynson, Caxton's rival and early printer of Chaucer, locates England's ancient history in relation not only to Greece and Rome, but also to Israel: "Brute came after the making of the world into the land of Albion in the time that Eli the priest of the law was in the land of Israel. New Troy (that is now called London) was founded by the making of Brute after the making of the world. Rome was founded by Remus and Romulus. Jesus Christ was conceived by the holy ghost in the maid Mary on a Friday." Chaucer is thus one point on an iconic scale begun with the ancient Brutus. But Chaucer's icon, identified specifically with English's original poetic language, shimmers with "Englishness." Chaucer is, for Edmund Spenser (1552–1599), "the well of English undefil'd."

Unlike their successors intent on defining modernity and cordoning off the past, people in the "Middle Ages" (a term introduced in 1616) did not see themselves as between eras, bounded on either side by the classical era and the Renaissance. Rather, their self-image was one of continuity with a Trojan and Roman past (even Charlemagne, crowned Holy Roman Emperor in 800, wore a toga to the ceremony) and of membership in a universal Christian church. The social, political, and economic changes for which we use the term "Renaissance" reflect the term's coinage in the mid-sixteenth century by the Italian artist George Vasari (1511–1574) to break with an ostensibly stultifying past. "Classic," which entered the English language in the seventeenth century, in its original use meant only "best"; its application to Greece and Rome, and to literature, became exclusive only in the eighteenth century. The popular vigor of the term "Renaissance" rises in the nineteenth century, spurred by the work of German historian Jacob Burckhardt (1818–1897) and responding to the pressure of modernity—in science, art, medicine, technology, and Western expansion—to reassert divisions between eras and deny other than quaint antiquarian interest in a medieval past. Like the term "Enlightenment," "Renaissance" paints its own era positively and its medieval antecedent negatively. The use of words like "Renaissance" and "classics" *creates* that break between epochs because it serves the "new" era's need to make itself distinct. Such a need was not a feature of medieval thought: instead, an era's diminution in light of a Golden Past, and a recognition that there was "nothing new under the sun," epitomizes what we would call medieval ideology. For Karl Marx, modernity's rage for the new supports a capital economy. Asserting modernity's superiority over the past assures capitalism's success.

Nevertheless, individuals like Stow and his work in literature (Chaucer), history (annals), and geography (London) enabled adoration of the ancient and remote in England's language and politics. Those who identified, gathered, and then made available antiquarian researches on English history produced

editions of Chaucer's works that were keen to solidify an economically, politically, and literarily apt identity for the English nation. The same antiquari-
anism and obsessive scholarship characterize the next edition of Chaucer's
works, produced at the end of the sixteenth century during the reign of Elizabeth I. The folio Thomas Speght published in 1598 and amplified in 1602
ratifies Chaucer's iconic status in a fashion especially sympathetic to modern
tastes: Speght provides a biography for Chaucer with the help of antiquarian
records and manuscript documents, since personal knowledge like Hoccleve's
was no longer available.

Biography did not have the cultural weight in the medieval era that it began
to have in the Renaissance. Medieval manuscript books frequently list no
authors' names, let alone any information about them. Much that we know
about named authors comes from research into legal documents rather than
by consulting autobiographies, which essentially did not exist as a specific
genre until later. Chaucer's first readers who encountered his name and work
in Hoccleve or even Stow expressed no need for biographical information
about the poet, perhaps because it was assumed they already knew him: at
least, that's how Chaucer's contemporary Hoccleve expresses it. The original
assumption of personal knowledge isn't so far-fetched: considering the limited
literate audience and scarce production of manuscripts, an early fifteenth-
century lay reader would likely move in court circles.

To identify text with biography in post-medieval books shapes the taste
of a readership newly broadened by the printing press. Modern readers take
for granted the way a life informs a work, and vice versa. In the opening
years of the seventeenth century, the expectations of authorship changed, and
the habits of print that include biography certify firmer identity between an
individual's creative work and life story. Perhaps Chaucer's biography was
thought to make up for his poor readability. Through the seventeenth century, the disused rules of the English language that governed pronunciation of
Chaucer's over 200-year-old verse continued to fade from collective memory.
Thus, while the volumes gather hundreds of pages of English poetry, they
were little read. Chaucer's iconic status rested on affirmation of his ancient
English character and reputation rather than on appreciation of his verse.

THE RIVAL POPULARITIES OF CHAUCER AND GOWER

But, even granting a dearth of real readers, Chaucer was not universally
admired in the sixteenth and seventeenth centuries. His *Canterbury Tales*
became, for some, a signal of moral degradation. From the middle of the
sixteenth century and to its end, Chaucer's rival for affection and adula-
tion as England's premiere national poet was his contemporary John Gower
(ca. 1330–1408). The historical Chaucer and Gower knew each other in
their lifetimes; they refer to each other in their poetry. Both Chaucer and
Gower were printed by Caxton: Gower's long English poem, *Confessio*

amantis, appeared in 1483, the same year Caxton printed Chaucer's *Canterbury Tales* and *Troilus and Criseyde*. Thomas Berthelet, the self-proclaimed
King's Printer, brought out the *Confessio* in 1532, the same year that Thynne
brought out his works of Chaucer—printed by Berthelet. The *Confessio* was
reprinted, perhaps by other hands, in 1554, as Thynne's Chaucer edition was
reprinted two more times before Stow's version appeared in 1561. The editions of Gower's *Confessio* do not have the weight of contemporary Chaucer folios: with about 190 leaves, or about 400 pages, they do not have the
heft of Chaucer's well over 500 pages. But despite a reduced number of editions and copies, and despite the fifteenth century's identification of Chaucer
as England's literary icon, sixteenth-century Gower gave sixteenth-century
Chaucer a run for his money. Gower's tomb, in London's Southwark Cathedral, predates Chaucer's in Westminster, but Southwark was smaller than
Westminster and was identified with the monastic Augustinians rather than
having the political foundation Westminster enjoyed: Southwark earned its
designation as cathedral in 1905. Gower had a hand in his tomb's design, although its modern version is in large part a reconstruction. Perhaps Gower's
interest in a permanent chantry for his remains says more about his self-
opinion and attempts to foster his reputation than it does about his piety.
But it is for his piety, especially as foil to Chaucer, that Gower was known in
the sixteenth century.

In the complicated religious politics of the successive reigns of Henry VIII's
three children, Gower possessed the epithet "moral Gower." The phrase was
used not only to tout his work but to distinguish it from Chaucer's. In an era
riven by sectarian politics and religious foment, reformist mentalities preferred
"moral Gower" to his opposing number's racy *Canterbury Tales*. Truth be
told, a fair number of *The Canterbury Tales* are naughty: "The Miller's Tale"
is the best-told dirty joke in the English language. YouTube versions of it run
a close second to "Pardoner's Tale" videos. As for the sixteenth century, some
writers use the phrase "Canterbury Tale" as a code for scurrility. One drama-
tist, Robert Greene (1558–1592), actually constructs a prose dream vision
in which Chaucer and Gower visit him as he struggles with his legacy and
the immoral books he has produced. The dream's Chaucer supports Green's
less-than-pious collection of stories as an excellent legacy, but "moral Gower"
lectures Green on the error of his ways (with not a joke in sight). Through the
intercession of a biblical *deus ex machina*, King Solomon advises Greene that
wisdom and theology should be his only study. Greene credits Gower with
showing him the way to repent of his works and immoral behavior, and, when
the vision ends, Greene promises to leave all thoughts of love, instead devoting
himself to produce fruit of better labors.

Besides moral Gower in Greene's book, other sixteenth- and seventeenth-
century references to Chaucer and Gower show that Greene's opinion had
traction. For instance, Sir Philip Sydney's *Apologie for Poetry* notes Chaucer's
"great wants." But in the number of sixteenth-century editions published,
Chaucer outshone Gower brightly. Gower's work saw printing only once in

the sixteenth century, in 1554, in contrast to the many printings of Chaucer's works. No seventeenth-century Gower edition exists. Indeed, Gower's work wasn't republished until the nineteenth century. Perhaps fame needs a racy edge to reach the height of iconic status. Chaucer's work, though little read, inhabited sixteenth-century literary history and nationalist narratives and found printers for editions in the seventeenth, eighteenth, and nineteenth centuries.

The world of narrative literature itself changed in the seventeenth and eighteenth centuries, and not just because of the availability of books. Perhaps it was Roger Ascham, Queen Elizabeth I's tutor, who praised Chaucer as the English Homer to keep alive Chaucer's reputation as excellent versifier and epic poet. The attribution seems somewhat forced in light of the difficulty readers had with Chaucer's Middle English, pronounced and poetically scanned differently from modern English. Perhaps this difficulty prompted Sir Philip Sydney in his classic *Apologie for Poetry* (1581) to forgive Chaucer his "great wants," his deficiencies, because he had in the main "beautified our mother tongue."

CHAUCER AND THE ENLIGHTENMENT

By the eighteenth century, the winds of taste blew away the ostensible messes Chaucer (and Shakespeare) had made of English literature in order to install a new English classicism. As already noted, "classicism" as both concept and word took off in the eighteenth century. Enlightenment poets concentrated on reviving not English classics but Greek and Latin classics translated into English. Chaucer's legacy eventually fell into the hands of Alexander Pope and other poets of England's Enlightenment era. These Augustan poets professed disdain for the quaint relics of the past. They nevertheless paid obeisance to Chaucer's Ghost, as one work (1672) termed it. But that reverence did not include new editions, only reprints of his work. Speght's edition was reprinted in 1672, and no new Chaucer edition appeared, nor were old ones reprinted again, before two decades of the eighteenth century had already passed. The seventeenth century transformed Chaucer from an important and original antique voice whose poetry was little read, and even then with difficulty, to a quaint curiosity unenlightened and unadmired but for his (accidental) Englishness. In his *God's Plenty* (1700), John Dryden labels Chaucer "a rough diamond" who "mingles trivial things with those of greater moment." The icon kept standing almost as a curiosity.

Still, Pope admired Chaucer's storytelling ability despite the contemporary taste for Latin- and Greek-sounding poetry. Perhaps it was Pope's Catholicism that allowed him to admire Chaucer's works. The historical Chaucer was, of course, Catholic insofar as any fourteenth-century Christian was "catholic." Perhaps Chaucer's sixteenth-century Protestant editors had amplified the non-Chaucerian works in their editions in order to remove the poet's Catholic taint. Certainly their addition of anti-Catholic polemics under Chaucer's name was meant to recoup Chaucer as an English Protestant *avant la lettre*. But despite the need to recreate Chaucer as English Protestant, and also to situate him in the thick of English literary history, not very many readers were doing more than handling Chaucer's texts in old editions. While Chaucer continued to be referred to as the "father of English poetry," as he had been for quite some time, his works themselves had little purchase on the reading classes of eighteenth-century England. Schooling may have been slightly more available in the eighteenth century, but higher education concentrated on the Greek and Roman classics and left English literature out in the cold. And, beside the near unreadability of Chaucer's texts, self-professed English writers like Daniel Defoe thought Chaucer's lewdness explained the justifiable burial of his works.

Support for Chaucer's poetry and iconic status in spite of his supposed scurrility and difficult language found one interested party at the beginning of the eighteenth century, and a new edition of Chaucer's works finally caught up with this new appreciation. Unlike Speght, who merely included a glossary of "hard words explained," John Urry in his 1721 edition modernized Chaucer's language and made his verse widely readable. At least now Chaucer's metrics had been codified and the pronunciation of his verse was better understood. Not that Urry neglects a glossary, a feature included in all Chaucer editions to this day. Urry's readable Chaucer still retains the poet's original flavor and touts his paternity of English letters. The edition's biography calls Chaucer "a great scholar, a pleasant wit, a candid critic, a sociable companion, a steadfast friend, a grave philosopher, a temperate economist [!] and a pious Christian." A witty economist Chaucer given to friendship and conviviality reflects the values of eighteenth-century society: protean Chaucer, retaining his iconic status, acquires an eighteenth-century impress that makes him simultaneously venerably revered and contemporarily recognizable. The impulse, if not the exact fashion, of modernization persists in YouTube productions of Chaucer.

Even when his poetry was little read, Chaucer's iconic status is verified by the fact that admirers and detractors alike had to reckon with his reputation as Father of English Poetry. Even those who lament his lack of decorum—a signal eighteenth-century literary value—still recognized his poetic virtuosity or, as one critic labeled it (Joseph Warton, 1782), "a mine of gold." Surely eighteenth-century England's ambivalent attitude toward its poetic icon comes from efforts of poets like Pope not only to find their poetic voices in classical antecedents but to denigrate as "barbarous" the inescapable Middle English in which Chaucer wrote. But the attraction of Chaucer's "barbarous" voice and his identity with England's Celtic and Saxon past gained a foothold in the mid-eighteenth century. A Gothic impulse, still familiar today in the television horror series *Tales from the Crypt* (1989–96) gave new inspiration to English novels like Horace Walpole's *The Castle of Otranto*. An antiquarian interest in and general revival of Scots bards and Welsh poets, even in patent forgeries like the Ossian poems, makes Chaucer look downright modern even as burgeoning Romantic attitudes began to celebrate the awesome and antique as essential and authentic.

CHAUCER IN THE NINETEENTH CENTURY

William Godwin (1756–1836), father of *Frankenstein*'s author, Mary Shelley, reflected this new adoration of the Gothic allied with Romantic heroism in his biography of Chaucer (1803). Moving his reader's imagination further back in time, past the already remote sixteenth century, Godwin pointed to the "times of Chaucer" as more obviously and unquestionably barbaric than the times of that other English barbarian, Shakespeare. Chaucer, unlike Shakespeare, had the "single mind" to effect a restoration of poetry and the Muses to England's rocky shore by "fix[ing] and naturalis[ing] the genuine art of poetry in our island." Chaucer thus became the uniquely rugged and effective individual, the man of genius every Romantic heart claimed for its own. In the hands of William Blake, in his engraving of the *Canterbury Tales* pilgrims, Chaucer becomes the "great poetical observer of men," as well as master, father, and superior. Chaucer caught the sacred inspiration, according to Shelley. Adoration of Chaucer's realism, aided and abetted by widely readable editions of his work, made him into a figure of his time who was ironically not only capable of transcending it but friendly to his readers in the bargain. What better definition of iconic status?

Mass production in the nineteenth century enabled an enormous monumentalizing of Chaucer's iconic status. His cause was taken up by the Arts and Crafts movement and William Morris, whose Kelmscott Press produced an illustrated *Canterbury Tales* of enormous popularity. The signal temperament of English nostalgia can be summed up in the phrase "Merrie Olde England," and Chaucer was made to stand at the head of this nostalgic attitude's parade. Not unlike the Romantic gestures that certified Chaucer's individual genius in the early part of the nineteenth century, the mid-nineteenth century identified him with the beginnings of English literary enterprise in relation to moral truth. John Ruskin, prolific Victorian critic, teacher, and moralizer, considered Chaucer for the English the equal of Virgil for the Latins, teaching the purest theology. This feat could be accomplished, of course, only by leaving *The Canterbury Tales* out of the curriculum. Be that as it may, Chaucer's iconic identity with the English mind was a mainstay of nineteenth-century appreciations of the poet. Other assessments followed the changing currents of nineteenth-century literary aspirations, such that the literary aesthetics of Chaucer's poetry began to take primary position.

The nineteenth century saw another change in its intellectual landscape that affected the way Chaucer was read and understood. Nineteenth-century philology and linguistics made the recognition and description of a language's predictable changes in sound a scientific enterprise. Moreover, manuscript studies in the later nineteenth and early twentieth century professionalized the reading of Chaucer's poetry and led to a disconnect between those who read Chaucer for pleasure and those who studied his poetry in the academy. The Modern Language Association fought for the reading of the "modern languages," such as English and French, alongside classical Greek and Latin, which were the stuff of a college education (in 1900 only 10 percent of the American population pursued a high school education, let alone attended college). Although a nostalgia for "Merrie Olde England" kept a mostly modernized form of Chaucer in the public eye, including in children's books, in the first part of the twentieth century the professionalization of literary criticism began to take hold.

CHAUCER AND THE TWENTIETH AND TWENTY-FIRST CENTURIES

Some twentieth-century poets found themselves in Chaucer. Yeats praised Chaucer for his masculinity and vitality. Others praised his refinement; still others, his earthy physicality. His cheerfulness did not match modernism's seriousness, but among Chaucer's best twentieth-century readers was Virginia Woolf. She tangled with an iconic Chaucer in her *Common Reader*, and she discerns Chaucer's interest in nature (like a Romantic poet) coupled with a keen, realistic eye (like a modern novelist) that helps readers "make out a meaning for ourselves." This liberal tendency, coupled with an admiration for realism, brought Chaucer's iconic status into the twentieth century, where, through the wonders of cinema and YouTube, he has persisted in the modern imagination. Even as the Academy claims expertise in Chaucer's language and tends to denigrate popular culture's regard for the poet, a healthy cadre of lay readers continue to enjoy Chaucer's poetry.

Perhaps not all contemporary medieval-themed enterprises that employ the icon of Geoffrey Chaucer cave as blatantly to modernization as *A Knight's Tale*, but many do. A very funny Chaucer comes to life in the visitor attraction "The Canterbury Tales: Medieval Misadventures," just minutes from Canterbury Cathedral in historic Kent (see www.canterburytales.org.uk/home.htm). In the attraction, life-sized figures move à la Disney to enact five of the *Tales*, not surprisingly the five most frequently anthologized: "The Knight's Tale," "The Miller's Tale," "The Wife of Bath's Tale," "The Nun's Priest's Tale," and "The Pardoner's Tale." A sound system carries the walk-through narrative and a mostly Modern English reading of selected passages from the *Tales*. Multilingual audio guides can be had for a price. Still, like all things coded "medieval," the animatronics remain in semi-darkness, a subtle coding of the earlier "Dark Ages." Although it's a stretch to find anything remotely sublime about the poetic icon in the tourist attraction, "The Canterbury Tales" re-certifies for twenty-first-century tourists not Chaucer's attachment to the cathedral but the creative engine of his imagination tangling the medieval literal—the pilgrimage and its trudging steps—with the medieval virtual— tale-telling and an infinite variety of stories. Chaucer's identity as both poet and pilgrim, his seemingly bumbling narrator persona, and his constant attempts to blur the line between reality and fiction serve as continuous features of an iconic Chaucer.

YouTube Chaucer videos are amateurish and short. On the other hand, British novelist and screenwriter Jonathan Myerson has written and directed a very slick three-part version of *The Canterbury Tales* (1998 and 2000) that employs Claymation and other techniques of animation. Joining twentieth-century professionalism with good old-fashioned business sense, Myerson consulted academic Chaucerians for details of his production while also signing up the BBC and HBO as distributors. Several teams of animators, using visually different styles, produced 10 tales in nine episodes (The tales of the Miller and the Reeve are combined). Myerson's series also includes the frame story of the pilgrimage to Canterbury and a set of links between the tales, and his Chaucer looks as an iconic Chaucer should: hooded eyes, pointed beard, slight paunch. Even Alexander Pope would recognize him. Just like the portraits in the Hoccleve manuscript and everywhere else, though produced with the wonders of animated plasticene, the forked beard, slight pot belly, and hooded eyes are paired with a gentle demeanor that strongly contrasts with the wild and wooly Miller. Myerson originally provided two soundtracks for his videos: one in Middle English, the other modernized. In this, Myerson harks back to a sensibility born in the eighteenth century that, through modernization, encouraged the reading of the *Tales,* instead of antiquarian or purely iconic admiration.

A network television phenomenon that has kept iconic Chaucer in the public eye is a live-action series made for the BBC of six updated *Canterbury Tales* (2003). Sally Wainwright adapted "The Wife of Bath's Tale" and set it on and behind the stage of a soap opera; Peter Bowker's "The Miller's Tale" updates the funniest narrative in English with a pub, karaoke night, and false promises of fame; "The Knight's Tale," adapted by Tony Marchant, begins with jail and two prisoners falling in love with their teacher; Avie Luthra's "The Sea Captain's [Shipman's] Tale" concerns a love triangle in an Asian community in Gravesend, Kent, outside London and on the Thames; Rochester, east of Gravesend, is the setting for the three drunken rioters of "The Pardoner's Tale," adapted by Tony Grounds; and Olivia Hetreed sets her adaptation of "The Man of Law's Tale" in Chatham, just down the road from Gravesend, with an amnesiac yet pious Nigerian filling in for the Christian Constance.

The problem with adaptations like this high-budget BBC effort is the relentless normalizing of Chaucer's social world, not to mention his language. The commercial structures of London, Gravesend, Rochester, and Chatham may arguably have their roots in the late Middle Ages, but the triumph of commercialism that controls the modern imagination could not have been envisioned in Chaucer's time. In addition, regularization and familiarization rob *The Canterbury Tales* of their alterity and shortchange the audience of an opportunity to grapple with that alterity. Of course, such adaptations of

Chaucer fit the long history of his iconic status: reshaped, refolded to fit alternately others' Protestant and Catholic, national and provincial, sublime and scurrilous agendas. Can we ever define a "real" Geoffrey Chaucer?

CONCLUSIONS

What is the future of Geoffrey Chaucer? Although in the United States the College Board no longer requires students to recognize Chaucer's poetry, the number of *Canterbury Tales* projects on YouTube indicates that Chaucer remains protean, funny, rhymed, and mischievously attractive for the twenty-first century. It's easy to consider Chaucer's icon as eternal, having lasted for six hundred years through adaptation, manipulation, and commercial viability. Chaucer became very quickly a totem for Englishness, at once linguistic, national, and personal. His poetry's ambiguities in voice, character, plot, and interpretation make his work stand the test of time. But Chaucer's iconic status is not all about Chaucer, nor is it under Chaucer's control. We see in our icons what we project onto them, even as the icons themselves must have a protean nature to survive that amount of projection. The past speaks to us through these icons, and we can get over our obsession with one kind of authenticity if we can accept an icon's fame as dynamic, rather than static. Moreover, in Chaucer's case (and maybe that of other poets too, but not other Fathers of English Poetry, for only one exists), the continuity of his iconic status is assured by the pleasing proliferation of YouTube Chaucers. Icons are more than images, and the ease with which Chaucer has entered the Internet age (how many YouTube William Wordsworths are there?) bodes well for his continued iconic presence as England's medieval poet *par excellence*.

FURTHER READING

Editions

Benson, Larry D., ed. *The Riverside Chaucer*. 3rd ed. Boston: Houghton Mifflin, 1987. (This is the edition on which all professional scholars depend.)

Ellis, Steve. *Chaucer: The Canterbury Tales*. London: Longman, 1998.

Kolve, V.A., ed. *The Canterbury Tales: Nine Tales and the General Prologue*. New York: Norton, 1989.

Lynch, Kathryn L., ed. *Geoffrey Chaucer: Dream Visions & Other Poems*. New York: Norton, 2007.

Guides

Boitani, Piero, and Jill Mann, eds. *The Cambridge Chaucer Companion*. Cambridge: Cambridge University Press, 1986.

Bowden, Muriel. *A Reader's Guide to Geoffrey Chaucer*. Syracuse, NY: Syracuse University Press, 2001.

Brewer, Derek. *An Introduction to Chaucer*. London: Longman, 1984.

Brewer, Derek. *A New Introduction to Chaucer*. London: Longman, 1998.

Cooper, Helen. *The Canterbury Tales*. Oxford Guides to Chaucer. Oxford: Oxford University Press, 1989.

Ellis, Steve, ed. *Chaucer: An Oxford Guide*. Oxford: Oxford University Press, 2005.

Gray, Douglas, ed. *The Oxford Companion to Chaucer*. New York: Oxford University Press, 2003.

Minnis, Alistair J. *The Shorter Poems*. Oxford Guides to Chaucer. Oxford: Oxford University Press, 1995.

Rossignol, Rosalyn. *Critical Companion to Chaucer: A Literary Reference to His Life and Works*. New York: Facts On File, 2007.

Windeatt, Barry. *Troilus and Criseyde*. Oxford Guides to Chaucer. Oxford: Oxford University Press, 1992.

Biography

Brewer, Derek. *Chaucer in His Time*. London: Nelson, 1963.

Crow, Martin M., and Claire C. Olson, eds. *Chaucer Life Records*. Oxford: Oxford University Press, 1966.

Gardner, John. *The Life and Times of Chaucer*. New York: Knopf, 1977.

Howard, Donald. *Chaucer: His Life, His Works, His World*. New York: Dutton, 1987.

Pearsall, Derek A. *The Life of Geoffrey Chaucer: A Critical Biography*. Oxford: Blackwell, 1992.

Language

Burnley, David J. *A Guide to Chaucer's Language*. Norman: University of Oklahoma Press, 1983.

Davis, Norman, Douglas Gray, Patricia Ingham, and Anne Wallace-Hadrill. *A Chaucer Glossary*. Oxford: Clarendon Press, 1979.

Dillon, Bert. *A Chaucer Dictionary: Proper Names and Allusions. Excluding Place Names*. Boston: G. K. Hall, 1974.

Reception

Barrington, Candace. *American Chaucers*. New York: Palgrave MacMillan, 2007.

Boswell, Jackson Campbell, and Sylvia Wallace Holton. *Chaucer's Fame in England: STC Chauceriana 1475–1640*. New York: MLA, 2004.

Brewer, Derek. *Geoffrey Chaucer: The Critical Heritage*. London: Routledge, 1995.

Bryan, W. F., and G. Dempster, eds. *Sources and Analogues of Chaucer's Canterbury Tales*. Chicago, 1941. (Currently being updated as *Sources and Analogues of the Canterbury Tales*. Gen. ed. Robert E. Correale; associate gen. ed. Mary Hamel. Cambridge: D. S. Brewer, from 2002 [two volumes have appeared].)

Dane, Joseph. *Who's Buried in Chaucer's Tomb? Studies in the Reception of Chaucer's Book*. East Lansing: Michigan State University Press, 1998.

Ellis, Steve. *Chaucer at Large: The Poet in the Modern Imagination*. Minneapolis: University of Minnesota Press, 2000.

Forni, Kathleen. *The Chaucerian Apocrypha: A Counterfeit Canon*. Gainesville: University Press of Florida, 2001.

Prendergast, Thomas A. *Chaucer's Dead Body: from Corpse to Corpus*. New York: Routledge, 2004.

Prendergast, Thomas A. *Rewriting Chaucer: Culture, Authority, and the Idea of the Authentic Text, 1400–1602*. Columbus: Ohio State University Press, 1999.

Spurgeon, C.F.E. *Five Hundred Years of Chaucer Criticism and Allusion, 1357–1900*. 3 vols. Cambridge: Cambridge University Press, 1925.

Trigg, Stephanie. *Congenial Souls: Reading Chaucer from Medieval to Postmodern*. Minneapolis: University of Minnesota Press, 2002.

Selected Critical Studies

Aers, David. *Chaucer, Langland and the Creative Imagination*. London: Routledge, 1980.

Dinshaw, Carolyn. *Chaucer's Sexual Poetics*. Madison: University of Wisconsin Press, 1989.

Gibaldi, Joseph, ed. *Approaches to Teaching Chaucer's Canterbury Tales*. New York: MLA,1980.

Muscatine, Charles. *Chaucer and the French Tradition: A Study in Style and Meaning*. Berkeley: University of California Press, 1957.

Strohm, Paul. *Social Chaucer*. Cambridge, MA: Harvard University Press, 1989.

Yearbook and Journal

For specialists, *Studies in the Age of Chaucer* is the annual publication of the New Chaucer Society. *The Chaucer Review* is another source for up-to-the-minute scholarship on Chaucer.

Websites

The Geoffrey Chaucer Website Homepage (materials used in Harvard University Chaucer courses): http://www.people.fas.harvard.edu/~chaucer/.

METRO (Middle English Teaching Resources Online), hosted by Harvard University (a resource for teaching Middle English, with much of the site devoted to Chaucer): http://metro.fas.harvard.edu.

The New Chaucer Society: http://artsci.wustl.edu/~chaucer/index.php.

Portrait of Chinggis Khan (ink and watercolor on silk), date unknown, Chinese.
(National Palace Museum, Taipei, Taiwan/The Bridgeman Art Library)

Chinggis Khan
(ca. 1167–1227)

George Lane

Chinggis Khan, conqueror of the world, loomed large in the nightmares of medieval Europeans, and his image haunts the conscience if not nightmares of European and American leaders today as they instigate the return of Mongol troops to the ruins of Baghdad in what some see as a rerun of history. The man who became the myth lives on through a legacy that is very much alive and thriving today in many different guises and a multitude of conceptions throughout the lands where he and his immediate descendants first established their writ. DNA analysis suggests that the man is literally responsible for as much as 1 percent of the male population of the planet and his legacy is peopling rather than de-peopling the world, the association that has so often been coupled with Eurasia's greatest hero, Chinggis Khan.

Freed from the shackles of Soviet political correctness, Russia's easterly neighbors have reinstated their most famous ruler to the heroic and sometimes even divine status of which he is more deserving than either the dismissive or the demonic status he "enjoyed" under Soviet patronage. The demonic Genghis Khan and his "Storm from the East" found himself seated alongside Hitler and Stalin as visitations from hell in the European pantheon of evil. Therefore when the newly liberated former communist states adopted Chinggis Khan as a role model and national hero and, in the case of Mongolia, as very much the national hero and the embodiment of the state, it shocked much of the world. However, this shock was not universal, and what was also surprising was the number of countries that shared, if not the hero worshipping of the Great Khan, certainly a deep respect and admiration for the Mongolian conqueror. China had adopted the Mongol emperors as their own, Turkey had always viewed the horsemen from the East with approval, Iran certainly recognized that the Mongol century represented a golden age in literature and the arts, and Central Asia was in the process of raising Timür Khan onto a pedestal while recognizing their own hero's debt to the Mongol conqueror.

Realizing that some kind of reassessment of history was urgently needed, scholars were quick to dust off the many long-neglected tomes and examine again the many florid words and illustrated manuscripts in a rich array of tongues and from a exotic collection of courts, composed by eyewitnesses and participants in the history of that time. What began as a revisionist trickle has since the year 2000 become an increasingly excited torrent, and today the study of Chinggis Khan and the Mongol Empire is a particularly exciting field of history in which to be involved.

Temüjin (the future Chinggis Khan) was born into the Turco-Mongol world of nomadic pastoralists who inhabited the vast steppes of Eurasia. Much of his early life is obscure and clouded in both mystery and myth. This includes the date of his birth, for which at least three dates are widely cited. The year 1155 is cited by Rashīd al-Dīn (d. 1318), the historian and grand wazir (the equivalent of prime minister) at the court of the Persian Mongols; 1162 by the *Yuan shi*, a history of the Mongol Yüan dynasty of China compiled and edited by Ming scholars (1368–1644); and 1167 by various traditions citing direct and indirect evidence. While May 3, 1162, remains his official date of birth in the Mongolian Republic and 1162 is accepted in China and Russia, it is the last date, 1167, that most Western historians consider most likely and that most logically ties in with later recorded events in the Conqueror's life.[1] However, de Rachewiltz, in his definitive edition of the anonymous *Secret History of the Mongols*, has backed 1162 as the year of Chinggis Khan's birth, and it is very probable that he will be granted the last word. What all the histories agree is that the infant was born in Del'iun-bolduk on the Onon River, and many embellish this fact with the tradition that tight in his tiny hand he was clutching a clot of blood as big as a knucklebone.[2] Temüjin was related to the Tayichi'ut, a forest tribe of hunters and fishers, through his father and was related to the Mongol Onggirat tribe on his mother's side.

The Tatars were the dominant Turco-Mongol tribe at that time and enjoyed the support of the powerful, sedentary Chin dynasty (1115–1234) of the Jurchens from the settled north of China. A symbiotic relationship existed between the steppe and the sown (that is, nomads and agriculturists), and though this association is often portrayed as marked by animosity and incompatibility, the bonds uniting the two were strong and deep. By tradition, the Chins would ally themselves with one of the nomadic steppe tribes to encourage rivalry and thereby increase their own security. Tatars were one of a number of nomadic Turco-Mongolian tribes, but it was their name that became a generic term for all the Turco-Mongol tribes in Europe, possibly because of its resemblance to the Latin *Tartar* meaning "hell," and by implication people who emanated from hell. Because it was also a generic term for the Mongol tribes in western Asia, the explanation for this widespread adoption of the generic term could simply be that the Tatars were early the most successful, well known, and powerful of the nomadic steppe tribes. However, the identification of the Mongols with the mythical Gog and Magog was common throughout the Islamo-Christian world. At that time, these foul monsters were commonly believed to have been imprisoned by Alexander the Great beyond "Alexander's Gate" (the Derband pass, Daghestan, Russia). According to the Book of Revelations, they would be unleashed upon Jerusalem and the world before the Final Judgment, thus the apocalyptic stories circulating about the Mongols seemed to be confirming the veracity of this prophecy.

The main literary sources for Chinggis Khan's early life are the anonymous *Secret History of the Mongols* and Rashīd al-Dīn's *Compendium of Chronicles*[3] (*Jāmiᶜ al-Tavārīkh*). The former is the only literary text written in Mongolian about the Mongol Empire. It presented historians with some unique problems when it was first discovered. Because Mongolian was not a written language before the rise of Chinggis Khan, the original *History* had been written down in an adaptation of the Uyghur script; however, the surviving texts are all copies of painstaking transcriptions into Chinese characters, divorced from their Chinese meaning, that were phonetically equivalent to spoken Mongolian. It was written in the Year of the Rat, which would correspond to either 1228, the year after Chinggis Khan's death, or 1240, the year before the death of Ögödei, Chinggis's son and successor. In fact, it seems likely that the original text might have been completed during Ögödei's enthronement and certain abridgments and additional material concerning Ögödei's reign added later, in which case both dates could be correct. In fact it is now believed that substantial editorial adjustments and additions were made during Ögödei's reign. The author or compilers of this unique work remain unknown, and the history's English translator, Arthur Waley, dismissed it as fiction and fable. However, the *Secret History* has formed the framework of most accounts of Chinggis Khan's early life, providing the essential chronology and background, and much of what the history relates can be corroborated in a general sense from other primary sources.

Corroboration and a test of the *Secret History*'s reliability can be gained from a work compiled some 80 or so years later. Rashīd al-Dīn's *Compendium of Histories* used various Chinese sources for its extensive portrayal of early Mongol and Turkish history. These early Oriental chronicles are no longer extant, and almost the only known description of their content and the sole source providing access to their knowledge is from Grand Wazir Rashīd al-Dīn's laboriously recorded chronicles. Rashīd al-Dīn, who was among many things a serious historian, had unparalleled access to Mongol and Chinese sources, many of which were forbidden to non-Mongols, through his friendship with the Mongol administrator, entrepreneur, cultural broker, and diplomat Bolad Aqa.[4] In particular, Rashīd al-Dīn was able to utilize the *Altan Debter*, an official Mongol history with a strictly restricted circulation, which independently corroborated much of the background and substance of the stories reported in the *Secret History*. Rashīd al-Dīn was commissioned to write his *Compendium of Histories*, the *Jāmiʿ al-Tavārīkh,* by Sultan Ghazan Khan, the first Mongol ruler of Iran to convert to Islam. Ghazan had a deep interest in history and recognized that scholars in the Mongol courts had unprecedented access to the representatives of peoples from all over the world.

> In these days when, thank God, all corners of the earth are under [Mongol] control, and philosophers, astronomers, scholars, and historians of all religions and nations . . . are gathered in droves . . . and each and every one of them possesses copies, stories, and beliefs of their own people . . . the opportunity is at hand, [for] the composition of such a [history] the likes of which no king has ever possessed.[5]

Central to Rashīd al-Dīn's history was of course Chinggis Khan, and the grand wazir and his team had unlimited access to all available, extant sources. Due to the wazir's friendship with the Yuan ambassador to the Ilkhanid court, the remarkable Mongol courtier and Renaissance man Bolad Aqa Chīnksānk, he also had access to restricted Mongol documents normally for the eyes of the Mongol nobility only.

Much speculation has been offered regarding the authorship of the *Secret History*, but all that appears certain is that it was written from within the Mongol court and while avoiding too exaggerated panegyrics, its author is sympathetic to the image of Temüjin succeeding despite the opposition and treachery of the other khans. Chinggis Khan's considerable political skills are downplayed while the inevitability of his rise and the defeat of those who sought to oppose him through intrigue and perfidy are stressed. Speculation has even extended to the history having been written by a woman, evidenced apparently by inclusion of such anecdotes as Temüjin's fear of dogs and his childhood murder of his half-brother. The history contains a wealth of detail concerning the minutiae of Mongol camp life, detail that puts to rest the traditional theory that the Mongols had no interest or aptitude for administration and bureaucracy.

EARLY LIFE

Temüjin's early life was punctuated by four defining incidents: the murder of his father and the family's subsequent fall into near destitution; his murder of Bekhter, his half-brother; his kidnapping by the Tayichi'ut; and the abduction of his bride, Börte Füjin.

Though not born into the nobility, Temüjin's early circumstances were respectable, and his father, Yesügei, the son of Bartan-Baghatur, is generally recognized as a minor chieftain though not as a khan. His grandfather, Qabul Khan, was recognized as a *khagan,* or chieftain, by the Chins. Qabul Khan was a grandson of Qaidu Khan, who is credited with being the first leader to attempt to unify the Mongol tribes.

Temüjin's mother, Hö'elun, was from the Olkhunut forest tribe; she had been abducted by Yesügei and his brothers from her newlywed husband of the Merkit tribe as she and her husband were traveling back to the Merkit camp. Yesügei then made Hö'elun his chief wife, who would bear his heirs. Though abduction was a common and traditional form of marriage, the custom continued to cause resentment and anger, and it was a common cause of hostility and intertribal warfare.

Temüjin's mother, Hö'elun, bore Yesügei Bahadur[6] three more sons, Khasar, Khajiun, and Temüge, and lastly one daughter, Temulin, born when her oldest was nine. There were also two other brothers, Bekhter and Belgutei, from a second wife. The family had their base by the River Onon, where the children learned riding and archery from an early age. During these years Temüjin formed a close friendship with Jamuka, a son from a neighboring family, with whom he formed a blood-brothership (*anda*) by exchanging knucklebones and arrows. The relationship between *andas* was often considered stronger than that between blood brothers and could not be lightly set aside. It was also during this time that Temüjin's father arranged his nine-year-old son's marriage to Börte Füjin, a daughter of Dei-sechen, from the Boskur tribe, a subgroup of a leading Mongol tribe, the Onggirad. Upon departing from the bride's father's camp, leaving his son with his new in-laws, Yesügei Bahadur passed by a group of Tatars who had struck camp to eat. He availed himself of the ancient nomadic custom of hospitality and was invited to share their meal. However, the Tatars recognized him as an enemy who had previously robbed them—"Yesügei the Kiyan has come"[7]—and so poisoned his food. He died upon reaching home and entrusted the loyal Mönglik with ensuring his eldest son's safe return.

After his father's murder, Temüjin's family fortunes declined abruptly, and as eldest son, on whom the responsibility of breadwinner fell, Temüjin was summoned home to provide for his family. His mother famously

> hoisted her skirts up . . . running upstream on the banks of the Onon, gathering wild pear, fruits of the region, nourishing the bellies and throats of her children . . . digging up roots to nourish her children, she fed them with onions, fed them with garlic, saw how the sons of her belly could flourish. . . . Thus on a diet of seeds they were nourished.[8]

This was a harsh and bitterly learned lesson that left a profound impression on his character. The family's predicament worsened when their relatives decided that continued loyalty to a departed leader was strategically prejudicial, politically inopportune, and economically detrimental. Dismissing the nine-year-old Temüjin as too young to lead the clan, Yesügei Bahadur's Tayichi'ut followers, his *nökhöd*, deserted the camp, declaring, "The deep water has dried up; the shining stone is worn away. It is over."[9]

It was not only the *nökhöd*, whose expectations of plunder and martial adventure had now been dashed, who deserted Yesügei's stricken family, but also less explicably the family's close relatives. According to steppe tradition, a widow should be taken in marriage and given protection by the youngest brother, in this case, Da'aritai-otchigin. Hö'elun declined, asserting her wish to raise her family alone. However, as Rashīd al-Dīn records that in fact the bereaved family did receive considerable support from family members including Yesügei's elder brother, Kuchar, this might well be the *Secret History* overdramatizing Temüjin's plight to portray the mounting adversities from which the future world conqueror was so determinedly and remarkably able to extricate himself. What is clear is that times became considerably harder for Hö'elun and her young family, and such filial occupations as horse-rustling became necessities rather than pastimes.

The murder, when he was 13 or 14, of his half-brother, Bekhter, is perhaps the most controversial of the four defining incidents from Temüjin's early life. It is an incident that figures prominently in the *Secret History* but appears to have been ignored in the *Altan Debter,* an official history. Ostensibly the reason behind the murder was the theft of a fish and a lark from Temüjin and his brother, Jochi-Kasar, by the two half-brothers, Bekhter and Belgutei, which highlighted a certain rivalry simmering between the two branches of the family. The official history, the *Altan Debter,* avoids reference to the incident, which undoubtedly besmirches the reputation of Chinggis Khan, whereas the *Secret History* does not hide Hö'elun's grief, shock, and anger at her sons, whom she brands murderers and destroyers.

In response to Bekhter's theft of a fish, an incident that followed accusations of the half-brothers' failure to share their hunting spoils (the division of spoils being a practice sanctified by Mongol custom and tradition), Temüjin and Kasar confronted the older brother, who, apparently accepting his fate, asked only that his younger brother, Belgutei, be spared. Bekhter was dispatched with horn-tipped arrows, and Belgutei was spared to eventually find honor and recognition serving his brother's murderer. Chinggis Khan was later to speak of both brothers, "It is to Belgutei's strength and Kasar's prowess as an archer that I owe the conquest of the World Empire."[10]

It seems likely that more was at stake than ownership of a fish to have caused this fratricide. The age of the half-brothers is not explicitly stated in the sources, and there is evidence suggesting that Bekhter might have been older than Temüjin, in which case he could have been perceived as a threat to Temüjin's leadership of the family. Had Temüjin been the oldest of the boys, such breaches of tradition as the theft and refusal to share hunting spoils could not have occurred, because his status could not have been questioned. Belgutei is reported by Rashīd al-Dīn to have voted in the election of Möngke Qa'an in 1251 before dying in 1255 at the age of 110. While assuming the figure of 110 to be exaggerated but indicative of unusual longevity, it could be that even the younger of the half-brothers was older than Temüjin. However, as the first son of the first wife, Temüjin would have regarded Bekhter's behavior as an infringement upon his privileges, almost as insurrection, and would have felt full justification in meting out appropriate punishment. Bekhter's apparent lack of resistance and his brother's failure to seek revenge suggests that they also understood Temüjin's response.

In the *Secret History*, Temüjin's kidnapping and imprisonment by the Tayichi'ut follow immediately after the account of the murder, though no suggestion is made that the two events were linked other than portraying Temüjin's treatment as that befitting a common criminal. Whether his capture was retribution for the killing or because Tarkutai-Kiriltuk, a leading noble of the Tayichi'ut, considered him a potential rival, or both, is never clarified, and Rashīd al-Dīn suggests that throughout his youth Temüjin suffered continually at the hands of not only relatives from the Tayichi'ut but also rivals from the Merkits, the Tatars, and other tribes. Such tribulations were hardly uncommon for the young Turco-Mongols, and kidnappings for ransom, for servants, or even for forced fighters were not uncommon, as the many examples mentioned in the *Secret History* testify.

The *Secret History* recounts how Temüjin cleverly planned and calmly executed his escape. He chose to flee on the night of a feast, when he knew his guards would be distracted. Still wearing the wooden *cangue* his captors had put him in (a sort of collar immobilizing the head and both arms), he plunged into a river. By using the *cangue* as a flotation device, he was able to lie on the bed of the river and keep his head above water. In this manner he bided his time. He was discovered by Sorqan-shira, of the small Suldus tribe, who rather than betraying him assisted the fugitive in his escape. Sorqan-shira, like others who were to follow him, said of Temüjin, "There is a fire in his eyes and a light in his face."[11] Rejecting the advice of his savior to head straight for his family's camp, Temüjin sought out the camp of Sorqan himself, where he knew Sorqan's children were sympathetic toward him. While the *Secret History* might well have embellished this anecdote somewhat, the essential elements of Temüjin's character remain evident. The careful planning, the self-control, the understanding of people, the awareness of his powers over others and young people in particular, the lack of impulsiveness—these were all qualities that he was to develop over the next decades. The lessons he learned from this encounter with the Tayichi'ut were never to be forgotten.

The fourth defining incident in Temüjin's early life resulted in a gradual turn in his fortunes and the beginning of his rise to unifier of the Turco-Mongol tribes. This incident was the kidnapping of his bride, Börte Füjin, by the Merkits, and the repercussions were to echo far into the future political history of the Mongol Empire.

Not long after his escape from the Tayichi'ut and having reached the age of 15, the Mongol age of majority, Temüjin returned to reclaim his bride Börte Füjin from her father, Dei-sechen. He also sought to consolidate himself as head of his small tribe and gather supporters and outside protection that he might never again to fall victim to the dictates and bullying of neighboring tribes. To this end, he summoned his friend and fellow horse-rustler, Bo'orchu; collected his brothers, Kasar with his bow and Belgutei with his axe; packed his wife's wedding gift, a sable cloak, as a very persuasive and valuable offering; and set off in search of a powerful protector.

Parallels between Temüjin and the leader he chose as his protector are possible. Toghrul, the leader of the powerful Keraits, had been abducted by the Merkits when he was a boy and, for a while, forced into hard labor. Later, at 13, he and his mother were carried off by the Tatars, and the young Toghrul was made to tend their camels. After the death of his father, the young Toghrul also murdered his brother and as a result became head of his family. This role was short-lived: as a consequence of the murder of his brother, his uncle forced him into exile. It was Temüjin's father who assisted the exiled Toghrul, the two becoming *anda,* and together they attacked Toghrul's uncle, the *gurkhan* (leader of the tribe). Thus Toghrul became the powerful leader of the Kerait, with the title of ong-khan or wang-khan, and at the time when Temüjin made his appearance to remind the Kerait ruler of his debt to Yesügei Bahadur, Toghrul's authority had spread from the River Onon over the Mongol homelands to the lands of the Chin emperor, to whom he paid tribute and from whom he received recognition in return.

When Toghrul accepted the sable cloak and with it Temüjin, as an adopted son, he gained a much-needed ally against the intrigues of his own family and in return bestowed some much-needed status and security on Temüjin. In recognition of this new status, Temüjin was presented with a "son" as a personal servant. This was Jelme, the future Mongol divisional commander. The value and advantages of this new alliance were to be made clear within a very short time.

The details of the abduction of Börte Füjin by the Merkit differ in the *Secret History* and in Rashīd al-Dīn's *Altan Debter*–based account. Both agree, however, that a force of Merkits attacked Temüjin's camp and seized Börte Füjin and also Belgutei's mother while the men and Hö'elun with her daughter Temulun on her lap escaped. Both accounts also agree that Temüjin sought immediate assistance from his adopted father, Toghrul, who was only too pleased to wreak revenge on his enemies of old, the Merkits. The Merkits were in fact exacting revenge themselves for the original abduction of Hö'elun from them by Temüjin's father, Yesügei.

The discrepancy in the accounts surrounding this episode is not difficult to explain. Temüjin's first son, Jochi, was born approximately nine months after Börte Füjin's abduction, and the uncertainty of his paternity reverberated down through his line, sons who became rulers of the Golden Horde, the *ulus* (the lands and people designated to be under a Mongol prince's command) that held sway over Russia, Eastern Europe, and the Pontic (Qipchaq) steppes. Women abducted from other tribes were awarded to members of the capturing tribe as a matter of course. Belgutei's mother was filled with shame after her release, not so much because she had been given to a Merkit as a wife but because the Merkit to whom she had been given was a mere commoner, while her sons were khans. Rashīd al-Dīn's account has Börte Füjin treated with the greatest respect by her abductors due to her pregnancy and claims that the Merkits happily turned her over to their sworn enemy the Kerait leader, Toghrul. Toghrul refused to take her as a wife because he considered her his daughter-in-law, returning her to Temüjin. This account is obviously contrived and implausible and served the political aim of avoiding embarrassing a neighboring Mongol dynasty and tarnishing the name of Börte Khātūn (Lady). Rashīd al-Dīn adds that Toghrul sought to "preserve her from the gaze of strangers and non-intimates,"[12] an obvious inaccuracy because the Keraits were not Muslim and would never have entertained such sentiments, unlike Rashīd al-Dīn himself and others in the Muslim Mongol court where he served.

Though not explicit, the *Secret History*, written for insiders who would have been well acquainted with the facts of this incident, does not weave any falsehoods around the events, while at the same time it romanticizes the eventual reunion of Temüjin and his "beloved" Börte Füjin, a depiction worthy of Hollywood.

> Then Lady Borte, who was fleeing for her life, heard Temüjin's voice and recognized it. She leaped from the still moving cart and came running to him. . . . By the light of the moon he saw her, and, as he jumped from his horse, he took her in his arms.[13]

Such romantic love and moonlight tenderness sits strangely with the fact that Temüjin had abandoned his beloved apparently without a second thought when the Merkits launched their attack. However, this might be explained by the fact that whereas Temüjin and the other men in the party and possibly even Hö'elun, who was also there, would have faced almost certain death had they been captured, young women were too valuable a commodity to wantonly dispose of, and though paternity of any children could be important, women were considered transferable among men in Mongol society. This attitude is clearly evident in the inheritance laws that stipulate that the wives and concubines of deceased Mongols were inherited by their nearest relatives, with sons inheriting their father's wives. Temüjin would therefore have realized that it was imperative that he escape rather than confront a stronger enemy and that he would later be in a position to impose his revenge and reclaim his bride.

Temüjin called on his adopted father, Toghrul, his *anda*, Jamuka, his brothers Kasar and Belgutei, his boon-companion (*nökor*), Bo'orchu, and his servant and *nökor*, Jelme, to assist him in rescuing his bride and his stepmother from the Merkits. Toghrul had not forgotten his pledge:

> Didn't I tell you last time that you could depend on me? Your father and I were sworn brothers, and when you brought me the sable jacket you asked me to be a father to you. . . .

> In return for this sable I shall trample the Merkit;
> Lady Börte shall be saved.
> In return for this sable I shall trample the Merkit;
> Lady Börte shall be rescued.[14]

The victory was total. However, having retrieved his bride and scattered his enemies, Temüjin called a halt to the assault and though he took some youngsters as slaves and women as concubines, he spared many of the Merkit men. In future encounters also this was often the case, and the defeated enemy were usually encouraged to join the growing Mongol forces and become incorporated into Chinggis's army, a welcome option for most, as it offered the likely prospect of plentiful booty and future reward. Temüjin had begun his rise to power.

THE RISE TO POWER

Temüjin's rise to supreme leader was neither smooth nor in any way assured. The break with his boyhood *anda*, Jamuka, is often cited as the event that signified the real start of his pursuit of power. Jamuka was also singularly ambitious, and the two would have scented in each other a dangerous rival. This rivalry split them as it would also split the Mongol tribes, and as this rivalry intensified both knew that there could be only one ultimate winner and that the price of losing would be dire.

Eighteen months after their successful campaign against the Merkits, the two *andas* broke camp and went their separate ways. Jamuka, as the legitimate ruler of the Jadarat tribe, could expect support from the more conservative and traditionalist Mongol elements, who upheld the solidarity of the nobility and the constitution of the tribe. Temüjin, whose noble lineage had been effectively severed by the defection of his own tribe following his father's death, relied on personal loyalty and on those who would question the traditional tribal hierarchy or who sought refuge from the claims and strictures of clan and bondage. The night that Temüjin swept away from the *andas'* shared camp, he was followed by a defecting detachment of Jamuka's men. Temüjin's reputation as a just and generous master who inspired and rewarded loyalty was growing. Those who joined his ranks came as individuals or in small groups, often defying their leaders who generally remained supportive of Jamuka. Among those groups who rallied to Temüjin's banner were ancestral subject tribes, *ötögus bo'ol*, such as the Jalair, the Soldu, and the Baya'ut. Individual serfs, *ötögu bo'ol*, were also welcomed, with the result that representatives from all the tribes and from every level of tribal society could be found within Temüjin's following.

With a growing power base of loyal followers and even talk of a heavenly mandate, Temüjin could now realistically aspire to leadership of the steppe tribes. He was proclaimed khan[15] by his supporters in 1185, even though many of them outranked him in the tribal hierarchy.

> We will make you khan,
> And when you are khan
> We shall gallop after all your enemies,
> Bring you girls and women of good complexion,
> Bring palace-tents and foreign girls with cheeks
> Like silk, bring geldings at the trot,
> And give them to you.[16]

Whereas Toghrul, the ong-khan of the Keraits, offered his congratulations to the new khan, Jamuka was determined to thwart his former *anda*'s ambitions, and using the pretext of revenge for an executed horse-thief, he rode at the head of 30,000 men from 14 tribes against his one-time brother. Temüjin was defeated and fled to the higher reaches of the Onon River. Behind him he abandoned some of his men to Jamuka's mercy—but Jamuka showed none. The unfortunates were boiled alive in 70 vats,[17] and their two leaders were decapitated, their heads later used as tail-adornment on Jamuka's horse. This action would seal Jamuka's eventual fate.

Before he could regroup and counterattack, however, Temüjin was summoned to the aid of his patron, the Kerait ong-khan. Temüjin's defeat at the hands of Jamuka had repercussions throughout the Turco-Mongol tribes, one of which was the toppling from power of Toghrul, and Temüjin's once-powerful patron was forced into exile under the protection of the Kara-Khitai.

In fact mystery surrounds this whole period in the sources, and a certain amount of conjecture is necessary to ascertain the events clearly. In his authoritative biography, Paul Ratchnevsky surmises that Temüjin was held, possibly as a captive, at the Chin court following his defeat by Ja-muka. Toghrul had ruled with the acquiescence of the Altan Khan ("Golden Khan"), as the nomads called the Chin emperor, and he would not have welcomed the Chinese ruler's downfall. When the Tatars, the Chins' acting police force during this obscure decade between 1186 and 1196, fell foul of the Altan Khan, Temüjin was on hand to offer his services and at the same time take some revenge for his father's murder. Whether Toghrul took part in the battle against the Tatars is disputed in the sources, but as a result of the victory Temüjin was awarded a title by the Chin emperor, and Toghrul, now an old man, had his title wang-khan confirmed and his leadership of the Keraits restored. By 1197 Temüjin and the wang-khan[18] were therefore both restored to positions of prestige and power.

Temüjin was content at this time to serve as the wang-khan's protégé, and their alliance brought success to both the Mongols and the Keraits. Jamuka continued to inspire envy and hatred against Temüjin's growing prestige, and discontented Merkits, Naimans, Tayichi'uts, Unggirats, and remnants of the Tatars allied against him. The climax to this steppe war pitting Temüjin and Toghrul against an alliance loosely gathered under Jamuka, who had been hastily elected *gurkhan* (khan of all the tribes) in 1201, was reached in 1201–2 in the foothills of the eastern Khinghan mountains. Temüjin secured a victory over the confederation and followed it up by forcing a confrontation the following year near the Khalkha River with his old, hated enemy. This bloody battle resulted in the massacre and near extermination of the Tatars, final revenge for the murder of Temüjin's father, Yesügei.

EARLY ANECDOTES

These decisive battles of 1201–2 have furnished historians with some endur-ing stories about Chinggis Khan the man, which—whether they be truth or fabrication—certainly reflect aspects of his character that history has shown to be accurate.

The *Secret History* records the surrender of some Shirkutu tribal leaders. On their way to surrender, they had captured their overlord, Tarqutai of the Tayichi'ut, but before reaching Temüjin's camp they had decided to release their former lord. They admitted this when they arrived, and Temüjin re-sponded thus:

> If you had laid hands on your own Khan, Tarqutai, I would have ex-ecuted you and all your brethren. No man should lay hands on his right-ful lord. But you did not forsake him and your hearts were sound.[19]

In another incident, Temüjin was interrogating some prisoners after the bat-tle when he demanded to know the identity of the soldier who had shot and killed his "yellow war-horse with the white mouth." A certain Jirqo'adai (Tödöge) stepped forward and admitted his guilt. Temüjin responded as follows:

> When a foe is faced with his enemies, with those he has killed, he usually keeps his mouth shut, too frightened to speak out. Not this man. Faced with his enemies, with those he has killed, he does not deny it, but admits it openly. That is the kind of man I want on my side. His name is Jirqo'adai, but because he shot my yellow war-horse with the white mouth in the neck, he shall hence forth be known as Jebe, which means "arrowhead." He shall be my arrow.[20]

Jebe was to become one of Chinggis Khan's four great generals (*noyens*)—one of his "Four Hounds"—and he would achieve great renown.[21]

Before launching his terminal attack on the Tatars, Temüjin announced a break with steppe tradition and a defining battle tactic.

> If we triumph, we should not stop for booty, but press home our advantage. Once victory is secure, the booty will be ours anyway, won't it? Then we can divide it amongst ourselves. If we are forced to retreat, let us regroup in the original spot where we began our attack. Anyone who does not come back will be executed.[22]

By ordering his troops to ignore the plunder and continue the battle, Temüjin was breaking with an ancient nomadic custom that saw the aim of warfare solely as the acquisition of booty and that gave the chiefs the sole right for the dispersal of these spoils. Temüjin knew that unquestioning discipline was essential if victory was to be achieved over a superior enemy, and he knew also that such a decree would be a trial of strength between him and his tribal leaders. In accordance with these orders, after the battle he dispatched Jebe and Qubilai to confiscate the booty acquired by three "princes" who had disregarded his orders. Though these three were later to defect, Temüjin's resounding victory had proved his point and reinforced his reputation as a strong, disciplined, and just ruler who valued such traits in others, especially courage and honesty, be they friend or foe.

THE FINAL FALL AND ITS AFTERMATH

Temüjin had won a decisive victory over the confederation that Jamuka had collected against him, but he had failed to defeat Jamuka. In 1202, the Tatars had been practically exterminated, but resentment against Temüjin was still widespread amongst the old steppe order, and many of the tribal princes, jealous of their independence and suspicious of this warrior's growing might, were open to suggestions of resistance. The whispers became a call to arms when the growing ill will between Wang-Khan Toghrul and his "son" became formal.

Temüjin's proposal that one of Toghrul's daughters be given to his eldest son, Jochi, in marriage and that one of his daughters be given to Toghrul's grandson, Nilka-Senggum's son, Tusaqa, had been rejected out of hand by Nilka-Senggum. Senggum in his arrogance had declared, "We shall not give Cha'ur-beki [his younger sister] to you," a refusal that greatly displeased Temüjin. Jamuka capitalized on this ill feeling and immediately began intriguing against his former *anda*.

Informed of a planned ambush by Toghrul and Jamuka, Temüjin was able to escape, but his forces suffered serious losses, only 4,600 men surviving with him. Ögötei, his second son, was badly injured. It is thought that the only reason Jamuka did not press the hunt for Temüjin afterward was that Jamuka considered his adversary a spent force and no longer any kind of threat to his own ambitions. In the year 1203, on the shores of Lake Baljuna, Temüjin began to regroup his forces and once again call on his allies for their support. Those who remained with him at Lake Baljuna were accorded the highest honors in the years to come.

Meanwhile, the Keraits had grown in power, but, now under the leadership of Senggum rather than the ailing wang-khan, signs of fragmentation had appeared, and many of their allies once again turned to the exiled Temüjin. The epic battle (1203) that eventually ensued lasted three days, but the Keraits, who had been taken unaware, were soundly defeated. Toghrul fled, but he was quickly captured and executed before his "son" could intervene. Senggum also escaped and fled, but he too was eventually killed. Anxious to avoid a repeat of the Tatar solution, Temüjin ordered that the defeated Kerait commanders not be punished but rather be offered the opportunity to pledge their allegiance and join the Mongol "nation." He made a point of commending the bravery of the Keraits' commander-in-chief. To further cement his absorption of the Keraits, he married off their leading princesses. Two of these princesses—Sorkaktani, the wang-khan's youngest daughter, and his granddaughter, Dokuz Khatun, both Nestorian Christians like many of the Keraits—were given to Temüjin's youngest son, Tolui, as wives and were to play a prominent political role in later events. Dokuz Khatun eventually became the principal wife of Hülegü Khan, the first Il-Khan of Persia.[23]

Temüjin now sat on the throne of his one-time protector, the wang-khan, but he still felt insecure knowing that one great tribal grouping, the Naiman, remained beyond his control and were also harboring enemies, including Jamuka. The Naiman dwelt in the regions northwest of the traditional Kerait lands, between the Selenga River and the Altai mountains. If he could defeat the Naiman, his enemies would have nowhere to shelter, and he would be undisputed leader of the unified Turco-Mongol steppe tribes. With so much at stake, Temüjin could not risk failure, and so he devised a careful and militarily prudent plan that would form the basis of his world-conquering army in the decades to come. The army was organized into decimal units of regiments (1000s), squadrons (100s), and troops (10s), with each unit headed by a commander and these units often composed of men from different tribes.

He appointed six commanders-in-chief. His own bodyguard consisted of the sons of the unit commanders as well as the sons of individual soldiers personally known to him. There were 80 night guards and 70 day guards, these facts being detailed in the *Secret History*.[24] On the day of the Feast of the Moon in the Year of the Rat (1204), Temüjin led his troops into battle. To bolster the morale of his own meager forces and intimidate the numerically superior Naiman waiting to greet him, Temüjin employed a strategy that he was to use to great effect in future conflicts. By lighting innumerable campfires, mounting dummies on their spare horses, and trailing branches and bushes from their own mounts, the Mongols were able to create the impression that their numbers were far greater than they actually were.

The Mongols' victory was total, and the Naiman were decimated. Following this victory, all the other tribes that had once had thoughts of independence were quick to pledge their full loyalty to the Mongol khan. Only the Merkits sought to escape, but within the same year they too had been destroyed. When eventually Jamuka, betrayed by his followers, was brought before Temüjin, these same treacherous companions and followers were first executed, reputedly at Jamuka's request, before Jamuka himself was killed. Temüjin considered treachery the gravest of sins and happily granted this wish. Temüjin was now undisputed leader of the united nomadic Turco-Mongol tribes of the Asiatic steppes.

It is from this period that one of the most notorious quotes from Chinggis Khan is recorded. The discussion was on the pleasures of life, and Bo'orchu and his other companions expressed their pleasure in falconry in the spring. But for Chinggis this was nothing compared to the pleasures of conquest.

> Man's greatest good fortune is to pursue and claim victory over his foe, seize all his possessions, abandon his wives lamenting and wailing, ride his geldings, use the bodies of his women as nightshirts and support, casting eyes upon and kissing their rosy breasts and sucking their lips which are as sweet as the berries on their breasts.[25]

During the period of Chinggis Khan's rise to power, China was divided into three separate kingdoms. South of Mongolia was Hsi Hsia, Tangut territory, in what is today the northwest. To the east of Mongolia, the Jurchens ruled northern China. The Jurchens were a semi-nomadic people from Manchuria who defeated the Khitan and the Sung and established their own dynasty, the Chin. They were more powerful than Tangut-dominated Hsi Hsia. The most powerful and sophisticated of the three kingdoms was in the south, often considered the real heartland of China. This kingdom south of the lands of the Chins' was ruled by the Sungs. The Sungs, who traced their heritage back hundreds of years, regarded themselves as a pure Chinese dynasty. The Sung empire was widely believed to be the most powerful and sophisticated in the world.

Traditional accounts of Chinggis's life say that once he had created the Mongol nation, he turned on China, to extend his empire. However, initially this was not the case, because traditionally the nomadic Mongol horsemen had never shown any real interest in conquest, their periodic raids providing all they needed from the urbanized and settled world. The conquest of China was not contemplated when Chinggis Khan rode forth in 1207. For the great khan and his "nation of archers," China was just a rich quarry to be plundered.

In 1209, Chinggis Khan launched a raid on the Tangut and forced them to retreat into their fortified capital. Chinggis had not come across such defenses before, and he had no immediate answer to this alien tactic of hiding behind fortifications. Although the Tangut king eventually accepted the Mongols' terms, it was an important lesson for the Mongols. The Tangut kingdom recognized Chinggis Khan as its overlord. The Tangut monarch pledged to supply future Mongol military operations with troops, and to cement the allegiance he presented Chinggis Khan with a princess as a new wife.

Chinggis's name first became widely known and feared with his campaign against the Chins in 1211, which catapulted the name of Chinggis Khan, with the associations of fear and rampage, onto the international stage. This campaign started with the time-honored Mongol practice of extorting money and other concessions. However, the Chins felt they had little to fear from these unsophisticated horsemen. They had constructed a series of fortified cities to protect their empire from invasions from the north; they also possessed a large and powerful army. Chinggis scattered units of his force across the northern part of the Chin Empire, systematically laying waste to the land as they rode. They avoided the major fortified cities until they were confronted with a vast Chin force at Huan-erh-tsui. Chinggis decided to attack them. In their first serious engagement with a large foreign army, the Mongol cavalry proved devastating. They completely outmaneuvered the Chins, virtually destroying a force of some 70,000 within a matter of hours. Jochi, Chinggis's eldest son, rode as far as the gates of Chung-tu (modern Peking), but, having no knowledge of siege warfare, he withdrew.

Although the Mongols had gained control of key passes into China and a number of small fortifications, they had no use for these; so, early in 1212, they rode back to Mongolia. They had failed to extort much out of the campaign, and the Chins quickly rebuilt the towns that Mongol invaders had destroyed. Chinggis learned an important lesson: even though they had routed a huge Chin army, they would never extract a submission from the Chin emperor as long as he and his government could retreat into their large, fortified cities.

Chinggis Khan returned to raid the Chins in 1213. By a series of overwhelming victories in the field and a few successes in the capture of fortifications deep within China, Chinggis extended his control as far south as the Great Wall. He also captured or extorted vast amounts of plunder in silks and gold and took hundreds of Chin captives, including engineers and soldiers. In his typically logical and determined fashion, Chinggis and his staff studied the problems of the assault of fortifications. With the help of the captured Chin engineers, they gradually developed the techniques and built the siege engines that would eventually make them the most successful besiegers in the history of warfare. Many of their captives were found to be willing advisors and recruits. These were Khitans who had been defeated and exiled a hundred years before, and their memories and resentments were still strong, as was their deeply felt animosity toward the Jurchens.

As often happens with newcomers, Chinggis and his generals, assisted by the Khitan specialists, were soon making their own improvements and developing their own techniques. The two Chinese engines that the Mongols adopted, and later modified when they compared them to the siege weapons of the Persians, were the light catapult, which could launch a two-pound missile over 100 yards and required a crew of 40 prisoners to create the tension on its ropes, and a heavier machine, with a crew of 100 that would fire a 25-pound projectile over 150 yards. Although the lighter device was limited in range, it had the advantage that it could be dismantled and carried with the main body of the army. Both of these machines could be used either to launch rocks at walls and gates or to hurl naphtha or burning tar into the enemy's ranks. After his campaign against the Persians, Chinggis adapted the siege machines captured from the Persian army. The Islamic design was adapted to the lighter Chinese models to create something similar to the European catapult or trebuchet, with a range of more than 350 yards. Chinggis's men also adapted the ballista, which looked like a giant crossbow and fired a heavy arrow over the same range as a catapult but with far more accuracy. Ballistas were light enough to be carried onto the battlefield.

But the most important type of weaponry that the Mongols adopted was explosives, a Chinese invention. Explosives were used either in the form of rockets, which were fired en masse into the enemy's ranks, causing little damage but much alarm; or as grenades—clay vessels packed with explosives and hurled either by catapult or by hand. Virtually every new military invention was snatched up and adapted by the Mongols, and with these arms they quickly developed the modern principles of artillery.

A prolonged battering from rocks, burning tar, grenades, and firebombs into the enemy lines would be followed up by an attack from mounted archers. These carefully rehearsed maneuvers depended on great mobility and discipline. Although the bombardment was not nearly as accurate as the mounted archers, it spread fear and confusion among the enemy and made the archers' job easier.

In 1215, Chinggis Khan's army besieged, captured, and sacked Chung-tu, one of the largest cities in Asia. Squadrons of Mongol horsemen rode the streets firing incendiary arrows into the wooden houses, while others put thousands of the civilian population to the sword. There was some method in this madness. Chinggis preferred to secure submission from his neighbors without resort to warfare. His military excess sent a signal to others. Those who surrendered would be spared, but those who resisted would be annihilated. As the Mongol armies massed before a target city, they would invariably issue an ominous message in warning: "If ye submit not, nor surrender, what know we thereof? The Ancient God, he knoweth."[26] In a letter from Guyuk Khan to Pope Innocent IV, a similar message was relayed: "And if ye do otherwise, what know we? God knoweth.'"

To the west, where the Uyghurs had pledged their loyalty to the Great Khan, events, political and military, were also unfurling. Küchlüg the Naiman, the last remaining enemy from the days of Temüjin's rise to power, still retained his oppressive grip on power over the Qara Khitai. Küchlüg was a Buddhist neophyte, and he ruled his newly acquired kingdom with a convert's zeal, the Muslim population suffering accordingly. Such was the hatred felt for Küchlüg by his Islamic subjects that the Mongols were viewed as potential liberators and Chinggis Khan as their savior. Their former rulers, the Qara Khitai, whom Küchlüg had brutally ousted, had been popular, and their ethnic ties to the Mongols were duly noted by the Muslims suffering under the cruel oppression of their new ruler, Küchlüg. For Chinggis Khan, Küchlüg, who had gathered to his cause the remnants of the rebel Naimans, represented a potential military threat and also unfinished business.

In the west, the first contact the Mongols had with the Islamic world was ultimately positive and, after the objectives of their advance became clear, one of welcome. This is often forgotten, and the Mongols' subsequent bloody confrontation with the armies and cities of the Khwārazmshāh is often erroneously interpreted as the Mongols' war on Islam.

The Qara Khitai (Black Cathays) were descendants of Khitans, semi-nomadic Turco-Mongols who fled westward in the 1120s after their defeat by the Jurchens from Manchuria. They left some of their people behind, who resentfully served their new masters the Jurchens, while under the leadership of Yelü Dashi (d. 1142), the Khitans were adopted by the Islamic world as their "Great Wall" against the barbarians to the north and east. They established a state in Transoxiana and Turkestan in 1141 after defeating the last Great Saljuq, Sultan Sanjar, at the historic battle of Qatwan.[27] They practiced the religious tolerance endemic to the Eurasian steppe societies, and Christians, Buddhists, Manichaeans, and Muslims all existed harmoniously under their decentralized regime. They were accepted and recognized by their Muslim subjects, but also very significantly by the wider Islamic world, including the caliph in Baghdad. The Muslim sources such as the 'Arundī's *Chahar Maqala* refer to the Qara Khitai in the most respectful and positive terms. Even though they were accepted and became an integral part of the Islamic world, the Qara Khitai never lost their dream of returning to their ancestral lands in northern China, usurped by the hated Jurchens. It was their defeat of the Muslim Saljuqs that gave rise to stories of the Christian king, Prester John, answering the call of the hard-pressed Crusaders in the Holy Lands. During the Chinggisid raids into Chin territory, many Khitans had defected to the Mongol forces, so with the arrival of the Mongols in neighboring Uyghur lands, many Qara Khitai saw a potential ally against the usurper, Küchlüg, rather than an invader. In 1218, Chinggis Khan sent his general Jebe, "the

Arrow," to dispose of the Naiman Küchlüg, a task he completed promptly and with the support of the Qara Khitai people. The rights and freedoms of the Muslims were restored, and the Mongols were welcomed. The incorporation of the lands and people of the Qara Khitai was one of the most significant phases in the development of the Mongol Empire, because it was these people whose influence was to be so crucially important and pervasive in the organization and administration of the growing empire. The Khitans shared common roots, traditions, and culture with the Mongols. However, they had already progressed far from their nomadic beginnings; the Qara Khitai had a fully developed state and the experience of statecraft and administration, and these were things they were now willing to share with their new masters and allies, the Mongols. Just as the top commands and military posts had gone to those who had shared Temüjin's lean times, many of the empire's top administrators emerged from the ranks of the Qara Khitai and the Uyghur.

One reason for the collapse of the Qara Khitai forces other than the widespread dislike of Küchlüg and the popular uprising at the appearance of Jebei Noyan was the weakness of the Qara Khitai army. With the connivance of Küchlüg, Sultan Mohammad, the Khwārazmshāh and vassal of the Qara Khitai, had risen in revolt against the *gurkhan* (the ruler of the Qara Khitai). While the sultan declared Khwārazm, Khorasan, Persia, Ghur (Afghanistan), and Transoxiana independent and under his sovereignty, Küchlüg imprisoned the *gurkhan* and made himself ruler of eastern Turkestan and the remaining lands still under nominal Qara Khitai control. The dispirited army he inherited was no match for the growing Mongol forces who arrived at his borders fresh from their victories in the east.

Chinggis Khan now found himself neighbor to one whom he held in the highest esteem, even awe, and his early communications with the Khwārazmshāh reflect this respect: "I am the sovereign of the Sun-rise, and thou the sovereign of the Sun-set."[28] However, the reality of Sultan Mohammad's kingdom matched neither his own grandiose vision nor the reputation believed by his new neighbor. Chinggis Khan had grave misgivings about assailing such a powerful ruler, yet the Khwārazmshāh was a paper tiger, and once hostilities had begun there was no real opposition to the relentless march of the great khan's armies. The bloated and strife-ridden Khwārazmian Empire crumpled because it had no cohesion and was unable to present a united front to the Mongol assault and also because it was led by a sultan who harbored grave illusions concerning the extent of his true authority and his military prowess. The Khwārazmshāh was a petty tyrant briefly sitting atop an artificially united bandit kingdom, whose delusions of his own grandeur were initially shared by Chinggis Khan.

There was a widespread belief that the caliph had been in secret communication with the Mongol leader and had asked him to attack his rival, though what he offered in return is unknown. This story is alluded to in the histories of Ibn al-Athīr. Though he goes into little detail, Ibn al-Athīr alludes to what was obviously a common belief at the time among the Iranians:

[The Caliph's] role in what the Persians attribute to him was correct, namely that he is the person who roused the Tatars' ambition for the lands of Islam and wrote to them about that. It was a very great disaster in comparison with which every serious sin becomes insignificant.[29]

It was the initial irruption of the Mongols into the Islamic world that sealed their reputation for brutality and barbarism, a reputation that unfortunately has never left them, even though the excesses of those early years were never again repeated. One campaign, in particular, ensured that the Mongols' reputation would be inextricably linked to pathological barbarism and wanton slaughter: the notorious reconnaissance trip around the Caspian Sea undertaken by Noyens (Generals) Jebe and Subodai in the years 1221 to 1224.

NOYENS JEBE AND SUBODAI

Subodai Bahadur (1176–1248) was the son of a blacksmith of the Uriangqadai clan and had joined Temüjin as a youth in 1190. By the age of 25 this large and imposing man had been appointed commander of cavalry. He was so large that the slight Mongol horses sometimes had problems carrying him, and he is recorded as being transported to battle in various forms of carriage. Subodai was utterly loyal to his master, and in mopping up operations before the great *quriltai* (assembly of leaders) of 1206, it was Subodai who pursued and terminally disposed of Kutu and Chila'un, sons of Chinggis's archenemy, the defeated Merkit leader, Tokhto. Such service and loyalty was rewarded. Subodai was made commander of a *tümen* (10,000) in the devastating wars against Hsi Hsia in 1209.

Subodai's most enduring claim to fame arose from his legendary reconnaissance trip around the Caspian Sea with his fellow general, Jebe Noyen. This trip, which ensured the pair's place securely in the annals of military history, commenced when Jebe and Subodai abandoned the search for the dying Khwārazmshāh in western Iran in 1221. On the island of Abaskun in the southeast corner of the Caspian Sea, Mohammad Khwārazmshāh was left to slowly die from his ills. He had brought terrible tragedy to his divided people and the people of western Asia, and he had opened the legendary gates of Īrānzamīn ("the land of Iran": "Greater Iran," referring to those regions subject to Iranian cultural influence) to the mythical hordes of Tūrān ("the land of the Tur": "Central Asia," the homeland of fierce rivals to the Iranians). Chinggis Khan had unleashed his armies to wreak vengeance-fed death and destruction on an unprecedented scale because the Khwārazmshāh had allowed, if not ordered, the unprovoked murder of a trade delegation composed mainly of Muslim merchants. In Bokhara, Chinggis Khan had addressed the assembled citizens to explain his presence: "I am the Punishment of God. If you had not committed great sins, God would not have sent a punishment like me upon you" (Juwaynī 105). If this had been the verdict on the people of

Bokhara, there must have been countless other people in the environs of the Caspian Sea and the Qipchaq Steppes who thought those words should apply equally to them after being visited by the two *noyens* Subodai and Jebe.

Having given up the hunt for the Khwārazmshāh, the two Mongol generals, with their armies, began their devastating journey, and their brief, bloody visits to the surrounding regions enshrine the reputation of the Mongols for barbarity and bloodletting for all time. Though the city of Tabriz managed to bribe the approaching army in time to avert catastrophe, other towns were not so fortunate, and the human wave of destruction engulfed them before they knew what was upon them. The Mongols swept through so quickly that the Georgian army under George IV was able to claim victory from their total defeat: After engaging the Mongol forces of 20,000 men and suffering calamitous defeat, the Caucasians fled in terror back to their capital, Tiflis, to await the inevitable siege. However, that siege never came; the Mongols merely continued on their way northward, the encounter being merely another skirmish for them on their circumnavigation of the Caspian. George IV, seeing the Mongols apparently in retreat, was able to convince himself that his decimated forces had in fact so impressed the invaders that they had fled rather than risk another encounter. There were few who believed his boasts.

The generals continued their unstoppable march north through the rugged Caucasus, cleaving asunder at Derbent the biblical barrier restraining Gog and Magog,[30] and into the open plains beyond encountering and defeating Cuman Turks from the Qipchaq steppe lands and Rus armies from what is today Russia. In the *Chronicle of Novgorod* the impact of their coming in 1224 is poignantly expressed in the few startling words of an observer.

> The same year, for our sins, an unknown tribe came, whom no one exactly knows, who they are, nor whence they came out, nor what their language is, nor of what race they are, nor what their faith is; but they call them Tartars. . . . God alone knows who they are and whence they came out.[31]

Their army was to meet up with the main Mongol armies in Khwarazm and leave it to others to consolidate their gains. In these two short years they had expanded the reach of the great khan's writ as far as the borders of Eastern Europe and the heartlands of the Islamic world. The tales of horror, heroism, cunning, blood and gore, desperation, and bravery that have filled the pages of many chronicles in almost as many languages associated with this epic journey are too numerous to recount here. However, the famous battle of Kalka,[32] fought on the river of the same name in the Crimea in 1223, deserves special mention. It was carried out with great tactical skill and classic Mongol cunning, and it left the alliance between the Qipchaq/Cuman/Polovtsian Turks and the Rus princes shattered and their armies routed. The victory feast was celebrated literally on top of the still-living bodies of the vanquished foes. After the remnants of the defeated Kievan army surrendered to the Mongols, a heavy wooden platform was placed on top of the bodies of the tightly bound Russian generals. As the joyful Mongol leaders celebrated their hard-won victory, their helpless foes slowly suffocated in a horrible death.

The Story of the coming of Jebe and Subeda'i to the province of Iraq and Azerbaijan and Aran and the killing and pillage in this land, and the passing from the road to Darband, Qipchag to Moghulistan.

When Sultan Jalāl al-Dīn fled from Nishapur and turned his thoughts to for Ghaznin, Jebe and Subeda'i sent a messenger to Chinggis Khan to say, that Sultan Muhammad no no more and his son Jalāl al-Dīn had fled and was coming in that direction. "We are no longer worried about him, and in accordance with your command we will spend a year or two conquering as many lands that lie before us as we can and then we will be able to return via Derband, the Qipchaq Gates to the rendezvous point as commanded in Mongolia, God willing and through Chinggis Khan's fortune. The authority of the Great God and the fortune of Chinggis Khan know that." Thereafter he dispatched envoys for the purpose of taking care of necessary business, and since provinces had still not been secured, no fewer than three or four hundred envoys went. In short, when they began the conquest of Iraq (Persia), they first took Khwar and Simnan. From there they came to the city of Ray, where they killed and plundered. Then they went to Qum, the people of which were all killed and the children of which they took away into captivity. And from there they went to Hamadan. Sayyid Majd al-Dīn Ala' al-dawla surrendered, sending tribute in steeds and garments and accepting to have a *shahna*. When they had heard that there was a large number of soldiers from the sultan's army assembled in Sanjas under the leadership of Beg-Tegin Silahi and Kuch Buqa Khan, they headed for them and "nothinged" (*nīst gardānīdan*) or annihilated them. From there they came to Zanjan, where they massacred many times more than they had done in other regions. They returned to Qazwin where they engaged in a fierce battle with the Qazwinis and took the city by force. The Qazwinis, as was their wont, fought inside the city with knives until nearly fifty thousand men had been killed on both sides. They massacred and plundered throughout the land of Iraq [i.e., Persia].

When winter set in, they engaged in a great battle in the vicinity of Ray. At that time Chinggis Khan was in the Nakhshab and Termez area. That year the cold was extreme. They headed for Azerbaijan, any place they encountered a hindrance [*godāz* 'gorge, ford'], they indulged in killing and looting in the customary manner, everywhere along the way. When they reached Tabriz, the governor, who was Atabeg Ozbeg, son of Jahan Pahl-avan, hid himself and sent someone to ask for a truce. He also sent much tribute and many animals. They turned back to spend the winter there under the truce before setting out for Arran on the road to Georgia.

Ten thousand Georgians faced them and engaged them in battle. The Georgians were defeated, and most were killed. Since most of the roads in Georgia were narrow and they foresaw difficulties in the hills, they turned back and headed for Maragheh. When they returned to Tabriz, the governor, Shams al-Dīn Tughra'i, sent out enough tribute to satisfy them, and they passed on. They laid siege to the city of Maragheh, and because at that time the ruler was a woman who ruled from Royin[diz], there was no one in the city who could offer resistance or think up a strategy. They therefore turned their hands to war. The Mongols put the Muslim prisoners out in front to attack the walls, and they killed anyone who turned back. They fought in this fashion for several days. In the end, they seized the city by force and put [both] high and low to death. Anything that could be easily carried they took away, and the rest they burned and smashed. Then they set out for Diyarbakr and Arbela, but when they heard the great fame of Muzaffar al-Dīn Kok-Bori's army, they turned back. Because Jamāl al-Dīn Aybeh, one of the Khwārazmshāh's slaves, had stirred up sedition again with a group of people, killed the *shahna* of Hamadan, seized Ala'al-Dawla for having submitted, and imprisoned him in the castle of Girit, a dependency of Lur, they went again toward Hamadan. Although Jamāl al-Dīn Aybeh came forth to surrender, it did him no good. He and his *nokers* ['vassals, lieutenants'] were martyred and the Mongols laid siege to the city and carried out a general massacre in Rajab 618 [August–September 1221].

After devastating Hamadan, they set out for Nakhichevan, which they captured and [in which] they massacred and looted. In the end Atabeg Khāmūsh surrendered and they gave him a royal seal ["*āl-tamqā*"] and a wooden *pāīza*. From there they went to Arran. First they took Saraw [Sarāb] and massacred and looted and [then] Ardabil in the same way. From there they went to the city of Baylaghan, which they took by storm, killing old and young [alike]. After that, they attacked Ganja, which was the greatest of the cities of Arran. They seized it and destroyed it too. From there they headed for Georgia, where the people had gathered an army and had prepared for battle. While they were facing off against each other, Jebe hid himself with five thousand soldiers in a secret recess, and Subeda'i advanced with the army. At the very beginning of the battle the Mongols retreated with the Georgians in pursuit. Jebe leapt from ambush and caught [the Georgians] in a trap. In an instant thirty thousand Georgians were killed. From there they headed for Derbent and Shirvan. Along the way they took the city of Shemakhī by siege, massacring the people and taking many captives. Since it was impossible to pass through Derbent, they sent a message to the Shirvanshah telling him to send representatives for peace talks. He dispatched ten of his nobles. The Mongols killed one of them and seized the others, saying, "If you show us the way through Derbent, we will spare your lives; otherwise we will kill you too." They guided them out of fear for their lives and [the Mongols] passed through.

When they reached the province of the Alans, there was a multitude of people there, and together with the Qipchaqs they engaged the Mongol army in battle and not one [managed to] escape. Afterwards the Mongols sent a message to the Qipchaqs, saying, "We and you are one tribe and of one sort. The Alans are aliens to us. We have made a pact with you not to harm one another. We will give you whatever gold and vestments you want. Leave them with us." And they dispatched a large quantity of goods.

The Qipchaqs turned back, and the Mongols achieved victory over the Alans, exerting themselves as much as they could in massacring and looting. The Qipchaqs, in hopes of peace, dispersed in safety in their own territory. Suddenly without warning the Mongols attacked them and killed everyone they found, taking double that which they had given [the Qipchaqs] before turning back. Some of the Qipchaqs who remained fled to the lands of the Rus. The Mongols wintered in that area, which was all pasture lands.

From there they went to the city of Sudaq on the coast of the sea that is connected to the Gulf of Constantinople. They took that city, and the people scattered. After that, they resolved to attack the towns of the Rus and the Qipchaqs who had gone there. They [the Rus and Qipchaqs] got ready and assembled a large army, and when the Mongols saw the formidable size they retreated.

The Qipchaqs and Rus thought they were retreating out of fear and pursued them at a distance of twelve-days. Then, without warning, the Mongols turned around and attacked them, and before they could re-group many were killed. They fought for a week, and in the end the Qipchaqs and Rus were routed. The Mongols went in pursuit and destroyed their towns. A great deal of their province was emptied of human beings. From there they traveled until they rejoined Chinggis Khan, who had returned from the province of the Tajiks.[33]

Subodai continued a celebrated military career, and his descendants added to his illustrious legacy. His last campaign was in Hungary, where he decimated the Hungarian troops after luring the already-defeated army into a trap that enabled the Mongol archers to pick off the fleeing enemy one by one. Reports claim that bodies littered the region for a distance of two days' march. By late 1241, Subodai was discussing plans with his generals for the invasion of Austria, Italy, and Germany. It was the death of the Great Khan Ögödei and the subsequent recall of all the leaders of the clans to Qaraqorum that saved Europe from the "Tatar yoke."

Subodai was dead by 1248, but his progeny continued in his military footsteps. His son, Uriyangkhadai, led Mongol armies into the jungles of what is today north Vietnam, while his grandson Bayan earned a reputation of which his grandfather would have been proud. He is credited with finally defeating the Sung armies of southern China in 1276.

A record exists of Chinggis Khan's last years due to his insistence on finding the elixir of life. He had heard tell of a certain holy man from the east who possessed the secret of eternal life, and the great khan duly summoned the great man, Ch'ang Ch'un, a Taoist sage. Ch'ang Ch'un explained that he knew the secret of eternal spiritual life but not of eternal earthly life, and Chinggis eventually became reconciled to that. A disciple of Ch'ang Ch'un recorded a diary of their journey across Asia and Turkestan to meet Chinggis Khan and has left a chronicle of life in those lands recently conquered by the Mongols and accounts of their meetings with the great khan.

Chinggis was determined he would return to Mongolia before meeting his fate, but before his end he wished to take final revenge upon the Tanguts of Hsi Hsia, the first people outside of the steppe that he had conquered 20 years previously. The Tanguts had failed to send him reinforcements to help him with his campaigns in the west, and for this perceived treachery he was determined to exterminate them. It has been said that the Mongols' actions were the first recorded act of deliberate genocide in recorded history; there no longer remains any trace of Tangut history in the region today. Chinggis Khan died in 1227 after a fall from a horse before he was actually able to personally kill the ruler of the Tanguts, though someone else murdered him shortly after. Chinggis Khan's burial site was a closely guarded secret, and it has never been found. Rashīd al-Dīn claims that all those involved in the actual burial were subsequently killed to preserve the secrecy of the site, but this story is not repeated elsewhere.

There may be another explanation for the disappearance of the Tanguts. Many of the peoples of the steppe gladly joined the Mongol army, and just as the various Turco-Mongol tribes were absorbed into the Mongol supra-tribe, so too were these other ethnic groups absorbed into those people who went under the banner of the Mongols.

> Now it has come about that the people of the Khitāī, Jurchen, Nankiyas (S. China), Uyghur, Qipchaq, Turkoman, Qarluq, Qalaj, and all the prisoners and Tajik races that have been brought up among the Mongols, are also called Mongols. All the assemblage takes pride in calling itself Mongol.[34]

CHINGGIS KHAN AND THE YASA

Another institution associated with Chinggis Khan and often erroneously dated to 1206 is the so-called Great Yasa of Chinggis Khan. The common assumption that a new steppe conqueror will "mark the foundation of his polity by the promulgation of laws"[35] has often been applied to Chinggis Khan, and the belief that the Great Yasa is just such an example has been held by many since within a few decades of the great conqueror's death.[36] The term *yasa* is a Mongol word meaning law, order, decree, judgment. As a verb, it implied the death sentence, as in "some were delivered to the *yasa*" usually meaning that an official execution was carried out. Until Professor David Morgan exploded the myth in 1986, it was the accepted wisdom that Chinggis Khan had laid down a basic legal code called the Great Yasa during the *quriltai* of 1206 and that written copies of his decrees were kept by the Mongol princes in their treasuries for future consultation. The Great Yasa was to be binding throughout the lands where Mongol rule prevailed, though strangely the actual texts of the code were to remain taboo, in the same way as the text of the *Altan Debter* was treated. This restriction on access to the text explains the fact that no copies of the Great Yasa have ever actually been recorded.

The Great Yasa became a body of laws governing the social and legal behavior of the Mongol tribes and the peoples of those lands that came under their control. Initially it was based on Mongol traditions, customary law, and precedent, but it was never rigid. It was always open to very flexible and liberal interpretation and quite able to adapt, adopt, and absorb other legal systems. Speaking of the *yasas*, the Muslim Juwaynī was able to declare, "There are many of these ordinances that are in conformity with the *Shariʿat* [i.e., Islamic law]."[37] The Great Yasa must therefore be viewed as an evolving body of customs and decrees that began long before Chinggis Khan's *quriltai* of 1206. His son Chaghatai was known to adhere strictly to the unwritten Mongol customary law, and many of his strictures and rulings would have been incorporated into the evolving body of law. Many of the rulings that appear to be part of this Great Yasa are based on quotations and *biligs* (maxims) of Chinggis Khan that are known to have been recorded. Another source of the laws that made up the Great Yasa is the Tatar Shigi-Qutuqu, Chinggis Khan's adopted brother, who was entrusted with judicial authority during the 1206 *quriltai*. He established the Mongol practice of recording in writing the various decisions he arrived at as head *yarghuchi* (judge). His decisions were recorded in the Uyghur script in a blue book (*kökö debter*) and were considered binding, thus creating an ad hoc body of case histories. However, this in itself did not represent the Great Yasa of Chinggis Khan, and it must be assumed that such a document never existed, even though in the years to come, the existence of just such a document became a widespread belief.

With or without the existence of a written Great Yasa, the Mongols, especially under Chinggis Khan, had a strict set of rules and laws to which they adhered, and their discipline was everywhere remarked on and admired. An intelligence report prepared by Franciscan friars led by Friar John of Plano Carpini, who visited Mongolia in the 1240s, commented as follows.

> Among themselves, however, they are peaceable, fornication and adultery are very rare, and their women excel those of other nations in chastity, except that they often use shameless words when jesting. Theft is unusual among them, and therefore their dwellings and all their property are not put under lock and key. If horses or oxen or other animal stock are found straying, they are either allowed to go free or are led back to

their own masters. . . . Rebellion is rarely raised among them, and it is no wonder if such is their way, for, as I have said above, transgressors are punished without mercy.[38]

Even the Muslim historian Jūzjānī does not hold back:

The Chinggis Khan . . . in [the administration of] justice was such, that, throughout his whole camp, it was impossible for any person to take up a fallen whip from the ground except he were the owner of it; and, throughout his whole army, no one could give indication of [the existence of] lying and theft.[39]

Nor does he refrain from treating Chinggis Khan's son and successor, Ögödei Qa'an, who was generally credited with having shown compassion and great sympathy for his Muslim subjects, with respect and positive treatment.

Religious tolerance became enshrined in the Yasa, though some would say that the Mongols were just playing safe by safeguarding religious leaders of all faiths. Priests and religious institutions were all exempted from taxation. Water was treated with great respect: it was strictly forbidden to wash or urinate in running water, because streams and rivers were considered as living entities. Execution was the reward for spying, treason, desertion, theft, adultery, or persistent bankruptcy in the case of merchants. Execution could take on various horrific forms, and one particularly gruesome example has been recorded by Rashīd al-Dīn: A rash Kurdish warlord had attempted to double-cross Hülegü Khan. He was apprehended and received this fate.

He [Hülegü] ordered that he [Malik Salih] be covered with sheep fat, trussed with felt and rope, and left in the summer sun. After a week, the fat got maggoty, and [the maggots] started devouring the poor man. He died of that torture within a month. He had a three-year-old son who was sent to Mosul, where he was cut in two on the banks of the Tigris and hung as an example on two sides of the city until his remains rotted away to nothing.[40]

Reflecting the Mongols' respect for and superstitious fear of aristocracy, they were fearful of shredding the blood of the highborn upon the earth. They therefore reserved a special form of execution for kings and the particularly mighty: such nobles, in recognition of their status, were wrapped in carpets and kicked to death.

In a grand *quriltai* (assembly) held near the source of the Onon River in the spring of the Year of the Tiger (1206), the assembled leaders, princes, and steppe nobility of the now-united Turco-Mongol tribes awarded Temüjin Khan the title Chinggis Khan, meaning Oceanic or Universal Ruler.[41] Why Chinggis Khan set out on his mission of world conquest can only be surmised, and explanations have been numerous, including those put forward in his own lifetime. Many of his people and indeed his enemies believe that he had a mandate from God and that he had been divinely inspired and commanded to go forth and spread his word and laws over the whole known world. Such a belief was eventually reflected in the messages demanding submission that his offspring sent to kings, popes, and emperors during the empire's rise to power. Chinggis Khan is famously quoted as haranguing the cowed people of Bokhara from the pulpit of their central mosque that he was a judgment from God.

> O People, know that you have committed great sins, and that the great ones among you have committed these sins. If you ask me what proof I have for these words, I say it is because I am the punishment of God. If you had not committed great sins, God would not have sent a punishment like me upon you.[42]

Most of those who experienced the Mongol onslaught and survived, and certainly those who heard tell of the invasion second- or third-hand were quite willing to believe that Chinggis Khan was indeed the "Punishment of God." His own followers and his family were also quite content for this belief to persist and also later the belief that his mission of conquest was sacred and his and their destiny was at least sanctioned if not written by God.

However, in the period around 1206 when Temüjin was awarded the leadership of the Eurasian steppe tribes and was proclaimed Chinggis Khan, there is no evidence that the would-be world conqueror regarded himself anything other than a very powerful and unstoppable warrior-king. He had fought, connived, plotted, intrigued, and battled his way to the top, and he had rewarded those who had remained loyal to him. But his rise had been difficult and demanding, and he had been given few breaks by smiling fortune. He owed his success to his own cunning, bravery, tenacity, and cold insight into the hearts of his fellow men. He knew that loyalty had usually to be bought and that for loyalty to be held, payments had to be forthcoming. The tribes flocked to his banner because of the promise of reward. His continued aggrandizement was dependent on his ability to replenish those coffers of promised plenty.

THE ARMY

Immediately after the *quriltai* of 1206 the great khan, Chinggis, began to consolidate power and reorganize his army in anticipation of dipping into the rich pickings of the Sung, the power center of China to the south. He continued the process of decimalization, and where possible he broke up tribal structures and rewarded with command postings those who had been loyal to him during the lean years. The breakup of the tribal makeup of his fighting force was to have profound effects on the loyalty, discipline, and effectiveness of his army. The *ordu* (base camp) was a tightly regulated unit, and its layout and organization were often uniform so that newcomers and visitors would immediately know where to find the armory, the physician's tent, or the chief. The fighting men, who included all males from 14 to 60 years, were organized into standard units: *arbans* (10 men), *jaguns* (100 men), *minghans* (1000 men), and *tümens* (10,000 men) and were overseen by the *tümen* quartermaster, the *jurtchi*. Such an organization meant that no order would ever have to be given to more than 10 men at any one time. Transfer between units was forbidden. Soldiers fought as part of a unit, not as individuals. Individual soldiers, however, were responsible for their equipment, weapons, and up to five mounts. Their families and even their herds would accompany them on foreign expeditions.

Soldiers wore protective silk undershirts, a practice learned from the Chinese. Even if an arrow pierced their mail or leather outer garment, the arrowhead was unlikely to pierce the silk. In this way, though a wound might be opened up in the flesh, the actual metal would be tightly bound in the silk and so would be prevented from causing more extensive harm and would also be easier to withdraw later. The silk undershirt would be worn beneath a tunic of thick leather, lamellar armor-plate, or mail and sometimes a cuirass of leather-covered iron scales. Whether the helmet was leather or metal depended on rank. Contemporary illustrations depict helmets with a central metal spike bending backward, and others ending in a ball with a plume and wide neck-guard shielding the shoulders and the jaws and neck. Shields were leather-covered wicker.

The Mongols were famous for their mastery of firing their arrows in any direction while mounted and galloping at full speed. Strapped to their backs, their quivers contained 60 arrows for use with two composite bows made of bamboo and yak horn. The light cavalry were armed with a small sword and two or three javelins, while the heavy horsemen carried a long lance (four meters) fitted with a hook, a heavy mace or axe, and a scimitar.

On campaign, all fighting men were expected to carry their equipment and provisions as well as their weaponry. A horsehair lasso, a coil of stout rope, an awl, needle and thread, cooking pots, leather water bottles, and a file for sharpening arrows would be among the utilities possibly carried in an inflatable saddlebag fashioned from a cow's stomach. When the horseman was fording a river, this saddlebag, if inflated, could double as a float.

Much is known about the Mongol fighting forces simply because they succeeded in causing such a wide impact, and artists of the pen, the brush, and the song as well as various artisans of all skills, media, and provenance have all vividly recorded in their different ways the details of the Mongol war machine, its composition, organization, and methods.[43]

Two other aspects of the army deserve mention before returning to the account of the Mongols' rise to greatness, because both were crucial to the success that Chinggis Khan achieved after the *quriltai* of 1206. One was the *nerge* (hunt or chase), which was not only a source of entertainment and food but vital in the training of the Mongol fighting force and in the installation of discipline and coordination into the tribe as a military unit. The other institution was the *yam* and *barid* or "postal" system, the communications network, the efficacy of which ensured the unity and cohesiveness of the empire and its armies.

The *nerge* formed an essential element in Mongol life. Juwaynī (d. 1282) was brought up in the Mongol court and later became governor of Baghdad under the Il-Khan Hülegü, and he must have witnessed, if not taken part in, the *nerge* many times. The *nerge* not only provided sustenance for the tribe, but served as an exercise in military training and discipline that was taken with the utmost seriousness. It was an event that was remarked upon by many, and accounts are many, from the earliest days of the nascent empire until the Golden Age of the Yuan and the Ilkhanate.

[Chinggis Khan] paid great attention to the chase and used to say that the hunting of wild beasts was a proper occupation for the commanders of armies; and that instruction and training therein was incumbent on warriors and men-at-arms, [who should learn] how the huntsmen come up with the quarry, how they hunt it, in what manner they array themselves and after what fashion they surround it according as the party is great or small. For when the Mongols wish to go a-hunting, they first send out scouts to ascertain what kinds of game are available and whether it is scarce or abundant. And when they are not engaged in warfare, they are ever eager for the chase and encourage their armies thus to occupy themselves; not for the sake of the game alone, but also in order that they may become accustomed and inured to hunting and familiarized with the handling of the bow and the endurance of hardships, Whenever the Khan sets out on the great hunt (which takes place at the beginning of the winter season), he issues orders that the troops stationed around his headquarters and in the neighbourhood of the *ordus* shall make preparations for the chase, mounting several men from each company of ten in accordance with instructions and distributing such equipment in the way of arms and other matters as are suitable for the locality where it is desired to hunt. The right wing, left wing and centre of the army are drawn up and entrusted to the great emirs; and they set out together with the Royal Ladies (*khavāṭīn*) and the concubines, as well as provisions of food and drink. For a month, or two, or three they form a hunting ring and drive the game slowly and gradually before them, taking care lest any escape from the ring. And if, unexpectedly, any game should break through, a minute inquiry is made into the cause and reason, and the commanders of thousands, hundreds and tens are clubbed therefor, and often even put to death. And if (for example) a man does not keep to the line (which they call *nerge*) but takes a step forwards or backwards, severe punishment is dealt out to him and is never remitted. For two or three months, by day and by night, they drive the game in this manner, like a flock of sheep, and dispatch messages to the Khan to inform him of the condition of the quarry, its scarcity or plenty, whither it has come and from whence it has been started. Finally, when the ring has been contracted to a diameter of two or three parasangs, they bind ropes together and cast felts over them; while the troops come to a halt all around the ring, standing shoulder to shoulder. The ring is now filled with the cries and commotion of every manner of game and the roaring and tumult of every kind of ferocious beast; all thinking that the appointed hour of "And when the wild beasts shall be gathered together" is come; lions becoming familiar with wild asses, hyenas friendly with foxes, wolves intimate with hares. When the ring has been so much contracted that the wild beasts are unable to stir, first the Khan rides in together with some of his retinue; then, after he has wearied of the sport, they dismount upon high ground in the centre of the *nerge* to watch the princes likewise entering the ring, and after them, in due order, the noyans, the commanders and the troops. Several days pass in this manner; then, when nothing is left of the game but a few wounded and emaciated stragglers, old men and greybeards humbly approach the Khan, offer up prayers for his well-being and intercede for the lives of the remaining animals asking that they be suffered to depart to some place nearer to grass and water. Thereupon they collect together all the game that they have bagged; and if the enumeration of every species of animal proves impracticable they count only the beasts of prey and the wild asses.[44]

The *yam*, the successor institution to the *barid*, was in essence a postal system and a means of communication for the reigning and the reigned. Though first mentioned by name during Ögödei Khan's reign, it must be assumed that the *yam* network was developed during Chinggis Khan's rule. In 1234 Ögödei set up a properly organized network that in future years was to so impress visitors and merchants to the Mongol Empire. *Yam* is a Mongol term and the term most commonly employed in the Persian sources of the time, whereas *barīd* is an Arabic term used to describe the horse relay stations of the Abbasids (749–1258) and the later communications network of the Mamluks of Egypt, which in fact was a development of the Mongols' *yam* system. Much of what is known of the functioning of the *yam* is from later sources that detail various reforms of the system and often lambaste the failings of the operation under former rulers. However, praise comes from many sources, including Marco Polo, who claims that distances of between 200 and 250 miles a day could be covered by the great khan's couriers, adding that "these strong, enduring messengers are highly prized men." The *yam* operating in China, where it originated, seems to have been more effectual than the Persian system, but whatever the criticisms of the sources (whose authors so often had their own agendas), this network of fresh horses, couriers, supply houses, and escorts succeeded in establishing a remarkable degree of cohesion and communication over such a vast empire.

The network was run by the army, and therefore it crisscrossed the whole expanse of Mongol-controlled territory, from Eastern Europe to the Sea of Japan. Post-houses were established every three or four *farsangs* (somewhere between 9 and 18 miles) and each *yam* had at least 15 horses in good condition and ready to go or, if Marco Polo is to be believed, between 200 and 400 ready mounts. Rashīd al-Dīn puts the figure at 500 mounts, but it can be assumed that different routes would have different requirements. *Īlchīs* (messengers or representatives) would be authorized to make use of these waiting horses as well as replenish their supplies or seek shelter if their journey was to be continued by another waiting *īlchī*. Though the army was entrusted with operating and replenishing these numerous *yam* stations, it was the local peasantry who supplied the food, fodder, and generous provisions that were made available to the *īlchīs* and others passing through. One of the abuses of the *yam* system that was rectified by later reforms was the frequent use made of these facilities by merchants. Officially only persons on official business and in possession of a tablet of authority, a *paiza,* made of wood, silver, or gold and engraved in the Uyghur script with a tiger or gerfalcon at its head were permitted to make use of the *yam* services. However, the heavy burden the *yam* stations inflicted on the locals suggest that many others benefited from the free horses, food, and provisions on offer. The frequent references in the sources to reforms of the system to curb misuse imply that such exploitation was widespread. Particularly urgent messages or documents could also be sent with runners who would also be on hand at the *yam* stations and at regular short intervals of a *farsang* or less in between. According to Marco Polo, they would wear belts of bells so that the runner at the next village would hear their approach and be able to make preparations to continue the relay. He further claimed that they carried not only urgent messages for the great khan but also fresh fruit. These runners or *paykān* would relay their packages from station to station, village to village, and they could cover between 30 to 40 *parsangs* in 24 hours. As with most figures recorded in medieval sources, numbers differ widely and cannot be relied on for accuracy. However, that the *yam* was a major institution and that it was crucial for the smooth and effective running of the empire cannot be questioned. The fact that someone of the prestige and status of Rashīd al-Dīn, the grand wazir to the Il-Khan of Persia, Ghazan Khan (r. 1295–1304), was put in charge of the *yam*'s operation and reform program speaks of the significance attached to this institution. Rashīd al-Dīn took responsibility for the *yam* stations away from the army and the burden of their financial upkeep from the local people and entrusted each *yam* to a great emir. Generous funds were allotted for maintenance, and strict regulations were laid down detailing exactly who was permitted use of the facilities. Documents requiring stamps and seals were issued to control unauthorized use of the horses, runners, and provisions of the *yam* stations. The *yam* under Ghazan Khan was a far more sophisticated institution than the improvised relay system that Chinggis Khan began adapting to his needs as his steppe empire began to emerge from its pastoralist past. It was certainly one of the more effective of the Mongols' imperial institutions, and it lived on in the *barīd* of the Egyptian Mamluks, the courier system found in the Delhi Sultanate, and even the *ulak* system of the Ottoman Turks.

CHINGGIS KHAN AND MUSLIMS

Although few now believe that the Mongol armies under Chinggis Khan or his successors had pointedly negative designs on the Muslim world, it is still widely believed that the advent of the Mongols bode ill for people and countries of the Islamic world. This view, however, has very little basis in fact and is increasingly being challenged. One recent biography of the great khan that appeared in 2007 was researched and penned by Michel Biran of the Hebrew University of Jerusalem. What is remarkable is that it is published by Oneworld Publications of Oxford in their series of "Makers of the Muslim World."[45] Chinggis Khan and his successors enjoyed positive and fruitful relationships with those Muslims they encountered and with whom they had political, cultural, and mercantile dealings.

There is a story related by the revered South Asian saint Shaykh Nizam al-Dīn Awliya (d. 1325) concerning Chinggis Khan that not only demonstrates the presence of influential Muslims at the heart of the Mongol court early in their campaigns but also the sophisticated and benign attitude of the world conqueror toward mankind. Though not specific, the narrative suggests the date in which the events occurred to be in the second decade of the thirteenth century. A certain Khwajeh 'Alī, the son of Khwajeh Rukn al-Dīn, the venerable Chishti saint, was taken prisoner by the Mongols. It so happened that when Khwajeh 'Alī was brought before Chinggis Khan to explain himself, there was present at the Mongol court one of the disciples of the Chishti Sufi order. Upon seeing a fellow Chishti Sufi, he at once began wondering how best to realize his release.

It has already been remarked on that with the initial encounter with the Islamic world, Jebe Noyen, one of Chinggis's four "Hounds of War," was regarded as a liberator and welcomed by the Uyghur Muslims of the former lands of the Qara Khitai as their deliverer from oppression. When the full force of the Mongol war machine was ranged against the Khwārazmshāh, the foremost representative of the Islamic world, there was a tradition emerging that the figure rallying the hosts of barbarism and ranks of infidels was not Chinggis Khan but in fact was the figure of the Sufi saint Shaykh Maṣlahat Khujandī.[46] Sufi tradition believes that God had sent the Mongols to punish the blasphemous Khwārazmshāh who had defied the caliph and who was an insult to the Islamic world. A fifteenth-century chronicler, Dawlatshāh, records the terror of the Khwārazmshāh who heard voices from the "unseen world" whispering, "Oh infidels, kill the evildoers"[47] and relates that some saw the Prophet Khizr leading the Tatar hosts. Other stories stress the central role of Shaykh Najm al-Dīn Kubrā in guiding and initiating the Mongol devastation of Khwārazm in fulfilment of God's designs. These stories were restricted to Sufi circles, but their significance lies in their reflection of the widespread ill will felt toward the Khwārazmshāh by the Muslim world and the acceptance of Chinggis Khan as an agent of the Divine.

The Mongols in the role as the Punishment of God was a common image of the time and one found in Armenian, Georgian, and Chinese, as well as Persian and Arabic, sources. The medieval mind saw the world in religious terms, and all events were played out on a spiritual chessboard. Nothing happened by chance, and divine intent could be discerned behind every eventuality. Juwaynī famously remarked after the fall of the Ismā'īlīs at their fortress of Alamut that now God's secret intent had become clear. It has often been assumed that Juwaynī, a troubled devout Sunni Muslim, was trying to assuage his guilt at working for the Mongols by seeing the annihilation of, in his eyes, a blasphemous sect as just retribution by a vengeful God. However, his words toward the end of his history of Chinggis Khan[48] were sentiments doubtless shared by many of his Muslim contemporaries. Not only had this perceived blasphemous scourge, the Ismā'īlīs, been destroyed, but the despised Khwarazmshah had also been removed and Islam had indeed been freed from its Arab homeland and freed upon the world. Juwaynī had traveled extensively, and he would have known the extent of Islam's penetration of China. Islam flourished in China far more vigorously than today. The port cities of Hangzhou, Quanzhou, and Guangzhou were Muslim strongholds, while the province of Yunnan, safeguarding the Mongol state's borders, had a Muslim governor, Sayyid 'Ajall, safely and fully entrenched. The Mongols played host to an international audience, and the stage was centered in Muslim Iran. Juwaynī's words were not hollow prayers for forgiveness but rather the realization that his judgment had been sound and that the Chinggisids represented a Muslim renaissance.

Muslim acceptance of the Mongols coincided with the emergence of the dominance of the Toluids, the Mongol rulers of Iran descended from Chinggis Khan's youngest son, Tolui. However, this acceptance was more to do with an identification with a new elite and a new world order that split not only the Mongol world but the Islamic world as well. It was the Persians and Turks who happily forgot about the injustices of the House of 'Abbas and the oppression of the Arabs and embraced a global vision and an economy and culture that spanned Asia from Kurdistan and Anatolia to Manzi and the three international port cities of Hangzhou, Quanzhou, and Guangzhou. Persian was the language spoken; Islam, Nestorian Christianity, and Buddhism were the religions practiced; and commerce was the cement. In Iran, the respected cleric and historian, Qāḍī Baḍāwī, had written and widely disseminated a "pocket history" that portrayed the Mongols as a legitimate and almost preordained Iranian dynasty. Written originally under Abaqa Khan (1234–1282), the second Mongol ruler of Iran from 1265, his little history found its way into every subsequent important historical bibliography, and the establishment of the Ilkhans so soon after their arrival suggests that the

Iranian delegation that petitioned Mongke Qa'an for a royal prince to rule over their province already envisaged absorbing themselves into the new Toluid empire that was emerging. In this brave new world, membership of the ruling elite was not dictated by ethnicity or religion. The Muslims of Iran and Turkistan were free to practice their religion, but their world was no longer bounded by the constraints of the past, and they were now members of a global community sometimes ruled over by infidels and sometimes ruling over infidels. This was the world that Chinggis Khan had left them, and this is the reason that so many Muslim rulers regarded Chinggis Khan and his successors as just and noble rulers.

NOTES

1. Igor de Rachewiltz, trans. and ann., *The Secret History of the Mongols: A Mongolian Epic Chronicle of the Thirteenth Century*, 2 vols. (Leiden: Brill, 2006), 1:320–21.

2. Urgunge Onon, trans., *Chinggis Khan: The Golden History of the Mongols* [i.e., the *Secret History*] (London: The Folio Society, 1993), 9.

3. Rashīd al-Dīn's work is translated and published as Rashiduddin Fazlullah, *Jami'u' t-tawarikh: A Compendium of Chronicles*, trans. and ann. Wheeler M. Thackston, 3 vols. (Cambridge, MA: Harvard University Press, 1998–1999; rpt. Ottoman Studies Foundation). Cited hereafter as Rashīd al-Dīn.

4. See Thomas T. Allsen, *Culture and Conquest in Mongol Eurasia* (Cambridge: Cambridge University Press, 2001).

5. Rashīd al-Dīn, *Jami'u' t-tawarikh*, 6 (text), 8–9.

6. "Bahadur" is a title awarded brave warrior leaders, used by both Rashīd al-Dīn and the *Secret History*. Chinggis Khan alone described his father as "khan."

7. de Rachewiltz, *The Secret History*, 1:16.

8. Onon, *Chinggis Khan*, 14–15.

9. Ibid., 14.

10. From the *Yuan Shi*, cited in Paul Ratchnevsky, *Genghis Khan: His Life and Legacy*, trans. and ed. Thomas Nivison Haining (Oxford: Blackwell, 1991), 24.

11. Onon, *Chinggis Khan*, 19.

12. Rashīd al-Dīn, *Jami'u' t-tawarikh*, 347.

13. Onon, *Chinggis Khan*, 33.

14. Ibid., 28–29.

15. The *Secret History* inaccurately claims the title "Chinggis Khan" was awarded at this time.

16. Onon, *Chinggis Khan*, 38–39.

17. On this form of execution, see Ratchnevsky, *Genghis Khan*, 46–47.

18. Toghrul was one of several historical persons who were identified as the legendary Prester John, tales of whom entranced Europe, as, indeed, was Chinggis Khan by the European Crusaders of the early thirteenth century.

19. Onon, *Chinggis Khan*, 56.

20. Ibid., 53.

21. Chinggis Khan's four "Hounds of War": Jelme, Kubilai, Jebe, and Subodai.

22. Onon, *Chinggis Khan*, 58.

23. Hülegü Khan, grandson of Chinggis Khan, founded the Il-Khanid dynasty, which ruled Iran from 1256 until 1335.

24. Onon, *Chinggis Khan*, 86–87.

25. Rashīd al-Dīn, *Jami'u' t-tawarikh*, 591; see also Ratchnevsky, *Genghis Khan*, 153.

26. Ata-Malik Juvaini, *Genghis Khan: The History of the World-Conqueror* [i.e., ʿAṭā Malik Juwaynī, *Tārīkh-i Jahān Gushā*], rev. ed., trans. and ed. John Andrew Boyle, introd. David O. Morgan, 2 vols., Manchester Medieval Studies (Manchester: Manchester University Press, 1997), 25–26. Cited hereafter as Juwaynī.

27. Michal Biran, "Like a Mighty Wall: the Armies of the Qara Khitai," *Jerusalem Studies in Arabic and Islam* 25 (2001): 44–91.

28. Minhāj Sirāj Jūzjānī, *The Tabakat-i-Nasiri of Minhaj-i-Saraj, Abu-Umar-i-Usman: A general history of the Muhammadan dynasties of Asia, including Hindustan from A. H. 194 (810 A. D.) to A. H. 658 (1260 A. D.), and the irruption of the infidel Mughals into Islam*, trans. Henry G. Raverty, Bibliotheca Indica, vol. 78 (Calcutta: Asiatic Society of Bengal, 1881; rpt. in 2 vols., New Delhi: Oriental Books Reprint Co., 1970), 966. Cited hereafter as Jūzjānī.

29. Ibn al-Athīr, *The Chronicle for the Crusading Period from al-Kāmil fi'l-ta'rīkh. Part 3. The Years 589–629/1193–1231: The Ayyubids after Saladin and the Mongol Menace*, trans. D. S. Richards (Aldershot, Hampshire: Ashgate, 2008), 261.

30. In the Bible, Gog is a hostile power that is ruled by Satan and will manifest itself immediately before the end of the world (Revelation 20). In the biblical passage in Revelation and in other Christian and Jewish apocalyptic literature, Gog is joined by a second hostile force, Magog; but elsewhere (Ezekiel 38; Genesis 10:2) Magog is apparently the place of Gog's origin. See the Encyclopædia Britannica Online, http://www.britannica.com/EBchecked/topic/237108/Gog-and-Magog.

31. *Chronicle of Novgorod, 1016–1471*, trans. Robert Mitchell and Nevill Forbes; introd. C. Raymond Beazley; account of the text A. A. Shakhmatov, Camden Society, 3rd Series, vol. 25 (London: Offices of the Society, 1914), 64.

32. David Nicolle and Viacheslav Shpakovsky, *Kalka River 1223: Genghiz Khan's Mongols Invade Russia* (Oxford: Osprey Publishing, 2001).

33. Rashīd al-Dīn, *Jami'u' t-tawarikh*, 531–35.

34. Rashīd al-Dīn, *Jāmi' al-Tavārīkh*, ed. M. Roushān and M. Mūsavī (Tehran, 1994), 78; Rashīd al-Dīn, *Jami'u' t-tawarikh* (trans. Thackston), 44.

35. Patricia Crone, *Slaves on Horses: The Evolution of the Islamic Polity* (Cambridge: Cambridge University Press, 1980), 20.

36. The debate has raged since Professor David Morgan published his now generally accepted paper on the subject, "The Great Yāsā of Chinggis Khān and Mongol Law in the Ilkhānate," *Bulletin of the School of Oriental and African Studies* 49, no. 1 (1986): 163–76.

37. Juwaynī, *Genghis Khan*, 25.

38. "The Tartar Relation," ed. George D. Painter, in *The Vinland Map and the Tartar Relation*, ed. R. A. Skelton, Thomas E. Marston, and George D. Painter, foreword by Alexander O. Vietor (New Haven, CT: Yale University Press, 1965), 96, 98.

39. Jūzjānī, *Tabakat-i-Nasiri*, 1078–79.

40. Rashīd al-Dīn, *Jami'u' t-tawarikh*, 1043, (trans. Thackston) 510–11.

41. Some sources, including the *Secret History*, suggest this title might have been awarded Temüjin by his own tribe at an earlier date and then endorsed in 1206.

42. Juwaynī, *Genghis Khan*, 105.

43. See, for example, Stephen R. Turnbull, *The Mongols*, illus. Angus McBride, Men at Arms Series 105 (Oxford: Osprey, 1980); Stephen R. Turnbull, *Mongol Warrior 1200–1350*, illus. Wayne Reynolds (Oxford: Osprey, 2003); Stephen R. Turnbull, *Genghis Khan and the Mongol Conquests 1190–1400*. (Oxford: Osprey, 2003); Antony Karasulas, *Mounted Archers of the Steppe 600 BC–AD 1300*, illus. Angus McBride (Oxford: Osprey, 2004); Timothy May, *The Mongol Art of War* (Yardley, PA: Westholme, 2007).

44. Juwaynī, *Genghis Khan*, 27–28.

45. Michal Biran, *Chinggis Khan* (Oxford: Oneworld, 2007).

46. Devin DeWeese, "'Stuck in the Throat of Chingīz Khān:' Envisioning the Mongol Conquests in Some Sufi Accounts from the 14th to 17th Centuries," in *History and Historiography of Post-Mongol Central Asia and the Middle East: Studies in Honor of John E. Woods*, ed. Judith Pfeiffer and Sholeh A. Quinn, with Ernest Tucker (Wiesbaden: Harrassowitz Verlag, 2006), 23–60.

47. *The Tadhkiratu 'Sh-Shu'ará ("Memoirs of the Poets") of Dawlatsháh bin 'Alá'u 'd-Dawla Bakhtísháh al-Ghází of Samarqand*, ed. Edward G. Browne, Persian Historical Texts Series 1 (London: Luzac & Co., 1901; rpt. on demand Whitefish, Montana: Kessinger, 2010), 134–35.

48. Juwaynī, *Genghis Khan*, 638.

FURTHER READING

Allsen, Thomas. *Culture and Conquest in Mongol Eurasia*. Cambridge: Cambridge University Press, 2001.

Amitai, Reuven. *The Mongols in the Islamic Lands: Studies in the History of the Ilkhanate*. Variorum Collected Studies Series. Aldershot, Hampshire: Ashgate, 2007.

Amitai, Reuven, and Michal Biran, eds. *Mongols, Turks, and Others: Eurasian Nomads and the Sedentary World*. Leiden: Brill, 2005.

Bar Hebraeus. *The Chronography of Gregory Ab'l Faraj the Son of Aaron Hebrew Physician Commonly Known as Bar Hebraeus. Being the First Part of His Political History of the World*. Translated by E. A. Wallis Budge. 2 vols. Oxford: Oxford University Press, 1932. Rpt. Gorgias Historical Texts 6, 7. Piscataway, NJ: Gorgias Press, 2003.

Biran, Michal. *Chinggis Khan*. Oxford: Oneworld Publications, 2006.

Browne, Edward G. *A History of Persian Literature under Tartar Domination (A.D. 1265–1502)*. Cambridge: Cambridge University Press, 1920; rpt. New Delhi: Munshiram Manoharlal Publishers, 1996. (Vol. 3 of Browne's *A Literary History of Persia*.)

Dunnell, Ruth W. *Chinggis Khan: World Conqueror*. The Library of World Biography. Boston: Longman, 2010.

Fitzhugh, William, Morris Rossabi, and William Honeychurch, eds. *Genghis Khan and the Mongol Empire*. [Media, PA]: Dino Don, 2009.

Juvaini, Ata-Malik. *Genghis Khan: The History of the World-Conqueror* [i.e., ʿAṭā Malik Juwaynī, *Tārīkh-i Jahān Gushā*]. Rev. ed. Translated and edited by John Andrew Boyle, with an introduction by David O. Morgan. 2 vols. Manchester Medieval Studies. Manchester: Manchester University Press, 1997.

Karasulas, Antony. *Mounted Archers of the Steppe 600 BC–AD 1300*. Illustrated by Angus McBride. Oxford: Osprey, 2004.

Krawulsky, Dorothea. *The Mongol Īlkhāns and Their Vizier Rashīd al-Dīn*. Frankfurt am Main: Peter Lang, 2011.

Komaroff, Linda. *Beyond the Legacy of Genghis Khan*. Leiden: Brill, 2006.

Komaroff, Linda, and Stefano Carboni, eds. *The Legacy of Genghis Khan: Courtly Art and Culture in Western Asia, 1256–1353*. New York: Metropolitan Museum of Art, 2002.

Lane, George. *Genghis Khan and Mongol Rule*. Westport, CT: Greenwood, 2004. Paperback rpt. Indianapolis: Hackett, 2009.

Lane, George. *Daily Life in the Mongol Empire*. Westport, CT: Greenwood, 2006. Paperback rpt. Indianapolis: Hackett, 2009.

Marco Polo. *The Book of Ser Marco Polo the Venetian, Concerning the Kingdoms and Marvels of the East*. Translated by Henry Yule and revised by Henri Cordier. Rpt. New Delhi: Munshiram Manoharlal Publishers, 1999. (The 3rd edition [London: John Murray, 1903] of Yule's translation, which was "revised throughout in the light of recent discoveries by Henri Cordier.")

Marshall, Robert. *Storm from the East: From Genghis Khan to Khubilai Khan*. Berkeley: University of California Press, 1993; London: BBC Books, 1993.

May, Timothy. *The Mongol Art of War*. Yardley, PA: Westholme, 2007.

Morgan, David O., and Reuven Amitai-Preiss, eds. *The Mongol Empire and Its Legacy*. Leiden: Brill, 1999.

Rashiduddin Fazlullah [Rashīd al-Dīn]. *Jami'u' t-tawarikh: A Compendium of Chronicles*. Translated and annotated by Wheeler M. Thackston. 3 vols. Cambridge, MA: Harvard University Press, 1998–1999. Rpt. Ottoman Studies Foundation.

Ratchnevsky, Paul. *Genghis Khan: His Life and Legacy*. Translated and edited by Thomas Nivison Haining. Oxford: Blackwell, 1991.

Turnbull, Stephen. *Genghis Khan and the Mongol Conquests 1190–1400*. Oxford: Osprey, 2003.

Turnbull, Stephen. *The Mongols*. Illustrated by Angus McBride. Men at Arms Series 105. Oxford: Osprey, 1980.

Turnbull, Stephen. *Mongol Warrior 1200–1350*. Illustrated by Wayne Reynolds. Oxford: Osprey, 2003.

Painting of Dante Alighieri by Renaissance painter Giotto di Bondone. Dante is considered one of the great Italian poets of the Middle Ages. His work helped form the basis for the modern Italian literary tradition. (Corel)

Dante Alighieri (1265–1321)

Elizabeth K. Haller

INTRODUCTION

Known in Italy as "il Sommo Poeta" ("the Supreme Poet"), Dante Alighieri's relatively short list of works contains some of the most highly influential pieces in the literary canon. Although he is most well-known for his epic poem *The Divine Comedy* (ca. 1308–21), Dante was a political thinker as well as a poet and prose writer. In fact, his influence also stretched beyond literature to language, contributing to the slow demise of Latin as a predominant literary tool. Latin was the prevailing written language of the time; all of the most scholarly individuals used it. Florence-born Dante, however, political free-thinking rebel that he was, chose to write in the language of his forefathers and countrymen: Italian. By doing so, Dante effectively turned Italian into a literary language, thereby securing his designation as "Father of the Italian Language," one of several honorary titles assigned to him.

With its solemn purpose and literary style, *The Divine Comedy* soon established that it was entirely possible for Italian to be used as a literary language. The Italian in which Dante wrote was mostly based on the regional dialect of Tuscany, with some elements of other regional dialects. His aim was to deliberately reach a diverse readership throughout Italy—not just people of scholarship or high status who understood and spoke Latin. By creating an epic poem, both structurally and in its philosophic purpose, he established that the Italian language was more than suitable for the highest form of literary expression.

Publishing works in Italian marked Dante as one of the first (though soon to be followed by other writers such as Chaucer and Boccaccio) to break free from the established standard of writing in Latin (the language of religion, history, and scholarly study as well as of lyric poetry). This break from the norm set a precedent and allowed more literature to be published in other languages for wider audiences—this would ultimately set the stage for higher levels of literacy. However, Dante did not really become widely read (that is, beyond Italy) until the Romantic era (approximately 1820–90), when he was viewed as an "original genius" and placed in stature alongside Shakespeare and Homer—pretty good company. Throughout the nineteenth century, Dante's reputation grew, and by the time of the centenary in 1865 of his birth, he was firmly viewed as one of the greatest literary icons of the Western world.

Now that we have noted the steady increase in Dante's fame, let us examine more closely the man behind the legend. In order to do so, we must go on a fact-finding mission through the works he has left behind. Why? Because Dante included numerous autobiographical references throughout his writings, and he placed himself as the central character taking the epic journey in *The Divine Comedy*. This is where our search begins. References he makes within this epic poem are our only indication of Dante's birth date. The exact year and date of his birth are unknown, but searching through *The Divine Comedy* we find his statement "Halfway through the journey we are living" (*The Inferno*). This is a clue. A foundation of Dante's Florentine culture was the Bible, and within this text (Ps. 90:10) a full lifespan is described as "three score and ten years," or 70. Therefore, if he is halfway through the journey of life, he must be roughly 35 years old. Because there is indication within the *The Divine Comedy* that the events take place in 1300, that would mean he was born around 1265. Now we have a hint of the year, but what about the date? In the *Paradiso* section of *The Divine Comedy,* he refers to his being born when the sun was in the constellation Gemini, which would place his birth date somewhere between mid-May and mid-June. Not as precise a date of birth as some might like, but it's a start. Why is it necessary for us to search Dante's writing in this manner for factual evidence of his life? By all accounts, Dante did not leave behind any autobiographical data other than references such as these found in his writings, what is made available in public records of the time, and what is recounted in Giovanni Boccaccio's formal life of Dante, *Trattatello in laude di Dante* (*Little Tractate in Praise of Dante*), written at some point after 1348.

It is largely through these public records and Boccaccio's account that we are able to gather information concerning Dante's childhood as well as his literary and political life. We know Dante's mother was Bella degli Abati, who died sometime before his tenth birthday. His father, Alighiero di Bellincione, soon remarried to Lapa di Chiarissimo Cialuffi, with whom he had two children, Dante's half-brother Francesco and half-sister Tana (Gaetana).

EDUCATION

We have no specifics regarding Dante's early childhood education, but given his family's relatively high social standing and religious belief system, it can be presumed that he studied at home or in a Florentine school included as part of a church or monastery. He informs us in his *La Vita Nuova* (*The New Life*) (ca. 1292) that he taught himself how to write verse. He studied poetry at a time when the Sicilian School (*Scuola poetica Siciliana*), a group from Sicily who wrote hundreds of courtly love poems between 1230 and 1266, was becoming well-known. He had an interest in Occitan, a romance language; poetry of the performing troubadours; and the classical Latin poetry of such famous and influential writers as Ovid, Cicero, and most especially Virgil, who would later become a leading figure in Dante's *Divine Comedy*.

Dante's interest in philosophy grew out of his readings, and he eventually dedicated himself to philosophical studies at religious schools, including the school located at the Dominican church in Santa Maria Novella. He also took part either overtly or indirectly in the debates between the two principal religious orders, Franciscan and Dominican, held in Florence. The Franciscans represented the doctrine of the mystics and of Saint Bonaventure, while the Dominicans supported the largely Aristotelian theories of Saint Thomas Aquinas. It was these Aristotelian theories that would most influence Dante.

When he was approximately 18 years old, Dante met contemporary poets and writers Lapo Gianni, Guido Cavalcanti, Brunetto Latini, and Cino da Pistoia. Together, they developed the *Dolce Stil Novo* (Sweet New Style) of writing, exploring themes of love. Brunetto would later receive special mention in *The Divine Comedy*, but it was Guido to whom Dante dedicated *The New Life* and who would later be referred to by Dante as "the first of my friends."

POLITICAL LIFE

Dante was born into a family who claimed allegiance to the Guelphs, one of two opposing factions (the Ghibellines being the other) that kept Italy divided through civil wars during the greater part of the Middle Ages (the thirteenth and fourteenth centuries). The Guelphs were primarily of the merchant middle classes and were sympathetic to the papacy (both the Pope himself and the church in general), while the Ghibellines were primarily of the aristocracy, held contempt for the church, and were instead sympathetic to the Holy Roman Emperor. Dante was born into a contentious period in Florence's history, with power bouncing back and forth between the Guelphs and the Ghibellines.

It helps to know the background of this contention to understand better the context of Dante's belief system, which so influenced his writing. The Ghibellines gained power in Florence in 1249 and immediately banished the Guelphs. Ezzelino da Romano was one of the leaders of the Ghibelline movement and had a reputation for cruelty. He is depicted by Dante as a tyrant in *The Divine Comedy*. When the Ghibelline leader, Frederick II, died in 1250, the Guelphs regained and retained power until 1260. By all accounts, Florence prospered politically and economically during this time. However, when the Guelphs were deemed responsible for the Florentine loss in the battle of Montaperti (1260), the Ghibellines resumed power once again, putting an end to the prosperous times Florence saw under Guelph rule. The ruling Ghibellines restored laws that favored their own party, exiled prominent Guelphs, and destroyed every building belonging to or associated with the principal leaders of the Guelph party in a deliberate campaign of revenge. Dante's father was not affected by this destruction or these exiles, suggesting that he either received some type of exemption or was of such low political standing among the Guelphs that he was deemed insignificant and not worthy of punishment.

Being born into this historic Florentine power struggle, it is no wonder Dante took an active position in the cause. We know that Dante's loyalties lay with the Guelphs, as there is a record of his fighting at the forefront of the Guelph cavalry at the battle of Campaldino (1289) against the Ghibellines. The Guelphs emerged victorious and took back the ruling authority of Florence from the Ghibellines. At this point, Dante took an active interest in politics, so much so that by 1295 he had earned quite a name for himself in Florentine political circles.

There was serious turmoil in the Guelph party, however, and by 1300, the Guelphs had split into two factions, the *Bianchi* (Whites) and the *Neri* (Blacks). The Whites emerged as the power in Florence. They supported the burgher government (made up of the democratic middle class, or merchant class) and the Ordinance of Justice (restrictive laws primarily directed against all Ghibelline sympathizers, who were primarily of the more noble classes, and requiring that anyone who wished to enter public office must first be actively enrolled in either a commercial or an artisan guild). The Whites were opposed to Pope Boniface VIII and wished to extend the political power of the Florentines as well as their intellectual dominance. The Blacks, though, supported the aristocracy and had the support of the Pope. Naturally, Dante supported the Whites. Dante followed the Aristotelian concept that man is a social/ political being, and he held firm to the belief that individuals should put their knowledge and skills to use in the service of their country. His philosophical mind and writing were just some of the skills that he possessed. Therefore, further conforming to the enrollment requirements set forth by the Ordinance of Justice, in 1295 Dante entered the Guild of Physicians and Apothecaries (the only guild suitable for philosophers). By 1300 he maintained an active political and public role with the White faction and was named prior (magistrate), one of the six highest-level magistrates in Florence. He is recorded as having spoken or voted in various councils of the republic. Unfortunately, a substantial portion of minutes from the meetings that took place between 1298 and 1300 were lost during the repercussions suffered by Italy in World War II. As a result, the specifics of Dante's involvement in Florentine councils of the republic remain relatively uncertain.

The dominance of the Whites was relatively short-lived, though, because in 1301 the Blacks were restored to power in Florence and sought payback against whom they deemed to be the more influential and outspoken Whites. As one might expect, Dante fell under the category of those to receive such payback and was one of the first to be ousted from public office. On a phony charge of corruption and hostility toward the church, he was sentenced in January 1302 to permanent exclusion from public office, including the Blacks' promise of death by burning should he ever go against this sentence. Ultimately, in April 1302, the Blacks succeeded in banishing the entire White faction, including Dante, from Florence. At this time Dante was married, with at least three children that we know of: Jacopo, Pietro, and Antonia. Once he was exiled, Dante never returned to Florence and never saw his wife, Gemma, again; his sons and his daughter would join him in later years.

Never seeing his wife again might seem a bit harsh, but there might be a reason why he did not seek out his wife or fight to have his family exiled along with him. As was common at the time, Dante's family promised him in marriage when he was 12 years old to Gemma di Manetto Donati (ca. 1265–1329/32), daughter of a prominent family in Florence. The actual marriage would take place between three and five years later. As the marriage was an arranged one, there is a good chance he did not have undying feelings toward Gemma. This is another instance in which exploring Dante's work provides some insights into events in his life. As it has been established that Dante tended to put much of himself in his writings, the fact that he didn't mention Gemma in any of his poems (not even a word or a scribble) is perhaps the best indication we have of a lack of passionate love toward her. Or, perhaps Gemma was aware of Dante's emotional devotion to another woman and so did not mind too much when he was exiled. While Gemma is glaringly absent from Dante's work, several of his poems mention or are singularly devoted to this "other woman"—Beatrice. Although they were apparently never involved in a romantic relationship, theirs is perhaps the most romantic of poet-muse relationships to exist in literature, and it is certainly the most popular.

When he was nine, Dante met and fell instantly in love with Beatrice di Folco Portinari ("Bice") (1266–1290), a girl differing only a few months in age from himself who would have a powerful presence in his life and in his writings and who would ultimately become one of the most celebrated fictionalized representations in all of literature. If he was so in love with Beatrice, why didn't Dante's family promise him in marriage to her instead of Gemma? Aside from the fact that love had very little to do with arranged marriages, we do not know for certain. It is quite possible, though, that Dante's family took into consideration her background (though we are unaware of the specifics of her family connections) and may have felt that a marriage to Gemma would prove more beneficial than a marriage to Beatrice.

Dante claimed in his writings that his love for Beatrice was transcendent, a spiritual and mystical love of true friendship rather than a passionate sexual or physical love (though cynics might claim that this sounds like a "we're just friends" defense). Who could blame Gemma for not joining Dante in exile?—transcendent love is a tough act to follow. It is, perhaps, not coincidental that Dante's daughter took the name of Sister Beatrice upon entering the convent at Santo Stefano degli Olivi at Ravenna. It is quite evident that the feelings Dante had for his Beatrice not only held sway over his emotions throughout his lifetime but also had a definite effect on his family. Gemma must have been an incredibly tolerant wife.

Sadly, Beatrice died in 1290, when Dante was in his mid-twenties. After Beatrice's death, Dante was overcome with grief and set out to memorialize his lost love by composing several poems dedicated to Beatrice. The collection he produced at this time was placed together with poems he had previously written and devoted to her in her lifetime. The result was *The New Life,* a collection of poems in which he recounts the first time he ever saw Beatrice ("the glorious lady" of his heart). *The New Life* ends with the promise that he would write of Beatrice "what has never before been written of any woman"—this would ultimately become the *Paradiso* section of *The Divine Comedy.*

LIFE IN EXILE

Where did Dante go during his exile? Some sources claim that he spent two years in Paris, from 1308 to 1310, and some time at Oxford, but these are largely unsubstantiated claims. There is no indication that Dante ever left Italy. He initially joined the other exiles in Arezzo, an area largely controlled by the Ghibellines. Themselves banished from Florence, the Ghibellines tended to sympathize with these newly exiled White Guelphs. We know that Dante attempted to gain his way back into Florence using Ghibelline force, because his name is included on a 1302 document naming the exiled Whites who were forming an alliance with the Ghibellines to enter into war with the Florentine Republic. However, in a similar signed document dated 1303, his name is no longer listed among those in the alliance. Sometime between 1302 and 1303, he sought refuge in Verona.

Dante's interest in philosophy and literary pursuits only deepened in exile, when his time was no longer taken up by Florentine domestic politics as a prior. It is during his exile that Dante wrote his most notable works: *The Divine Comedy*, *The Banquet*, *On the Eloquence of the Vernacular*, and *On Monarchy*. He was quite outspoken during his time in exile, as evidenced by his writings. He openly criticized what he saw as the obvious ecclesiastical corruption of the times and condemned most of the contemporary popes, leading some, both now and then, to question whether or not Dante was a heretic. *The Divine Comedy* has been closely analyzed by contemporary and modern critics and scholars for any signs of heresy, but there is no trace that Dante ever spoke against the supreme doctrine of the church. In fact, from childhood he had always held the highest respect for the divine power of the church. It was the perceived political power of the church that he had problems with: he strongly disagreed with the position that the pope could grant political authority upon Roman Emperors—a strong position he would later explore in *On Monarchy*. In hindsight, we can see Dante's outspokenness against certain ecclesiastical power issues as a forerunner of prominent thoughts leading to the Reformation.

In 1304, he is documented as living in Bologna, where he began (but left unfinished) his Latin treatise *De vulgari eloquentia* (*On the Eloquence of the Vernacular*; ca. 1304–7). In 1306, however, all Florentine exiles were barred from Bologna, and Dante was once again displaced. Later that year we find him in Padua and Lunigiana. His writing during this time centers on lyrical poems, more particularly a series of 14 *canzones* that are primarily allegorical (figurative symbols) and didactic (instructional) in nature. These poems eventually connected *The New Life* with *The Divine Comedy*. In one of the odes he wrote at this time, the "Canzone of the Three Ladies," Dante expresses his outlook on the situation in which he finds himself. In the ode, Dante is visited in his banishment by the personification of Justice and her spiritual children, exiled like him, and he declares that with these as his companions in his misfortune, his counts his exile as an honor.

In 1308, Henry of Luxembourg was elected emperor as Henry VII. In him Dante saw a new hope for Italy, a healer of its bitter wounds, with the potential to retake Florence from the Black Guelphs. Although he had remained outside of an active involvement in politics since beginning his exile, this new hope for the salvation of his homeland drew him back into a life of political action. This involvement, however, would not end well for Dante. In 1309, highly anticipating the emperor's 1310 arrival in Italy, Dante wrote his famous work, *On Monarchy*, in three books, which proposed a universal monarchy under Henry VII. In 1310, Henry marched 5,000 troops into Italy. In September 1310, Dante enthusiastically announced his hopes regarding Henry VII in a letter to the princes and peoples of Italy. He also sent a letter to Henry VII demanding that he destroy the Black Guelphs in Florence and suggesting several particular targets who just happened to coincide with those he felt were his personal enemies. In 1311, however, Dante wrote to the Florentine government, "the most wicked Florentines within," and blatantly criticized their opposition to the emperor, and later he wrote to Henry VII admonishing him for his delay in taking back the city of Florence. This did not make the Black Guelphs too happy, obviously, and on a decree dated September 2, 1311, Dante was included in the list of those who were permanently exempted from all amnesty and grace by the Florentine republic.

Early in 1312, Dante joined other exiles in Pisa, where the emperor was readying a revolt against the Black Guelphs in Florence. It is believed that Dante's undying reverence for the city of his birth kept him from joining the imperial army as they besieged Florence later that year. The attack on the city, however, proved unsuccessful. The White Guelphs quickly began to disintegrate after this loss and completely deteriorated in August 1313 with the death of Henry VII. With the failure of the Whites and the death of the emperor, Dante's hopes for what could and should be accomplished in Florence were effectively destroyed.

He took refuge at a convent in Santa Croce de Fonte Avellana and later traveled to Lucca under the protection of Uguccione della Faggiuola, a Ghibelline soldier who had temporarily made himself lord of that city. In 1315, as a consequence of his association with this soldier, the Florentines renewed the threat of Dante's death sentence and, perhaps to further ensure Dante's lack of political involvement, included his family in the condemnation as well. His sons and daughter would eventually join him in exile.

In 1316, more amnesty decrees were passed in Florence, and although there appears to have been some attempt made to have Dante included in the list of those to receive amnesty, Dante was vehemently against it. Knowing his innocence in the matters that led to his exile, he refused to return to Florence under such shameful conditions. Later that year, Dante went back to Verona, where he met Cangrande della Scala, an imperial cleric who ruled a large portion of Eastern Lombardy. In Cangrande, Dante saw a personification of the knightly ideal and a replacement for Henry VII as another possible new hope for Italy. Many commentators suggest that Dante represents Cangrande in *The Divine Comedy* as the "Veltro," or greyhound, the hero whose coming is prophesied at the beginning of *The Inferno*, and who is to put into effect the imperial ideals of his *On Monarchy*, succeeding where Henry VII had failed. Dante dedicated *The Paradiso* to Cangrande.

Throughout his exile, although Dante moved around quite a bit in Italy, he remained eternally devoted to Florence. In *Il Convivio* (*The Banquet*) (ca. 1304–07), Dante provides an emotional account of the poverty and misery he endured during his exile. He also recounts this misery in *The Paradiso*:

. . . Tu lascerai ogne cosa diletta	. . . You shall leave everything you
più caramente; e questo è quello strale	love most:
che l'arco de lo essilio pria saetta.	this is the arrow that the bow of exile
Tu proverai sì come sa di sale	shoots first. You are to know the
lo pane altrui, e come è duro calle	bitter taste
lo scendere e 'l salir per l'altrui	of others' bread, how salty it is, and
scale . . .	know
	how hard a path it is for one who goes
	ascending and descending others'
	stairs . . .

In 1319, Dante received a letter from Giovanni del Virgilio, a lecturer in Latin at the University of Bologna, inviting him to come to Bologna and receive the laurel crown in that city. This circular wreath-like crown, made of interlocking leaves and branches, is generally presented to accomplished individuals with worthy and notable works in their field of study. It is most often seen in portraits of medieval poets, philosophers, and scholars. Several portraits of Dante show him wearing the laurel crown, but this crown is representative of the honor he should have received in life but never did. Dante expressed his unalterable resolution to receive the laurel crown only from Florence—a resolve filled with his intent to one day be recognized by Florence not only for his literary accomplishments but also for his innocence of the crimes for which he was banished. He describes this resolve in *The Paradiso*:

Se mai continga che 'l poema sacro	If it ever comes to pass that the sacred
al quale ha posto mano e cielo e terra,	poem
sì che m'ha fatto per molti anni macro,	To which both heaven and earth have
vinca la crudeltà che fuor mi serra	set their hand
del bello ovile ov'io dormi' agnello,	So as to have made me lean for many
nimico ai lupi che li danno guerra;	years
con altra voce omai, con altro vello	should overcome the cruelty that
ritornerò poeta, e in sul fonte	bars me
del mio battesmo prenderò	from the fair sheepfold where I slept
'l cappello . . .	as a lamb,
	an enemy to the wolves that make
	war on it,
	with another voice now and other
	fleece
	I shall return a poet and at the font
	of my baptism take the laurel
	crown . . .

In 1317, Dante settled at Ravenna, and it was here that he would complete *The Divine Comedy*. He died in exile in Ravenna in 1321, where his daughter, the nun Beatrice, had by this time joined him in his exile and cared for him until his death. Dante never returned to Florence and was buried in Ravenna at the Church of San Pier Maggiore. In his final years Dante was admirably received in many noble houses of Italy, most notably by Guido Novello da Polenta, the nephew of the tragic Francesca (represented in *The Inferno*), in Ravenna. Guido saw to it that Dante was given an honorable burial. His funeral was attended by the leading poets and writers of the time. Guido was with Dante at his death, and he requested that he be able to deliver Dante's funeral eulogy—a high honor, showing how highly he favored Dante.

By 1483 Dante's literary contributions were well known, and Bernardo Bembo, a Venetian magistrate, ordered a better tomb be built to house Dante's remains. On his tomb, Bernardo Canaccio, a friend of Dante, had etched the phrase "parvi Florentia mater amoris" ("Florence, mother of little love"). Eventually, after several decades of change, Florence came to regret Dante's exile and made repeated requests to Ravenna for the return of his remains. The church guardians of Dante's body, however, refused to comply. At one point, however, they feared Florence might try to take the bones by force, so they concealed Dante's remains in a false wall of the monastery. In 1829, a tomb was built for him in Florence in the basilica of Santa Croce, but the tomb remains empty to this day, with Dante's body remaining in his tomb in Ravenna. On the front of his Florence tomb is etched a phrase from his *Inferno*: "Onorate l'altissimo poeta" ("Honor the most exalted poet"). In *The Inferno*, this quote depicts Virgil's welcome as he returns among the great ancient poets spending eternity in Limbo. The rest of the line, "L'ombra sua torna, ch'era dipartita" ("his spirit, which had left us, returns") is absent from the empty tomb.

MOST NOTABLE WORKS

La Vita Nuova *(The New Life; ca. 1292)*

The New Life was a celebration of Dante's love for Beatrice. This work was a medley of lyrical verse and poetic prose, also known as *prosimetrum*. It is the first of two collections of verse that Dante would make in his lifetime (the other is *The Banquet*). In each collection, the prose form is a device for binding together poems composed over a 10-year period. *The New Life* brought together Dante's poetic efforts from before 1283 to roughly 1292–93; *The Banquet* contains his most important poetic compositions from just prior to 1294 to the time of *The Divine Comedy* (begun in ca. 1308).

Dante referred to *The New Life* as his *libello* (small book). It contains 42 chapters with commentaries on 25 sonnets, 1 ballad, and 4 canzones; a fifth canzone is left interrupted by Beatrice's death. The prose commentary provides the story of the collection, which tells of the first time Dante saw Beatrice (when they were nine), the measures he took to conceal his love for her, his anguish at the possibility that she might ignore him, his determination to rise above this anguish and sing only of Beatrice's virtues, and finally his mourning over her death. In the last chapter, Dante expresses his desire to write about her "that which has never been written of any woman"—the writing he is referring to will become his *Paradiso*, in which Beatrice is the ultimate symbol of salvation in *The Divine Comedy*.

The New Life contains many of Dante's love poems in Italian. One of the most famous poems in *The New Life* is "Tanto gentile e tanto onesta pare":

Tanto gentile e tanto onesta pare	So winsome and so worthy seems to me my lady,
La donna mia quand'ella altrui saluta,	when she greets a passer-by,
Ch'ogni lingua divien tremando muta	that every tongue can only babble shy
E gli occhi non ardiscon di guardare.	and eager glances lose temerity.
Ella sen va, sentendosi laudare	Sweetly and dressed in all humility,
Benignamente d'umilta`vestuta,	away she walks from all she's praisèd by,
E par che sia una cosa venuta	and truly seems a thing come from the sky
Di cielo in terra a miracol mostrare.	to show on earth what miracles can be.
Mostrasi si' piacente a chi la mira,	So much she pleases every gazing eye,
Che da' per gli occhi una dolcezza al core,	she gives a sweetness through it to the heart,
Che intender non la puo' chi non la prova.	which he who does not feel it fails to guess.
E par che della sua labbia si muova	A spirit full of love and tenderness
Uno spirto soave e pien d'amore,	seems from her features ever to depart,
Che va dicendo all'anima: sospira	that, reaching for the soul, says softly "Sigh."

Dante's commentary on his own work is also in Italian—both in *The New Life* and in *The Banquet*—instead of the Latin that was almost universally used at the time.

Il Convivio (The Banquet; ca. 1304–7)

The Banquet is a collection of allegorical commentaries in prose on several of Dante's own poems. While he projected 15 treatises, the work contains only 4—an introduction and three commentaries. These treatises tell how Dante became a lover of Philosophy, personified as a mystical woman whose soul is love and whose body is wisdom, she "whose true abode is in the most secret place of the Divine Mind."

In the introduction, Dante represents this work as a metaphorical banquet made of wisdom, in which the poems are the meat and the commentaries the bread. The guests to this banquet are primarily all who are eager for philosophical knowledge but who may be too consumed by political life.

De vulgari eloquentia (On the Eloquence of the Vernacular; ca. 1304–7)

A Latin treatise, *On the Eloquence of the Vernacular* is the first theoretical discussion of the Italian literary language. In it, Dante attempts to discover the ideal Italian language, the noblest form of the vernacular, and then to show how it should be used when composing poems. Of the four books he planned, only the first and part of the second were written.

De Monarchia (On Monarchy; 1309)

His close involvement in the political controversies of the time led Dante to write *On Monarchy*, one of the major tracts of medieval political philosophy. It is written in Latin to underscore its accessibility to those whom Dante felt most needed to read it—those in power. *On Monarchy* argues for the necessity of a universal monarchy in order to establish universal peace, and this monarchy's relationship to the Roman Church is a necessity as a guide to eternal peace. Entirely familiar with the writers of classical tradition, Dante drew on works from Cicero, Virgil, and Boethius in making his argument.

In *On Monarchy*, Dante attempts to show that a single supreme and earthly monarchy is necessary for the well-being of the world. He writes that the Roman people acquired universal sovereign sway by divine right and that the authority of the emperor is not dependent upon the pope but descends upon him directly from God.

Dante states that man is intended for two purposes: blessedness of this life and blessedness of life eternal. To these two ends man must come by diverse means, for to the first "we attain by the teachings of philosophy, following them by acting in accordance with the moral and intellectual virtues. To the second by spiritual teachings, which transcend human reason, as we follow them by acting according to theological virtues." Although these ends seem clear to Dante, he believed that man would invariably reject them if they were not somehow guided by a universal monarchy: "Wherefore man had need of a twofold directive power according to his twofold end, to wit, the Supreme Pontiff, to lead the human race in accordance with things revealed, to eternal life; and the Emperor, to direct the human race to temporal felicity in accordance with the teachings of philosophy." According to Dante, it is therefore the duty of the emperor to establish freedom and peace "on this threshing floor of mortality."

Inevitably, *On Monarchy* was condemned by the Black Guelphs and burned after Dante's death in 1321.

La Divina Commedia *(The Divine Comedy; ca. 1308–21)*

"Abandon hope, all ye who enter here" is surely one of the most well known and memorable lines in literature, drawn from Dante's *Divine Comedy.* In approximately 1308, Dante began work on this most notable literary feat and finished it just prior to his death in 1321. Originally called *Commedia* and later called "*divina*" by Boccaccio, this monumental epic poem became known and referred to as *The Divine Comedy.* It is often considered the greatest literary work composed in the Italian language and a masterpiece of world literature. With the trials Dante suffered in exile, it is perhaps even more poignant that he was never able to hear such validation and acclamations of this work during his lifetime.

One of the earliest outside indications that the poem was under way in 1308 is a notice by the law professor Francesco da Barberino in his *I Documenti d'Amore* (*Lessons of Love*) and written circa 1314. He speaks of Virgil and notes an appreciation that Dante followed the classic poet in a poem called the *Comedy* and that at least part of the poem was set in Hell—the *Inferno* portion of *The Divine Comedy.* Da Barberino does not specifically indicate whether or not he had seen or read *The Inferno,* but this does indicate that Dante was quite far along in the poem at this time. *The Inferno* was in circulation by 1317, a year established by contemporary marginal quotes found within dated records from Bologna.

The Divine Comedy is the last great work of the Italian Middle Ages. It effectively sums up the knowledge of the centuries and gives a detailed picture of Catholicism in thirteenth-century Italy. In this sacred poem, Dante presents a Christian vision of human earthly and eternal destiny. It models the spiritual journey through acknowledgment of sin, repentance, and penance, leading to salvation. On its most personal level, *The Divine Comedy* draws on Dante's experience of exile. Dante spoke of truth as a force that transcends any philosophical school of thought or "earthly paradise." He wrote of a truth that he believed the entirety of mankind longs for: the transcendent, universal light. *The Divine Comedy* is written as an allegory in the form of a pilgrim's journey through *Inferno* (Hell) and *Purgatorio* (Purgatory), guided by the classic Roman poet Virgil, and on through to *Paradiso* (Paradise), guided by Dante's love Beatrice. It is from the classical tradition that Dante seems to have derived his conception of the epic poem, a framing story that is large enough to cover the most pressing issues of his time.

While the vision of Hell may be fairly vivid for modern readers, the religious ideas present in Purgatory and Paradise require a certain amount of knowledge to appreciate. This is perhaps why most modern renditions of Dante's poem tend to focus on *The Inferno,* as it is the more accessible work for readers without prior historical or theological knowledge. *The Purgatorio,* the most lyrical of the three, also mentions the most poets. *The Paradiso,* the most heavily religious in nature, contains beautiful passages in which Dante tries to describe what he confesses he is unable to convey. For example, when Dante looks into the face of God, he states: "all'alta fantasia qui mancò possa" ("at this high moment, ability failed my capacity to describe").

Readers often have difficulty understanding how a poem with such an obviously serious nature came to be titled a comedy. The word "comedy" in the classical sense refers to works that reflect a belief in an ordered universe, in which events move toward a happy or contented ending, generally an ending influenced by divine intervention. By this meaning of the word, as Dante wrote in a letter to Cangrande, the progression of his pilgrimage from Hell to Paradise is a model of classical comedy, because the work begins with his moral confusion and ends with the vision of God.

In the most basic terms, *The Divine Comedy* is an allegory of human life in the form of a vision of the world beyond the grave, written with a purpose, according to Dante, of converting a corrupt society to righteousness: "to remove those living in this life from the state of misery, and lead them to the state of felicity." It is composed of 100 cantos written in terza rima (see the section on his "Influence on Other Prominent Writers" below for more information on terza rima) and grouped together into three canticles, or sections: Hell, Purgatory, and Paradise. Nearly 20 years have passed since the time of the events contained therein when Dante conveys these events to his reader. The life-changing event occurred in 1300, during the year of Jubilee, and consists of an extended vision granted to Dante for his own salvation from a sinful life, taking place over the course of seven days (beginning on the morning of Good Friday). By writing of these events, Dante is able not only to reference his exile in the poem but also to explain the means by which he came to cope with this personal tragedy and to offer suggestions for the resolution of Italy's troubles. Thus, the exile of an individual becomes a representation of the problems of a country. As he passed through the varying realms of Hell, Purgatory, and Paradise, he spoke with the souls in each realm and heard what God had in store for him and for the world.

Virgil, representing human philosophy, guides Dante by the light of natural reason through and away from the dark woods of alienation from God (where the beasts of lust, pride, and greed prevent man from ascending the Mountain of the Lord). Once Dante's journey with Virgil is complete, his companion is Beatrice, representing divine philosophy and revelation, who leads him up through the nine moving heavens of intellectual preparation into the true paradise of eternal life that is found in the sight of God.

It is to Hell that we find condemned the "dear and kind paternal image" of Brunetto Latini, in one of the most moving passages in the poem, as a sinner against nature, though from him Dante learned "how man makes himself eternal." It is strange that he should place Brunetto here, especially as he places Constantine in Paradise, although it is to him Dante attributes the corruption of the church and the ruin of the world. The pity and terror of certain episodes in Hell—the fatal love of Francesca da Rimini, the useless nobility of Farinata degli Uberti, the fall of Guido da Montefeltro, the fate of Count Ugolino—are extreme portrayals of tragedy.

Dante's conception of Purgatory is a mountain rising out of the ocean in the southern hemisphere and leading up to the Garden of Eden. His meeting with Beatrice on the banks of Lethe, with Dante's personal confession to her of an unworthy past, effectively concludes the story of *The New Life* after the bitter experiences and disillusions of his lifetime.

It is believed that the essence of Dante's philosophy in *The Divine Comedy* is that all virtues and all vices proceed from love. Hell shows how love is abused or manipulated, and Purgatory shows how love is to be prioritized, while Paradise shows how love is made perfect in successive stages of enlightenment until it reaches a union with God's divine love.

Dante was not the first poet to explore Hell. Homer's *Odyssey* (ca. 800 BCE) and Virgil's *Aeneid* (ca. 19 BCE) both represent a visit to the land of the dead in the middle of their poems because this is where the essential values of life are revealed within the poem. Dante, however, begins his journey with the visit to the land of the dead. It is in Hell that Dante must begin his journey and be cleared of harmful values that may somehow prevent him from rising to Paradise.

The visit to Hell, as Virgil and Beatrice explain, is extreme, but it is a painful yet necessary deed before his real recovery can begin. Some readers are disappointed by the lack of drama or severe emotions in the encounter with Satan in *The Inferno*. However, because Dante's journey through Hell is symbolic of the necessary process of separation from harmful vices, and is the first step in full human development, it must then end with a scene that is distinctively anticlimactic. The final revelation of Satan can have nothing new to offer: the sad effects of his presence in human history have already become apparent throughout *The Inferno*.

In *The Purgatorio*, Dante's painful process of spiritual rehabilitation begins. Here Dante suppresses his own personality in order that he may fully ascend into Paradise. In contrast to Hell, where Dante is confronted with a series of exemplary models that he must both recognize and discard, in Purgatory few exemplary models are presented; all of the penitents here are pilgrims along the road of life. Dante, rather than being a fearful and hesitant observer, as he is often represented in *The Inferno*, is represented here as an active participant. In Purgatory he learns to accept life as a pilgrimage, an essentially Christian image. Beatrice reminds Dante that he must learn to reject all deceptive promises of the earthly world and look forward to those promises of the divine world.

Purgatory, then, is the realm of spiritual awakening. It is here that historical, political, and moral landscapes are opened up to Dante. *The Purgatorio* is widely considered as the section devoted to poetry and the arts. After leaving Hell, Dante proclaims: "But here let poetry rise again from the dead." In Purgatory, Dante encounters the poet Sordello and hears of the destiny of Guido Guinizelli and Guido Cavalcanti. Shortly after he encounters Guido Guinizelli, we have the long-awaited and much anticipated reunion with Beatrice in the earthly Paradise.

Virgil, Dante's guide thus far, must hand over his position to another leader, and in a canticle generally absent of drama, the rejection of Virgil becomes a singularly dramatic event. Dante's use of Virgil is considered one of the richest cultural representations in literature. To begin, with his inclusion of Virgil in this poem, it is clear that Dante is an advocate of classical reason. Virgil is also a historical figure, and he is presented as such in *The Inferno*: "once I was a man, and my parents were Lombards, both Mantuan by birth. I was born *sub Julio,* though late in his time, and I lived in Rome under the good Augustus, in the time of the false and lying gods." Virgil is also associated with Dante's homeland (his references are to contemporary Italian places), and he has an imperial background (born under Julius Caesar, he extolled Augustus Caesar). He is presented quite aptly as a poet; the theme of his great epic *Aeneid* sounds remarkably similar to that of Dante's poem: "I was a poet and sang of that just son of Anchises who came from Troy after proud Ilium was burned." Dante also sings of the just son of a city, in this case Florence, who was unjustly exiled and forced to search, as Aeneas had done—it is clear he speaks of himself—for a better city, a heavenly city.

In his early years, Dante studied Virgil carefully and appropriated his beautiful poetic style. But during his exile, Dante had lost touch with the works of Virgil, so when the spirit of Virgil returns to him, it is a spirit that seems weak from an extended silence. The Virgil that returns to Dante, however, is a poet who has become a *saggio,* a sage or moral teacher.

Though an advocate of reason, Virgil has become a messenger of divine grace, and his return in the poem is part of the revival of those simpler faiths associated with Dante's earlier years. Dante does not reject Virgil; rather he sadly comes to the realization that nowhere in Virgil's work—that is, in his own consciousness—was there found any sense of personal liberation from the allure of history and its processes. In essence, Virgil provided Dante with a moral instruction in the ways of survival as an exile, which is the theme of his own poem (*Aeneid*) as well as Dante's. However, in *The [????] Aeneid* Virgil clung to his faith in history and the Roman Empire and was consoled by this. Dante, though, was determined to go beyond history because it had proven for him to be such a profound nightmare of injustice.

In *The Paradiso*, Dante achieves true heroic fulfillment. It is in *The Paradiso* that the authority of Aristotle, whom Dante held in high esteem, is ranked in supremacy next to that of the scriptures. His poem ultimately gives expression to those historical and literary figures of the past (such as Virgil and Aristotle) who seem, at least to him, to defy death. *The Paradiso* is consequently a poem of fulfillment, retrospection, and completion.

INFLUENCE ON OTHER PROMINENT WRITERS

Dante invented the three-line rhyme scheme he used in *The Divine Comedy*. It is called *terza rima*, a form that consists of 10- or 11-syllable lines in tercets (three-line stanzas) using the rhyme scheme aba bcb cdc ded, and so on. Later English poets who used terza rima include Geoffrey Chaucer, John Milton, Percy Bysshe Shelley, and W. H. Auden.

Giovanni Boccaccio (1313–1375)

Aside from writing the first formal life of Dante, from 1373 to 1374 Boccaccio's commentaries on *The Inferno* were the first public lectures on *The Divine Comedy*. Effectively, as a result of these lectures, Dante was the first of the moderns whose work found its place with the ancient classics in a university course.

The subtitle of Boccaccio's famous framed narrative *The Decameron* (1350–53) is *Prencipe Galeotto*, or Galeotto, the middle man in Lancelot and Guinevere's tragic love. Boccaccio is referencing Dante's allusion to Galeotto, who was blamed for the arousal of lust in the episode of Paolo and Francesca in *The Inferno*.

Throughout *The Decameron* there runs the common medieval theme of Lady Fortune and how quickly one can rise and fall under the influence of the Wheel of Fortune or Destiny. Boccaccio was educated in the tradition of Dante's *Divine Comedy*, which we know used allegorical techniques to show connections between literal events within the story and the Christian message Dante wished to portray. However, *The Decameron* uses Dante's allegorical model not to educate the reader but to satirize this method of learning. This was part of a wider historical trend at the time that openly criticized the powers of the church after the estimated 1.5 million deaths from the bubonic plague ("Black Death") (1348–50) were attributed to unanswered prayers of deliverance.

Geoffrey Chaucer (ca. 1343–1400)

A large portion of Chaucer's *Canterbury Tales*, including "The Monk's Tale," were written in the 1370s, shortly after Chaucer's visit to Italy, where he was exposed to Boccaccio's *Decameron* and *Concerning the Falls of Illustrious Men*. In "The Monk's Tale," Chaucer hails Dante: "the grete poete of Itaille that highte Dant" ("The great poet of Italy who was named Dante"). Additionally, one eight-line stanza of Chaucer's "A Complaynt to His Lady," an early short poem, is written in terza rima. His *House of Fame*, a dream vision in which the narrator is guided through the heavens by an otherworldly guide, is a parody of *The Divine Comedy*. The beginning of the last stanza in his *Troilus and Criseyde* is modeled after a passage in *The Paradiso*.

Edmund Spenser (ca. 1552–1599) and John Milton (1608–1674)

Though neither necessarily admitted to being influenced by Dante in their two most famous poems, it is clear that they were both aware of him and his works. Each wrote one epic poem that just happened to carry similar allegorical themes to Dante's *Divine Comedy*.

Though written to celebrate Queen Elizabeth I and the Tudor dynasty, Spenser's epic poem *The Faerie Queen* is an extended allegory about the moral life and what makes for a life of virtue. With its themes of Man's Creation, Fall, and Salvation, Milton's epic allegorical poem *Paradise Lost* (1657) is perhaps most closely associated with Dante's *Divine Comedy* by means of comparison.

Milton put Dante's insistence on the separation of worldly and religious power to use in his treatise *Of Reformation* (1641), where he explicitly cites *The Inferno*. Additionally, Beatrice's condemnation of corrupt and neglectful preachers, found in *The Paradiso* ("so that the wretched sheep, in ignorance, / return from pasture, having fed on wind"), is translated and adapted in Milton's lyrical poem *Lycidas* (1638): "The hungry Sheep look up, and are not fed, / But swoln with wind, and the rank mist they draw," when Milton condemns corrupt clergy.

George Gordon, Lord Byron (1788–1824)

Lord Byron employed terza rima in his "Prophecy of Dante" (1821). Through the main character, Dante, Byron ponders what it means to be a poet and all of the social and political aspects that go along with that title. Its central theme is the relationship between life and art.

Percy Bysshe Shelley (1792–1822)

Shelley pays tribute to Dante in his "Epipsychidion" (1820), the "Triumph of Life" (1822), and "A Defence of Poetry" (1840). In "Epipsychidion" he drew creatively upon Dante's celebration of eternal, constant love in *The New Life*. "Triumph of Life" is a terza rima poem and Shelley's most obvious adaptation of Dante, borrowing not only his verse form but also a Virgil-like figure in Rousseau and a parade of souls in death. In his prose work "A Defence of Poetry," written in 1821 and published posthumously in 1840, Shelley's intent was to demonstrate the similarities and to resolve the differences between Dante and himself. It is in this work Shelley made his famous claim that the "poets are the unacknowledged legislators of the world"—similar to Dante's thoughts on philosophers.

Alfred, Lord Tennyson (1809–1892)

Although the character of Ulysses (Odysseus) has been widely explored throughout classical literature (most notably in Homer's *Iliad* and *Odyssey*, ca. 800–700 BCE), Tennyson's poem "Ulysses" (1833) is the first modern account and seems to draw most closely on Dante's Ulisse from his *Inferno*. In Dante's retelling, Ulisse is condemned to Hell among the false counselors, both for his pursuit of knowledge beyond human bounds and for his adventures in disregard of his family.

Robert Browning (1812–1889)

Browning admired Dante and his work, and his influence or name is seen in several of Browning's poems, including "One Word More" (1855), "Ixion" (1883), *The Ring and the Book* (1868), and most notably "Childe Roland to the Dark Tower Came" (1855). The "Childe Roland" landscape has been described as Hell-like either as a place embodying the possibility of eternal damnation or as a projection of the poem's traveler's state of mind (a psychological Hell). Several critics have noted "Childe Roland" as an adaptation of *The Divine Comedy*.

Dante Gabriel Rossetti (1828–1882)

Originally named Gabriel Charles Dante Rossetti, on his art and in his published works he placed the name Dante first, in honor of the great Italian poet. He worked on translations of Dante's *New Life* and adopted some of Dante's stylistic characteristics in his own writing.

William Butler Yeats (1865–1939)

Yeats referred to Dante as "the chief imagination of Christendom." The first two stanzas of Yeats's poem "Byzantium" (1928) closely echo Canto VIII of Dante's *Purgatorio*.

E. M. Forster (1879–1970)

In Forster's novel *Where Angels Fear to Tread* (1905), the character Gino Carella, when first introducing himself, quotes the initial lines of Dante's *Inferno* ("Abandon hope all ye who enter here"). This novel also includes several references to Dante's *New Life*.

Ezra Pound (1885–1972)

Pound's epic poem *The Cantos* (1915–62) (consisting of 120 sections, or cantos) takes as a direct model Dante's *Divine Comedy*. The opening canto echoes Dante's opening and the poet Pound also descends into Hell to interrogate the dead. Here are some of the more prominent mentions. Cantos 14 and 15 conclude with a vision of Hell, using the convention of *The Divine Comedy* to present Pound moving through a Hell populated by bankers, newspaper editors, hack writers, and other "perverters of language" and the social order. In Canto 15, Plotinus takes the role of a Virgil-like guide. In Canto 16, Pound emerges from Hell into an earthly paradise where he sees some of the people he encountered in earlier cantos. Canto 38 opens with a quote from Dante in which he accuses Albert of Germany of falsifying money. Canto 93 looks at examples of benevolent action by public figures, including Dante and his writing *On Monarchy*. *The Cantos* close with a reference to the following lines from Dante's *Paradiso*:

O voi che siete in piccioletta barca,	O ye who are in a little bark,
desiderosi d'ascoltar, seguiti	desirous to listen, following
dietro al mio legno che cantando	behind my craft which singing passes
varca,	on,
tornate a riveder li vostri liti:	turn to see again your shores:
non vi mettete in pelago, ché forse,	put not out upon the deep, for haply,
perdendo me, rimarreste smarriti.	losing me, ye would remain astray.

This reference to Dante's *Paradiso* signaled Pound's intent to close his poem with a final volume based on his own Paradise-like vision.

T. S. Eliot (1888–1965)

Modernist poet Eliot elevated Dante to a preeminence he felt was shared by only one other poet, William Shakespeare: "[They] divide the modern world between them. There is no third." Eliot declared that Dante's poetry exercised a persistent and deep influence on his work. The spiritual quest in Dante's *Divine Comedy* greatly influenced the central theme of Eliot's "The Waste Land" (1922), the individual's quest for spiritual meaning through a kind of psychological hell. Eliot uses allusions to *The Divine Comedy,* specifically *The Inferno,* throughout "The Waste Land." Eliot also cites *The Inferno* as an epigraph to "The Love Song of J. Alfred Prufrock" (1915). He also cites heavily from and alludes to Dante in *Prufrock and Other Observations* (1917) and "Ara vus prec" (1920).

TRANSLATIONS

The first complete translation of *The Divine Comedy* into English was completed in 1802 by Irishman Henry Boyd (1748/9–1832). He had previously published a translation of *The Inferno* in 1785. The first translation of *The Divine Comedy* by an American was completed in 1867 by Henry Wadsworth

Longfellow (1807–1882). Longfellow spent several years translating this work and recruited the aid of friends in perfecting the translation and reviewing early drafts. He invited friends to weekly meetings, which came to be known as the "Dante Club" starting in 1864. Novelist Matthew Pearl's 2003 novel titled *The Dante Club* tells the story of various American poets translating *The Divine Comedy* in post–Civil War Boston. Longfellow's full three-volume translation was eventually published in 1867, but Longfellow continued to revise the translation; it went through four printings in its first year. Longfellow also wrote a poem titled "Mezzo Cammin" (1845) alluding to the first line of *The Divine Comedy,* and a sonnet sequence (of six sonnets) under the title "Divina Commedia" (1867), published as flyleaves to his translation of Dante's work.

American poet and critic John Ciardi (1916–1986) published a translation of *The Divine Comedy* that is considered to be one of the more accessible translations available. His translation of *The Inferno* was published in 1954, *The Purgatorio* in 1961, and *The Paradiso* in 1970. It is his translation that is now widely used in university literature courses.

DANTE TODAY

The most pressing needs of Dante scholarship today are additional textual study of his work, more thorough acquaintance with every aspect of his more minor works, and a fuller investigation of Dante's position with regard to the great philosophies of the Middle Ages. Several societies have popped up with connections to Dante in an attempt to bring to light some of those needs I just mentioned. The most noteworthy of these societies is the "Società Dantesca Italiana" (Italian Dante Society), established in 1888, with headquarters in Florence (www.dantesca.it/eng/). It welcomes non-Italian-speaking members and is distinguished for its high scholarship. In addition to sponsoring and delivering courses and lectures throughout Italy, the society publishes a quarterly "Bulletino," and a survey of contemporary Dante literature; it has released several volumes in a series of critical editions of Dante's smaller works.

INFLUENCE ON MODERN POPULAR CULTURE

Dante has an active presence in popular culture. A visit to www.4degreez .com/misc/dante-inferno-test.mv allows you to take a quiz that will calculate what circle of Hell you belong to. Dante is infiltrating not only the Internet but also our living rooms; there is a *Dante's Inferno* video game! Electronic Arts released its highly anticipated action adventure in February 2011, for PlayStation 3, Xbox 360, and PSP. *Dante's Inferno* the video game takes players on a colorful (and often gruesome) adventure through Dante's nine circles of Hell. Somehow, the allegory is lost in the translation of hand-eye coordination. The release of this video game comes on the heels of the comic book/graphic novel on which it is based and the direct-to-DVD film spinoff, though the latter appears to have no obvious relation to the graphic novel or the video game other than its possession of the same title.

The film *Dante's Inferno* (www.dantefilm.com/about.html) was released on DVD in 2008 and places a thoroughly modern spin on the classic poem. It is retold through intricately hand-drawn paper puppets and miniature sets, without the use of CGI. In this world, Dante (voiced by Dermot Mulroney) is a hoodie-wearing alcoholic of indiscriminate age who wakes up (physically and metaphorically) from the previous evening's drunken pass-out to find that he is in a strangely unfamiliar part of town. He asks the first person he sees for some help: enter Virgil (voiced by James Cromwell) sporting a mullet and wearing a brown robe of the bath variety. Because he has no idea where he is or how he will survive alone, Dante follows Virgil on a journey through the depths of Hell, which resembles a decayed urban landscape. There is a cast of contemporary presidents, politicians, popes, and pop-culture icons sentenced to eternal and horrific suffering. Dante eventually comes to understand Hell's merciless punishment and emerges a new man convinced of the necessity to change the course of his life—while still drinking heavily.

Unlike the more modernized film version, the six-issue graphic novel miniseries *Dante's Inferno* stays fairly close to the more traditional version of Hell set forth in Dante's poem. Like the video game, the graphics are telling and disturbing. The first issue was released by DC Comics in 2009 to relatively wide acclaim.

For a version of Dante's *Divine Comedy* that attempts a contemporary political setting, one need look no further than the Bread and Puppet Theater rendition of "The Divine Reality Comedy" (www.loho10002.com/wordpress/?p=1079). "The Divine Reality Comedy" is geared toward adults and is a new and unique translation of Dante's *Divine Comedy* divided into four parts. According to the website, in "Paradise," the old human Born-to-Die gene is replaced by the brand-new Born-to-Buy gene. In "Post-Paradise Horsemanship," a herd of white equestrian cutouts (of all sizes) is manipulated by a crowd of dancers in a picturesque, prancing dance. In "Purgatory," the shadows of the indefinitely detained speak to you. In "Hell," the Guantanamo interrogation process is staged with an eight-inch papier maché population, which recites actual interrogation transcripts and then witnesses three cases of torture as demonstrated on three larger-than-life-size puppets.

If you would like to have the same benefits of the Bread and Puppet Theater in the palm of your hand, the *Dante's Inferno* puppet show available on YouTube for viewing on a cell phone or computer is your best bet (www.youtube.com/watch?v=TVM1vRm9GI8). This is an imaginative 11-minute stick-figure, sock-puppet, masked-figure rendition of Dante's *Inferno*. There is also iDante, an interactive version of the poem for the iPhone and iPad. The iPad version features fully colorized illustrations, 3-D reconstructions of key environments, and maps of Hell, Purgatory, and Paradise.

NOTABLE REPRESENTATIONS IN FILM

The 1911 silent film *L'Inferno,* directed by Giuseppe de Liguoro and starring Salvatore Papa, was released on DVD in 2004, with a newly adapted soundtrack by Tangerine Dream. The 1935 film *Dante's Inferno,* directed by Harry Lachman and starring Spencer Tracy, centers on a fairground attraction based on *The Inferno.* In the 1946 Merrie Melodies cartoon "Book Revue," starring Daffy Duck, the Big Bad Wolf falls into the book *The Inferno.* The 1995 film *Se7en,* directed by David Fincher, stars Brad Pitt and Morgan Freeman as two detectives who investigate a series of ritualistic murders inspired by the seven deadly sins. The film makes several references to Dante's *Divine Comedy.*

Perhaps the most visually breathtaking rendition of Dante's *Divine Comedy* is the 1998 film *What Dreams May Come,* directed by Vincent Ward and starring Robin Williams, Annabella Sciorra, and Cuba Gooding Jr. Based on Richard Matheson's 1978 novel, this film makes several connections with and references to the *Divine Comedy,* including its depiction of Hell. The lead character, Chris (Williams), tragically loses his children in a car accident. His wife (Sciorra) retreats from her life as a result of the loss and commits suicide. Chris goes on a journey through Hell, with Gooding as the Virgil character, to redeem his wife and himself and find happiness once again with their children.

FURTHER READING

Alison, Morgan. *Dante and the Medieval Other World.* Cambridge: Cambridge University Press, 1990.

Auerbach, Erich. *Dante: Poet of the Secular World.* New York: New York Review of Books, 2007.

Auerbach, Erich. *Scenes from the Drama of European Literature.* Translated by Ralph Manheim, Catherine Garvin, and Erich Auerbach. Minneapolis: University of Minnesota Press, 1984.

Barolini, Teodolinda. *Dante's Poets: Textuality and Truth in the Comedy.* Princeton, NJ: Princeton University Press, 1984.

Barolini, Teodolinda. *The Undivine Comedy: Detheologizing Dante.* Princeton, NJ: Princeton University Press, 1992.

Botterill, Steve. *Dante and the Mystical Tradition: The Figure of St. Bernard in Dante's Commedia.* Cambridge: Cambridge University Press, 1994.

Boyde, Patrick. *Perception and Passion in Dante's Comedy.* Cambridge: Cambridge University Press, 1994.

Cervigni, Dino. *Dante's Poetry of Dreams.* Florence: Olschki, 1986.

Dronke, Peter. *Dante and Medieval Latin Traditions.* Cambridge: Cambridge University Press, 1986.

Ferrante, Joan M. *The Political Vision of the Divine Comedy*. Princeton, NJ: Princeton University Press, 1984.

Freccero, John. *The Poetics of Conversion*. Cambridge, MA: Harvard University Press, 1986.

Hollander, Robert. *Dante's Epistle to Cangrande*. Ann Arbor: University of Michigan Press, 1993.

Jacoff, Rachel, ed. *The Cambridge Companion to Dante*. Cambridge: Cambridge University Press, 1993.

Jacoff, Rachel, and Jeffrey T. Schnapp, eds. *The Poetry of Allusion: Virgil and Ovid in Dante's Commedia*. Stanford, CA: Stanford University Press, 1991.

Lane, William Coolidge. *The Dante Collections in the Harvard College and Boston Public Libraries*. Cambridge, MA: Issued by the Library of Harvard University, 1890.

Lansing, Richard, ed. *The Dante Encyclopedia*. New York: Garland, 2000.

Masciandaro, Franco. *The Myth of the Earthly Paradise and Tragic Vision in the Divine Comedy*. Philadelphia: University of Pennsylvania Press, 1991.

Matthews, Joseph Chelsey. *Dante's Influence on American Writers*. New York: Published for the Dante Society of America by Griffon House Publications, 1977.

Mazzotta, Giuseppe. *Dante's Vision and the Circle of Knowledge*. Princeton, NJ: Princeton University Press, 1993.

Schnapp, Jeffrey T. *The Transfiguration of History at the Center of Dante's Paradiso*. Princeton, NJ: Princeton University Press, 1986.

Some Notable English Translations

Ciardi, John, trans. *Dante: The Divine Comedy*. New York: Norton, 1977.

Halpern, Daniel, ed. *Dante's Inferno: Translations by 20 Contemporary Poets*. Hopewell, NJ: Ecco Press, 1993.

Longfellow, Henry Wadsworth, trans. *The Divine Comedy of Dante Alighieri*. Boston and New York: Houghton, Mifflin, and Co., 1867.

Mandelbaum, Allen, trans. *The Divine Comedy of Dante Alighieri*. Illustrated by Barry Moser. 3 vols. Berkeley: University of California Press, 1980.

Pinsky, Robert, trans. *The Inferno of Dante*. New York: Farrar, Strauss, and Giroux, 1994.

Raffel, Burton, trans. *The Divine Comedy*. Commentary by Henry L. Carrigan. Evanston, IL: Northwestern University Press, 2010.

Sinclair, John D., trans. *Dante: The Divine Comedy*. 3 vols. London: Bodley Head, 1958.

Singleton, Charles, trans. *Dante: The Divine Comedy*. Princeton, NJ: Princeton University Press, 1970.

Recordings and Websites

The Dartmouth Digital Dante Project: http://dante.dartmouth.edu/.

Digital Dante: http://dante.ilt.columbia.edu/new/.

The Orb: On-Line Reference Book for Medieval Studies: http://the-orb.net/encyclop/culture/lit/italian/danindex.html.

The Princeton Dante Project: http://etcweb.princeton.edu/dante/index.html.

Film and Video Documentaries
La Porte de L'enfer d'Auguste Rodin

46 min. Color. 35mm. 1991. France.

Director: Philippe Sollers. Examines "The Gates of Hell" by French sculptor Auguste Rodin (1840–1917). On August 16, 1880, the Musée des Arts Decoratifs commissioned Rodin to create a sculpted bronze door based on the work of Dante Alighieri. Over 30 years in creation, the door was never completed. Based on an original text by Philippe Sollers.

A TV Dante

34 programs, 11 min. each. Color. Video. 1985. Great Britain.

Directors: Peter Greenaway and Tom Phillips. A video adaptation of Dante's *Inferno*, combining archival and recent footage with computer-generated paintbox images. Dante's text, translated by Phillips, is juxtaposed with images from modern times that conjure up a contemporary vision of Hell: a vast bureaucracy shaped by two world wars and daily tabloid headlines. Each of the 34 cantos is presented as an individual segment.

APPENDIX: CHRONOLOGY OF DANTE'S LIFE

ca. 1265	Dante born in May or June in Florence to Alighiero and Bella.
1274	Dante sees Beatrice for the first time. (According to *The New Life*, he falls in love with her the moment they meet.)
1275–1282	Dante studies at the convents of Santa Croce and Santa Maria Novella.
1283	Dante's father dies.
	Dante marries Gemma Donati (with whom he will have four children: Jacopo, Pietro, Giovanni, and Antonia).
	Writes his first sonnets.
1285	Dante becomes a soldier and takes part in the battle of the Sienese against the Aretines at Poggio Santa Cecilia.
1288	Dante writes the ballad "Ladies who have intelligence of love" and the two sonnets "Love is one with the gentle heart" and "My lady bears love in her eyes."
1289	Dante takes part in the battle of Campaldino. (He recalls this battle in *The Purgatorio*.)
1290	Beatrice dies.
1292	Dante writes *La Vita Nuova* (*The New Life*).
1294	Dante meets Charles Martel of Anjou king of Hungary and heir to the kingdom of Naples and the county of Provence, and establishes a friendship with him. (Dante recounts their meeting in *The Paradiso*.)
1295	Dante enrolls in the Guild of Physicians and Apothecaries and enters Florentine political life.
	Elected to the council of the Heads of the Arts in order to cooperate with the Captain of the People in the selection of new priors.
1296	Dante takes part in the Council of the Hundred.
1300	Pope Boniface VIII proclaims the Jubilee Year.
	Dante named a prior, one of the six highest magistrates in Florence.
	(Eastertime) Fictional date of the journey of *The Divine Comedy*.
1301	Dante takes the floor in the Council of the Hundred to oppose helping Boniface VIII fight the Santafiora of Maremma.
	Sent to Rome as an ambassador to Boniface VIII to convince him to recall Charles de Valois, whom the Pope has sent to Florence as a mediator.
	The Black Guelph Corso Donati reenters Florence and wreaks vengeance on the Whites while Dante detained in Rome by Pope Boniface VIII.
1302	Dante accused of treachery and receives a fine and banishment for two years with permanent exclusion from public office.

1302	After failure to appear in court (due to the Pope's detaining him in Rome), Dante condemned to death in absentia.
1303	Pope Boniface VIII dies.
1304	Dante writes *De vulgari eloquentia* (*On the Eloquence of the Vernacular*). During this same period, writes *Il Convivio* (*The Banquet*).
1306	Dante moves to Lunigiana and appointed procurator to the Marquesses Malaspina.
1308	Dante begins writing *La Divina Commedia* (*The Divine Comedy*).
1309	Dante writes *De Monarchia* (*On Monarchy*).
1310	At the news of the arrival in Italy of Henry VII of Luxembourg, Dante goes to meet his fellow exiles at Forli.
	With other exiles, goes to Asti to pay homage to Henry VII.
1311	Emperor Henry VII crowned King of Italy in Milan.
	Dante writes a letter to Henry VII inviting him to come to Tuscany and restore peace to Florence.
1312	Dante joins Henry VII in Pisa.
	Henry VII camps under the walls of Florence.
1313	Henry VII moves from Pisa toward the Kingdom of Naples. He dies of fever during the journey.
1314	Dante guest of Cangrande della Scala in Verona.
	The Inferno, the first part of *The Divine Comedy*, published.
1315	Dante leaves Verona for Lucca.
	Renewed Florentine sentence against Dante extends to family.
	Dante moves to Verona as guest of Cangrande della Scala. Works on *The Purgatorio* and *The Paradiso* and writes the *Questio de aqua et terra* (*Question Concerning Water and Earth*).
1316–1319	Dante travels between Verona, the Marca Trevigiana, Romagna, and Tuscany.
1319	Dante moves to Ravenna, where he is the guest of Guido Novello da Polenta, lord of that city.
1321	Dante completes *The Divine Comedy*.
	Is ambassador to Venice. On a mission for Guido Novello, stricken with fever and returns to Ravenna. Dies on September 13.
	Guido buries Dante in the Church of Saint Francis, with full honors.

Effigy of Eleanor of Aquitaine, Fontevrault Abbey, France. Eleanor died in 1204. (Erich Lessing/Art Resource, NY)

Eleanor of Aquitaine (ca. 1122–1204)

Dominique T. Hoche

INTRODUCTION

Eleanor of Aquitaine is known as the Queen of the Troubadours and served, at least in part, as a model for King Arthur's Guinevere in the medieval romance tradition; she was also responsible for the spread of the folk tradition about the fairy Melusine. She was also one of the richest and most powerful women in Europe in the Middle Ages, but we know relatively little about her or her life. She left no autobiographical records and only three letters written in her own hand. What we know about her comes from the writings of chroniclers in her own time and those of centuries later, both of which could be very hostile to her, describing her more along the lines of a whorish Messalina or a witchy Morgan Le Fay. We know a lot about the men in her life, but about her personally all we have are insinuations: that she was a bad wife and a neglectful mother, that she was very beautiful and vain even into old age, that her eyes were blue or gray—yet we don't know many simple details such as the color of her hair.

OVERVIEW

Born in 1122 (an estimated date—her parents were married in 1121), Eleanor was the eldest daughter of Guillaume X duke of Aquitaine and his duchess, Aenor de Châtellerault. When Guillaume X died while on pilgrimage in 1137, Eleanor inherited his lands; now duchess of the richest and largest province in France (Aquitaine, in southwestern France, stretched from the river Loire to the Pyrenees and functioned like a separate nation) and also countess of Poitiers, the teenage Eleanor was the most eligible bride in Europe. A marriage was arranged for her with King Louis VII of France, and he fell deeply in love with her. The two even went on a Crusade to Damascus together—but failed in the attempt to rescue the Frankish kingdoms. After many years their marriage began to fail as well, especially because they had managed to produce only two daughters, and Louis needed a son for the throne. In 1152, they dissolved the marriage by mutual consent, being granted an annulment due to consanguinity (their bloodlines were too close, being third cousins), leaving them free to marry again.

Within six weeks of the annulment, Eleanor married Henry count of Anjou and duke of Normandy. When he became King Henry II of England, the merger of their landholdings created an empire. With Henry, Eleanor had five sons and three daughters over the next 13 years: William, Henry, Richard, Geoffrey, John, Matilda, Eleanor, and Joanna. The years between Henry's accession and the birth of Prince John were tumultuous: the fight to claim Toulouse, the inheritance of Eleanor's grandmother and father, was a failure; and the feud between the king and Thomas Becket, the archbishop of Canterbury, became known all over the continent (see the chapter on Thomas Becket). By late 1166, after the birth of her final child, Eleanor separated from Henry and moved home to Poitiers.

It was in Poitiers that the famous "Court of Love" or "Court of Ladies" began. Away from Henry's adulteries and constant warfare, Eleanor was able to develop her own court that encouraged music, literature, and what we think of today as "chivalric" manners. In 1173, however, the younger Henry made a bid for power against the king, along with his brothers Richard and Geoffrey, and the ensuing revolt resulted in Eleanor being imprisoned for the next 16 years. Upon Henry II's death in 1189, she was freed, and Richard became king. While Richard went off on the Third Crusade, she ruled England in his stead, and, after he died, she helped King John rule as well, even in her late seventies. She died in 1204 at the surprisingly advanced age of 82 and was buried in Fontevrault Abbey.

THE YOUNG DUCHESS

Eleanor was a colorful character, but she came by her color honestly: her grandfather was Duke Guillaume IX of Aquitaine. When he fell in love with Dangereuse, the wife of his vassal the viscount of Châtellerault, he carried her off and made a luxury apartment for her in a newly built tower in his palace at Poitiers. His wife Philippa, who had had enough of his philandering, left him and moved to the Abbey of Fontevrault, though the wayward Guillaume IX cared little what the church might say about his actions because he had been excommunicated the previous year. When the church found out, he was excommunicated a second time for his scandalously immoral behavior. Guillaume and Dangereuse could not marry in this situation, so they did the next best thing: they married Guillaume's son to Dangereuse's daughter Aenor in 1121. From that marriage, Eleanor (possibly derived from *alia Aenor* or "the other Aenor" in Latin) was soon born, and her sister Petronilla arrived in 1124, with a brother—named, of course, Guillaume—arriving a few years later.

Eleanor was a very well educated girl: she learned to read and speak Latin, proved talented in music and literary arts, and was schooled in riding, falconry, and hunting. She learned the business of ruling a land even at her father's knee—when her parents brought her on tours around their realms, she watched the duke and duchess receive homage, hold court, conduct business, and disagree and be reconciled with rebellious and unruly vassals. In 1130, her young brother died; her mother died a few months later, and so by 1136 her father began to worry about who would inherit, and he began to look for a new wife. Yet he soon died, confirming Eleanor as heiress of his vast dominions, and she became the ward of his overlord, King Louis VI "the Fat" of France. Louis himself was gravely ill, and he hurriedly made arrangements for the teenage Eleanor to marry his second son (his heir since 1131), 16-year-old Louis. The young man, along with a huge retinue of barons, knights, and troops, set off to marry his young fiancée, and after expensive and lavish celebrations and feastings, the marriage was celebrated on July 25, 1137. On

August 1, Louis VI died, and suddenly Louis was not just her husband but King Louis VII, and Eleanor became queen of France as well as duchess of Aquitaine.

THE QUEEN OF FRANCE

Young Eleanor's new husband, Louis, was a pious man who had been expected to enter the church, as was common for second sons, who did not stand to inherit. Even though he was supposedly gentle, devout, and very unworldly, he fell madly in love with his sophisticated, fun-loving wife and granted her every wish, including remodeling the Cité Palace in Paris to suit her love of beauty and domestic finery. Her power over him even extended to getting him to fight wars for her. In 1141, Louis became involved in a war with Count Theobald of Champagne, using the excuse of helping Raoul I count of Vermandois to divorce his wife and marry Petronilla, Eleanor's sister. The fact that Petronilla was 18 and Raoul was in his late fifties did not seem to disturb either party, and if all the machinations and warfare went according to plan, Louis would also regain the county of Toulouse for France. The war lasted for two years (1142–44) and greatly angered the pope. The burning of the church in the town of Vitry, where more than 1,300 people died in the flames, earned Eleanor a scolding by Bernard (later Saint Bernard) of Clairvaux. Bernard was a very persuasive and intelligent man with a sharp tongue, but confronted by Eleanor's clever excuse (that she had encouraged her husband to go to war because she was frustrated they had not yet managed to conceive) he became much more kind to her and offered to pray for her to have a child in exchange for her influencing the king to back down from warfare and agree to the church's wishes. It took only a few weeks for peace to return to France, and in April 1145, Eleanor had a daughter named Marie.

Louis felt very guilty about the massacre at Vitry, and, as pious young men often did, he decided to make a pilgrimage to the Holy Land to atone for his sins. The pope seized upon this opportunity and asked Louis to rescue the Frankish kingdoms in the Middle East—and so on Christmas Day in 1145, Louis announced he was going on crusade.

THE CRUSADER

Eleanor did not stay at home—she decided to go with her husband as a result of a sermon preached by Bernard—insisting upon taking part in the Crusade because she was the feudal leader of the knights in Aquitaine. Months of preparation followed, and on March 31, Easter Sunday, Louis started the march to the Holy Land, intending to meet the army of the Holy Roman Emperor Conrad in Constantinople. While a Crusade was meant to be uncomfortable, full of penance and hardship, Eleanor's participation was marked by theatrics and luxury: she launched her own forces from Vézelay, the supposed location of Mary Magdalene's tomb, to emphasize the role of women in the campaign, and not only did she bring her royal ladies-in-waiting and 300 non-noble vassals, she had a huge train of servants and baggage—and there is a rumor that she and her ladies dressed as Amazons, with one breast bare to dazzle the troops.

While the Crusade itself accomplished little, it meant a lot to Eleanor. She was able to travel, see new places and exotic cultures, and visit friendly foreign monarchs. The Byzantine emperor Manuel Comnenus threw a party for Louis and Eleanor; the Greek historian Nicetas Choniates compared her to Penthesilea, the mythical queen of the Amazons, and it was his report that said she earned the epithet *chrysopous* ("golden-foot") from the fringe of golden cloth that decorated her robe. After Constantinople, though, the Crusade began to go very badly. Food began to be scarce, and the Crusaders were harassed and ambushed by Turks almost every step of the way. They discovered that Conrad's army had been almost annihilated by the Turks in Dorylaeum, and near Mount Cadmos an attack almost cost Louis his life, but they pushed on, hoping to reach Antioch and the court of Prince Raymond of Poitiers, Eleanor's uncle. When they arrived, the army was without food or water, having had to drink the blood of their horses and even eat the flesh of horses and asses killed in the fighting. Eleanor's baggage train had been pitched into a deep canyon, and they were without money, while the army was dressed in rags, starving and sick.

The rest at Prince Raymond's court was exactly what Eleanor and Louis needed, and while they stayed there, she discovered a great friend in her uncle. John of Salisbury (a notorious gossip) reported in his *Historia pontificalis* that she and Prince Raymond were often together, speaking in "constant, almost continuous conversations" that left Louis out. Raymond was Eleanor's father's youngest brother, and like many of her line, was tall, handsome, athletic, aggressive, and very masculine—all things that Louis was not. Raymond was also only eight years older than Eleanor, which fed the rumors that she fell into an adulterous (and incestuous) affair. Despite their like-mindedness, it is quite probable that Raymond simply hoped for military aid to protect Antioch against the Turks and was doing all he could to get it and save his city. Eleanor, for her part, was learning about maritime conventions, which would later become the basis of admiralty law, and she brought those conventions to her own lands, to the island of Oléron, in 1160 and later to England as well. She also was learning how to create trade agreements with Constantinople and trading centers in the Mediterranean and the Holy Land. And so when the jealous Louis demanded to leave Antioch (without helping Raymond with his problems with the Turks) and go at once to Jerusalem, Eleanor balked—she wanted to stay with her uncle and help him fight—and Louis had her dragged out by force and made her come with him to Jerusalem.

Louis and the barely recovered Emperor Conrad, upon discovering that Jerusalem was not in immediate danger of attack, decided to attack the Muslim state of Damascus—ironically, the only Muslim state willing to be on good terms with Christians—and the Muslim leader called upon his allies to defend him. When Louis heard that a vast army was approaching, he wisely turned his own army back to Jerusalem, then decided to sail home. Eleanor is not mentioned in the chronicles of this period, but it was no doubt because of her quarrel with Louis that they took separate ships home. After an adventure of being shipwrecked and lost for several months, the disillusioned couple sought out the pope for an annulment in 1149, arguing that they were too closely related in blood (an issue of consanguinity) and that was why their union had displeased God and in 12 years only produced one daughter. Pope Eugenius III tried to reconcile the couple, even getting them to sleep in a specially prepared bed so that Eleanor would have sexual intercourse with Louis. Their second child—Alix of France—was the result, but, being a girl, she was useless for dynastic purposes, and the marriage was doomed.

THE ANNULMENT

On March 11, 1152, Eleanor and Louis met at the royal castle of Beaugency to dissolve the marriage under the eyes of Archbishop Hugh Sense, Primate of France, and on March 21 annulment was granted based on consanguinity within the fourth degree (they were indeed third cousins, descended from Robert II of France). Louis received custody of the daughters, and Eleanor's lands were restored to her.

Eleanor's marriage on May 18, 1152, to Henry count of Anjou and duke of Normandy has puzzled historians because it happened within six weeks of the annulment of her marriage to Louis on grounds of consanguinity and because of the fact that Eleanor was more closely related to Henry than to Louis: they were half third cousins (both related to Ermengarde of Anjou and descendents of Robert II of Normandy). This was a marriage that must have been plotted many months, possibly years, before.

In August 1151, Geoffrey Plantagenet count of Anjou and duke of Normandy visited the court of King Louis with his 17-year-old son, Henry, in order to pay homage to Louis for the fief of Normandy and to gain help in the civil war that was being fought between Empress Matilda and the noble-born usurper, Stephen of England. By all accounts, Geoffrey and his son were impressive: handsome, athletic, energetic, and decisive, aspects that must have reminded Eleanor of her own kin. She must have known the annulment was coming and been thinking about what she would do with herself and her lands afterward. She would have to marry . . . but to whom? Geoffrey was still married to Empress Matilda, rightful heir to the throne of England and duchy of Normandy. His son, though, would make a delightful husband—especially because his French domains united with Eleanor's would create a power base greater than Louis's—an advantage for both of them in the match. Eleanor was 29 years old, and by the time of the marriage, Henry was 18, and the chroniclers say that she was beautiful. She was vastly wealthy, well traveled and educated, and in her sexual prime. And so after the annulment, she went home to Poitiers (two opportunistic suitors tried to abduct her on the journey) and canceled every treaty she had made with Louis. Eleanor's marriage to Henry ignored feudal law because the participants failed to seek the consent of their suzerain, Louis. Louis responded by invading Normandy with the help of the usurping King Stephen of England, but Henry was an able military commander and counterattacked Louis's territories, generally making life miserable for the monkish king. Eleanor toured her own territories, asserting her authority and receiving homage. Her seal at the time shows her great titles: "Eleanor, by the grace of God, duchess of Aquitaine and Normandy, countess of Anjou, Poitou, and Maine." In August 1152, she and Henry spent four months together, and by January 1153 Eleanor was pregnant. When King Stephen of England lost his sons to an illness, he wisely met with Henry and, in order to end the civil war, agreed to adopt him as his heir. In the peace treaty, Stephen was to rule for the rest of his life, and Henry would inherit the kingdom after his death. Indeed, in October 1154, King Stephen died at the age of 58, and on December 19 Henry and Eleanor were crowned king and queen of England.

THE QUEEN OF ENGLAND

Prince William was born in the fall of 1153, and Eleanor quickly became pregnant again when Henry returned from his travels and joined her in June 1154. She had a second son in February 1155, named Henry. With two sons in her lap, a handsome husband, and her own income from her own lands, the newly crowned queen of England enjoyed a luxurious lifestyle: both Eleanor and Henry appreciated the thrill of hunting, enjoyed musicians and poets who could offer sophisticated entertainment at court, and welcomed foreign visitors who gave her gossip about the newest in literature, culture, fashion, and the daring new polyphonic music. Henry deserved his moments of relaxation and amusement, as he worked feverishly to restore order to England after it had been torn apart by the long years of civil war. Eleanor actively helped him with the business of government, often acting as his deputy when Henry was required to oversee his domains in France. While Eleanor had Henry's full confidence in her statecraft, they never met up more than once or twice a year for the first 12 years of marriage, and yet these meetings were very fruitful, as each time Eleanor conceived a child. After William in 1153 and Henry in 1155, Matilda was born in 1156, Richard in 1157, Geoffrey in 1158, Eleanor in 1161, Joanna in 1165, and finally John in 1166 when Eleanor was 44 years old. Henry was expectedly unfaithful, being away from his wife for months at a time, and sired many illegitimate children—including one with a notorious prostitute named Ykenai. Henry brought the woman's son to court, perhaps as a playmate for Prince William, who was a few months older, and Eleanor became fond of the boy, whom the king named Geoffrey of York. Sadly, Prince William died at the age of three, but Eleanor raised the illegitimate Geoffrey with affection, and when he grew up he had a celebrated career in the church.

Henry was much more difficult to influence than the indecisive Louis had been, but Eleanor managed to have her way despite Henry's stubbornness. The situation with Thomas Becket is a good example: Henry adored the man, giving riches and honors to his friend and constant companion while ignoring his wife. One of the honors Henry steered Becket's way was the archbishopric of Canterbury in 1162—but much to Henry's chagrin, Becket took the position very seriously, transforming from the king's loyal friend into a champion of the church's views, privileges, and authority. Feeling betrayed, Henry fought with Becket for eight years over issues small and large, and ultimately Becket was murdered in 1170. Behind the scenes, there is a strong tradition that Eleanor, who disliked Becket, encouraged Henry to find fault with the man and resent him.

After John was born, it appeared that Eleanor had enough of both Henry and childbearing (although she must have been past the age by the late 1160s) and increased the amount of time she spent in her French territories. The dynasty was settled when in 1170 young Prince Henry was crowned the Young King (while Henry II yet lived) and Prince Richard was confirmed as duke of Aquitaine. Eleanor moved her court to Poitiers and focused on being a patron of the arts.

THE QUEEN OF THE TROUBADOURS

Both Eleanor and Henry loved literature, especially stories about King Arthur. Henry encouraged the tales of fighting and brave knights in order to support his claim to the throne and to strengthen the psychological connection between Arthur's Camelot and his own court, a form of publicity or, perhaps, propaganda. Eleanor, on the other hand, enjoyed the new kind of literature called the romance, and the earliest surviving romances, such as *Tristan* by Thomas of England and *Lancelot* (*The Knight of the Cart*) by Chrétien de Troyes, were written during Eleanor and Henry's reign. The court in which Eleanor grew up was a very cultured place, heavily influenced by the Spanish courts of the Moors, and home to the famous troubadours Cercamon and Marcabru along with dozens of lesser musicians and poets. An extrovert, she responded to fashion and sophistication instinctively, and growing up in a court where the social model was an early version of "courtly love," she was surrounded by clever, witty, educated men who admired Love.

Thus, while Eleanor and her court were in Poitiers, she (along with her daughter Marie of Champagne and Marie de France, a close relative of Henry II) encouraged and developed what has come to be called "the court of love" or "courtly love." Although all but fragmented records of this court have been lost, the writings of Andreas Capellanus give us an idea of what the festivities were: 12 men and women would hear "cases of love" between individuals, deciding issues of fidelity, vows, proper behavior, and worthiness of love. (This court was later used by Eleanor in a more secular way as a forerunner of the jury system.) Eleanor herself was the subject of songs and poetry, many of which openly convey the poet's sexual desire for her or express hopeless passion for a mistress who is far above him in rank. This type of untouchable love is often called *fin' amors*, a love that not only exists outside of marriage but is actually incompatible with marriage. Lovers give each other love freely, but married people must obey each other out of duty. A husband has a right to enjoy his wife's favors, and a wife her husband's, but a lover must earn his favors, if any, from his lady. Thus a husband gains no worth or virtue in pursuing his wife, but a lover can gain worth in his endeavors or quests to gain favor from his lady. For the men who played this game, Love was an end in itself, and the beloved Woman was an object of worship, unattainable due to the fact of her superior rank and usually her preexisting marriage. The man was the supplicant and had no power over her; indeed, his prayers and wishes were usually denied, and he was supposed to suffer ghastly torments because of this denial. Placing women (who were considered to be powerless by both church and state) in this position was revolutionary because it gave women complete dominance over their lovers, indeed over the whole relationship. Eleanor created a court where, for the first time in Western history, a man's status was based (partly) on his behavior toward women. Some scholars see this as an elaborate intellectual game played solely by aristocrats, an ironic literary joke enjoyed by Eleanor's court, while others see it as an actual cultural shift, the blossoming of the light of chivalry out of the darker androcratic ideals of the time—and today we still see the results of this game, in that men are (or used to be) taught to open doors for "ladies" and to stand up when a lady walks into the room.

In addition to Eleanor's love of romance, her love of music and song led her to support the troubadour style that her grandfather Guillaume IX had introduced in Aquitaine, where this aristocratic music had developed based on Poitevin, the area's vernacular language. Her father, Guillaume X, continued to patronize the troubadours, encouraging their music to become a tradition in its own right. Troubadours were always welcome at her court; in fact she found them to be a necessity and took them wherever she went in her travels: as a patron can create a demand for artists, Eleanor's favoring of the music encouraged other aristocratic circles to welcome the musicians. The budding art form, seen memorably in the *lais* of Marie de France, spread to other courts to meet the demand for the new and fashionable. The music and song soon expanded beyond the Poitevin language barrier and became a style of its own, called *trouvère* music. Eleanor's importation of troubadours to her court in England spread the music to that country and strongly influenced later English music and vernacular song. Her son Richard was a troubadour himself, and her two daughters by Louis helped spread the music throughout northern France, passing on the tradition of patronage. Eleanor's need for intellectual diversion, her love of music and troubadours, and her desire to turn unruly young men into proper courtiers were powerful factors in the creation of courtly literature as we know it. Without Eleanor's patronage the Celtic legends that she enjoyed might never have been introduced into the literature of educated Europe, nor would the exploits of King Arthur and his court, the love of Guinevere and Lancelot or Tristan and Isolde, the magic of Merlin and Morgan Le Fay, or the tender heroism of Gawain be remembered and cherished today.

THE POWER-BROKER AND PRISONER

The marriage between Henry and Eleanor had a lot of drama and arguments, intrigue and unfaithfulness, but in one of the few letters that we have from Eleanor, she does admit that her marriage to Henry was "a much happier one than my marriage to Louis." It does appear that they loved each other in their own way and definitely respected each other. But the lure of power, and Eleanor's own need to control her own life and children, got in the way of domestic peace in the royal household. For example, when the young Henry quarreled with his father in 1173, Eleanor took her son's side and defended and backed him openly. The king had not allowed young Henry any real power, thus making his son angry and resentful. They fought, and the king forced his son to accompany him north to Normandy, but at Chinon, where they had stopped overnight, the Young King escaped his house arrest and fled south again to Poitou and Eleanor's court. There, he plotted with Eleanor and his brothers Richard and Geoffrey to take over the throne of England.

The revolt of 1173–74 was a family quarrel made large: the king ordered his family to join him, but his sons fled to Paris to seek the help of King Louis in their revolt. Eleanor intended at first to stay in Poitiers, but, upon hearing that Henry was marching south, she decided to flee to Paris disguised as a man. She was captured and handed over to her husband, and he, realizing her deep influence upon their sons, decided to imprison her—an imprisonment that would last for 16 years. Henry disbanded her court at Poitiers and sent the queen to live at Salisbury Castle, but he allowed his sons to make peace with him as long as they promised to obey him. We do not have many records of Eleanor for the next 10 years, although we know she was moved around to various locations in England and was released to see her children on occasions such as Easter and Christmas.

Here we must mention Henry's mistress, Rosamund Clifford. A great beauty, Rosamund had first met Henry in 1166, and they began an affair in 1173—an affair that was so deeply emotional that Henry considered divorcing Eleanor, and he had no problem flaunting Rosamund in front of his wife in 1175 so that Eleanor would become angry and try to annul the marriage, but Eleanor was too wise to be provoked. Rosamund died suddenly in 1176, and rumors soon arose—and suspicions remain—that the queen had Henry's mistress poisoned for revenge.

Henry the Young King again fought with his father in 1183, but this time the end was not reconciliation, but death. His angry father cut off his allowance, and so Henry tried to relieve his debts by plundering the shrine of Rocamandour; not only did his plan fail, but he contracted dysentery. When Henry realized he was dying, he sent his father a message to free his mother, then he lay down on a bed of ashes to show his penitence and died on June 11, aged 28. After the Young King's death, Eleanor was allowed more freedom—not complete freedom, as she always had to travel with a warden—but freedom enough. In 1184 she traveled to France to tour her lands, then returned to England at Christmas to spend the holidays with Richard, John, and Geoffrey (the historical setting of James Goldman's famous play/film, *The Lion in Winter*).

THE WIDOW

Who would now be the future king of England? Henry preferred John, making him king of Ireland in anticipation of his rule over England; Eleanor favored Richard, and when Richard asked Henry to confirm him as heir, Henry refused. To add insult to injury, the king had seduced Princess Alice, half-sister to the new king of France, Philip II (known as Philip Augustus), and taken her as his mistress even though she was betrothed to Richard—who was himself rumored to have been Philip's lover. In 1189, Richard and Philip combined forces to attack Henry's cities of Le Mans and Tours, but instead of a glorious war all they got was a peace treaty from Henry, because he had been injured in a joust and was dying from an ulcerated wound. Henry died on July 6, 1189, and Richard inherited the throne. One of his first acts was to release his mother, and she ruled England in his stead while he went on the Third Crusade to recover Jerusalem from the victorious Saladin. Eleanor was now 67 years old, but that did not stop her from arranging a marriage between Richard and Princess Berengaria, daughter of King Sancho of Navarre. In 1192 she negotiated Richard's ransom after he was shipwrecked and taken prisoner by Duke Leopold of Austria and held in the Holy Roman Emperor's castle at Hagenau. Eleanor spent most of 1193 collecting the ransom, which amounted to 35 tons of silver. Richard was released in December, and he and his mother toured their French and English territories and arranged a new coronation for Richard in celebration of his return from captivity.

The stress of intense power-brokering and intrigue took its toll on Eleanor, and in 1194 she retired to the Abbey of Fontevrault, her favorite place to rest and find peace. She stayed there for five years, lending her influence as needed, but was called out in 1199 when Richard was wounded in battle on March 25. He had been struck by an arrow; the wound turned gangrenous, and he sent for Eleanor when it was apparent that he would die. She raced the hundred miles to the fortress of Châlus to be with him, and he died in her arms on April 6. Now that Eleanor had left the abbey, she resumed her active involvement in politics and power-brokering: Richard had named John as his heir, and Eleanor managed to outmaneuver the scheming King Philip II, who was trying to put Arthur, Geoffrey's son, on the throne of England. At the grand age of 77, Eleanor took control of Richard's mercenary forces and helped John recapture territories lost during the fight for the throne, defended his lands while he was crowned at Westminster, took a tour of Aquitaine to remind its inhabitants who their duchess was, and went to Spain in 1200 to fetch her granddaughter Blanche of Castile, who was to marry Philip's son and heir Louis.

In 1202, Eleanor was again drawn out of retirement when Philip tried yet again to seize French territories. In alliance with Arthur of Brittany, Philip attacked Normandy and then marched on Poitiers. Eleanor made her way to Poitiers to prevent Arthur—her grandson, but John's enemy—from taking control, yet Arthur showed no respect for his 80-year-old grandmother and besieged her castle at Mirabeau. John fortunately arrived quickly and captured Arthur by surprise at dawn, taking all of his men as well. Arthur's forces at the siege constituted almost all the rebels fighting against John, so this fiasco put an end to the civil war and secured John's place on the throne of England, though since he soon alienated his allies and lost almost all of the continental empire of the Angevins to King Philip of France.

The crisis, however, took its toll on Eleanor's health. In March 1204, she fell into a coma, in which she died peacefully on April 1. She was entombed in Fontevrault Abbey next to her husband Henry and her son Richard, and her effigy on the tomb shows her reading a Bible, her figure beautifully decorated with jewelry.

THE MYTH

It is surprising how much has been written about Eleanor, as we know so very little about her. Her creation of the "Court of Love" is for many scholars her greatest invention, even though there is little to no evidence that she actually created anything of the sort. Even in writing the present biography, it has not always been possible to stay solely with the facts: some speculation, rumor, and gossip must be invoked in order for the reader to understand not only how she lived, but also how she was perceived. Her myth is a rich mixture of traditions—and, to paraphrase Winston Churchill, she remains a mysterious and enigmatic riddle.

The ingredients of the Eleanor legend can be seen in the concerns of her time: the constantly tilting political balance between France and England, the growing cult of the Virgin Mary in the church, and the resurgence of Celtic literature and mythological figures all used Eleanor as a foundation for their growth, and she in turn used them as well to augment her prestige and achieve her own goals. Eleanor was first queen of France, and then queen of England, helping England rise in power and strength: to portray her in myth as an evil queen who had gone over to the enemy gave the French a wonderful personage to blame for their troubles. It may be surprising to claim Eleanor as a religious symbol, but when her poets elevated her to the pedestal that women stand on in courtly literature and poetry, she became an ideal: woman as earthly mother, with children of her own, and as a mother to her country, but she also became a spiritual mother, connected to the cult of the Virgin Mary, the intermediary between God and men. Eleanor also became representative of the rebirth of the feminine myth seen in Celtic tales, especially the ancient myth of Melusine, a fairy queen who helped her husband, Raimondin, build his country and his fortune. Melusine was well known from Scotland to the south of France, a half-human fairy princess who married a king and had many strong but strangely gifted children. She would disappear for weeks at a time, but her absences would correspond to the arrival of a new church or castle to add to Raimondin's wealth. In legend, as in history, we have a woman who was the source for a nobleman's chance to become rich and powerful. With her fairy ancestry, Eleanor was easily accepted as a woman who offered a different, alternate world through her love of troubadours, music, and courtly literature, especially the idea of a round table where all men were equal—a social group based on confidence and esteem instead of on aggression and strength—and a place where women were free to choose their lovers and offer their bodies as they willed, instead of being seen as chattels.

As of this date, we do not have a final academic or professional biography of Eleanor of Aquitaine, probably because so little factual evidence survives— even in her own time, chroniclers had to speculate about her life and motivations, and later writers frequently took negative gossip as fact, and thus many of the nasty rumors that arose during her life became "history" after her death—but nevertheless, Eleanor marks a turning point in the history of European civilization. Despite the valid historiographical need to separate fact from fiction, it must be admitted that much of her attraction to readers stems not from her life, but from her magnificent legend.

FURTHER READING

Fripp, Robert. *Power of a Woman. Memoirs of a Turbulent Life: Eleanor of Aquitaine.* Toronto: Shillingstone Press, 2008.

Hopkins, Andrea. *Six Medieval Women.* New York: Barnes & Noble, 1999.

Konigsburg, E. L. *A Proud Taste for Scarlet and Miniver.* New York: Atheneum, 1973.

Markale, Jean. *Eleanor of Aquitaine: Queen of the Troubadours.* Translated by Jon E. Graham. Rochester, VT: Inner Traditions, 2007.

Meade, Marion. *Eleanor of Aquitaine: A Biography.* New York: Penguin Books, 1977.

Wheeler, Bonnie, and John C. Parsons, eds. *Eleanor of Aquitaine: Lord and Lady.* New York: Palgrave Macmillan, 2002.

APPENDIX: CHRONOLOGY OF THE LIFE OF ELEANOR OF AQUITAINE

1121	Eleanor's parents, Guillaume X and Aenor, marry.
ca. 1122	Eleanor born at Belin, near Bordeaux, or at Nieul.
1127	Geoffrey of Anjou marries Empress Matilda of Saxony.
1129	Philip, son of Louis VI, crowned (associated with his father) as future king of France.
1130	Eleanor's mother and brother (Guillaume, age 8), die.
1131	A fall kills Philip, the crowned heir to France.
1133	The future King Henry II of England, son of Geoffrey of Anjou, born at Le Mans March 5.
1135	King Henry I of England dies at Rouen December 1. A 19-year civil war for the crown of England ensues.
1137	Eleanor's father, Guillaume X, dies at Compostela on Good Friday.
	Abbot Suger leads King Louis VI's embassy to Eleanor in June.
	Eleanor marries Louis VI's son, Louis, in Bordeaux July 25.
	Louis VI dies in Paris August 1. Louis VII and Eleanor assume titles at Poitiers August 8. Eleanor enters Paris as Louis VII's queen.
	Louis VII crowned at Bourges December 25.
1141/43	Trouble at Bourges. Louis sacks Champagne, burns the church at Vitry.
1145	Eleanor's first child by Louis, Marie, born.
	News reaches Paris of Muslim victories in the Holy Land.
	Louis announces intention to go on crusade December 25.
1146	Bernard of Clairvaux calls for Crusade.
	Emperor Conrad accepts Crusade December 25.
1147	Louis and Eleanor march out of Paris May 12.
	French and Angevin armies march on crusade June 11.
	Louis and Eleanor enter Constantinople October 4.
	Armies waste time while leaders tarry in Constantinople in October.
1148	In spring, arguments over strategy strain relations with Raymond. Create rift between Louis and Eleanor. Army leaves Antioch. Jerusalem welcomes Frankish army.
	Later, Louis VII and Eleanor tarry in Palestine.
1149	Louis and Eleanor take separate ships from Palestine after Easter. Both come ashore separately in Roger of Sicily's lands in late July.
	Pope Eugenius refuses Eleanor's divorce plea in October.
1150	Eleanor's second daughter, Alix, born midwinter.
1151	Count Geoffrey (Plantagenet) of Anjou and his son Henry visit Paris in August. Count Geoffrey dies September 7.
1152	Louis VII and Eleanor divorce March 21. Eleanor sets up her court at Poitiers.

	Eleanor marries Henry of Anjou May 18. Henry beats back punitive raids by Louis and allies.
	Eleanor and Henry tour her lands in summer.
1153	Henry leaves for England in January. Eleanor based in Angers.
	King Stephen's heir to England, Eustace, dies in summer.
	William, Eleanor's first child by Henry, born August 17.
	Negotiations for peace in England succeed in December.
1154	Stephen accepts Henry as his heir January 13.
	Henry returns from England in April after negotiating for the throne.
	King Stephen dies at Dover October 25.
	Henry II and Eleanor crowned at Westminster in December.
1155	Thomas Becket named as Henry's chancellor.
	Prince Henry of England born February 28.
1156	Matilda born at London in June.
1157	Prince Richard (the Lionhearted) born September 8 or 13.
1158	Prince Geoffrey of England born September 23.
1160	Eleanor summoned to bring Prince Henry to Normandy in October.
	Strategic marriage of Prince Henry, age 5, to Marguerite, age 2, November 5. Henry seizes the Vexin, Marguerite's dowry.
1162	Henry appoints Becket archbishop of Canterbury after Easter.
	Eleanor of England born October 13.
1163	Henry and Eleanor return to England after long absence January 25.
	Welsh and Scots rulers do homage to Henry and Prince Henry July 1.
1164	Joanna of England born.
1165	Henry, at war in Wales, meets "Fair Rosamund" Clifford in summer.
	Philip, the future Philip II (known as Philip Augustus), born at Paris August 22.
1165	Henry divides time between law-making and affair with Rosamund in the winter.
1166	Prince John of England born December 24.
1167	Henry's mother, the empress Matilda, dies.
	Eleanor decides to separate from Henry. Leaves England, establishes Court of Ladies at Poitiers.
1168	Young Matilda marries Henry the Lion of Saxony February 1.
1169	Eleanor proclaims Richard duke of Aquitaine in April.
	Young Eleanor betrothed to Alfonso, heir to Castile.
1170	Prince Henry crowned "the Young King" in Westminster Abbey June 14.
	Henry and Becket attempt reconciliation. Becket returns to England, lands at Sandwich December 1. Is murdered in Canterbury Cathedral by four knights December 29.
1172	Thomas Becket canonized in spring.

Prince Henry crowned again, with Marguerite, August 27.

Henry does penance for Becket's death in autumn.

1173   Rift between Henry II and sons, abetted by Eleanor, in spring. Prince Henry flees his father, finds refuge in Paris March 24. Richard and Geoffrey also flee to Paris.

Henry and three sons attempt reconciliation in autumn.

1174   Henry ransacks Eleanor's allies and her court at Poitiers in spring. Exiles royal women, including Eleanor, to England in June.

Henry does penance for Becket's death, at Canterbury, in summer.

Louis, Young Henry and Philip of Flanders besiege Rouen in July. Henry II beats off the allies' attack on Rouen August 11.

1175   Eleanor refuses Henry's demand for a divorce in October.

1176   Rosamund Clifford dies.

Joanna marries William II of Sicily February 13.

1177   The curia denies Henry's plea to divorce Eleanor.

Eleanor of England ("Leonor") marries Alfonso September 22.

1179   Henry compels Eleanor to cede lands to Richard.

Richard wars on rebellious vassals, razes Taillebourg in May.

Philip (Philip Augustus) crowned (associated with his father) on All Saints' Day.

1180   King Philip assumes his father's regal powers in February.

King Philip's first marriage, to Isabelle of Hainault, April 28. The two are crowned May 29.

King Louis VII dies at the abbey of Saint-Port September 18.

1182   Henry II and Richard crush rebels in Aquitaine in summer.

1183   Strife between Henry II and two sons in spring.

Prince Henry (the Young King) dies June 11.

Henry II and King Philip confer in December.

1186   Henry, Eleanor, and sons confer at Windsor in summer.

Geoffrey dies at Paris August 18.

1187   Saladin's forces capture Jerusalem September 17.

1188   Henry and Philip make peace, take the cross January 21–22.

Henry prepares English and Welsh barons for Crusade in February.

1189   Henry lies ill in Le Mans during Lent.

Matilda dies at Brunswick June 28.

King Philip and Richard dictate terms to the dying Henry at Chinon. Henry II dies July 6. Eleanor freed, assumes regency of England.

Richard invested as duke of Normandy July 20.

King Richard crowned September 3. Decides to go on Crusade December 11.

1190   Richard and Philip agree on Crusade strategy, leave Vezelay July 4.

Richard sails, ahead of army, from Marseilles August 7. Lands at

Messina, Sicily, ahead of troops September 24. Philip joins Richard at Messina in autumn.

Richard rescues sister Joanna and property from Tancred in winter.

1191	Richard and Philip quarrel over Joanna and Alix February 2. Eleanor brings Richard's bride, Berengaria, to Messina March 30. Richard marries Berengaria May 12.
1192	Christians and Muslims reach a "three-year truce" August 9. Richard leaves Palestine October 9. Captured by Leopold near Vienna December 20.
1193	Eleanor works to collect Richard's ransom. Escorts Richard's ransom to Mainz in December.
1194	Richard released; he and Eleanor return to England February 3.
1195	Death of Alix, Eleanor's second daughter by Louis.
1198	Death of Marie of Champagne, Eleanor's firstborn, March 11. Eleanor's grandson Otto crowned emperor July 12.
1199	Pope Innocent III imposes a truce on Richard and Philip January 13. Richard dies April 6. John becomes duke of Normandy April 25. Crowned king of England at Westminster May 27. Joanna delivers a son at Rouen; both die, September 4.
1200	Eleanor travels to Castile January 1. In February, selects Blanche to marry French heir. Blanche marries future Louis VIII May 23. Widower John marries Isabella August 26. Isabella crowned at Westminster October 8.
1201	John and Isabella return to Normandy in summer. Amicable relations between Kings John and Philip in July.
1202	Philip, Arthur, and Lusignans attack Normandy in spring. Eleanor flees Fontevrault for greater safety in Poitiers in July. Arthur of Brittany besieges Eleanor at Mirebeau July 30. John's forces break the siege, capture Arthur August 1.
1203	Probable death of Arthur in John's custody on Good Friday Eve.
1204	Eleanor dies April 1; buried at Fontevrault.

Thorfinn Karlsefne (*left*), Guðriðr ("Gudrior"), and Leif Eriksson ("the Lucky," *right*), from a stained-glass window cartoon by Edward Burne-Jones of the William Morris firm, about 1883. (Lisle, Fortunee de. *Burne-Jones*, 1906)

Leif Eriksson
(ca. 975–1020)

Paul Acker

INTRODUCTION

Leif Eriksson (spelled Leifr Eiríksson in Old Icelandic)[1] is known primarily as the first European to set foot on North American soil, almost 500 years before Columbus. According to one version of events, the continent was actually discovered even earlier, by one of Leif's countrymen: Bjarni Herjólfsson spotted parts of it a few years earlier when blown off course while sailing from Norway to Iceland and on to (he thought) Greenland. But Bjarni did not step ashore on the strange land; he turned back to Greenland, for which many people there "thought him short on curiosity." (*The Greenlanders' Saga*, ch. 2, trans. Kunz).[2] Leif retraced Bjarni's voyage and explored a region he named Vínland, staying over the winter, perhaps building and sheltering in the very houses that archaeologists in the early 1960s uncovered in L'Anse aux Meadows at the tip of Newfoundland.[3] Before that site was excavated, the Norse claim could not be substantiated, and Leif's landfall was proposed all up and down the Atlantic coast. As things look now, Leif may have been the first European explorer of (modern) Canada, but perhaps not the United States (of course Christopher Columbus did not make it to [modern] U.S. shores either).

Leif is sometimes also known as the man who converted Norse medieval Greenland to Christianity; indeed, U.S. President George H. W. Bush, in officially proclaiming Leif Erikson (so spelled) Day in 1989, called Leif a "courageous Norse missionary and explorer."[4] The earliest firmly datable account of Leif describes him in this connection.[5] In about 1230, Snorri Sturluson in his historical work *Heimskringla* mentions that Iceland was Christianized (in the year 999 or 1000), and then:

> That same spring King Olaf [Tryggvason] dispatched Leif Eriksson to Greenland to preach Christianity there, and he left that summer for Greenland. He rescued at sea a crew of men who had been shipwrecked, and then he discovered Vínland the Good. He arrived in the summer in Greenland and had brought with him a priest and clerics. He went to stay with his father Erik at Brattahlíð. Thereafter people called him Leif the Lucky, but his father Erik said that the two things balanced each other out: Leif had rescued the ship's crew, but he had also brought to Greenland a great imposter, namely the priest. (ch. 104)[6]

Clearly Erik, who died a pagan, was less than grateful for Leif's missionary activity, especially when his wife (and Leif's mother) Thjóðhild converted and then refused to sleep with him (*Erik the Red's Saga*, ch. 5). Her little chapel has been excavated in Greenland and a reconstruction of it can now be seen there, doubtless haunted by Erik's grumpy old ghost.[7]

Other than Snorri's account, the main sources for material about Leif Eriksson are the two so-called Vínland sagas: *The Greenlanders' Saga* and *Erik the Red's Saga*.[8] The former was written down in a manuscript called the *Flatey*

Book (*Flateyjarbók*) in the year 1387, where it is woven into *The Saga of Olaf Tryggvason* (king of Norway 995–1000). *Erik the Red's Saga* was written down in two different manuscripts in about 1306 and 1420. Opinions differ widely about how much earlier than their manuscripts the Vínland sagas might have been first composed, and about which saga was composed first; they may both go back as far as 1200 in something like their preserved form. The two sagas differ considerably in their accounts of the voyages to Vínland taken by Leif and his kinsfolk and thus likely derive ultimately from different oral traditions.

THE LIFE OF LEIF IN *THE VÍNLAND SAGAS*

The story of Leif Eriksson begins with his father, Erik the Red (Eiríkr inn rauði). Like many early Icelanders, Erik had come to Iceland from western Norway, in his case because of "some killings" he had committed there. Erik arrived around 970, well after the initial Icelandic Settlement Period (874–930), so that most of the good land had already been taken. He settled in Drangar in the far north-northwest (a desolate place known for its lack of farmland) but married into a better situation farther south in Haukardalr, at a farm called (predictably) Eiriksstaðir (Erik's Stead). His wife Thjoðhild was descended from such notable Icelandic settlers as Helgi the Lean and Auð (or Unn) the Deep-Minded; their son Leif was born at Eiríksstaðir in about 975. Erik's disposition does not seem to have improved much, however. When his thralls started a landslide that destroyed a nearby farm and were killed for it, Erik killed the killer (named Eyjolf the Filthy) and then another man named Hrafn (Raven) the Dueller, who doubtless deserved it. Erik was banished to some nearby islands, then outlawed from there, after which he set out to re-discover and explore a land he had heard about farther west. He stayed the first winter at Erik's Island, then sailed into Erik's Fjord (now Tunulliarfik Fjord) and stayed in Erik's Isles.[9] He snuck back to Iceland briefly and told all his friends they should come live with him in this new land, which he named Greenland, saying "people would be attracted there if it had a favorable name" (*The Greenlanders' Saga*, ch. 1, tr. Magnusson and Pálsson; cf. *Erik the Red's Saga*, ch. 2). He brought his wife and children with him, sailed into Erik's Fjord, and named his new farm not, surprisingly, Erik's Stead II, but rather Brattahlíð (Steep Slope; now Qassiarsuk). It was in one of the greenest spots in all of Greenland. Living there with Leif were his half-sister Freydís and his brothers Thorstein and Thorvald, the last named for Erik's father Thorvald; indeed, it has been suggested that Leif's full name was Thorleif, so that the names of all Erik's children paid homage to the Norse gods Thor and Frey.[10] Leif's brother Thorstein married a woman called Gudrid (Old Norse Guðriðr), a Christian woman who nonetheless had knowledge of pagan songs and sang them for a seeress named Thorbjörg to help with her prophecy (*Erik the Red's Saga*, ch. 4).

Leif started out as a bit of a "bad boy," impregnating a woman in the Hebrides of whom it was said that "she knew a thing or two" (*Erik the Red's Saga*, ch. 5). The love child (named Thorgils) eventually made it to Greenland and was said to be a bit odd, but we are given no details by which to judge (the late-Victorian translator of *Erik the Red's Saga*, John Sephton, suppresses this entire episode).[11] Leif left the Hebrides and went to Norway, where King Olaf asked him to go back and convert Greenland. According to *Erik the Red's Saga* (ch. 5), it was on this voyage back to Greenland that Leif got blown off course and discovered a land of "self-sown wheat and [grape] vines."[12] On his way back to Greenland he rescued a shipwrecked crew, earning the name "Leif the Lucky" (*Leifr inn heppni*), as we have already heard tell from Snorri Sturluson. The saga writer comments: "He showed his great magnanimity and goodness by bringing Christianity to the country and by rescuing these men" (ch. 5, tr. Magnusson and Pálsson).

The Greenlanders' Saga tells a longer version of this voyage, which Leif undertakes on purpose to explore the land Bjarni Herjólfsson had already glimpsed. Leif crosses west and then sails south, naming the regions Helluland (Stone Slab Land, usually identified as Baffin Island); Markland (Forest Land, on the Labrador coast) and Vínland (Wineland). The Vikings sail up a river teeming with salmon. A crewman named Tyrkir comes back to the group acting a bit strangely (drunkenly?) and carrying grapes, which he recognizes from his childhood in Germany. Current scholarly opinion (which is to say, the scholarly opinion that I most agree with) holds that in that era, river-grapes grew as far north as New Brunswick, and salmon bred as far south as the Gulf of Saint Lawrence; hence Vínland was most likely the region from the tip of Newfoundland down into the Gulf of Saint Lawrence.[13] Leif and company build some houses ("Leif's booths"), stay the winter, and then return to Greenland with a load of grapes and grape-wood. During its account of this expedition, *The Greenlanders' Saga* describes Leif thus: "Leif was a large, strong man, of very striking appearance and wise, as well as being a man of moderation in all things" (ch. 2(3), trans. Kunz). The accent on moderation aims at distinguishing him from his father Erik.

Subsequent voyages to Vínland were attempted by Leif's brother Thorstein (who never found it); Thorvald (who was killed by an indigenous arrow, *The Greenlanders' Saga*, ch. 5, or a Plinian "uniped," *Erik the Red's Saga*, ch. 12);[14] his former sister-in-law Gudrid with her new husband Thorfinn *karlsefni* (who were hugely successful, until they were overrun by natives called *skrælingar* in skin canoes); and his sister Freydís (who was successful but homicidal, having inherited the paternal temperament; at one point she frightens off the *skrælingar* by slapping her naked breast with a sword; see *Erik the Red's Saga*, ch. 11).[15]

While I do not present a full summary of these voyages because Leif is not involved, a few other details are picked up by later retellings that I discuss below. On his voyage (as more fully recounted in *Erik the Red's Saga*, ch. 7–12), Thorfinn *karlsefni* (his nickname means "manly stuff") names additional locales, among them *Furðustrandir* (Wonder Strands, perhaps along the

Labrador coast), *Straumsfjörðr* (Stream Fjord, perhaps the Strait of Belle Isle), and Hóp (Tidal Pool, perhaps Miramichi Bay).[16] With Thorfinn's crew was a man called Thorhall the Hunter, who prayed to the god Thor for food and a whale washed ashore; its meat, however, made the others ill, so they prayed to the Christian God to better effect. Also among the crew are two Scottish runners, Haki and Hekja, whom King Olaf had given to Leif (*Erik the Red's Saga,* ch. 8). Thorfinn trades milk (*The Greenlanders' Saga,* ch. 7) or red cloth (*Erik the Red's Saga,* ch. 11) with the natives for furs and other goods. They are frightened by the Vikings' bellowing bull but when the natives return in numbers, the Vikings kill one for trying to steal weapons (*The Greenlanders' Saga,* ch. 7) and then a wholesale battle ensues, in which a number on both sides are killed, including Thorbrand Snorrason (*Erik the Red's Saga,* ch. 11).[17] While in Vínland, Gudrid had given birth to a boy they named Snorri (who is therefore the first European said to be born in the New World); on their way back to Greenland, Thorfinn and his crew capture two *skraeling* boys and baptize them (*Erik the Red's Saga,* ch. 12). Thorfinn and Gudrid later return to Iceland; after her husband dies, Gudrid goes on a pilgrimage to Rome.

LATER NOTICES OF THE VÍNLAND VOYAGES

The Vínland voyages begin to be mentioned in print in the seventeenth century, with the 1629 publication of Adam of Bremen's "Descriptio insularum Aqvuilonis," appended to his *Gesta Hammaburgensis ecclesiae pontificum*; and two works by Arngrímur Jónsson, *Specimen de Islandiæ historicvm* (1643) and *Gronlandia* (written ca. 1600 but not published until 1688; it mentions Leif specifically, for the first time), followed by the 1715 *Historia Vinlandiæ Antiquæ* of Torfaeus (Thormóður Torfason).[18] In his *Introduction à l'histoire de Dannemarc* (1755), Paul Henri Mallet paraphrased *The Greenlanders' Saga* based on Torfaeus, and his work was translated into English by Thomas Percy as *Northern Antiquities* (1770).[19] Late eighteenth-century historians, such as David Crantz, author of *The History of Greenland* (London, 1767), also helped disseminate Mallet's account. But the major impetus for the modern reemergence of the legend of Leif is Carl Rafn's *Antiquitates Americanæ* (1837), which included texts of *The Greenlanders' Saga* and *Erik the Red's Saga* with translations into Danish and Latin. The matter became known almost immediately in English, through reviews of Rafn, his English abstracts in 1838, and in the form of a "dramatic dialogue" or mock debate published by Joshua Toulmin Smith in 1839.

VÍNLAND IN LITERATURE

Unfortunately, much of the nineteenth-century debate centered not on Leif but on the location of Vínland (which always seemed to be more or less in

the author's backyard, usually in New England) and on the authenticity of
such spurious monuments as the Newport Tower, built not by Vikings but by
a colonial governor of Rhode Island in about 1670.[20] The Tower figured in
Longfellow's 1841 poem "The Skeleton in Armour," mainly inspired by another spurious Viking artifact, the skeleton (of an Indian, actually) unearthed
in 1832 in Fall River, Massachusetts.[21] The poem, mainly spoken by the skeleton itself, tells how a Viking abducted a princess but was blown off course
(to America) by a hurricane:

> As with his wings aslant,
> Sails the fierce cormorant,
> Seeking some rocky haunt,
>   With his prey laden,
> So toward the open main,
> Beating to sea again,
> Through the wild hurricane
>   Bore I the maiden. (39)

This Viking erected the tower "for [his] lady's bower," but she dies in child-
birth, so he buries her under the tower, then wanders off (to Fall River, presumably) and kills himself by falling on his spear. He ascends, apparently to
Valhalla:

> Thus, seamed with many scars
> Bursting these prison bars,
> Up to its native stars
>   My soul ascended!
> There from the flowing bowl
> Deep drinks the warrior's soul,
> *Skoal!* to the Northland! *skoal!*
>   —Thus the tale ended. (41)

The poem was illustrated in a wall painting by Walter Crane as part of
the decoration for a Newport mansion called Vínland, which also included
stained-glass windows designed by the William Morris firm (see below).[22]

Similarly, John Greenleaf Whittier wrote a poem called "The Norsemen"
(1841), which took its cue from "the Bradford statue," a chunk of stone that
had in fact been chiseled in colonial times.[23] It was found along the Merri-
mack River in Massachusetts. Whittier asks in Blakean mode:

> Who from its bed of primal rock
> First wrenched thy dark, unshapely block?
> Whose hand, of curious skill untaught,
> Thy rude and savage outline wrought?

The poet is transported in a dream to the Viking times of its purported making:

> But hard!—from wood and rock flung back,
> What sound come up the Merrimac?
> What sea-worn barks are those which throw
> The light spray from each rushing prow?
> Have they not in the North Sea's blast
> Bowed to the waves the straining mast?
> Their frozen sails the low, pale sun
> Of Thulë's night has shone upon;
> Flapped by the sea-wind's gusty sweep
> Round icy drift, and headland steep.
> . . .
> A sound of smitten shields I hear,
> Keeping a harsh and fitting time
> To Saga's chant, and Runic rhyme;
> Such lays as Zetland's [Shetland's] Scald has sung.

Whittier shows at least that not only British Victorians were inspired by the skaldic muse (on which, see Wawn's *The Vikings and the Victorians*).

The Vínland voyages themselves (rather than their dubious artifacts) had given rise to verse as early as 1819, when Scottish poet James Montgomery in "Greenland: A Poem, in Five Cantos" spurns the heroic and monkish muses:

> Rather the muse would stretch a mightier wing,
>   Of a new world the earliest dawn to sing
> How,—long ere Science, in a dream of thought,
>   Earth's younger daughter to Columbus brought,
>   And sent him, like the Faerie Prince, in quest
>   Of *that* "bright vestal thron'd in the west."
>   —Greenland's bold sons, by instinct, sallied forth
>   On barks, like icebergs drifting from the north,
>   Cross'd without magnet undiscover'd seas. (4.145–53)

Of these Viking adventurers, only Leif Eriksson's German crewman Tyrker is mentioned by name; just before he finds grapes, he crosses a river "Swarming with alligator-shoals" (4.169). Montgomery thus imagines Leif and company as discovering in effect all of North and South America.[24]

The New Englander James Russell Lowell (1819–1891) wrote a poem called "The Voyage to Vinland" (1850–1868), which however mostly passes over Leif to muse on Bjarni Herjólfsson as a figure of lost opportunity and Gudrid as prophetess for the New Land.[25] Gudrid's stanzas are alliterative and echo the Eddic cosmological poem *Völuspá*, finding the Twilight of the

Gods and the rebirth of the White Christ (as he was called by Scandinavian missionaries) in the New World:

> Looms there the New Land:
> Locked in the shadow
> Long the gods shut it,
> Niggards of newness
> They, the o'er-old.[26]

Sidney Lanier, a native of Georgia, drew on the Vínland voyages for his compendious historical poem "Psalm of the West," completed in 1876 in time for the nation's centennial:

> Then Leif, bold son of Eric the Red,
>   To the South of the West doth flee—
> Past slaty Helluland is sped,
>   Past Markland's woody lea,
> Till round about fair Vinland's head,
>   Where Taunton helps the sea.
> The Norseman calls, the anchor falls,
>   The mariners hurry a-strand,
> They wassail with fore-drunken skals
>   Where prophet wild grapes stand,
> They lift the Leifsbooth's hasty walls,
>   They stride about the land—
> New England, thee! (p. 121)

The mention of the Taunton River (in Massachusetts) is no doubt due to the Dighton Picture Rock located nearby, another of the (spurious) New England Viking antiquities mentioned by Rafn.[27] Leif's booths are the temporary homes he built, mentioned in the Vínland sagas, and now sometimes identified with the buildings excavated in L'Anse aux Meadows, Newfoundland.

THE WILLIAM MORRIS VÍNLAND WINDOWS IN NEWPORT, RHODE ISLAND

Toward the end of the nineteenth century, a New England devotee of Leif Eriksson and the Vínland voyages was responsible for perhaps the most aesthetically significant visual arts monument to them. In Newport, Rhode Island, which as we have already seen was home to the so-called Viking Tower, a wealthy tobacco heiress named Catherine Lorillard Wolfe had begun construction of a "cottage" (the Newport term for a mansion or stately home) to be named Vínland. No mansion was complete without stained-glass windows, so Wolfe in 1883 commissioned the firm of William Morris and Co. to design appropriately themed windows for her. Some of Morris's letters to her (and her decorator) survive, and they record Morris deliberating about which figures to include. Erik the Red had never actually made it to Vínland, and Freydís was "a horrible wretch according to the Leif's Saga whereas Guðriðr has something pleasing and womanly about her."[28] Thorfinn Karlsefne and Leif the Lucky would make up the other two portraits flanking Guðriðr.

While unfortunately the windows were removed in 1934 and sold into private hands in 1937, there survives a cartoon for the windows.[29] One can see that all three figures are standing on rock platforms amid a sea of blue, swirling waves with the paler blue sky (rendered in a kind of brickwork pattern) above them, where their names are written on scrolls. According to Morris, Guðriðr holds a rune-staff to represent her knowledge of pagan incantations (*Erik the Red's Saga,* ch. 4). Thorfinn holds a shield and spear, Leif a shield and ax.

Above the Vínland adventurers (as he called them), Morris (and his chief designer for stained glass, Edward Burne-Jones) arranged three figures of Norse gods (Thor, Odin, and Frey), accompanied by their associated beasts and attributes. Above them appear Sol, the sun; Luna, the moon; and a Viking ship, with the golden boar of Frey gleaming on its sails; the handsome window for this last is now owned by the Delaware Art Museum and toured in a recent exhibition.[30]

Morris, who had become a socialist and an advocate for relief to the poverty-stricken Iceland of his time, could not help but comment on the political irony involved in the fact that "the poor fishermen & sheep farmers of Greenland & Iceland have so curiously found a place among the worthies connected with the great Modern Commonwealth."[31]

LEIF ERIKSSON IN JUVENILE LITERATURE

In the later nineteenth and early twentieth centuries, Leif and his companions (real and imagined) began to figure in novels for juveniles such as (in the United Kingdom) R. M. Ballantyne's *The Norsemen in the West* (1872) and J. F. Hodgett's *Edric the Norseman* (published serially in *The Boy's Own Paper,* 1887–88)[32] and (in the United States) Ottilie Liljencrantz's *The Thrall of Leif the Lucky* (1902; later adapted into a silent film; see below) and Jennie Hall's *Viking Tales* (1902; see the illustrated chapters "Leif and His New Land" and "Wineland the Good"). In her appended "Suggestions to Teachers," Jennie Hall comments:

> The historical value of the story of Leif Ericsson and the others seems to me to be not to learn the fact that Norsemen discovered America before Columbus did, but to gain a conception of the conditions of early navigation, of the length of the voyage, of the dangers of the sea, and a consequent realization of the reason for the fact that America was

unknown to mediæval Europe, of why the Norsemen did not travel, of what was necessary to be done before men should strike out across the ocean. Norse story is only one chapter in that tale of American discovery. (202–3)

RUDYARD KIPLING, "THE FINEST STORY IN THE WORLD" (1891)

Another sometime writer for juveniles from this period, Rudyard Kipling, also paid homage to the legends of Leif. In 1891, a few years before he wrote *The Jungle Book* (1894), Kipling published a story titled "The Finest Story in the World."[33] Its anonymous narrator is a writer acquainted with a Charlie Mears. Mears is a young London banker but with literary ambitions; when he has trouble with a story he is attempting to write, the narrator offers to hear it. The narrator thinks that the story fragment Mears presents him with is badly written but that when told out loud, the "notion" behind the story is really quite fine. As he relates his story, it becomes clear to the narrator that Mears, who has never been at sea, knows in astonishing detail about the daily life of an ancient Greek galley-slave; that indeed in a former life he must have been the very slave who features in his story. Moreover, when Mears says he (the slave) had also rowed to the Long and Wonderful Beaches, the narrator asks, "Furdurstrandi[r]?" realizing that Mears had gone to Wineland in America with Thorfin Karlsefne. Unfortunately, Mears has begun to read prodigiously and becomes more interested in quoting from Longfellow about Viking voyages than recounting his own firsthand experiences. On another occasion, however, he blurts out, "When they heard *our* bulls bellow the Skrœlings ran away." The narrator muses:

> Now it is written in the Saga of Eric the Red, or that of Thorfin Karlsefne, that nine hundred years ago when Karlsefne's galleys came to Leif's booths, which Leif had erected in the unknown land called Markland, which may or may not have been Rhode Island, the Skrœlings—and the Lord He knows who these may or may not have been—came to trade with the Vikings, and ran away because they were frightened at the bellowing of the cattle which Thorfin had brought with him in the ships. But what in the world could a Greek slave know of that affair?

He concludes that Mears's soul must have known "half a dozen several and separate existences spent on blue water in the morning of the world!" The narrator longs for an opportunity to transcribe an hour's worth of Mears talking uninterrupted. As he muses about the possibilities, he is accosted by a young Bengali law student he knows, named Grish Chunder. He tells the Hindu about Mears's case, knowing that Chunder will be familiar with the "remembering of previous experiences." Grish tells him that Mears will soon begin to forget, especially once he meets a woman: "One kiss that he gives back again and remembers will cure all this nonsense."

Mears visits the narrator and reads an awful poem he has composed, and will only impart a bit more of his Viking adventures. Without Mears's full account, the narrator realizes any story he writes "would be nothing more than a faked, false-varnished, sham-rusted piece of Wardour Street work at the end." (It is interesting to note here that William Morris's archaizing translations of Old Norse sagas and other ancient works were sometimes denigrated as "Wardour Street antiques," after the Soho street where sham-antiques were sold.)[34] On another occasion Mears tells some more about his adventures with the "red-haired man" (Thorfin), rowing for three days among floating ice. But the next time Mears visits, he has written a love poem and produces a photograph of a girl "with a curly head and a foolish slack mouth." The narrator concludes, "Grish Chunder was right. Charlie had tasted the love of woman that kills remembrance, and the finest story in the world would never be written."

The story plays cleverly with both the pretensions of bad, youthful writers and the longing for fame of more accomplished ones. Kipling himself of course hardly needed help in spinning a fine adventure yarn. For him, the voyage to Vínland serves as one of most wondrous adventures in history, if perhaps too remote a source for genuine rather than Wardour Street fiction. To emphasize this note of wonder, Kipling has Mears begin with the "Long and Wonderful Beaches" of Thorfinn's discoveries rather than the Wineland of Leif. We can perhaps blame Mears's scatteredness for conflating Markland (a forested area clearly north of Vínland, most likely in Labrador) with Leif's booths, which "may or may not have been" in Rhode Island.

LEIF ERIKSSON AND THE SCANDINAVIAN AMERICAN COMMUNITY

In the decades running up to 1892 and the 400th anniversary celebrations of Columbus's encounter with the New World, Scandinavian Americans sought to advance the cause of Leif Eriksson, who (they claimed, although the matter was not regarded as proven) had come to America almost five centuries before the Italian sailor. Professor Rasmus Anderson proposed a monument and recruited Ole Bull in the effort, a violinist who was one of the best-known Scandinavians of his day (a sort of nineteenth-century Victor Borge). The statue was planned for the University of Wisconsin campus in Madison, where Anderson taught, to help make it a chief center of Scandinavian studies in the nation (which indeed it is to this day). Attention shifted to Cambridge and Boston, however (where Leif Eriksson and Vínland fever were strong, spurred by baking-powder magnate Eben Horsford), and in 1887 a statue by Ann Whitney was erected on Commonwealth Avenue overlooking Back Bay, Boston. In his autobiography, Anderson comments: "The statue is subject to criticism. Miss Whitney made a figure more or less resembling Ole Bull. Leif Erikson has a smooth face, and upon the whole it is in all its outlines more a Roman than a Norse work of art, but is a great work of art nevertheless" (207). He might have added that the figure's circular breast plates, long flowing hair, miniskirt-length tunic, and half-akimbo posture (as he scans the horizon) make him look a little less than rugged. An inscription in Norse and runic letters translates as "Leif the Lucky, Eric's son." In the same year, a replica was commissioned for Milwaukee, Wisconsin.

For the 1893 Columbian celebrations themselves (aka the Chicago World's Fair), a replica of the recently unearthed Gokstad ship sailed from Bergen, Norway, to Newfoundland, to New York, and ultimately via the Erie Canal to the Great Lakes and Chicago. (The ship would then reside in Lincoln Park until it was moved in 1996 to Geneva, Illinois, where it awaits restoration.)[35] Of course replicas of the *Niña*, the *Pinta*, and the *Santa Maria* also sailed to Chicago, from Spain. With regard to Leif, the most significant event was the commission of a painting by Norwegian artist Christian Krohg (1852–1925). Titled "Leif Erikson Discovering America," the painting is perhaps the best-known artistic representation of our hero.[36]

Statues of Leif continued apace; Norwegians in Chicago funded another statue (by Sigvald Asbjørnsen), erected in 1901. Perhaps the best-known Leif Eriksson statue was erected in Reykjavík in 1930, a gift from the United States to commemorate the 1,000th anniversary of Iceland's Althing, its parliament. It was sculpted by Stirling Calder, father of the famous maker of mobiles Alexander Calder; the competition runner-up to Calder's statue, by Nína Sæmundsson, now stands at Eiríksstaðir in Iceland.[37] The *Milwaukee Journal* (August 5, 1931) noted that Calder's statue showed a "sturdier Viking" than their own. Indeed, the lantern-jawed visage does connote a tough customer, a bit like Klaus Kinski in the film *Aguirre, Wrath of God* (dir. Werner Herzog, 1972).[38]

Rasmus Anderson lived to see another one of his pet projects realized, the proclamation of a Leif Eriksson Day, signed into law in Wisconsin in 1929. President Franklin Roosevelt proclaimed the day in 1935, but it seems to have needed continual reinforcement; President Johnson proclaimed it in 1964, and President George W. Bush during each year of his presidency. The day chosen, October 9, is sometimes said to commemorate the first Norwegian immigrant ship to America on that day in 1825. But Anderson reportedly suggested "that a day be fixed in the first or second week of October because that is the time of ripe grapes."[39] Nor was it likely mere coincidence that the timing, as Inga Dóra Björnsdóttir expresses it, enabled "Scandinavian-Americans to pre-empt Columbus Day by some seventy-two hours."[40]

LITERARY AND FILM ADAPTATIONS IN THE TWENTIETH CENTURY

Perry Marshall, Vinland, or The Norse Discovery of America; An Historical Poem *(ca. 1920)*

To return to literary adaptations, in about 1920, Perry Marshall, a minister and medical doctor living in New Salem, Massachusetts, published *Vinland, or The Norse Discovery of America; An Historical Poem*. According to his preface (p. 3), Marshall's source is the *Saga of Thorsefni* (i.e., *Erik The Red's Saga*) as recorded in the manuscript *Hauksbók*. The saga's account had been "sifted anew" by Professor Fiske—that is, John Fiske, a professor of history at Washington University in Saint Louis, author of *The Discovery of America* (Boston, 1892). Accordingly, Marshall feels he can claim: "I dare indeed to call my Thorfinn story true." Marshall interweaves a claim for Boston as the site of Leif Eriksson's landing (where, as noted above, a statue of Leif had been erected in 1886):

> Nine hours, precisely, was the winter's shortest day,
> Which marks the latitude, exact, of Boston Bay,
> And when upon the wings of spring the south winds came,
> Ten hundred one, brave Leif reloads his ship of fame
> With timber, such as oft before Norse eyes had seen
> Afloat and sought to trace unto its sources green;
> And with this freight he started toward his father's land. (14)

Despite his claim for a historic authenticity, one of Marshall's more interesting contributions to Vínland lore is pure fiction: he provides a death scene for Leif Eriksson. As we read in *The Greenlanders' Saga* (and not in fact *Erik the Red's Saga*), Leif, retired in Greenland, hears that his sister Freydís murdered many of her co-voyagers to Vínland, to increase her own profits. But he does not have the heart to punish his sister as she deserves (ch. 9). It is the last we hear of Leif in *The Greenlanders' Saga*. But Marshall adds that Leif took the news mortally hard:

> Brave Leif had often wiped an iron eye and brow,
> But sorrow gathers on his silvered features now.
> "My bones to Vinland take and bury by the main,"
> And then expired in sorrow for his sister's slain. (26)

William Carlos Williams, "Red Eric" (1925)

Beginning in 1922, a poet of more lasting fame, William Carlos Williams, undertook a series of historical essays that would eventually be called *In the American Grain* (1925). The book begins with a piece called "Red Eric," a monologue in the voice of Eric the Red, who interests Williams primarily as an outlaw: "Rather the ice than their way," he begins, referring to his exile from Norway to Iceland. Eric continues in the manner of a swashbuckler or Western film hero: ". . . a man that can throw a spear, take a girl, steer a ship, till the soil, plant, care for the cattle . . . but they have branded me." He first mentions his son Lief (spelled thus) as having sailed to Norway and back from "a new country" (Vínland): "At the same stroke he brings me pride and joy-in-his-deed . . . and poison," in the form of Christianity. "Thorhild bars me, godless, from her bed . . . Let her build a church and sleep in it."

Eric then goes on to narrate the voyages of Karlsefne and Freydis (following first *Erik the Red's Saga* and then *The Greenlanders' Saga*). He concludes:

> In Greenland, Lief, now head of the family, has no heart to punish his sister as she deserves: But this I predict of them, that there is little prosperity in store for their offspring. Hence it came to pass that no one from that time forward thought them worthy of aught but evil. Eric in his grave. (9)

The Viking *(1928, dir. Roy William Neill)*

Mention was made above of a juvenile novel, Ottilie Liljencrantz's *The Thrall of Leif the Lucky* (1902). It has the distinction of having been made into a two-strip Technicolor silent film called *The Viking* in 1928, starring Donald Crisp. Since this is the only cinematic version of Leif that I have found (aside from documentaries, and an animated feature I will discuss below), I will give it a full summary.[41] Unlike the novel upon which it was based (in which Alwin is "barely seventeen," and Helga "a year or two younger"), the film begins with its protagonists as adults, and it begins in Northumbria rather than Norway.

Lord Alwin returns home to his castle in Northumbria and greets his mother at her needlework (we can tell he is English because he has trimmed black hair and eyebrows and no facial hair, unlike the Vikings who have long fair or red hair and sport beards and/or mustaches). His sister is at her Bible and offers up a version of the famous Irish prayer: "From the sword and the chains of the Vikings, O Lord, deliver us and from all other manner of evil, protect us, O Lord." Unfortunately, the Vikings choose that moment to attack (as announced in a title card where the words grow ever larger: THE VIKINGS!). The Vikings take their plunder back to a trading post in Norway, where a big Viking and a dwarf take inventory of the loot, including the needlework of Alwin's mother, which he, now a captive, looks upon with sadness.

A Viking rides up and dumps a young warrior woman on the ground: Helga Nilsson, "an orphan of noble blood—living the life of a Viking sea rover under the protection of the famous Leif Ericsson." She has the winged helmet and strapless chainmail of a valkyrie, and indeed Richard Wagner's *Ride of the Valkyries* is her musical theme. Her friend Sigurd buys a Greek slave woman from the trader. Helga decides to buy Alwin and take him back to Leif Ericsson's camp, where Egil the Black, "Leif's Danish sailing master," is practicing his swordplay. Sigurd gives the female slave to his (beefy) wife, and Helga shows her slave Alwin to Egil, but they scuffle. Helga tells Alwin to lead her horse to the pens. He mounts it and starts to gallop off, but Helga stops him, saying horses are not for slaves. She chastises Egil for lifting a sword against a slave, at which he confesses his jealousy and love. She suggests they just stay friends, words piercing enough to make the fiercest Viking grow disconsolate.

At the court of King Olaf, a man is receiving the Christian faith. Vikings look on, including "Leif Ericsson, famed throughout the North for his strength, courage and justice." After the other Vikings pass out drunk, Leif discusses with Olaf his intention to sail west of Greenland, which his father, Eric the Red, had discovered. He points on a map to where the edge of the world drops off into the clutches of dragons. Olaf gives Leif a cross to put around his neck and wishes him success on his journey.

Back at camp, Alwin has snuck off to go read a book, so Helga attempts to whip him. Egil draws his sword, Alwin calls for a weapon, and the Vikings laugh, but the noble Leif rides up and asks, "Since when have Vikings scoffed at a man of courage?" Alwin and Egil duel until Egil's sword breaks and Alwin spares him in Helga's name. She decides to give Alwin over to Leif, who, in contrast to Helga, simply admires Alwin's horsemanship as he rides off.

Leif and company set sail for Greenland. Alwin disobeys Kark, Leif's chief slave, and is taken again and whipped against the mast. Helga intervenes and then Leif shows Alwin the dragon map; Alwin is not afraid. Above deck Leif strokes the hair of Helga, who has doffed her chainmail, but she gazes upon Alwin.

In Bratthahlid, Greenland (where "hard, stubborn paganism still held sway"), Eric the Red adjudicates a case and has the men bow to a statue of Thor. One is reluctant and is exposed as a Christian, at which Eric strikes him down with his ax.

Back on Leif's ship, Alwin continues to ignore Helga despite her several costume changes. She inquires about his diffidence and he rejoins, "You forget that I am still a slave." He shows a bit of pluck when she nuzzles his shoulder, but then he turns away again, sobbing.

Leif and his men arrive at Greenland's shores, and Leif confesses to his parents his plans to marry Helga. Egil is displeased to hear this, and he eggs on Kark, whose place Leif has now given to Alwin. Kark's father confronts Leif for favoring this Christian slave, and Leif is forced to confess that he, too, is Christian. Erik throws his ax at Leif, and a scuffle ensues, while Leif gets his men to take stores from the granary for his voyage. Leif tells Helga she must stay behind, but she dons a false beard and stows away. As Leif and his crew make it back to his ship, Eric is forced to admit, "Christian or no Christian, he is a son of Eric the Red!"[42]

On board, Alwin discovers Helga, who promptly jumps his Northumbrian bones, at which point he finally kisses her. Leif does not see this, however, and announces his plan to marry her on board. Meanwhile, some crewmen fear they are nearing the edge of the world and are again egged on by Egil. Kark seizes Leif's crucifix and throws it overboard. A mutiny threatens, until Leif adopts a heroic stance by the ship's ropes and exhorts his crew: "We are bound on the greatest adventure man has ever known—and we do not turn back!" Steersman Sigurd beats time, and they all set to their oars.

The marriage ceremony begins, but just as Egil is about to strike Leif with his sword, Alwin intervenes and takes the blow instead. Leif then fatally stabs

Egil. Alwin lies wounded on the deck, with Helga embracing him. She kisses him, and when Leif looks on, dumbfounded, she announces, "I love him!" Leif is on the verge of striking Alwin when he recalls his Christian principles, touching the cross around his neck. Sigurd stands by Egil, who confesses, "It was all for love of Helga," and then dies. Leif stands against the mast but then the music stirs, the crew act excited, and a title card reads, "LAND! LAND!"

Leif steps onshore with a cross made of oars. Subsequently, "as his Viking fathers had done in other lands, Leif built a watch tower of stone." In front of this tower, Leif puts a cross around the neck of a native leader (as King Olaf had done to him). Alwin and Helga exult in their happiness in this "fresh new land," intending to stay with some of the crew while Leif returns to Greenland. "What became of this Viking colony, no one knows. . . . But the watch tower they built stands today in Newport, Rhode Island." The film closes with a shot of this tower in the present day (an out-of-focus car drives by it) and we hear on the soundtrack: "o'er the land of the free, and the home of the brave."[43]

Some aspects of this adaptation of the Leif Eriksson material deserve comment (aside from any further sniggering about its comical helmets and mustachios). As we have seen, Leif was never involved in any love triangle (or quadrilateral, if we count Egil), but in fact some Icelandic sagas do involve a (more rugged) version of this theme.[44] Leif's crewmen never mention the edge of the world, although Norse cosmogony did conceive of the world as a disk encircled by a giant serpent. Nor do they threaten mutiny, although the concurrent theme of Christianity triumphing over paganism is present in *Erik the Red's Saga* especially. As previously noted, Leif converted while his father Erik did not, and in one instance in *Erik the Red's Saga*, Christian prayers succeeded while pagan ones did not (see above, regarding the pagan Thorhall). Leif's genial demeanor and tolerant governance suits the traditional American view of its leaders, but also has some counterpart in Leif's character as described in the Vínland sagas. *The Viking* presents Leif's voyage as "the greatest adventure by sea that man had ever known," appropriately enough for a film of love and adventure. When Leif plants a makeshift cross, the title card reads "the first white man set foot on the shore of the New World," which is still the main American gloss put on his voyage (though we certainly prefer now to substitute "European" for "white man"). The film is confident in this assertion, and offers as historical evidence the Newport Tower, thus taking a firm stance on the Viking versus Columbus controversies, and the American (New England) versus Canadian location of Vínland, with the soundtrack's final notes weaving in the finale of the American national anthem.

Henry Chapin, Leifsaga (1934)

A more highbrow, epic attempt at retelling our hero's story was made in *Leif-saga* (1934), by Henry Chapin, a minor poet who at least had some major friends, F. Scott Fitzgerald and Robert Frost.[45] The poem follows the Vínland sagas with one principal added motif, that of Leif the Lucky's ill luck in love. In *Eric the Red's Saga* (ch. 5), the Hebridean woman Thorgunna had made some ominous statements to Leif when he left her unwed and pregnant. For Chapin, this threat takes the form of a curse. In her Complaint, which swells beyond the usual iambic pentameter, Thorgunna avers:

> . . . nor rest nor peace shall he,
> The horizon-breaker, at the end of the whale-path find;
> Never a nesting place for the wild bird of his mind.
> . . . he himself shall be
> Lodestar for love of eager women, but they shall find
> That a gold-bright, sorrowful ghost possesses his mind. (11)

(The lines also show something of what Chapin takes from Old English and Old Icelandic verse, especially in the kenning "whale-path.") Towards the end of the poem, Thorgunna's bastard son Thorgils makes a surprise appearance as a surly confidant of Leif's sister, accompanying her to Vínland. When Freydís adopts her memorable warrior stance against the natives (*Eric the Red's Saga,* ch. 11), Thorgils (hiding behind the name Gest) is placed rather unconvincingly alongside her:

> She foamed with berserk rage, she stripped her shift,
> and waved her naked blade and slapped it hard
> against her great up-standing breasts and howled.
> Gest stood beside her grinning, and these two
> there turned the tide of battle for the Norse. (101)

Both hyperbole and iambic pentameter are to blame for turning Freydís's one exposed breast into [two] "great up-standing breasts." An added bit of drama concludes the poem, when back in Greenland Freydís's murders are revealed and Leif outlaws her henchman "Gest." He attacks, but Leif slits his throat:

> Gest looked surprised. He slumped upon the ground.
> His hand went up; his life came squirting out
> between his five great fingers. Freydis cried,
> . . . "'Tis Thorgils dead. This Leif has killed his son.
> This lucky Leif. Thorgunna's lucky Leif." (108–9)

Surprised indeed. This time, while the number of his fingers (five) cannot be said to be exaggerated, the poetic effect is both more and less than epic.

The poem has a few good touches, mainly in passages describing northern, maritime life:

> The wall of ice retreated up the coasts.
> On the dark mountain-sides the silver-quick

and many-gleaming snakes of melting snow
raced down the barren fells and met the sea.

Nonetheless, a contemporary reviewer (S. I. Hayakawa) in the magazine *Poetry* was unimpressed by the poet's facility in iambic pentameter, singling out such lines as "'Now listen, chief,' says Gunnar, 'I am plain. / I never was a man for lofty thoughts'" (63; Gunnar, an added, ostensibly comic first mate, is unimpressed by the delights of Vínland because there are no women about). Reading the poem reminds me of a dismissive comment I once heard made by a contemporary poet (Robert Bly, perhaps?) that after some practice one could easily learn to speak in iambic pentameter (and thus our observations all would mark their wordy course in iambs, five by five). Or one could repeat Chapin's own mournful admission at the age of 89: "But it's narrative verse. People don't read it today."[46]

Ingri and Edgar Parin d'Aulaire, Leif the Lucky (1941)

In the same year that Donald Crisp (the actor who had played Leif in *The Viking*) won an Oscar for *How Green Was My Valley* (1941), a children's book appeared, *Leif the Lucky*, that merits attention. It was written and illustrated by Ingri and Edgar Parin d'Aulaire, a husband and wife team originally from Norway and Germany respectively, many of whose books are still in print, including their *Book of Greek Myths* and *Book of Norse Myths*. The illustrations incorporate design motifs from Old Scandinavian woodcarving, especially the gripping beasts from the Oseberg, Norway, ship burial (Erik's dragon-head prow carving is modeled on its Oseberg counterpart).

The story follows a synthesis of the two Vínland Sagas, although with many elements tailored for an audience of children. Accordingly, Erik is banned from Norway and then Iceland not for killing his countrymen but because "his temper was wild," causing him "to quarrel and fight." A number of pages are devoted to the young Leif growing up in Greenland, whose shores he gazes upon: "his eyes were keen as the eyes of a snake and blue as steel as he watched the rows of waves rising like a thousand fences between him and his new home in the West." Erik steers the ship ashore (his name is carved in runes on the rudder), and Leif removes the dragon head from the prow so as not to "anger the spirits of the land." On his farm, Erik sacrifices to Odin, whom Leif imagines he sees in the Northern Lights above him. Young Leif hunts for seals at their breathing holes in the ice, and he plays with a (muzzled) polar bear cub indoors by the fire.

A sailor named Bjarne tells of distant "forest-clad shores still further west" (as in *The Greenlanders' Saga*), and now teenage Leif sails to Norway. He meets King Olaf, who asks him to convert Greenland to Christianity and gives him two fleet-footed Scottish thralls (this detail is thus inserted in its proper place, rather than as an afterthought as in *Erik the Red's Saga*, ch. 8). He sails back toward Greenland but is blown off course and sights Vínland (as in *Erik the Red's Saga*), his piercing eyes and pointing finger the only parts of him visible in the fog. The Scottish pair (here called Haig and Haigie) are sent to reconnoiter, jogging about in the garment called a *kjafal* in *Erik the Red's Saga,* chapter 8, here depicted as a hooded white leotard. Leif builds houses and spends the summer (rather than the winter, as in *The Greenlanders' Saga*), enjoying the wild grains and grapes (the drunken Tyrkir, a poor role model no doubt, is not mentioned, but a man is shown stomping grapes).

Leif sails back to Greenland, rescuing the shipwrecked crew and their goods, for which he is called Leif the Lucky. Later, Gudrid and Torfinn Karlsevne (a Norwegianized form of Thorfinn *karlsefni*) sail to Vínland, stopping off on an island where "there were so many birds and eggs there was hardly room to put a foot" (cf. *Erik the Red's Saga*, ch. 8). These birds are depicted as the flightless, hapless, and now extinct great auks; a couple in the background is shown frying their endangered eggs in a skillet, sunny-side up. Gudrid gives birth to Snorre, and she and Torfinn begin to trade with the Skraellinger (see *The Greenlanders' Saga*, ch. 7, and *Erik the Red's Saga*, ch. 11), who later attack until they see "a Viking woman sharpening a sword on her own skin" (i.e., the pregnant Freydís slapping a sword upon her naked breast, cf. *Erik the Red's Saga*, ch. 11). The Norsemen sail back to Greenland, picking up two Skraelling boys along the coast (*Erik the Red's Saga*, ch. 12). Back in Greenland, these two get to ride Norse hobbyhorses while Leif tosses young Snorre up in the air.

The book ends by bringing the reader up to date. For "hundreds of years," ships continued to go to America to bring timber, but the Greenlanders suffered long periods of cold (i.e., the so-called Little Ice Age) and began to grow smaller, ultimately blending in with the Eskimos. Across the sea, "for many hundred years the Indians in America could enjoy their land in peace." (It is true the Norse Greenland colony died out sometime after 1408, although the cause is debated.[47]

"Jimmy Olsen's Viking Sweetheart" (1963)

Moving ahead to the literature of my own youth, we find Leif Eriksson making a surprise appearance in the comic *Superman's Pal Jimmy Olsen*, number 69, from June 1963.[48] Cub reporter Jimmy, together with members of his fan club, goes to a ski resort, where his heartthrob Lucy Lane snubs him for Olympic ski champion Ron Baxter. Thinking to impress her, he attempts to leap across Daredevil Chasm, where he crashes, concusses, and awakens to hear a woman's voice calling to him from beneath a snowdrift, in the Old Norse language (her speech balloon in fact says "Hilf"—i.e., "Help" in German, written in runes!). He frees her, and she calls him Leif, mistaking him for Leif Ericsson because of his red hair.[49] She tells her story: she had landed on the shores of Vineland with Leif, her beloved, but some days later fell into a snowbank (Eeeyah!). Her name is Holga; thinking to help her, Jimmy takes her hands, and they are cold—not because she has been frozen for nearly a millennium, but because she is in fact a robot being manipulated by Jimmy's fan club! They plan to use her to make Lucy Lane, whom they want to fall for their Jimmy, get jealous.

Holga manages to jump Daredevil Chasm (as Jimmy says, "The Vikings invented skis"), and Lucy does indeed start to reevaluate the freckle-faced doofus. Holga becomes a national celebrity and is invited to the White House, where she is given a model of a Viking ship as a memento by none other than First Lady Jacqueline Kennedy. When Jimmy and Holga board a plane, stewardess Lucy observes them; later, in the fan club, she discovers the monitor and control panel and realizes Holga is a robot. To punish him, she presses the "treat Jimmy coldly" button, at which Holga dumps him, discarding the gift he had just given her, which Lucy had assumed was an engagement ring. But in fact it was her amulet, accompanied by a note saying that he, Jimmy, can only love Lucy, no matter how much she scorns him. The discovery makes Lucy melt, and she kisses Jimmy in his Leif Ericsson outfit. The members of the fan club congratulate themselves while watching on their monitor. Will Lucy marry Jimmy? Keep reading *Jimmy Olsen* to find out!

The allusion to Leif Eriksson in this opus is not particularly integral to the narrative, except that Jimmy under the influence of the Viking princess's (programmed) love takes on the guise of the Vínland explorer, as a manly Nordic counterpart to his Olympic skier rival (he even dresses as Leif toward the end of the story "for publicity pictures"). The main focus, however, is on a motif I remember well: the robot imposter. I suppose if science fiction films of the 1950s reenvisioned lurking communists as alien body snatchers, then the comics of the early 1960s did something similar with robots; or else pre–sexual revolution anxieties turned seemingly interested partners into deceiving robots; or else we are all just pawns of fanboys watching us on closed-circuit TV.

Charles Olson, The Maximus Poems (1975)

American poet Charles Olson is the first of our writers to take into account the discovery of Norse ruins in L'Anse aux Meadows in Newfoundland, having read Ingstad's 1964 account of it in *National Geographic*.[50] In 1965, Olson composed a poem that reads a bit like some notes taken from Ingstad, if in Olson's characteristically jaunty fashion. He begins with George Decker, the man who first pointed Ingstad to the site, who thus deserves to be at least a minor hero in the modern Vínland saga. Olson later incorporated the sketch into his ongoing opus *The Maximus Poems* (3.76, 1975):

And George Decker (when he got there) sd
Anything goes on

at Lancey Meadow
I know—there is
evidence down at
Black Duck Beach.
There was. Norse
persons,
by carbon date
1006 had
come ashore
here Had built
houses, had set up
a peat bog iron
forge. Were
living
Lancey Meadow
1006
AD

(The section goes on to mention the Skraelings, or Indians, as having been there first. Black Duck Beach was, in Ingstad's account, Black Duck Brook, and Ingstad gives a range of dates rather than 1006 specifically.)

George Mackay Brown, Vinland *(1992)*

In 1992, Orkney native George Mackay Brown published the historical novel *Vinland,* about Ranald Sigmundsson, son of a foul-tempered sea trader, Sigmund Firemouth. Sigmund intends to bring a load of timber to Greenland, having heard that it is "the most fertile and delightful place in the world"— that is, he has heard tell and accepted Erik the Red's propaganda about Greenland being green. His wife, Thora, sensibly wonders why such a fertile and green place would need a load of timber, but Sigmund tells her to mind her own affairs, slamming a board with his fist for emphasis. Sigmund plans to take young Ranald with him on his voyage despite the objections of his mother, who wants the boy to become a farmer like his grandfather.

Once on board ship, Sigmund shows his bad temper by striking a man whom he says had fallen asleep on his watch. The crew lands in Reykjavik, where Ranald sees a skipper who is "a tall handsome man, who didn't need to shout like his own father to get things done." The ship is called *West Seeker* and its skipper is Leif Ericson. He wants to "sail west as far as we can," but first is headed for Greenland. Sigmund calls for Ranald, and when they meet he strikes his son furiously and repeatedly for having wandered off.

Next day at first light Leif's ship departs. At breakfast time, Wolf the cook finds Ranald stowed away among the ale barrels. Leif's ship is a far happier one than Sigmund's, and Leif is much liked as a skipper. Ranald is viewed as a lucky omen and is accepted by the crew. The cook wonders if they will find the "Stoor-Worm" at the world's end (an Orkney folk tale version of the Norse World Serpent). A poet, Ard, improvises about the many shapes of water (Norse skaldic poets liked to collect and employ many different names for poetic concepts). Leif mentions how welcome their cargo of timber will be in Greenland; next morning the wooden fragments of a wrecked ship float past, and Ranald realizes his father has drowned.

Leif swiftly takes care of his affairs in Greenland and then sets off toward the west. The crew hear splashing noises and see dark shapes, and the cook mentions the Stoor-Worm again, but Leif knows it is only a company of whales, "seeking pastures among the ice floes." After the wind swings round, Leif lets loose a caged raven; it flies high and then shoots "westward like an arrow," and Leif claims land is near. The crew have to keep rowing in the becalmed sea, but Leif insists he can hear the shore; an old sailor comments that Leif "had ears as keen as a wolf" (in *The Greenlanders' Saga*, it is said that Leif had keener eyesight than his crew). Ranald hears something too, and soon the crew spies a low headland. They go ashore, and while the crew drink and celebrate, Leif sketches a map with coal on a piece of parchment. He says they will spend the winter and remarks that "this new-found-land is a far more promising place than Greenland." He also comments on the lack of any other inhabitants, but after dusk Ranald spies a young boy, who waves at him.

Next morning the shore is lined with natives, their faces painted and with feathers in their hair. Their chief cries out like a bird and then more men come, carrying baskets filled with salmon, venison, and "bunches of small fruit." These Leif tastes and identifies as grapes, but the old sailor (like many an antiquarian scholar before him) pronounces it impossible to find grapes so far north. Leif offers the natives ale, a bad idea because they soon start to get a bit wild, but it is one of his men who strikes and kills first. As the crew retreats, they are beset with arrows, and Ranald is struck by a stone thrown by the boy he had seen before. Leif decides they should sail farther south, but first he names the place Vínland.

They come to a place that is even more fertile, teeming with fish and game, and they begin to build log houses, hoping they have frightened off the "skraelings." Ranald goes wandering in the woods and espies the native boy again. Ranald waves, but his hand is struck by a bone knife thrown by the boy. Next morning the natives attack in force but are driven off and do not attack again. Some time passes, and the poet Ard recites ancient poems (one is recognizable as the Eddic poem *Grottasöngr*). But Ranald, wandering along the shore, sees a pattern of shells pointing at their settlement and once again sees the skraeling boy staring at him.

One day some watchmen fail to return, and that night on board ship Leif sees his house on fire. In the morning they find one of the watchmen dead and scalped. After they care for the body, Leif announces that they might find better prospects yet farther south, but for now they should return to Greenland. As they sail off, the natives watch them go, the boy among them. On their return trip, Leif shares navigational lore with Ranald. A whale spouts near the ship, and the crew wish they could kill it. Leif, however, thinks it a good thing that "there are still some creatures too big and strong for the greed of men to compass" but that eventually "men will devise weapons to kill even the greatest whale. The skraelings, that we thought so savage and ignorant, were wiser than us in this respect. . . . Did you not see what reverence the Vínlanders had for the animals and the trees and for all living things?"

Ranald stays a while with Leif in Greenland, where he proves a fine horseman. People talk of returning to Vínland, but Leif has had a dream that the "skraelings and the animals and trees were dancing together" until they were joined by a blue-eyed man in a gold mask. The dancers left one by one, until in the end "only the man in the gold mask was left on that shore." Leif will not return to Vínland, and although Ranald would like to, he must first return to Orkney. He does so, and for the remainder of the novel his adventures shift to a different historical source, the events pertaining to the earls of Orkney as told in the *Orkneyinga saga*. At the end of his life, he does dream of returning to Vínland, a mystical place that has become overlaid in his mind with Saint Brendan's Island of the Blessed and the Celtic land of Tir-nan-og. "I'd like to make peace with that skraeling lad before I die." On an Easter Monday morning, Ranald sets off along the shore toward the village of his birth, stumbling in the seaweed, until one last time when he falls and fails to get up again.

The first section of *Vinland* has much in common with historical novels for juveniles, with the young lad stowing away on the famous sailing adventure and meeting another young lad on the other side of the world. Brown's Leif has the qualities of moderation and seamanship that derive appropriately enough from the older Vínland sagas, but he has also taken on some 1980s environmentalism. He must have been quite a proto-anthropologist indeed to have intuited the skraelings' "deep ecology" while dodging their rain of arrows. But in this regard the novel shares one other detail of the sagas: the Norsemen kill first.[51]

LEIF ERIKSSON: THE MILLENNIUM CELEBRATIONS

The year 2000, aside from bringing the dreaded Y2K scare, marked the millennium of Leif's voyage to Vínland. There were certainly more academic studies published in 2000 that commemorated the millennial apocalypticism of Europe (when the world failed to end in 1000, fortunately) than Leif's more hopeful discovery, but a few books and activities honored our hero. Three books about Vínland that have been cited often in this study appeared in or about 2000: Fitzhugh and Ward's *Vikings: The North Atlantic Saga* (in connection with a touring exhibition from the Smithsonian Institute, 2000); Geraldine Barnes's *Viking America: The First Millennium* (2001); and Andrew Wawn and Þórunn Sigurðardóttir's *Approaches to Vinland* (2001). The first complete translation of all the Icelandic family sagas into English had been issued in Reykjavík in 1997 by a publisher invented for the occasion, Leifur Eiríksson Publishing. A copy was given to Hillary Clinton when she visited Iceland in the year 2000 (as two of my own translations were included in the volumes, this is the closest I have ever come to the reins of power). The 2000 paperback selection from Penguin Publishing highlighted the Vínland sagas, with an introduction by Jane Smiley, author of *The Greenlanders*. In the same year, Snorri Sturluson, who had written about Leif in his *Heimskringla* (ca. 1230), was named Icelandic scholar of the millennium.

Iceland cooperated with Greenland on "Project Leif," and a Viking ship called "Íslendingur" (Icelander) sailed from Erik the Red's home in Iceland to his home in Greenland in July 2000, piloted by a 28th-generation direct descendant of Leif Eriksson (it should perhaps be pointed out that in the close-knit society of Iceland, almost everyone can be shown to descend from Leif or, more often, Snorri Sturluson). The ship went on to L'Anse aux Meadows in Newfoundland and eventually to Manhattan, where it was greeted by Hillary Clinton. The replica of Thjodhild's church in Greenland was inaugurated as part of the festivities, and a "three-metre tall" statue of Leif was raised looking out to sea from Erik's farm (a copy of the statue erected at the Seattle World's Fair, mentioned above).

Leif Ericson: The Boy Who Discovered America *(2000, dir. Phil Nibbelink)*

The year 2000 also saw the release of an animated feature, *Leif Ericson: The Boy Who Discovered America*. Writer, director, and animator Phil Nibbelink, who had worked with Walt Disney Studios on *Who Framed Roger Rabbit* (1988) and Stephen Spielberg on *An American Tail: Fievel Goes West* (1991), left to become an independent animator, working very much on the cheap. He made *Leif Ericson* on an Amiga computer with *Deluxe Paint*.[52] The foreground features tend to waver back and forth against backgrounds executed without much detail and sometimes incorporating video effects (of fire, for instance). Occasionally the technique is sufficient, as when young Leif is stranded among some ice floes in Greenland, but more often it is difficult to see past the film's technical limitations.

The story focuses on young Leif, first in Iceland when his father is outlawed, then in Greenland, and on his quest to acquire luck. Vínland discoverer Bjarni Herjólfsson is made into a long-faced villain with a falcon sidekick, not unlike Jafar and parrot Iago in *Aladdin* (1992). When Eric returns to Greenland with a boatload of settlers, having taken Bjarni's slave girl (and Leif's love interest) Thorgunna, Bjarni attacks them with his crew until a subterranean volcano disrupts the proceedings. Bjarni chances upon a new land inhabited only by the wolf Fenrir (a figure borrowed from Norse mythology). Back in Greenland, Bjarni makes it seem as if Leif has killed his father, so Leif sails off to the new land himself, where Fenrir (Leif's spirit guide, apparently) tells him he must make his own luck. Young Leif sails back to Greenland, rescuing a shipwrecked Thorgunna on the way, and saves his father with the help of the ethereal Fenrir. The settlers shout "Leif the Lucky," and the voiceover tells us that "In the fullness of time, Leif became chieftain of Greenland. Because farmland was scarce, others followed Leif's trail and settled in Newfoundland.[53] Leif never returned to the New Land he discovered." Leif watches from atop a cliff as a wobbly Viking ship heads toward Newfoundland on a shining, digital sea.

LEIF ERIKSSON AND TOURISM

The Leif Eriksson tourist industry is not particularly robust, except that one can visit the (rather remote) site and reconstruction at L'Anse aux Meadows, Newfoundland; take a cruise ship to Erik's farm and his wife Thjoðhild's church at Brattahlið, Greenland; or fly into Leifur Eiríksson Terminal in Keflavík, Iceland, and make one's way from Reykjavík about two hours north to the Leifur Eiríksson Heritage Centre (Leifsbuð) in Búðardalur near Eiríksstaðir in Iceland, where Leif was born.[54] Here one may view a newly created "Vínland Tapestry," designed by Sigurjón Jóhansson.[55]

The Vinland Tapestry

The tapestry (really a backlit wall display) depicts scenes from the Vínland sagas drawn in the style of the Bayeux Tapestry and incorporating some of its imagery (the Bayeux Tapestry or embroidery depicts the Norman William the Conqueror, the English King Harold Godwinsson, and events leading up to and including the Battle of Hastings in 1066). The four scenes are set within top and bottom borders; some figures at the top are copies of the confronted lions and griffins often depicted in the Bayeux Tapestry borders. But the artist has added in some properly Vínland items: butternuts, grapes, Viking axes, a stone cross, a Thor's hammer, and the Norse pin found at L'Anse aux Meadows. The first scene shows the wonders of Vínland: a woman on the left carries "self-sown wheat"; a small man (Tyrkir, based on a servant at William's feast) carries bunches of grapes; big fish leap from the bottom border straight into the hands of man at the right. The pointing or calling figure at his right [Leif?] is based on young Harold at William's court. As if to signal this wondrous bounty, the hand of God reaches down from the clouds (cf. the Bayeux Tapestry scene depicting Edward's funeral). In the bottom border, a man threatens a bear with his sword, in reference to the bear killed at Bear Island (*Erik the Red's Saga,* ch. 8). The depiction is from a bottom border of the Bayeux Tapestry, beneath an early scene of William's messengers on horseback.

The second scene shows men building a boat (as William's men do in the Bayeux Tapestry, before the Battle of Hastings) and other men smelting iron. Excavations at L'Anse aux Meadows showed that Vikings there had made boat repairs and smelted iron for boat nails. The griffins in the top border most resemble those in the Bayeux Tapestry above a scene of Harold on a ship returning from France. In the bottom border, a man slings stones at some birds (from a bottom border in the Bayeux Tapestry, below the depiction of the dwarf Turold). At the right are the two Scottish runners, Haki and Hekja (*Erik the Red's Saga*, ch. 8).

The third scene shows Vikings trading red cloth for furs from the Indians (as Thorfinn *karlsefni* does in *Erik the Red's Saga*, ch. 11). The peculiar tree at the center is of the type often seen in the Bayeux Tapestry. The mustachioed man with the red cloth (Thorfinn) is modeled on King Harold, seen in the prow of his ship about to land in France. In the bottom border, a uniped takes aim at Thorvald in his ship (*Erik the Red's Saga*, ch. 12) and three natives carry a bag on a stick (the mysterious weapon mentioned in *Erik the Red's Saga*, ch. 11).

The fourth and final scene shows natives in loincloths attacking (some based on Norman archers) while a bull bellows and Freydís bares her breast (*Erik the Red's Saga*, ch. 11; the bull is taken from a scene where William's men seize food before the Battle of Hastings). Gudrid stands at the right, holding the infant Snorri. The borders below this scene cull naked figures from early on in the Bayeux Tapestry (the bosomy centaur is from above the scene of William's messengers; the squatting nude man is found under the Tapestry's depiction of Ælfgyfa and the cleric; and the nude pair appear under a scene of Harold and William on horseback carrying their hawks).

WOMEN RIVALS TO LEIF ERIKSSON

Although Leif may never be totally eclipsed as the first European to encounter North America, he has had to stand lately in the shadow of Gudrid Thorbjarnardóttir (Guðríðr Þorbjarnardóttir), one of the first Icelandic (temporary) settlers in America and mother of its first European infant, Snorri Thorfinnsson. We have already seen that William Morris chose her as one of three Vínland adventurers to depict in stained glass. In 1998, Jónas Kristjánsson, former director of the Icelandic Manuscript Institute (later the Árni Magnússon Institute), wrote a novel called *Veröld víð* (*The Wide World*), the subtitle of which translates as "a novel about the life and destiny of Guðríður Þorbjarnardóttir, the most widely traveled woman in the Middle Ages." In the year 2000, the catalog for an exhibition entitled *Living and Reliving the Icelandic Sagas* featured "sagas that describe the Norse encounter with North America and the life of Guðríður Þorbjarnardóttir, a remarkable Icelandic woman whose journeys carried her to the New World and to Rome." Despite the exhibition being partly supported by the Leifur Eiríksson Millennium Commission of Iceland, Leif does not get a mention in this New World connection.[56] Also in 2000 Margaret Elphinstone, a Scottish author of historical novels (living in Shetland, a group of islands once settled by Vikings) published *The Sea Road*, "an ambitious re-telling of the Viking exploration of the North Atlantic from the viewpoint of one extraordinary woman," according to its back cover, on which also Magnus Magnusson writes "for a thousand years [Guðríðr] has deserved a saga in her own right. Margaret Elphinstone has made good the omission at last." Most recently, Nancy Marie Brown has published a beautifully written re-creation of Guðríðr and the world she lived in, entitled *The Far Traveler: Voyages of a Viking Woman*. The book was released on Leif Eriksson Day, 2007.[57]

NOTES

1. The –r at the end of the Icelandic form is a nominative ending and is vocalized, so the name is pronounced as in the tennis player (Rod) *Laver*. The Americanized version is usually pronounced "leaf" rather than (more properly) "lafe." Leif's surname (patronymic) is spelled in numerous ways, often Erics(s)on. The first –s is genitive: Erik's son.

2. The Magnusson and Pálsson translation includes as its first chapter a section concerning Erik the Red from earlier on in the manuscript (*Flateyjarbók*). Kunz omits this chapter, so the chapter numeration of the two translations differs by one.

3. See Helge Ingstad, "Vinland Ruins Prove Vikings Found the New World," *National Geographic* 126, no. 5 (November 1964): 708–34, and the more recent works of Birgitta Wallace.

4. In the presidential proclamation of Leif Erikson Day (October 9) in 1988, President Ronald Reagan remarked that "This explorer with a missionary spirit challenged the unknown with courage and faith," while President Bush's proclamation of 1990 noted Leif's conversion to Christianity and "his return to Greenland as a missionary," characterizing him as "This daring navigator with a missionary zeal." Reagan was the first president to emphasize that Leif was "to spread religion among the Greenland settlers" (1982, though he didn't specify "Christianity" except in 1985–87); Bush dropped the religious references in 1992 and they have not reappeared since, being replaced by paeans to Nordic immigrants, cooperation, and shared freedom. [note by LMM]

5. Vínland alone is mentioned earlier, by Adam of Bremen ca. 1075; in the Icelandic annals for 1121; and in Ari the Wise's *Íslendingabók*, ca. 1133. Some scholars find it "historically doubtful" that Leif was "Óláfr Tryggvason's agent in the Christianizing of Greenland." Geraldine Barnes, *Viking America: The First Millennium* (Cambridge: D. S. Brewer, 2001), 75.

6. Translation mine from the text online at Netútgáfan (fornrit), http://www.snerpa.is/net/snorri/heimskri.htm. A similar version of this account is found in *Erik the Red's Saga*, ch. 5.

7. Erik plays a brief role in *Flóamanna saga*, which records that "Some men said that Eirik held onto the ancient beliefs" (ch. 25; ed. Viðar Hreinsson, 3.295).

8. *Erik the Red's Saga* has sometimes been called *Thorfinn karlsefni's Saga* (e.g., by Rafn), since it does in fact treat Thorfinn more than it does Erik.

9. Erik's discovery of Greenland is also mentioned in *Eyrbyggja saga*, where it is said to have happened "fourteen years before Christianity was adopted by law in Iceland," i.e., 986 (ch. 24; ed. Viðar Hreinsson, 5.157).

10. See Ólafur Halldórsson, "The Vínland Sagas," in *Approaches to Vinland*, ed. A. Wawn and P. Sigurðardóttir (Reykjavík: Sigurður Nordal Institute, 2001), 39. Old Norse names are usually made up of two separate elements, although there are also some shortened forms. Leif by itself means "leaving" or inheritance. (Leif's sons also have Thor- names; see below.) Leif is mentioned briefly as living with Erik in Greenland in *Bárðar saga* (ch. 5; ed. Viðar Hreinsson, 2.242).

11. According to *Fóstbrœðra saga* (ch. 20; ed. Viðar Hreinsson, 2.373), Leif had a (second?) son named Thorkell, who was head chieftain after him in Erik's Fjord.

12. The detail of "self-sown wheat" sounds like it may originate from tales of a paradisiacal land at the edge of the known world; in Norse mythology, when the world arises again after final battle of Ragnarök, it is said that the fields will grow "without sowing." Carolyne Larrington, trans., "Völuspá," in *The Poetic Edda* (Oxford: Oxford University Press, 1996), ed. C. Larrington, st. 62. On the other hand, Vínland scholars have often compared various beach grasses, such as strand wheat (Elymus arenarius), which may have seemed particularly noteworthy given the comparative lack of tall grasses on Icelandic or Greenlandic beaches.

13. See Birgitta Wallace [Ferguson], "L'Anse aux Meadows and Vínland," in *Approaches to Vinland*, ed. Wawn and Sigurðardóttir, 142–43. Other details point to this same general area, such as the use of skin canoes by the natives; according to Wallace, canoes were "only rarely used south of central Maine" (143). She concludes: "Anyone sailing due west from the Western Settlement [of Greenland] ends up in Baffin Island, or north of Labrador if leaving from the Eastern Settlement. Proceeding south from there leads automatically along the Labrador coast to the Strait of Belle Isle. The Strait forms a funnel into the Gulf of St. Lawrence. This is by far the most natural route from Greenland to resources such as those described for Vínland." (144)

14. In *The Saga of the Greenlanders* (ch. 5), Thorvald and his men come upon nine natives under their skin boats; they capture eight and then kill them, with no reason given. The ninth presumably informs his tribesmen and they attack, killing Thorvald. Barnes discusses nineteenth-century American commentary on the incident in *Viking America*, 80–87.

15. Leif is mentioned briefly for the last time in *The Saga of Greenlanders* (ch. 9) when he hears in Greenland about Freydís's having murdered other members of her expedition. He decides not to punish her but foretells that she and her descendants will not prosper.

16. I provide the geographical equivalents favored by Wallace; for a chart (by Gísli Sigurðsson) showing locales proposed by 15 scholars from Rafn to Wallace, see Keneva Kunz, trans., *The Vinland Sagas* (London: Penguin Books, 2008), 66–67. In chapter 8 of *Erik the Red's Saga*, in the Hauksbók manuscript only, Vínland is called Vínland the Good (so also in *Heimskringla*), a name adopted by some later writers (such as Jennie Hall and William Carlos Williams).

17. According to *Eyrbyggja saga*, ch. 48 (ed. Viðar Hreinsson 5.195), the man killed in Vínland the Good was Snorri Thorbrandsson. Another member of Thorfinn's crew, Thorhall Gamlason (not the same man as Thorhall the Hunter) is called "the Vínlander" in *Grettis saga* (ch. 30; ed. Viðar Hreinsson 2.97).

18. The Icelandic annals for 1121 mention that Vínland was sought in that year by Eiríkr Gnúpsson, bishop of Greenland. In his *Grønlandske Cronica*, printed in 1608, C. C. Lyschander mentions Vínland in this connection (see Barnes, *Viking America*, 71). Adam of Bremen mentions an island called Winland for the grapevines found there.

19. The 1847 edition adds material from *Erik the Red's Saga*, based on Rafn.

20. See Carl Christian Rafn, *Antiquitates Americanæ. Supplement* (Copenhagen: Royal Society of Northern Antiquities, 1841), 3–10, with illustrations at the end of the volume. In his 1827 novel *Red Rover*, James Fenimore Cooper describes the tower and comments that it "has suddenly become the study and the theme of that very learned sort of individual, the American antiquarian" (ch. 3, p. 82). Characters discuss whether it might have been a mill or a fortress, but no reference is made to any Viking origins.

21. See Birgitta Linderoth Wallace and William W. Fitzhugh, "Stumbles and Pitfalls in the Search for Viking America," in *Vikings: The North Atlantic Saga*, ed. W. Fitzhugh and E. Ward (Washington, DC: Smithsonian Institute, 2000), 377–78.

22. For the Crane fresco, see Stephen Wildman, *Waking Dreams: The Art of the Pre-Raphaelites from the Delaware Art Museum* (Alexandria, VA: Art Services International, 2004), 136–37.

23. See Barnes, *Viking America,* 120–21.

24. In his notes to the poem (142–44), Montgomery retells *The Greenlanders' Saga*, citing David Crantz's *History of Greenland* (1767; see above). James Montgomery, *Greenland and Other Poems* (London: Printed by Strahan and Spottiswoode, for Longman, Hurst, Rees, Orme, and Brown, 1819), http://www.archive.org/details/greenlandandothe00montuoft.

25. See Barnes, *Viking America*, 128–30.

26. Ibid., 131.

27. See Rafn, *Antiquitates Americanæ,* 356–61. For an account of these and other "Viking hoaxes," see Erik Wahlgren, *The Vikings and America* (London: Thames and Hudson, 1986), and, Wallace and Fitzhugh, "Stumbles and Pitfalls," 374–84. The most spectacular is probably the Kensington Rune Stone, whose runes tells of a group of Vikings who make the Northwest Passage in 1362 and end up in Minnesota, burying their runestone in what would eventually become the farmyard of a late nineteenth-century Swedish immigrant with some knowledge of runes. More recently the so-called Vinland Map, acquired by Yale University in 1965, continues to be debunked and re-vindicated.

28. Norman Kelvin, ed., *The Collected Letters of William Morris* (Princeton, NJ: Princeton University Press, 1984), 2.1.182–83 and 2.2.422–25.

29. See Charles A. Sewter, *The Stained Glass of William Morris and His Circle*, 2 vols. (New Haven, CT: Yale University Press, 1974–75), 2.224–25, and Edward R. Bosley, "Two Sides of the River: Morris and American Arts and Crafts," in *'The Beauty of Life': William Morris and the Art of Design,* ed. Diane Waggoner (New York: Thames & Hudson, 2003), 134–67 at 140–43, with a color reproduction on p. 142. The color cartoon is actually for an installation in Folkestone, Kent; Morris and Co. often re-used their designs in several locations. Burne-Jones's gray cartoons for the Vínland windows are owned by the Birmingham Museum and Art Gallery.

30. See Wildman, *Waking Dreams,* with color reproduction on p. 293. For the Vínland windows, Morris planned runic scrolls in the windows flanking the Viking Ship, rather than the Sol and Luna used for Folkestone. Kelvin, *The Collected Letters,* 2.1.181.

31. Kelvin, *The Collected Letters,* 2.1.183.

32. For commentary on these novels, see Andrew Wawn, *The Vikings and the Victorians: Inventing the Old North in Nineteenth-Century Britain* (Cambridge: D. S. Brewer, 2000), 322–25, and Barnes, *Viking America,* 92–103.

33. The story was first published in *The Contemporary Review* and then included in *Many Inventions* in 1893.

34. The term was used memorably by Archibald Ballantyne in 1888, with reference to Morris's translation of the *Odyssey*. For a list of Morris's translations, see the Morris Online Edition.

35. See the "Friends of the Viking Ship," http://www.vikingship.us/.

36. In Norwegian, "Leiv Eriksson oppdager Amerika." Another picture with the same title was painted by Hans Dahl (1881–1919), with Leif onshore in a pose not unlike at the end of the film *The Viking* (see below).

37. See Peter van der Krogt, "Leif Eriksson Monuments Pages," http://www.vanderkrogt.net/leiferiksson/index.php (accessed March 7, 2011). A copy of the Calder statue was placed in Newport News, Virginia, in about 1938; it also figures on a six-cent stamp issued on Leif Eriksson Day in 1968 and on a commemorative Icelandic coin issued in connection with a U.S. silver dollar in the millennial year 2000.

38. There is also a statue of Leif by John Karl Daniels in Leif Ericson Park, Duluth, Minnesota (erected 1956) and another by August Werner in Shilshole Bay Marina, Seattle, Washington (erected in 1962 in connection with the Seattle World's Fair). Both locations were areas of modern Scandinavian immigration. A statue by Einar Jónsson of another Vínland adventurer, Thorfinn *karlsefni*, was erected in Philadelphia in 1920. For statues of Gudrid and her son Snorri, see below.

39. Sundby-Hansen, "Saga of Leiv," 2.

40. Inga Dóra Björnsdóttir, "Leifr Eiríksson versus Christopher Columbus: The Use of Leifr Eiríksson in American Political and Cultural Discourse," in *Approaches to Vinland*, ed. Wawn and Sigurðardóttir, 224. An episode of the children's animated TV series "SpongeBob SquarePants," originally aired in 2000, begins with SpongeBob waking up in a Viking helmet and red beard, saying, "Hey everybody, it's Leif Ericsson Day! Hinga dinga durgen!" (The relevant excerpt may be seen on YouTube.)

41. Although I have not seen any of the documentaries, one IMAX version, called *Vikings: Journey to New Worlds* (dir. Marc Fafard, 2004), has location footage in Iceland, Greenland, and Newfoundland, and digital graphics to illustrate shipbuilding techniques. One could also mention films in which Vikings (but not Leif) come to the New World: *The Norseman* (dir. Charles B. Pierce, 1978); *Pathfinder* (dir. Marcus Nispel, 2007); *Severed Ways: The Norse Discovery of America* (dir. Tony Stone, 2007); and the truly peculiar *Valhalla Rising* (dir. Nicholas Winding Refn, 2009). A TV show called *Tales of the Vikings* (1959–60) featured a main character named Leif Ericson (see imdb.com); I do not know whether he goes to the New World or otherwise relates to our hero in any way other than as a generic Viking.

42. In the novel, Leif stops the fight and there is a further Greenlandic interlude, during which he converts a number of Greenlanders and Alwin learns from a seeress (a version of Thorbjörg) that his fate lies to the west, in the land first seen by Biorn Herjulfsson (Bjarni Herjólfsson).

43. By contrast, the novel follows the sagas a bit more closely at least insofar as Leif and company stay a while in Vínland, finding self-sown wheat and grapes and so on, until they encounter savage natives, after which they all depart for Greenland, Helga and Alwin included. There is no mention of the Newport Tower or a Lost Colony (on which see Barnes, *Viking America*, 76–77).

44. See Robert Cook, "Gunnar and Hallgerðr: A Failed Romance," in *Romance and Love in Late Medieval and Early Modern Iceland: Essays in Honor of Marianne*

Kalinke, ed. Kirsten Wolf and Johanna Denzel, Islandica, 54 (Ithaca, NY: Cornell University Press, 2008), 5–31.

45. See E. M. Broner and Paul Pines, "A Poet's Perspective: An Interview with Henry Chapin," *North American Review* 257, no. 1 (March 1982): 55–58.

46. Broner and Pines, "A Poet's Perspective," 58.

47. For possible explanations, see McGovern; also Jane Smiley's novel, *The Greenlanders,* 1988).

48. The story is entitled "Jimmy Olsen's Viking Sweetheart" and was reprinted in no. 122, September 1969 (DC Comics). Most but not quite all the panels of the reprint are reproduced online by Mister Kitty and Friends, under Stupid Comics, http://www.misterkitty.org/extras/stupidcovers/stupidcomics55.html.

49. In the first version of the comic, she in fact calls Jimmy Eric the Red, which is changed to Leif Ericsson in the 1969 printing. Eric the Red's (presumed) red hair matched Jimmy Olsen's, but the authors must have realized in the interim that Eric never made it to Vínland.

50. As Butterick points out, 581–82.

51. See the note above concerning Thorvald and the natives in *The Saga of the Greenlanders.*

52. See the interview at http://coldhardflash.com/2006/10/one-man-one-movie-112000-drawings.html.

53. In fact the archaeological evidence indicates that Vikings stayed only a short while on Newfoundland. The Vínland sagas also report that the would-be settlers of Vínland had to return to Greenland.

54. In Eiríksstaðir itself, one may visit a picturesquely located reconstruction of Erik's longhouse.

55. Images of the tapestry, no longer labeled as such, can be found with some difficulty on the site www.leif.is (choose English, then choice of leisure and travel options, then Búðardalur, then "see more" for Leifsbuð / Leifur Eiríksson Heritage Centre).

56. According to its author Cullen Murphy (http://www.theatlantic.com/past/docs/issues/99dec/9912murphy.htm), the comic strip *Prince Valiant* in 1999 also commemorated the Vínland millennium by incorporating not Leif but instead a character named Gudrid. Three copies of a statue of Gudrid and her son Snorri by Ásmundur Sveinsson (1893–1982; the original was first exhibited in 1940) were erected in Iceland and in Ottawa in 2000; see van der Krogt, "Leif Eriksson Monuments Pages."

57. Some of the research for this article made use of the Fiske Icelandic Collection, Cornell University Library. I thank Patrick J. Stevens and Thomas D. Hill for their hospitality.

FURTHER READING

Note: Icelandic authors are alphabetized under their first names.

Anderson, Rasmus B., and Albert O. Barton. *Life Story of Rasmus B. Anderson.* Madison, WI: [n.p.], 1915. Online.

Arngrímur Jónsson. *Gronlandia.* 1688. Published in facsimile with an introduction in English by Jón Helgason. Monumenta Typographica Islandica 6. Ed. Sigurður Nordal. Copenhagen: Munksgaard, 1942.

Ballantyne, Archibald. "Wardour-Street English." *Longman's Magazine* 12 (October 1888): 585–94. Online.

Barnes, Geraldine. *Viking America: The First Millennium.* Cambridge: D. S. Brewer, 2001.

Bosley, Edward R. "Two Sides of the River: Morris and American Arts and Crafts." *'The Beauty of Life': William Morris and the Art of Design,* edited by Diane Waggoner, 134–67. New York: Thames & Hudson, 2003.

Broner, E. M., and Paul Pines. "A Poet's Perspective: An Interview with Henry Chapin." *North American Review* 267, no. 1 (March 1982): 55–58.

Brown, George Mackay. *Vinland.* London: John Murray, 1992.

Brown, Nancy Marie. *The Far Traveler: Voyages of a Viking Woman.* Orlando, FL: Harcourt, 2007.

Butterick, George F. *A Guide to the Maximus Poems of Charles Olson.* Berkeley: University of California Press, 1978.

Chapin, Henry. *Leifsaga: A Narrative Poem of the Norse Discoveries of America.* New York: Farrar & Rinehart, 1934.

Cook, Robert. "Gunnar and Hallgerðr: A Failed Romance." In *Romance and Love in Late Medieval and Early Modern Iceland: Essays in Honor of Marianne Kalinke,* edited by Kirsten Wolf and Johanna Denzel, 5–31. Islandica, 54. Ithaca, NY: Cornell University Press, 2008.

Cooper, James Fenimore. *The Red Rover.* Paris: Lachevardiere, 1827. Online.

D'Arcy, Julian Meldon. "George Mackay Brown and *Orkneyinga Saga.*" In *Northern Antiquity: The Post-Medieval Reception of Edda and Saga,* edited by Andrew Wawn, 305–27. Enfield Lock, Middlesex, UK: Hisarlik, 1994.

Elphinstone, Margaret. *The Sea Road.* Edinburgh: Canongate, 2000.

Fitzhugh, William W., and Elisabeth I. Ward, eds. *Vikings: The North Atlantic Saga.* Washington, DC: Smithsonian Institute, 2000.

Hall, Jennie. *Viking Tales.* Illustrated by Victor R. Lambdin. Chicago: Rand McNally, 1902. Online.

Halldór Hermannsson. *The Problem of Wineland.* Islandica, 25. Ithaca, NY: Cornell University Press, 1936.

Hayakawa, S. Ichiyé. "Heroism Libeled." *Poetry* 47, no. 5 (February 1936): 287–90.

Inga Dóra Björnsdóttir. "Leifr Eiríksson versus Christopher Columbus: The Use of Leifr Eiríksson in American Political and Cultural Discourse." In *Approaches to Vinland,* edited by A. Wawn and P. Sigurðardóttir, 220–26. Reykjavík: Sigurður Nordal Institute, 2001.

Ingstad, Helge. "Vinland Ruins Prove Vikings Found the New World." *National Geographic* 126, no. 5 (November 1964): 708–34.

Jónas Kristjánsson. *Veröld víð.* Reykjavík: Vaka-Helgafell, 1998.

Kelvin, Norman, ed. *The Collected Letters of William Morris.* Princeton, NJ: Princeton University Press, 1984.

Kipling, Rudyard. "The Finest Story in the World." *Many Inventions.* New York: Appleton, 1893, pp. 106–50. Online.

Kunz, Keneva, trans. *The Vinland Sagas.* London: Penguin Books, 2008.

Lanier, Sidney. "Psalm of the West." *Poems of Sidney Lanier.* New York: Scribner's, 1908, 114–38. Online.

Larrington, Carolyne, trans. *The Poetic Edda.* Oxford: Oxford University Press, 1996.

Leif Ericson: The Boy Who Discovered America. Dir. Phil Nibbelink. 2000. [Film]

Liljencrantz, Ottilie A. *The Thrall of Leif the Lucky*. Chicago: McClurg, 1902. Online.

Living and Reliving the Icelandic Sagas. Exhibition Catalog. Compiled by Kristín Bragadóttir and Patrick J. Stevens. Ithaca, NY: Cornell University Library, 2000.

Longfellow, Henry Wadsworth. "The Skeleton in Armour." *Ballads and Other Poems*. Cambridge: J. Owen, 1842, 29–41. Online.

Lowell, James Russell. "Voyage to Vinland." *Under the Willows and Other Poems*. London: Macmillan, 1869, 123–39. Online.

Magnusson, Magnus, and Hermann Pálsson, trans. *The Vinland Sagas: The Norse Discovery of America*. Harmondsworth: Penguin Books, 1965.

Marshall, Perry. *Vinland, or The Norse Discovery of America; An Historical Poem*. Chicago: Charles H. Kerr, [ca. 1920].

McGovern, Thomas H. "The Demise of Norse Greenland." In *Vikings: The North Atlantic Saga*, edited by W. Fitzhugh and E. Ward, 327–39. Washington, DC: Smithsonian Institute, 2000.

Montgomery, James. *Greenland and Other Poems*. London: Printed by Strahan and Spottiswoode, for Longman, Hurst, Rees, Orme, and Brown, 1819. Online.

Ólafur Halldórsson. "The Vínland Sagas." In *Approaches to Vinland*, edited by A. Wawn and P. Sigurðardóttir, 39–51. Reykjavík: Sigurður Nordal Institute, 2001.

Olson, Charles. *The Maximus Poems*. Edited by George F. Butterick. Berkeley: University of California Press, 1983.

Rafn, Carl Christian. *America Discovered in the Tenth Century*. New York: Jackson, 1838.

Rafn, Carl Christian. *Antiquitates Americanæ*. Kongelige nordiske oldskrftselskab. Copenhagen: Schultz, 1837.

Rafn, Carl Christian. *Antiquitates Americanæ. Supplement*. Copenhagen: Royal Society of Northern Antiquities, 1841.

Sewter, A. Charles. *The Stained Glass of William Morris and His Circle*. 2 vols. New Haven, CT: Yale University Press, 1974–75.

Smith, Joshua Toulmin. *The Northmen in New England or America in the Tenth Century*. Boston: Hilliard, Gray, 1839.

Sundby-Hansen, H. "The Saga of Leiv and his Voyages." *Leiv Eiriksson Review* 9 (October 1935). Supplement to *Nordisk Tidende*, Brooklyn, NY.

van der Krogt, Peter. "Leif Eriksson Monuments Pages." Available online at http://www.vanderkrogt.net/leiferiksson/index.php (accessed March 7, 2011).

Viking, The. Dir. Roy William Neill. 1928. [Film]

Viðar Hreinsson, ed. *The Complete Sagas of Icelanders (Including 49 Tales)*. Reykjavík: Leifur Eiríksson, 1997.

Wahlgren, Erik. *The Vikings and America*. London: Thames and Hudson, 1986.

Wallace, Birgitta Linderoth. "The Viking Settlement at L'Anse aux Meadows." In *Vikings: The North Atlantic Saga*, edited by W. Fitzhugh and E. Ward, 208–16. Washington, DC: Smithsonian Institute, 2000.

Wallace, Birgitta Linderoth, and William W. Fitzhugh. "Stumbles and Pitfalls in the Search for Viking America." In *Vikings: The North Atlantic Saga*, edited by W. Fitzhugh and E. Ward, 374–84. Washington, DC: Smithsonian Institute, 2000.

Wallace [Ferguson], Birgitta. "L'Anse aux Meadows and Vínland." In *Approaches to Vinland*, edited by A. Wawn and P. Sigurðardóttir, 134–46. Reykjavík: Sigurður Nordal Institute, 2001.

Wawn, Andrew. *The Vikings and the Victorians: Inventing the Old North in Nineteenth-Century Britain*. Cambridge: D. S. Brewer, 2000.

Wawn, Andrew, and Þórunn Sigurðardóttir, eds. *Approaches to Vinland*. Reykjavík: Sigurður Nordal Institute, 2001.

Whittier, John Greenleaf. "The Norsemen." *Folklore Ballads*. ed. D. L. Ashliman. Pittsburgh: University of Pittsburgh Press, 1998–2002. Online.

Wildman, Stephen. *Waking Dreams: The Art of the Pre-Raphaelites from the Delaware Art Museum*. Alexandria, VA: Art Services International, 2004.

Williams, William Carlos. *In the American Grain*. Norfolk: New Directions, 1925.

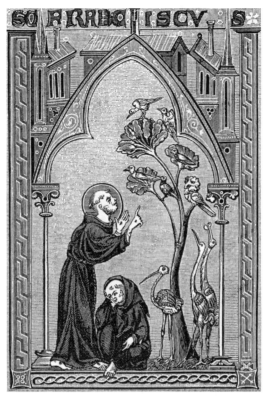

Saint Francis of Assisi talking to the birds. Engraving from a thirteenth-century psalter. (Steven Wynn Photography)

Francis of Assisi (1181/1182–1226)

Anna Kirkwood Graham

INTRODUCTION

Saint Francis of Assisi is one of the best known and most beloved figures of the medieval era. Although the scion of a privileged class, he has inspired generations of followers through his radical renunciation of wealth and physical comforts and through his works of charity, to the extent that his influence today reaches most of the nations of the world and well beyond the limits of the Catholic Church. His embrace of absolute poverty made him both an exemplar and a thorn in the side of the thirteenth-century church, which found him useful to counteract the image of the luxury-loving priesthood and also to elevate the status of the poor and humble, but he also served to embarrass some by the contrast and worry others who saw the necessity of possessions toward the future stability of his Order. He founded the three Franciscan Orders—the First, the Order of Friars Minor or OFM; the Second, the Order of Saint Clare or Poor Clares; and the Third or Tertiary Order of Saint Francis (which allows members of the laity to observe vows of poverty, chastity, and obedience within their stations in secular life)—all of which thrive today. Although he was personally a little suspicious of learning, his followers would include some of the great philosophers and theologians of the late Middle Ages. His love of nature and of animals has rendered him dear to many who might not be moved by more conventional forms of religious piety. He was a nature mystic, and he is today the patron saint of animals and ecology. He was responsible for staging the first living Nativity scene, or crèche, in Christian history; and he was also Christianity's first stigmatic. He shares the honor of being patron saint of Italy with Saint Catherine of Siena. His feast day is celebrated on October 4, the day of his death; many churches, including the Anglican, Lutheran, and Episcopal churches, commemorate this with a blessing of the animals.

Saint Francis's sanctity was acknowledged immediately after his death, with the result that his life was well documented from the first, in part by eyewitnesses and people who knew him and accompanied him on his travels. This occurred initially at the behest of Pope Gregory IX, toward the process of canonization. One of these early authors was Thomas of Celano, who wrote Francis's *First Life* (1228), *Second Life* (1247), and *Treatise on the Miracles of Blessed Francis* (1253). Thomas of Celano is, however, unreliable and contradictory on details of Francis's youth, and it is very difficult to construct a chronology from his works. A second whose writings contributed to our knowledge was Francis's secretary and confessor, Brother Leo, along with Brothers Angelo di Tancredi and Rufino; their reminiscences provide the basis for the thirteenth-century *Legend of the Three Companions* and *The Assisi Compilation*: "both texts provide facts about and insights into Francis not found in the earlier lives and, as such, are indispensable in knowing the details of his life and vision."[1] These latter two have been described as the most authentic of the early lives, because they contain many anecdotes that could come only from everyday association with Francis. The authorship of many of the early documents (aside from Thomas of Celano's) has been much debated; both of the authoritative anthologies of works by and about Saint Francis (see below) contain the arguments of various scholars in the introductions to each work, and it is not necessary to address the issue here.

In addition to the earliest figures, the great Saint Bonaventure, elected Minister General of the Friars Minor in 1257, wrote two early biographies of Francis, the *Major* and *Minor Legends,* by 1263, but it is unlikely that he ever met Francis, despite legends to the contrary. The thirteenth-century Anglo-Norman poet Henry of Avranches wrote one of the most important literary artifacts of the era, a life of Saint Francis in Latin verse, shortly after Francis's canonization. Although it was based on Thomas of Celano's *First Life,* it contains many "poetic expansions and embellishments" and a "much more critical account of [Francis's] misspent youth."[2] A number of other lesser, early biographies exist, in addition to the many that have been written more recently.

A difficulty in dealing with the early accounts of Francis's life, as with all medieval hagiography (and medieval biography in general), is that medieval saints' lives are very formulaic: they abound with stories and images that are repeated in one life after another, so that what survives today is often more symbolic of the general virtues that saints are supposed to have had—and that Francis undoubtedly had in abundance—rather than authentic and individualized portraits of characters. Thomas of Celano's work is more characteristic of this tendency than the more authentic-seeming works by Leo and his companions. The very language used by early hagiographers like Thomas can be highly ritualized. As A. G. Rigg[3] puts it: "[hagiography] was at times a minor literary industry," and hagiographers, as "professional" writers, were familiar with all of the *topoi* available for portraying their lives: "over time a collection of traditional themes or *topoi* emerged which reoccur in accounts of saints' lives . . . one of the consequences of this is that it is possible to group together saints whose stories follow a common pattern."[4] The early lives of Francis are by no means free from this tendency, and it is necessary to sift through them carefully to present a more factual account of Francis's life.

For instance, in accounts of his individual dealings with lepers, it is probably wiser to view the episodes in general as representative of his kindness to them and other unfortunates, because other saints are associated with lepers and, indeed, the Order of Saint Lazarus was founded for their care.[5] On the other hand, there is no doubt that Francis and the Franciscan friars made a point of helping lepers and other outcasts and frequented their dwellings and hospitals, and some of the episodes described are probably rooted in fact. The same may be said of many of the legends of Francis and his dealings with birds and animals; an ability to communicate with animals and birds is a frequent *topos* of a certain category of saints' lives (Saint Cuthbert, who spent years in hermitage off the coast of Scotland, communing only with seals and birds, springs to mind). But this is not at all to say that Francis did not love nature and demonstrate kindness to creatures, and whole books have been written on the topic. Other *topoi* of saints' lives concern the dreams and visions that saints had or others had about them, their encounters with other holy men or women, their forbearance in suffering, their misspent youths, and the like. All of this said, we are very fortunate in having so much detail about Francis's life that must be regarded as authentic; the same cannot be said about many another saint.

Francis himself was the author of a number of works, dictated most probably to Brother Leo, although two examples exist in Francis's own handwriting: a *Letter to Brother Leo* and the *Praises of God,* written for Leo. Francis wrote in both Latin and Umbrian Italian (he also spoke French); his Latin is not of a very high quality. In addition to the two works aforementioned, Francis wrote a number of letters and prayers, his *Testament* on his deathbed, and two versions of a rule for his order, one in 1209/10 (the original lost today, but existing still as revised in 1221) and one in 1223. Of these rules, the prominent scholar and biographer of Francis, Paul Sabatier, believed that the early or "primitive" rule was closer to Francis's true intent, and that "the latter Rule represented not what Francis wanted for his order, but what Cardinal Ugolino and the Church forced upon Francis." Sabatier was not a Catholic, however, and it is possible that he overstates the degree to which Francis was compelled against his will: a later, Catholic theologian suggests instead that the *Rule* of 1223 was simply the primitive rule expanded by revisions in 1221 and then rendered more legalistic in 1223.[6] Other writings by Francis are known to be lost. One last work that must be mentioned is the beloved *Canticle of Brother Sun,* perhaps the work most popularly known today, so expressive of both Francis's love of creation and his profound faith:

> "All praise be yours, my Lord, through all that you have made,
>   And first my lord Brother Sun,
>   Who brings the day; and light you give to us through him."

Francis's works, however, were never intended to be autobiographical, so it is primarily to his biographers that one must look for the details of his life.

Physical artifacts and early artistic depictions of Saint Francis abound. At Greccio, which Francis first visited in 1217 and where he sited one of his favorite hermitages, there is a depiction of him on a wood panel dating from the early thirteenth century (possibly during his lifetime) and originating from the accounts of people who knew him and could describe his appearance; it shows him mopping his eyes because of the eye affliction (possibly trachoma) from which he suffered beginning around 1220. His burial place, the Basilica di San Francesco in Assisi, built in his honor shortly after his death, contains frescoes by Giotto and Cimabue illustrating his life, as well as the twelfth-century crucifix from San Damiano that inspired his pivotal experience of religious conversion. Samples of his own handwriting remain, most notably on a parchment containing his *Blessing for Leo*; Leo's handwritten description of Francis's experience at La Verna exists on the same parchment, housed at the Basilica (which also houses one of his habits). His very remains were exhumed in 1978 to provide for scientific analysis and then, after a special rite, reinterred in the lower church of the Basilica. Indeed, it is not common for a figure from the Middle Ages, other than royalty, to be so well and early documented and depicted.

EARLY LIFE

The man we know today as Saint Francis was born Giovanni di Pietro di Bernardone in Assisi, a town in Umbria, Italy, in 1181 or 1182. Perhaps to reflect his love for France, where he traveled often in the course of business, the young Giovanni's father changed his name to Francesco soon after his birth. His parents were Pietro and Pica di Bernardone. The family belonged to the wealthy merchant class; his father dealt in cloth, and the young Francis was brought up to follow in his father's footsteps. His father was indeed one of the wealthiest men in Umbria and owned a number of estates in the vicinity of Assisi as well as dealing widely in cloth.

Although the amount of education that Francis received is debated, it is clear that he received enough to express himself eloquently in a variety of ways. He attended the parish school of San Giorgio near his home. He was never intended to be a scholar, though his biographers describe him as clever; much spoiled by his parents, he grew up instead pursuing pleasure. His mother, in particular, who may well have come from France, instilled in him a love of poetry and song, of courtly manners and chivalry; his model then was the troubadour. Many sources tell us that the young Francis had a strong interest in the Arthurian legends and that he and his future followers shared the secular value of chivalry, whatever the church may have felt about it. Early sources are very kind to Pica, but much less so in their descriptions of Pietro, despite the fact that his father would seem to have indulged Francis's excesses rather than to have driven him very hard.

The young Francis led a very different life from the one he would later lead. He enjoyed finery and lavish parties, spending a great deal of money and running around with a wild crowd of youths who ate and drank too much and scandalized the community, although more by wildness than by viciousness; both Thomas of Celano and Henry of Avranches suggest that he was by no means celibate at this period of his life. In appearance he was small and slight, "his face a bit long and prominent," dark-haired and dark-eyed, "his nose symmetrical, thin and straight" (*First Life* 83); later he would sport a tonsure and a beard, but he dressed like a popinjay in his youth.

Although he helped his father with the family business, he showed little interest in settling down to anything serious at all, and in fact Thomas of Celano notes that "he squandered and wasted his time miserably . . . outdid all his contemporaries in vanities and came to be a promoter of evil" until his twenty-fifth year. Even his faults, however, reflected the generosity, gaiety, and charm that would make him so charismatic as a religious leader; he early demonstrated the love of nature that would make him the patron saint of animals and ecology in later eras, as well. He never, before or after his religious conversion, displayed the animosity against and contempt for women so characteristic of clerics of the time, adopting instead an attitude of friendship, respect, and chivalry.

We know that Francis accompanied his father to France in 1197, to the cloth fair in Champagne; Pietro Bernardone had the reputation (as well as the success) of a ruthless businessman, and no doubt when Francis accompanied and assisted his father, he was expected to follow suit. On their return, however, they found a region thrown into turmoil by the death of the Holy Roman Emperor, Henry VI. Tensions among rival cities across Italy were exacerbated, including one between Perugia and neighboring towns in Umbria. Francis got caught up in the conflict, first as a builder, helping to fortify Assisi against attack, then as a soldier himself, in 1202 at the Battle of Collestrada. Unfortunately, the force that Assisi sent forth against the Perugians was inadequate to the task; the battle was described as a massacre, and the Assisians soundly beaten. Mistaken for a noble, Francis was taken prisoner rather than put to death, and he found himself imprisoned for almost a year, until a ransom was negotiated and paid by his father; his cellmate was Angelo di Tancredi, who would become his lifelong friend. His health, and perhaps his soul, was permanently affected by his imprisonment; some scholars believe that he contracted tuberculosis and that this would be the ultimate cause of his death.

His character, at least, was not immediately affected. He left prison emaciated and weakened, but he still sought out revelry and indulgence, and he toyed with the notion of a military career. He even ventured forth to become a soldier in the retinue of Walter de Brienne, in 1205, but a second illness and a fateful dream sent him back to Assisi—or perhaps it was the death of Walter in Apulia (later he would encounter Walter's brother, John de Brienne, in Egypt; see below). At any rate, Francis would return home from this experience to spend the next year discerning his mission; part of this discernment involved a pilgrimage to Rome and another, consultation with his lifelong mentor, Bishop Guido of Assisi. The latter had arrived in Assisi in 1204, and hearing accounts of a prodigal youth who may have seemed debauched by night, but who gave away quantities of money and food to the poor all the while, was one of the first to recognize religious genius in Francis. He would frequently assist Francis in negotiating the intricacies of church politics and hierarchy as Francis's mission became more concrete.

Perhaps with Guido's encouragement, Francis journeyed to Rome at the end of 1205 or the beginning of 1206; here he had his first experience of begging, when he exchanged clothing with a beggar and stood in his shoes for a day. He witnessed the abject poverty of the beggars there, in the midst of the grandeur of the city and the wealth of the church. His return to Assisi marked a new sobriety in him.

In medieval Europe at this time, most people felt an almost supernatural horror of leprosy (probably a blanket name for a number of diseases with similar symptoms, including leprosy, *Mycobacterium leprae,* itself), which led to the ostracism and mistreatment of the unfortunates who were afflicted by it. Lepers were condemned to live outside the walls of the city, to abandon their homes, families, and livelihoods, to wear distinctive clothing and carry clappers to warn people of their approach, and to beg for their living. Many stories surround Francis's humane treatment of lepers who lived around Assisi, including his charity to them at this critical period of his life, when he was said to have first dismounted and kissed the hand of a leper, suppressing physical revulsion at the sight and smell, and then to have taken a great sum of money to the leper hospital and distributed it to the inmates there, kissing each one's hand as he did so. Later, he would use the humane treatment of lepers by new recruits to the Order as a sort of "trial by fire," for them to demonstrate their poverty and humility: "thus at the beginning of the religion, after the brothers grew in number, he wanted the brothers to stay in hospitals of lepers to serve them . . . whenever commoners or nobles came to the religion . . . they had to serve the lepers and stay in their houses" (*Assisi Compilation* 9).

Although he still spent his evenings in revelry, his companions noticed a new sobriety in him; when asked whether he would be married, "'Yes', he replied, 'I am about to take a wife of surpassing fairness.' She was no other than Lady Poverty whom Dante and Giotto have wedded to his name, and whom even now he had begun to love."[7]

Another phenomenon that marked this period of Francis's life was his increasing need to find seclusion for prayer and his continual lapses into trances; he underwent constant emotional turmoil, constant vacillation between doubt and faith, in this process of discernment. He began to retreat to Mount Subasio, to the southeast of Assisi, where he sought out caves in which he could spend time in contemplation, first demonstrating his profound bent toward finding God in nature. He probably became known to the Benedictine monks who inhabited the monastery of San Benedetto on Subasio at this time; they were to become his friends and benefactors.

One day in 1206, Francis visited the church of San Damiano, which lay, neglected and in poor repair, to the south of Assisi. *The Legend of the Three Companions* tells us that Francis knelt in front of the crucifix there to pray, and while absorbed in the image of the suffering Christ, heard a voice saying, "Francis, don't you see that my house is being destroyed? Go, then, and rebuild it for me." Trembling and amazed, he undertook what he was commanded, and as the legend continues, "From that hour his heart was stricken with melting love and compassion for the passion of Christ; and for the rest of his life he carried in it the wounds of the Lord Jesus" (*Legend of the Three Companions* 13–14). While it might be that the legend of this experience was embroidered, there is no doubt that Francis was always deeply devoted to the cult of the crucified Christ and his sufferings on the cross.

At first Francis simply gave the priest in charge of San Damiano some money to keep the lamp burning in the church. But a sense of mission grew in him until he did something that would seem rather disgraceful today—although Francis and his followers would undoubtedly hold that the real disgrace lay in the condition of the church and the disparity of wealth that left some poor and others with more than they needed—he "stole" bolts of his father's most valuable cloth while his father was away, took them to Foligno, and sold them (along with the very horse that he rode), and then returned to San Damiano to attempt to give the priest there the money to restore the church. The priest, doubting that Francis could be serious, sent him on his way again without taking it, but Francis persisted, trying to rebuild the church with his own hands. When Pietro returned, he was indeed furious about the theft from his stores and demanded that Francis return the money. Francis hid from his father for weeks.

When Francis emerged from hiding, filthy and unshaven, and returned to Assisi looking like a madman, the people of Assisi, including his relatives, pelted him with filth and abuse, and rather than helping him, Pietro seized him and kept him imprisoned for awhile. This was the beginning of the rift with his son that would last until the end of Pietro's life; no doubt Pietro felt betrayed by Francis and embarrassed by his erratic behavior. When the soft-hearted Pica freed him at length, Francis took leave of his home once more and returned to San Damiano to continue the work of building the church; no plea or demand from Pietro moved him. Throughout this time, however, Bishop Guido had remained Francis's friend and would now mediate between father and son. When brought before the bishop and ordered by him to repay his father's money, Francis did so immediately, but did more besides: he stripped himself naked and returned the bundle of his clothing to his father as well. He renounced Pietro and embraced God as his true father, leaving Pietro to stalk home in anger and grief, bearing Francis's clothes with him, while Guido wrapped him in his own cloak: "he realized that a great mystery lay behind the scene he had just witnessed, and from now on helped and watched over Francis with loving concern" (*Legend of the Three Companions* 20).

THE EMBRACE OF LADY POVERTY

The course of Francis's life hereafter must be understood in the context of his radical devotion to the poverty of Christ and to his sufferings on the cross: for Francis, the poor and the sick were (in the wording of *The Assisi Compilation* 114) "a mirror for us in which we should see and consider lovingly the poverty and weakness of our Lord Jesus Christ which he endured in His body for the salvation of the human race." Possessions were a barrier between man and God. This indeed was the mission that Francis gave the Franciscan order in his *First Rule* (9): to abandon all worldly goods, abase the self, and serve the poor, trusting in the charity of others to provide for one's daily needs.

"Alms are an inheritance and a right which is due to the poor because our Lord Jesus Christ acquired this inheritance for us." He viewed even the unjust poor—for instance, robbers—as worthy of Christ's mercy, and in emulating Christ, his companions were admonished to give everything they had to alleviate the distress of others. Hence it is that, even today, a postulant to the Franciscan Order is required to give away all of his or her worldly possessions before entering orders; Francis kept only breeches, robe, and cincture, gave everything else he had to give to the poor, and begged for his daily sustenance, when he embraced his religious life.

Poverty as a form of religious discipline was a problem for the church then, and it is difficult to overstate how critical an issue it would become for the Franciscan Orders. Both the religious and laypeople could and did criticize the church for its wealth and possessions, while the church hierarchy preferred that even monastic foundations have common possessions in the form of endowments for their maintenance, rather than depending on alms. The church vigorously suppressed groups that practiced extreme asceticism, like the Cathars and Waldensians, which it considered heretical, and which criticized it in turn for its materiality. On the other hand, how could the church restrain a genuine desire to live as Christ did himself? The genius of the movement that Francis originated lay in its adaptation of radical poverty to the rules and approval of the church. These early Franciscans were ardent supporters of the papacy and were granted the so-called privilege of poverty in return.

Poverty, however, would be more problematic for the women who followed Saint Francis under the future leadership of his beloved friend and protégé, Clare di Favarone. Clare, born in Assisi in 1193 or 1194, was a nobleman's daughter who ran away from her family and the comforts of her home before she was 20, to follow Saint Francis and establish a women's foundation on his model; this became the Second Order of Franciscans, and later the Poor Clares. Clare idolized Francis, and she seems to have shared the gifts of sincere fervor and charisma that made Francis so magnetic a leader, besides showing remarkable maturity and skills of leadership. Before long, she attracted almost as many followers as Francis himself. The church did not permit women religious to beg for alms, however, and Clare and her followers were not initially allowed to adopt absolute poverty formally, despite their desire to; friars provided for them instead. Finally, the privilege of poverty was granted to her foundation as well, though there is debate about when this happened. Clare died in 1253; soon afterward, in 1255, the church canonized her. Her body is interred in the church dedicated to her, Santa Chiara of Assisi, not far distant from the Basilica di San Francesco.

Francis also adopted active bodily mortifications for himself, although he forbade the most extreme for his followers. He neglected his own health: "the love that filled his soul since his conversion to Christ was so ardent that, despite the prayers of his brothers and of many other men moved by compassion and pity, he did not trouble himself about taking care of his sicknesses" (*Legend of the Three Companions* 37). Francis's mortifications of the flesh and fasting undoubtedly diminished the span of his life: "when he was exhumed in 1978 his skeleton bore the signs of osteoporosis and advanced if not fatal malnutrition."[8]

Francis's deep and direct experience of Christ's sufferings reflects his profound mysticism. Mysticism, as a religious practice, involves a direct union of the soul with the Divine, which often occurs while the subject is in a trancelike state. Such a trancelike state might be induced by meditation and repetitive prayer, much the way transcendental meditation might be practiced today; it might also be produced by fasting and physical mortification, in some cases. Francis, of course, engaged in all of these activities, and whatever the cause, experienced many visions and dreams that influenced his own behavior and that of others. Thus Francis's greatness (or perhaps wisdom) as a theologian, as a preacher, and as a teacher stemmed not from formal education or from a great intellect as we would define it today, but from genuine goodness and, as a mystic, a direct experience of God. But much of the aforesaid was still in the future for Francis and Clare, after Francis had founded an order, after he had met Clare, and after she had followed him.

RELIGIOUS LIFE

When Francis parted from his father and home for good, in 1206, he intended to return to his mission of repairing San Damiano. But as he walked through the forest outside Assisi, robbers beat and robbed him of his last possession, the cloak that Bishop Guido had given him; even so, "he jumped out of the ditch . . . [and] glad with great joy, he began to call out the praises of God" (*Legend of the Three Companions* 23). This great joy in the face of adversity or in the most ordinary moments of life was one of the most distinctive parts of Francis's character.

To support himself and win materials for rebuilding San Damiano, he begged in the streets of Assisi, using his skills as an actor and minstrel as much to entertain as to beg. He received scraps of food (some spoiled) and ate them, first with distaste but then joyfully, and managed to drag vast amounts of stone back, but his begging and antics mortified and grieved his family: "when his father saw him in this pitiful plight, he was filled with sorrow . . . he was both grieved and ashamed to see his son half dead from penance and hardships and . . . he cursed Francis" (*Ibid.*). Francis paid no attention to his father's curses or the mockery of his brother but persisted until the work was done, living as a hermit near San Damiano all the while and winning the admiration of passersby for his patience.

Soon he became inspired to share his insights by preaching in public; this was when he began to attract followers. Francis and the early Franciscans preached with a direct and heartfelt simplicity, in the vernacular, in a style that was far removed from the dry Latin sermons that the people would have heard in church. Two of his first followers were Bernard di Quintavalle, a wealthy property owner of Assisi, and Peter of Catanio, a lawyer. Both gave all of their worldly possessions to the poor, donned the habit, and joined Francis in wandering the streets in search of materials and rebuilding another church, San Pietro della Spina. Next to join was Brother Giles, a man of Assisi. And they continued to come—Sabbatino, Morico, John of Capella, Barbaro, Bernard of Viridente, Philip the Long; even Angelo di Tancredi, Francis's childhood friend and a noble, joined them soon—until there were 12; a number of these first adherents would be Francis's closest companions for the rest of his life. They endured mockery and suspicion (their ragged and dirty appearance being against them) but persevered in preaching publicly, not only in Assisi but in the surrounding countryside, and in repairing churches, until Francis realized that he was there not only to rebuild small churches but to renew the whole institution of the church. During this period, Francis attended Mass regularly at Santa Maria degli Angeli, which was associated with the Abbey of San Benedetto; it later became the mother church of the Franciscan Order.

Through the example of their lives, their works of service and charity, and most important, the charisma and energy (Adrian House calls it "an almost radioactive energy") of Francis, the Franciscans became increasingly influential around Assisi and well beyond. Much of their effort during this phase was directed at missionary work: they wandered about Italy and beyond in pairs looking for new recruits who would help them to expand. Bernard and Giles even ventured through France and Spain, as pilgrims to Santiago de Compostela. Although sometimes the early friars were received with suspicion, mockery, or violence, on other occasions they were given food and shelter—Francis would not allow them to accept money as alms—and, best of all, their message began to take hold.

They called themselves the Friars Minor, the Lesser Brothers. As Francis would say, "the Lord has willed that they be called Lesser Brothers, because they are the people whom the Son of God asked of the Father . . . *what you did for one of these, the least of my brothers, you did it for me*" (*Assisi Compilation* 101). The designation marked their humility, and it would be codified in their first Rule.

With the advent of followers and the expansion of the original mission, it became necessary to formalize a rule to guide them. The Rules that were in place for other monastic orders or for the regular clergy did not work for Francis's ragged little band. The problem that it presented for the norm was in the novelty of a mendicant order of friars: they did not inhabit a monastery, like the Benedictines or other monastic orders that already existed; they roamed freely, rejecting permanent houses and living in wattle huts, caves, or other rough shelters instead. They begged for their sustenance as opposed to depending on endowed funds or farming extensive estates, as many monastic foundations did. They had no possessions in common, not even books; Francis's original intent was that they would own nothing at all. What Francis would have seen around him was monks and priests living in relative ease—if not luxury—in sturdy and comfortable houses with steady supplies of food and books to use for liturgical purposes as well as for education and edification—well above the standards that the truly poor were forced to endure. And for another thing, few of Francis's followers were priests, as yet; Francis himself was never to become one. (A priest of Assisi named Silvester, who had earlier chiseled extra money out of Francis for stones that he had already sold him, had a change of heart and became the first priest of the fledgling First Order.) So Francis devised a new rule, drawing mostly on passages from scripture; it was simple on the surface, but deceptively so: there was no doubt that Francis expected rigid adherence to his precepts. His way of life, then, might well have threatened established norms and been suppressed, had it not been for his personal magnetism and the enthusiasm that he raised in his listeners, as well as his complete devotion to the church as an institution.

Francis's First Rule exists today as revised in 1221. First and foremost it requires obedience and reverence to the pope and his successors, but immediately upon that, it enjoins obedience to one another, chastity, and abnegation of property. A postulant to the Order will be given "two tunics without a hood, a cord and trousers, and a caperon reaching to the cord" (*First Rule* 2), the sum total of permissible possessions; the brothers were frequently observed giving even these few garments away to someone in need of them. The rule goes on to prescribe modes of prayer and fasting, of punishment and service to the poor and sick, of missionary work (including missions to the Saracens), and of relations with women. Friars are forbidden to ride on horseback unless compelled by sickness—early stories tell of barefoot traveling friars leaving bloody footsteps in the snow.

Francis's Rule, like any other, required approval from the church in order not to be deemed heterodox. Fortunately for Francis, it was evident to church authorities even early on that the popular religious movement that he would inspire would be beneficial to them.

Francis and his band accordingly set off to Rome to visit the Papal See. Here they encountered their old friend, Bishop Guido of Assisi, who was able to advise and assist them in negotiating the bureaucracy of the See. After conferring with lesser figures for a few days, they were eventually granted an audience with Pope Innocent III himself. Thomas of Celano reports that Innocent had had a vision shortly before, of the Lateran basilica about to fall into ruin, "when a certain religious, small and despised, propped it up by putting his own back under it lest it fall" (*Second Life* 17). When Innocent met and talked to Francis, he was supposed to have recognized that small and despised man who would save the church, and he readily granted his approval of the Rule. This dream was famously depicted by Giotto di Bondone among the frescoes on the walls of Francis's basilica. Francis became a great admirer of Pope Innocent III, and Innocent promoted the interests of the Order in turn, recognizing its great value in evangelizing among the poor and humble and countering the popular perception of the clergy as addicted to luxury and leisure.

After their visit to Rome, the friars returned to the valley of Spoleto. They had previously inhabited a variety of hermitages, but now they shared a single cowshed. They occupied themselves in labor and prayer, continuing to beg for food, according to the rule of poverty. As yet, Francis did not allow them even to own prayer books, so they prayed from memory and in contemplation of the cross. They slept on the floor, each in the space allotted for him; Francis himself wrote their names on the beams under which each had his place. Soon, however, it became clear that they would need a place for prayer, so they erected an oratory made of reeds, along with a cell for private meditation. Here they lived until a peasant claimed it as a stall for his ass.

When they were evicted from this initial abode, Abbot Maccabeo of the Benedictine monastery of San Benedetto offered them the church of Santa Maria degli Angeli, "a dilapidated little chapel in a forest . . . [which] with the surrounding land was also known as the Porziuncula, or Little Portion,"[9] outside Assisi, where Francis had been attending Mass. Francis accepted with a proviso: as they could not own property, they would be considered to be renting it for an annual fee of a basket of fish from the river. This was the condition that Francis wished to impose on any house that the Order would occupy in the future—that it be known that the friars were mere renters, not owners, of the property—and it would be a sore point as the Order grew.

Here, around the mother church of the Order and the permanent home of Saint Francis, the friars built huts in which to live. There was no abbot, Francis having refused such a designation for himself; all were to be equal in rank. Eventually there would be priors of individual settlements and a Minister General of the Order, but it would not officially be Francis, who always refused to appoint himself leader, even when most regarded him as such. He did retain control of admitting novices to the Order in the early days, however, as well as dictating the terms of membership in his Rule. He was determined to admit no one who could not comply with his understanding of absolute poverty.

The Third Order, the lay order of people who embraced poverty, chastity, and obedience appropriate to their stations in life, perhaps arose during this phase (between 1209 and 1215; some insist that it was considerably later), when laypeople in the area chose to follow Francis more closely, inspired by his early disciples. And the Second Order, founded by Clare in 1212, grew almost as rapidly as the First; the women were granted San Damiano as a headquarters by the bishop.

The First and Second Orders maintained close connections in the early days, visiting freely with one another; indeed, the friars begged for alms to support the nuns, because everyone recognized that it would be unadvisable for them to do so on their own behalf. The friendship between Francis and Clare was especially intense and might be described as romantic, although unquestionably platonic—a meeting of minds and understandings of spirituality. Theirs was an unusual conjunction of two charismatic and inspired leaders who had the ability to sway many followers from a wide variety of stations and places.

Many of Francis's best-known followers and closest companions were in place by 1215: the first 12, of course; Brother Leo, a priest who would be Francis's confessor and secretary; Rufino di Scipione, scion of a wealthy and influential family of Assisi; Masseo di Massignano; Brother Juniper, who became the trusted companion of Clare; and later the biographer Thomas of Celano, the troubadour Brother Pacifico, and the scholar Brother Elias, whose future would be so brilliant and so troubled.

During the period from 1212 to 1215, Francis made two abortive attempts to evangelize the Saracens. The first, in 1212, found Francis en route to Syria, but he was shipwrecked on the way and forced to return to Italy. Again, in 1214, he set out for Morocco, but was sidelined in Spain by illness. In the meantime, he occupied himself with preaching in Central Italy and in contemplative retreats at his mountain refuge of La Verna, but he never forgot his desire not only to convert the infidels but to bring peace between warring Christians and Muslims. Across Europe, the rhetoric surrounding crusades inspired a number of sad attempts: the Children's Crusade of 1212, which ended at the Mediterranean shores of Italy with many of the children dying of disease or starvation, or straggling home in failure; a second children's effort, wherein the children were sold into slavery by the men who offered to take them to Jerusalem; and a third featuring adults in Spain, which had the limited success of confining the Moors to Andalusia.

HIERARCHY

In 1215, Innocent convened the Fourth Lateran Council, which Francis attended. Here he brushed shoulders with the princes of the church and made the acquaintance of Dominic de Guzman, the founder of another great thirteenth-century mendicant order, the Dominicans, the Order of Preachers. Before Dominic founded his own order, in 1216, he attempted to join the Franciscans, but because he did not forego a regular income, Francis would not admit him. Ultimately, Dominic did renounce worldly possessions on his own behalf and that of his order. Francis and Dominic remained friends until Dominic's death in 1221. And the Dominicans would produce one of the great minds of the Middle Ages in Saint Thomas Aquinas.

Two items on Innocent's agenda for the council affected the Franciscans in particular: the attempt to regularize the mendicant orders and to compel them to accept property in common, and the call for a fifth crusade. The former distressed the early Franciscans and especially Clare, because it burdened the women's houses to a greater degree, but the latter appealed to Francis and would shape his future, while other reforms were more palatable from the outset—that the mendicant orders should contain more regularly trained priests, in particular. Innocent is said to have granted the privilege of poverty verbally to Claire when she appealed to him directly after the council, although officially it was not granted until just before her death. Innocent died not long after the Lateran Council and was succeeded by Cencio Savelli, who took the name Honorius III.

Another rising luminary whom Francis would have encountered at the council was Ugolino dei Conti di Segni, later (after Honorius's death in 1227) Pope Gregory IX. Pope Honorius III appointed Ugolino plenipotentiary legate to Northern Italy in 1217; as such, he would exert much influence on the fledgling Order, in which he took an interest sometimes for the better, and sometimes not. In particular he kept his thumb on the Second Order, frequently compelling the women to adopt practices and policies that they did not desire; conversely, he was among Clare's greatest admirers (in fact, all of the churchmen with whom Clare had dealings came to view her with extraordinary respect). Two of Francis's practices worried Ugolino especially: his embrace of absolute poverty and his rejection of "book learning" and of the very books themselves. Not surprisingly, Ugolino was convinced that endowments and education would help the Order become more stable and influential.

Francis's suspicion of education and prohibition of books might strike modern readers as uncharacteristically narrow-minded. Francis, on the other hand, might retort that Jesus Christ, his Lord and his paradigm, was a carpenter, not a theologian. Francis experienced theological truth through the most direct method possible: received *sapientia,* or wisdom, rather than through years of training in school acquiring mere *scientia,* or knowledge; he might be said to represent what Etienne Gilson called the Augustinian family of philosopher theologians, who believed that "all the rational truth about God that had been taught by the philosophers could be grasped at once, pure of all errors, and enriched with many a more than philosophical truth by the simple act of faith of the most illiterate among the faithful."[10] Francis's narrow-mindedness might be said to lie more in not recognizing that this direct route was not available to all of his followers than in rejecting knowledge for its own sake. He believed, most fundamentally, that the quest for knowledge interfered with simplicity and humility, and that the friars would benefit more by spending time in prayer than in poring over books: "blessed Francis did not want his brothers to be desirous of learning and books, but wanted and preached to the brothers to be eager to have and imitate pure and holy simplicity, holy prayer, and Lady Poverty, on which the holy and first brothers had built" (*Assisi Compilation* 103). For Francis, brothers who forsook simplicity for education, who preached to impress others, had abandoned their vocation and would become puffed up in vanity and self-congratulation. But his position on education would ultimately fail, as more men entered the First Order: some of the finest and best-educated minds of the thirteenth and fourteenth centuries would be Franciscans, including Saint Bonaventure, Roger Bacon, William of Ockham, Ramon Llull (who was a tertiary), Saint Antony of Padua, John Duns Scotus, and a number of others less well known.

As the Order grew in its first decade of existence, then, and particularly between 1215 and 1220, Francis lost control over the process of recruitment. Newer recruits came in who had a desire for better accommodations and also for books and the opportunity for education. Their motives for joining the Order became less focused on Francis's ideals—for some, entering upon a religious life was actually a road to better living, education, and advancement, and the Franciscan Order, which enjoyed the high favor of the church, might well advance their cause. And so, during this period and beyond, there was continual tension between those who wanted to follow Francis absolutely, renouncing everything, and those who favored a more liberal approach to the religious life (Ugolino tended to side with the latter). The former eventually split off into the suborder known as the Spiritual Franciscans, who endured persecutions of their own, as heretics, in the fourteenth century; some were burned at the stake. There was a sad and fundamental irony in this: that the more Francis-like Franciscans were the ones who became the heretics, in the end.

Increasing numbers also made it necessary to organize the Order into 12 provinces—8 in Italy and 4 beyond the Alps—under the supervision of Ministers elected by their subordinates; these provinces would meet at semiannual General Chapters at Porziuncula. The first General Chapter was held at Pentecost in May 1217; the second yearly conference would be held at Michaelmas. Among the things decided at the first General Chapter was that missionaries would be sent out on more ambitious journeys, across Europe and even to Outremer (the crusader states of the Middle East: the County of Edessa, the Principality of Antioch, the County of Tripoli, and the Kingdom of Jerusalem), to found missions and gain recruits. The notion of hierarchy, in which one man was master over others, did not please Francis, but he acknowledged that the weight of numbers made it necessary. New recruits insisted on regarding Francis as Minister General, although he never claimed the title for himself and wished to be considered instead one of the humblest of the brothers.

Francis was finally forced to accept that they all would need permanent accommodations, and so he began to permit houses and chapels to be built for them in lieu of caves and hermitages, and he reluctantly allowed the possession of a few service books in common—Franciscan service books are known for their small size, making them not only more portable but less costly and ostentatious. He also adopted the observance of the Divine Office to organize their days, which made them increasingly like other monastic foundations. Francis himself and his ideal of apostolic poverty had become remote to the majority of the friars.

As had been decided at the General Chapter, much of the work of the Order became focused on missions abroad, including Outremer, a mission to which Brother Elias was dispatched as leader immediately after the first chapter. Although Francis wished to focus on France for his own missionary work, he was dissuaded by Ugolino, who recognized his value at home. So Francis spent much of the year 1218 roaming Italy, arousing extraordinary enthusiasm among his listeners and inspiring a popular religious movement that was of great interest and utility to the church, because first and foremost, it emphasized obedience to church tenets, and it also discouraged lawsuits and complaints that might be levied against the hierarchy. Francis usually preached outdoors, in simple but enthusiastic and approachable language that the common people loved. His listeners sometimes snatched at his clothing, hoping to tear off a piece of it as a relic of the holy man: "So great was the faith of the men and women, so great their devotion toward the holy man of God, that he pronounced himself happy who could but touch his garment" (*First Life* 62).

THE FIFTH CRUSADE AND ITS AFTERMATH

In 1219, Francis made the fateful decision to join the Fifth Crusade, as a peacemaker rather than a soldier. The *Second Life* (30) records that he went with "the desire for martyrdom"; he would be a knight for Christ in the best chivalric tradition. He left for Acre in the summer, accompanied by Peter of Catanio (this was not the same Peter of Catanio who was one of the early members of the order, who had died before this date) and a handful of others. Brother Elias was in charge of the mission in Acre, and after a brief sojourn in his company, Francis continued on with one companion (or several, according to Sabatier), Brother Illuminato, to the crusaders' camps outside the Muslim city of Damietta, at the mouth of the Nile in Egypt. These camps were the bustling headquarters of perhaps 40,000 Christian soldiers under the secular leadership of John de Brienne, king of Jerusalem in exile. Unfortunately for the mission, Pope Honorius had also put Cardinal Pelagius of Saint Lucia as legate in charge of his own expedition to Damietta, and Pelagius began to dispute the strategy and command with John of Brienne. Their mission was to recover Jerusalem from the Muslim forces and the Ayyubid dynasty, but in the course of this undertaking, they made a base outside Damietta and laid siege to the city, which they wished to turn into a center for trade. This siege began in May 1218 and lasted until after Francis's arrival in Egypt; when it began, the city had some 80,000 inhabitants and was an important and prosperous trading port in the Mediterranean. A surprise attack won the defensive watchtower of the city, situated on a small island in the Nile, for the crusaders in August 1218.

The news of the fall of the tower of Damietta, its first and perhaps most important line of defense, caused the death of the elderly sultan al-Adil. His son al-Malik al-Kamil became sultan of Egypt; he had already been the leader of the forces trying to battle the crusaders. Now the crusaders were able to besiege the city in earnest, and the situation became more critical for al-Kamil and the Muslim forces. The siege went on through the blistering heat of two Egyptian summers, during which the crusaders and the occupants of Damietta alike were wracked by plagues of disease-bearing flies and epidemics of dysentery and scurvy.[11] By the time Francis and Illuminato arrived, gangrene and disease were rampant not only in the camps, but also in the city.

Tensions rose inevitably as conditions worsened. It became clear that battle could not be postponed much longer. The *Second Life* (30) describes a vision that Saint Francis had, in which the Lord showed him that if the battle were to take place, it would not go well for the Christians. After some hesitation, he went before the Christian forces "with salutary warnings, forbidding the war, denouncing the reason for it." And indeed, the Christian forces were turned back on August 29, when some 5,000 crusaders may have died. It was then that Francis resolved to approach the sultan toward an attempt at peacemaking.

When Francis and Illuminato approached Sultan al-Kamil, they may first have been seized and maltreated: "for before he gained access to the sultan . . . he was captured by the sultan's soldiers, was insulted and beaten" (*First Life* 57). They were then received "very honorably" by the Sultan himself, given gifts, and listened to courteously, but sent away empty-handed (although with a protective escort), succeeding neither in converting the sultan nor in achieving peace. Steven Runciman describes his visit in terms that are not complimentary to Francis but evocative of the circumstances:

> The battle had been watched with sad dismay by a distinguished visitor to the camp, Brother Francis of Assisi. He had come to the East believing, as many good and unwise persons before and after him have believed, that a peace-mission can bring about peace. He now asked Pelagius to go to see the sultan. After some hesitation, Pelagius agreed, and sent him under a flag of truce to Fariskur. The Moslem guards were suspicious at first but soon decided that anyone so simple, so gentle, and so dirty must be mad, and treated him with the respect due to a man who had been touched by God. He was taken to the Sultan al-Kamil who was charmed by him and listened patiently to his appeal. . . . Francis was offered many gifts, which he refused, and was sent back with an honourable escort to the Christians.[12]

Not long after his visit, however, the sultan, determined to save Damietta, offered a trade to the crusaders: he would cede them Palestine, if they would leave Egypt. Although John of Brienne and his troops were eager to accept the offer, Cardinal Pelagius would not agree. And thus the stage was set for the final disgraceful episode of the siege of Damietta. The crusaders stormed the city walls on November 4 and found a mere 3,000 emaciated inhabitants alive, the other 70,000-odd souls having died of disease or starvation. The Christians promptly looted the city, raping and beating the last sickly inhabitants, or taking them to sell into slavery. To all of this were Francis and Illuminato witnesses, no doubt appalled by the savagery surrounding them.

Brother Elias and the other missionaries came from Syria to join them. The brothers spent their time in prayer and caring for the sick and the wounded. Francis wore himself out in caring for others; his health, never vigorous, was permanently broken, and he would return to Europe in 1220 with a chronic inflammation of the eyes that would eventually leave him blind. No doubt he also experienced traumas of the spirit after witnessing the ugliness of war and the behavior of the crusaders.

In 1935, medical historian Edward Frederick Hartung collated all of the symptoms Francis suffered after his time in Egypt and concluded that the affliction of the eyes from which Francis would suffer for the rest of his life was trachoma, which even today is the world's most common infectious cause of blindness and endemic in Egypt since ancient times. Today, the disease can be treated (if caught early enough) with antibiotics; untreated, it causes constant discharge, with other symptoms similar to pinkeye. Blisters on the eyelids and their eventual inversion follow; the inversion causes constant abrasion by the eyelashes, which in turn causes ulceration of the corneas and ultimately blindness. Hartung's diagnosis fits the symptoms described by Francis's biographers well, but of course it is impossible to know for sure. In Francis's day, trachoma was a chronic, painful, and debilitating disease for which there was no effective treatment: "for it St. Francis' physicians applied eye bindings, salves, plasters and *urina virginis pueri*, the sovereign eye wash [of the time]. In final resort the doctors applied hot irons to the Saint's face."[13] Hartung also speculated on the cause of Francis's stigmata and death (see further below).

While the crusaders won the day at Damietta, they would not win the war. The Fifth Crusade ultimately saw the crusaders return home in shame, with nothing to show for their efforts and Damietta again in the hands of the infidel. Runciman, in his three-volume history of the Crusades, categorizes the Fifth among "Misguided Crusades."

Following Francis's time in Damietta and before he returned to Acre, there is a gap in the records. No one knows where he was or how he spent his time; perhaps lying sick somewhere in the Middle East between the two cities, perhaps journeying to sites in the Holy Land. Even today, following the Franciscan mission to Acre led by Elias and Francis's time in Egypt and Syria, the Franciscans retain a special right of access to and care of Christian sites in the Holy Land.

RETURN TO EUROPE

Francis returned to Italy unhealthy and subdued. He spent some time in retreat on an island near Venice, praying and preparing for his return to Assisi and the altered circumstances that he knew he would find there. His order had changed in his absence: the vicars Gregory and Matthew whom he had left in charge had brought the Franciscan houses even further into line with the established monastic orders and further away from their simple beginnings.

New fasts, even more rigorous than the old, had been prescribed. Ugolino had imposed a rule, his *Constitutions*, on the Second Order that rendered them little different from Benedictine nuns, without regard for their unique beginnings or their desire to live as their male counterparts did. John of Capella was attempting to split off from the rest to found an order of lepers. Friar Peter of Staccia was known to be living in a comfortable house in Bologna with a library of books and a group of other friars, in utter disregard of Francis's wishes. Several friars had been martyred in Spain, the first Franciscan martyrs.[14] Furthermore, a rumor that Francis had died abroad left many uncertain of their future direction. Francis undoubtedly had much to deal with on his return, and little energy with which to do it.

Francis, uncharacteristically enraged, swept the house in Bologna clean of its inhabitants, even the sick who were lying there, much in the spirit of Christ purging the Temple of its money-changers. Then he proceeded directly to Pope Honorius at Orvieto, there to bare his soul to the pope and seek his guidance. Honorius, while sympathetic, did not waver: the Order was to be led by the dictates of the Lateran Council, the curia, and the pope. Ugolino would be the Order's Protector, and it would be to him that Francis would now appeal. To Ugolino's credit, at Francis's appeal he reversed some of the more objectionable innovations that he had previously sanctioned or prescribed, but Francis resigned any role of leadership in the Order, and bowed to the inevitable.

At some time before this period, Francis was said to have had a vision of a small black hen that "had so many chicks that it was unable to gather them all under its wings, and so they wandered all around her in circles" (*Legend of the Three Companions* 63). He recognized himself in the hen, and his brethren in her chicks, his many sons whom he could no longer protect. From this he learned the lesson that he must resign his order into the care of the church, but he hesitated to burden Honorius himself with the charge. And so he was glad to hand them over to Ugolino as protector, despite their differences. As Pope Gregory IX, Ugolino would be "a remarkable benefactor and protector of the brothers as well as of other religious, and above all, of Christ's poor" (*Legend of the Three Companions* 67).

Peter of Catanio then became Vicar General of the Order (or Minister General; the terms are often confused in the sources); when Peter died shortly afterward, the position went to the brilliant but flawed Brother Elias. Elias was extremely devoted to Francis and was appointed by the pope to oversee the construction of Saint Francis's Basilica in Assisi, but power corrupted him in the end. He lapsed into luxury and treated his confreres so highhandedly that he had to be ousted and excommunicated.

Another outcome of Francis's exile and return was that Ugolino had ended the informal and easygoing relations between the men's houses and the women's. Francis could no longer spend time in long conversation with Clare. Nor did he take an active interest in women's foundations, despite Clare's wishes; in part, this was at Elias's insistence, but it was also in line with Ugolino's *Constitutions*. Francis was perhaps more willing to part company with the women's houses than they were to lose him and the brothers. Ugolino became most truly the guide of the Second Order, in Francis's absence, although the friars continued to act as visitors to the houses and deliver sermons, hear confessions, and administer the sacraments, generally performing the services that the sisters were unable to perform on their own behalf.

ILLNESS AND DEATH

By 1221, Francis "suffered from infirmity of the eyes, stomach, spleen, and liver" (*Second Life* 96); accordingly, his behavior and temper had become erratic. Perhaps his most trying behavior toward others involved his rejection of books; one poor novice begged him repeatedly to be allowed to own a breviary or a psalter, and Francis seems to have lost his temper with him repeatedly:

> The same one spoke to him again about a psalter. And blessed Francis told him: After you have a psalter, you will desire and want to have a breviary; after you have a breviary, you will sit in a fancy chair, like a great prelate telling your brother: 'Bring me the breviary.' And speaking in this way with great intensity of spirit, he took some ashes in his hand, put them on his head rubbing them around his head as though he were washing it, saying: 'I, a breviary! I, a breviary!' He spoke this way many times, passing his hand over his head. The brother was stunned and ashamed. (*Assisi Compilation* 104)

This stubbornness extended to property and to his own health, as well; when the friars implored him to seek the aid of a doctor (which would have availed nothing in any case, given his ailments and the state of medical practice at the time), he refused to do so; when he finally gave in to their wishes, his situation was too dire to treat. Thomas of Celano attributed his ill health to his lifestyle, "in as much as he had chastised his body and brought it into subjection during the many years that had preceded . . . his body had had little or no rest while he traveled" (*First Life* 97) in order to spread the message of God. It was necessary for him now to ride an ass rather than walk to do his customary outdoor preaching and evangelizing, but he prayed standing erect, not sitting. His primary concern was never the care of his body, only the preservation of spiritual joy: "Blessed Francis had this as his highest and main goal: he was always careful to have and preserve in himself spiritual joy internally and externally, even though from the beginning of his conversion until the day of his death he greatly afflicted his body" (*Assisi Compilation* 120).

Despite his illnesses, Francis traveled to Rome as needed. In 1223, he was there to discuss the revision of his rule with Ugolino, for which purpose he was housed in the cardinal's palace; the Rule of 1223 was approved in November of that year and has remained in place ever since. *The Assisi Compilation* (97) tells that even while he was a guest in Ugolino's palace, he went out to beg for alms on the street and not only ate the scraps of food that he received but shared them with the dignitaries who were also guests, to Ugolino's embarrassment. Once, when returning from a visit to Rome, it was raining, and "since he was very sick, he was riding on horseback, but he got off his horse [to pray], standing on the road side despite the rain which completely soaked him." His manifold sufferings seem to have intensified in him the mystic's fervor, or, as Adrian House puts it, "as his body decayed, 'the inner man was renewed' and burned even brighter."[15]

Another frequent destination of Francis during this period was Greccio, a site south of Assisi where he had a hermitage. Here, also in 1223, Francis introduced a Christmas tradition that lives on today: he staged the first living crèche in history. He had a manger prepared, and to call to memory the birth of Christ, he set before living eyes the hay in which the infant lay, the ox, the ass, and the miracle of Bethlehem: "the night was lighted up like the day, and it delighted men and beasts" (*First Life* 85). The people present were filled with joy, and communities throughout the Christian world adopted the living Nativity scene.

According to the *Little Flowers of St. Francis,* in 1224, Francis decided to spend the 40 days before the feast of Saint Michael in fasting at his retreat at La Verna. He traveled there with his old companions, Angelo, Masseo, and Leo, who insisted that he ride on an ass, because he was ill and the summer was hot. Here he lived in a hut made of wattles, and he spent his time at first in teaching the others "the observance of holy poverty" and how to live in hermitage. Later, as he meditated alone, he was observed by his brothers "rapt in God and raised from the ground . . . sometimes as high as three feet, sometimes four, at others times halfway up or at the top of the beech trees."[16] Leo would go to him then, and embrace and kiss his feet, if they were in reach. Francis sought out a location even more remote, had a hut made for him there, and withdrew from the others; only Leo could come to him with bread and water for him to eat, and they would celebrate matins together.

In this hut, Francis kept fast "with great abstinence and severity," prayed fervently, and scourged his already dying flesh; at the same time, he increased in virtue and inspiration. He received visits from both devils and angels and, more mundanely, wild birds. *The Little Flowers* tells us that Francis was visited there by a seraph, a six-winged angel, during whose appearance the whole mountain appeared to be on fire, and shepherds keeping watch in the fields were afraid. Most miraculously of all, during this vigil the stigmata of Christ's crucifixion were imprinted on Francis's hands, feet, and side, where they would remain for the remainder of his life, making him the first stigmatic in history. The wound in his side, the mark of the spear wound in Christ's side, oozed blood constantly and left marks on his clothing and dressings, while his hands and feet needed to be bandaged, and for the first time in years, Francis was forced to wear foot coverings.

Francis tried to keep these wounds a secret, although several of his brothers, including Leo, Angelo, Rufino, and Elias, all caught glimpses of them, and ultimately everyone knew. After his death, his body was examined, and the church was satisfied that not only were the wounds real, but they were neither self-inflicted nor caused in some way by the friars: "the undeniable truth of those stigmata appeared most brilliantly through sight and contact not only in his life and death, but also after his death, the Lord revealed their truth even more brilliantly by many miracles shown in different parts of the world" (*Legend of the Three Companions* 17). Even today the Catholic Church regards their appearance as a bona fide miracle. Others have sought a scientific explanation: could they have been psychosomatic, for instance? Or caused by a disease like tuberculosis, malaria, or leprosy, all of which can cause skin lesions and damage to the extremities, and all of which are plausible given Francis's other symptoms? Adrian House's biography of Francis contains an extended discussion of the possible scientific and medical causes of the stigmata; his own thesis is that they were caused by lymph-node tuberculosis, *Lupus vulgaris* or scrofula, which causes pink or reddish nodules, ulcers, and scarring of the tissue, which happen suddenly as tissue deteriorates.[17] He thus accounts for the lung hemorrhages as well. No matter what the cause, natural or supernatural, the stigmata have always been accounted among the proofs of Francis's sanctity, and since then, hundreds of stigmatics have been documented.

Francis became more reclusive as he neared the end of his life. He could no longer bear sunlight because of the pain it caused in his eyes, and he preferred darkness to lamplight at night. Clare had a hut made for him outside her own accommodations at San Damiano, where she could tend to him; according to *The Assisi Compilation* (83), he lay there for 50 days. He suffered continual pain and sleeplessness, which he embraced, composing praises and consolations for Clare and his male companions, which he dictated as he lay in the darkness. This was the period during which he composed the beloved *Canticle of Brother Sun*, which became an immediate success: he bade his brothers to go forth, preach to the people, and sing it to them afterward, and so it was popularized around the countryside. *The Assisi Compilation* tells us that Francis recited it daily until his death.

Finally, Ugolino prevailed on him to receive treatment: "Brother, you do not do well in not allowing yourself to be helped with your eye disease, for your health and your life are of great value not only to yourself but also to others . . . you must not be cruel to yourself in such a serious and manifest need and illness" (*Assisi Compilation* 83). Brother Elias, by now General Minister of the Order, also commanded him to receive treatment and expressed a desire to be present when it happened.

With a special *capuche* (hood) covering his head and more especially his eyes, he was brought on horseback to a specialist in Rieti, Master Nicholas. Here Francis postponed his treatment as long as possible until Elias could arrive, but Elias was detained by business, so the treatment began without him.

The only remedy that the doctor could suggest was cauterization of the tissue "from the jaw to the eyebrow of the weaker eye" (*Assisi Compilation* 84). This terrible solution, in an era without anesthetic, might possibly end the continual discharge from his eyes. At the time of the procedure, Francis prayed to Brother Fire for mercy while the doctor heated the iron instrument. Witnesses fled in dread of watching his torment, but when they returned, Francis chided them for lack of faith: "I felt no pain nor even heat from the fire. In fact, if it's not well cooked, cook it some more!" (*Ibid.*). While his biographers attributed this lack of sensation to the generosity of the fire, it too has been explained by modern scholars as a symptom of his underlying disease. A characteristic symptom of leprosy, for instance, is the loss of sensation in the affected area; if Francis was suffering from advanced leprosy, given his prolonged exposure to the lepers whom he was trying to help, this could account for why he was able to withstand the unbearable pain of the cauterization.[18] Unfortunately, the procedure did no good whatsoever.

He was spared from fire on another occasion as well. Once, while sitting close to the fire, his breeches caught on fire. Untroubled by this, he refused at first to put them out. It was necessary for someone else to do it for him. In *The Canticle of Brother Sun*, Francis praised fire among the other elements as part of God's creation: "All praise be yours, my Lord, through Brother Fire, through whom you brighten up the night. How beautiful is he, how gay! Full of power and strength."[19]

Another doctor tried puncturing Francis's eardrums to solve the problem; not only did this not work, but Francis suffered a great deal in the process. He was fortunate only in receiving careful and constant attendance: "[he] was continuously cared for by his closest and most devoted companions, all experts in nursing the sick, all familiar with the problems of his stigmata and the agony from his lungs, stomach and eyes."[20] Indeed, accounts of his final year present a poignant picture of constant suffering in general and the decline of his strength and senses, as well as the patience with which he bore it and his concern for other beings and things in spite of it. Even while suffering desperately himself, for instance, he was eager to help a poor woman who came to his doctor for help for her own eye ailment. He sent her a mantle, pretending that it had been borrowed from her and then returned again along with loaves of bread, and saw that she received food regularly afterward. He apologized to his caregivers for his weakness and assured them that God would reward them, not for helping him, but for the good works that God knew they would have done if they had not been preoccupied with him. Many other such stories surround the last few months of Francis's life; he continued to deprive himself and give his scanty possessions to those in greater need until the end, while praying constantly and offering praises to God and creation.

Accounts of miracles performed by him abound during this period, as well. The miracles of his insensitivity to fire, of hearing beautiful music from nowhere, of restoring wine to a distracted caregiver when it had all been drunk by his clerical admirers while visiting him, all occurred during his final months. His companions moved him about as best they were able, from one city to another in search of medical assistance, and from hermitage to hermitage in search of respite. A crowd greeted him whenever he entered a new town, while he was sometimes driven even from his hermitages by visitors. Elias kept a watchful eye over his care, seeing that his dearest companions were able to be with him even while others complained of favoritism.

At a friary north of Siena, Francis began to vomit blood. Many believed that the time of his death was imminent; they begged him for final words. He encouraged them again to embrace Lady Poverty and obey the church, but he did recover enough to be moved on toward Assisi. They continued to break their journey at hermitages; at La Celle, where he suffered a relapse, his symptoms were described as "bleeding from the stomach and an enlarged liver and spleen," suggesting that "apart from chronic undernourishment and possible TB, he was suffering from a peptic stomach ulcer and the side effects of malaria. His abdomen began to swell—his hands and feet too—from dropsy; he could take no solid food."[21] He was very near the end.

By early September 1226, he was in Assisi, blind and weak, but still mentally alert. Soldiers carried him to Bishop Guido's palace there near his parents' house, where he welcomed Sister Death, dictated a final verse of his *Canticle* in praise of her, and looked forward with joy to union with God; Elias was forced to reproach him for the unseemly joy that he was experiencing at the approach of death, when he might be contemplating sin and death instead, but Francis would leave life as he had led it—in joy and celebration of Creator and creation. Here he dictated his *Testament* from his bed: "Many find its forty simple sentences the purest and most moving distillation of his *modus vivendi* because it emerged straight from his heart" without intervention by church authority.[22] In a way, it contradicted the formal Rule of the Order approved by the church, because it resurrected the absolute poverty that Francis had always desired for the friars without the admixture of possessions imposed by Ugolino. But Ugolino would have the final say.

Finally, sensing that he had but days to live, Francis had himself conveyed back to Porziuncula. This was always his home, then and now the geographical heart of the Order, although the official headquarters is the Basilica de San Francesco. He lay on the earth naked for awhile, but was persuaded to dress again in obedience to his comrades. He began to dictate final letters to those dearest to him, including beloved Clare, who was too ill to visit and afraid that she might die without seeing him again. She would see him again, but only after his death. His dear friend and patron of the order Giacoma de Settesoli of Rome brought him a shroud, candles, and some almond cookies of which he was especially fond, even as he was dictating a letter to her asking for those very things, another of the miraculous events surrounding his dying and death. The gatekeeper admitted her despite the rule against commingling of the sexes, at Francis's behest.

At the end, Francis summoned all of his dearest companions to his bedside—those present included Bernard of Quintavalle, first of the brothers to renounce every worldly good on his behalf; Elias; Angelo, his boyhood friend; and Giles. And after blessing them all and, through them, all of his order, commending the order into their care, and reciting Psalm 142, Francis slipped into death on the evening of October 3, 1226, at the age of 44 (in the reckoning of the day, this was already October 4, which is why Francis's feast day is celebrated on October 4 today). Giacoma, too, was there, while friars had come from many countries and from all over Italy to keep vigil. In accordance with one of Francis's final wishes, they laid his naked body on the earth, giving expression to the poverty and humility in which he had lived, and to the love that he had for the earth and all creation.

FRANCIS, THE PATRON SAINT OF ANIMALS AND ECOLOGY

Professor Lynn White Jr., the eminent historian of science, wrote the following in his 1967 essay, *The Historical Roots of Our Ecological Crisis*:

> Possibly we should ponder the greatest radical in Christian history since Christ: Saint Francis of Assisi. . . . The key to an understanding of Francis is his belief in the virtue of humility—not merely for the individual but for man as a species. Francis tried to depose man from his monarchy over creation and set up a democracy of all God's creatures. With him the ant is no longer simply a homily for the lazy, flames a sign of the thrust of the soul toward union with God; now they are Brother Ant and Sister Fire, praising the Creator in their own ways as Brother Man does in his.

It was he who first suggested that Saint Francis be recognized as the patron saint of ecology, a designation that he was granted formally in 1979, by Pope John Paul II. Roger D. Sorrell puts it this way: "He showed how much he valued [creatures] in the way he applied standards of chivalric behavior to them, in his beliefs about the proper use of creation's bounty as food, and in his contemplative experiences amid the glories of creation."[23]

Sorrell finds "chivalric compliment" in the form of address that Francis uses in the *Canticle of Brother Sun*: "And first my lord Brother Sun . . . through Sister Moon and Stars," and so forth. This was "Francis' unique way of showing his high regard for creatures by giving them the same type of chivalric honors he also gave to his human 'companions of the Round Table.'"[24] Chivalry is related to almsgiving for Francis as well; magnanimity demonstrated to the poor reflects well on the giver, and it is part of *noblesse oblige*.

One of the most famous episodes involving Francis and creatures was his sermon to the birds, during the summer of 1213. Here, according to Thomas of Celano, Francis "ran eagerly" to a flock of various kinds of birds that he encountered along the way, and, finding that they seemed to expect something, began to address them in a sermon: "My brothers, birds, you should praise your Creator very much and always love him: he gave you feathers to clothe you, wings so that you can fly, and whatever else was necessary for you. God made you noble among his creatures" (*First Life* 58). The birds listened to him with rapt attention, and Francis resolved then never to neglect to include birds, animals, and "even creatures that have no feeling" in his evangelizing. This indeed was not simply to treat them with concern and affection, but also to acknowledge that they had intellects and perhaps even souls that could be stirred to love of God.

As noted above, it is sometimes difficult to know how much credence to give individual anecdotes in saints' lives. Where powers of communication with birds and animals are concerned, many saints have been said to have possessed them. What Lynn White recognized in Francis was that, rather than exerting power over creatures to demonstrate that they were within human dominion, he exerted power over them by acknowledging their equality with him as fellow parts of God's creation (although more orthodox theology would not admit the degree of equality that Professor White and others have found in Francis's beliefs). There is, finally, no real reason to doubt that Francis truly loved and drew inspiration from the natural world—every account of his life and deeds abounds with such joy in nature that this becomes the dominant sensibility underlying all else. Another saint might perhaps have been named patron of Italy in his place; no other saint but Francis could have been named as patron of animals and ecology.

Francis always sought out wild and beautiful places for his solitudes with God, from the first throes of his conversion until the end of his life; indeed, many have observed that central Italy is riddled with caves and groves associated with his hermitages. In the account of Francis's fateful days at La Verna in 1224, *The Little Flowers* abounds in natural description, vividly portraying not only the dramatic scenery surrounding the friars but also Francis's contemplation of it: "Francis began to study the location and the scenery," and

> a few days later St. Francis was standing beside that cell, gazing at the form of the mountain and marveling at the great chasms and openings in the massive rocks. And he began to pray, and then it was revealed to him by God that those striking chasms had been made in a miraculous way at the hour of Christ's Passion when, as the Gospel says, "the rocks split."

Francis's propensity for seeking out the wilderness and his standing rapt in contemplations reflect the medieval notion that all of creation consists of visible signs by which the Creator can be known, and that every creature symbolizes some truth about God: "from these visible things, therefore, one mounts to considering the power and wisdom and goodness of God as being, living, and understanding," in the words of Francis's follower Saint Bonaventure, in *The Mind's Road to God*.[25]

If one truly believes that all of creation is a road to union with the Creator, one cannot help but treat all of creation with extraordinary care. Francis demonstrated such care to every creature that he encountered. He released birds and rabbits from traps, and he set fish free when they were caught. He pleaded for room for flowers among the vegetables—"He used to tell the brother who took care of the garden not to cultivate all the ground . . . for vegetables, but to leave a piece . . . that would produce wild plants that in their season would produce 'Brother Flowers'" (*Assisi Compilation* 88)—and for some part of each tree that was cut to be spared to allow it to regenerate. He made a pet of a pheasant that he had been sent for food. He moved frogs, toads, worms, and other creatures out of danger. He even converted a "dangerous" wolf to Christianity and sent it on its way tamed. Late in life, he befriended a crow, who was said to have followed his coffin to the grave and to have pined away after his death. In a world where the smallest of God's creatures was a symbol of the greatness and mystery of God's works, Francis seems to have been one of few who had the depth to see and apply this ethos consistently. No wonder, then, that even a scientist mourning mankind's destructive role in the natural world could appreciate and recognize the wisdom and chivalry of Saint Francis.

AFTERLIFE

After they raised Francis from the earth again, the friars washed his body and anointed him with spices. All who were present were then witnesses to the stigmata, although many there already knew of it. Witnesses reported as well that his body was restored to youth and suppleness. Elias made the stigmata known then to all of those keeping vigil outside, as well; during the night that followed he allowed the friars sometimes to kiss them and sometimes merely to see them.

Messengers were sent to bring word of Francis's passing to Clare, the church authorities, and secular leaders. Clare could not come, owing to her own illness, but others came to pay respects and to witness the stigmata.

Francis's body was finally placed in a coffin and carried in a procession toward Assisi and the church of San Giorgio, Francis's childhood church and school. Singing, on the way there, they stopped by San Damiano, where Clare and the nuns could mourn and then rejoice over his life. They kissed his wounded hands and sent him again on his way home to Assisi. His requiem Mass was then held in San Giorgio; many attendees waited in the piazza outside because the church could not accommodate them all. San Giorgio would be his first resting place.

In 1227, Ugolino succeeded Pope Honorius as Pope Gregory IX. By then, so many miracles had occurred since Francis's death and through his intervention that Pope Gregory had no hesitation in beginning the process of his canonization; besides, Gregory knew the living Francis so well and, despite their differences, revered him so highly that he bore personal witness to Francis's sanctity. On July 16, 1228, Francis was proclaimed a saint in the Piazza del Comune in Assisi; the pope's procession included John of Brienne king of Jerusalem among other dignitaries. Bishop Guido, Francis's lifelong patron, was able to be present as well, although he would die the same year.

On the day following the canonization, the cornerstone of his basilica was laid by Pope Gregory himself. Elias, who had been passed over initially as the new minister general of the order, was put in charge of the building. Francis would be interred here for good, although his body was moved once within it, in 1978.

The Franciscan Order continued to be vexed by the question of poverty after Francis's death. His most faithful adherents, including Clare, continued to petition for Francis's ideal, whereby brothers and sisters would own nothing, not even the buildings they lived in, while Pope Gregory and brothers like Elias insisted that money could be held in common for their needs, that they could have large and permanent dwellings for their housing, and that they could own books and become educated. There are still streams in the First Franciscan order—Friars Minor Conventual, Friars Minor, and Friars Minor Capuchin—some more strict, like Francis, and others more relaxed, but they all abide by the governance of the Papal See, in the end. After being elected Minister General in 1232 and supervising the construction of the basilica, Elias became so devoted to his possessions that they became his downfall; his opulent lifestyle and arrogant behavior were a subject of disgrace throughout the Order, and he was replaced and ultimately excommunicated; a sad ending for a man who seemed truly to have loved Francis while living and who had great ability. Today there are some 30,000 members of the three branches of the First Order.

Clare died in 1253. She was attended in her last illness by Giles, Leo, Angelo, Rufino, and Juniper, Francis's own favorite companions. Pope Innocent IV, Gregory's successor, was her great admirer, and before her death, he finally approved the rule that she desired for her order—poverty as Francis had understood it. Innocent wanted to proclaim her a saint immediately but was prevailed upon to begin a formal process instead. She was canonized in 1255, and her body lies in her own basilica in Assisi. Thomas of Celano wrote of her life, as well. The Poor Clares, as the Second Order was officially renamed around 1263, now number around 18,000 members.

And finally, there are hundreds of thousands of members of the Third Order, some living in community, some in the world, all inspired by the life of history's humblest man.

CONCLUSION

It can be difficult for moderns, living in a skeptical world where almost everything can be explained by science, to understand the medieval notion of sanctity, of miracles, and of the supernatural, at least among non-Catholics. Why indeed would not bathing for years, wearing hair shirts and scourging the flesh until the body was abscessed and oozing, eating fetid scraps, or kissing the decaying lips of a leper be particularly "holy" behavior? Why would anyone believe accounts of someone resisting the torments of demons, when there are no demons, and pronounce that man or woman holy? And if there are no miracles, how can they be proof of sainthood? It is difficult for most people living today to enter into a past world where the supernatural was vividly real; where scourging oneself reflected the humility and suffering of Christ and a willingness to assume burdens for his and for others' behalf; where everything that was, was a sign of God or some sacred truth of his; and where miracles were ever-present signs of a voice interceding for salvation with God.

Perhaps what makes Francis so charismatic, so enduring, and so far-reaching today is that anyone can understand what made him a saint. It was not just his mortifications of the flesh that made him holy, it was also the love and humility that compelled him to spare others' sufferings, to offer every little thing he had to someone poorer. It was not just his belief in the omnipresent supernatural forces of good and evil, of the signs and symbols of God's work in the natural world, it was also his appreciation of the natural as beautiful and intrinsically worthwhile, and of man's humble place in both the natural and the supernatural spheres. And it was not just the miracles performed by him and through his name that made him so revered through the ages, but the manifest goodness, profound faith, joyousness, and true charity of his life that enabled and still enable him to touch believers and skeptics alike, making followers of them all. He remains for many the best exemplar of true Christianity who ever lived, after Christ himself.

NOTES

1. *Francis of Assisi: Early Documents, Vol. II: The Founder,* ed. Regis J. Armstrong, J. A. Wayne Hellmann, and William J. Short (New York: New York City Press, 2000), 62: this three-volume set on Francis of Assisi contains all of the early documentation of Francis's life in the most recent edition and translation available.

2. A. G. Rigg, *A History of Anglo-Latin Literature: 1066–1422* (Cambridge: Cambridge University Press, 1992), 184.

3. Ibid., 12.

4. University of York, *Pilgrims and Pilgrimage: Saints in Medieval Society,* at http://www.york.ac.uk/projects/pilgrimage/content/med_saint.html.

5. See Luke Demaitre, *Leprosy in Premodern Medicine* (Baltimore: Johns Hopkins University Press, 2007), 147: "[Saints] were venerated as models of charitable dedication, who suppressed the revulsion toward loathsomeness. Saint Francis . . . was portrayed as kissing a leprous wanderer (on the lips, in some iconography) and then hastening to the leprosarium of Assisi, where he distributed alms to the inmates. Saint Elizabeth of Hungary (1207–1231) reportedly nursed a leprous beggar and took him into her bed."

6. This demonstrates that modern biographers are no more free of biases than their medieval counterparts, with some trying to ascribe behaviors and miracles to

post-traumatic stress and psychoses and others eager to defend the truth of sanctity, the church, and miracles; the truth is undoubtedly somewhere near the middle.

7. Paschal Robinson, "St. Francis of Assisi," in *The Catholic Encyclopedia: Vol. 6* (New York: Robert Appleton Company, 1909). Available at http://www.newadvent. org/cathen/06221a.htm (accessed Nov. 18, 2010).

8. Adrian House, *Francis of Assisi: A Revolutionary Life* (Mahwah, NJ: Hiddenspring, 2001), 170.

9. Ibid., 79–80.

10. Etienne Gilson, *Reason and Revelation in the Middle Ages* (New York: Charles Scribner's Sons, 1938), 16–17.

11. House, *Francis of Assisi,* 207.

12. Steven Runciman, *A History of the Crusades: Volume III. The Kingdom of Acre and the Later Crusades* (London: The Folio Society, 1994), 134–35.

13. "Medicine: St. Francis' Stigmata," in *Time* magazine, Monday, 11 March, 1935, available online at http://www.time.com/time/magazine/article/0,9171,883261,00. html.

14. "During the General Chapter of 1219 Francis sent a group of six friars to the missions of North Africa. Their names were Vitale, Berardo, Pietro, Accursio, Adiuto and Ottone. Vitale, the superior, fell sick in Spain, and had to abandon his resolve to go to Morocco to evangelise the moors. The others proceeded under the leadership of Berardo. They first went to Seville, in southern Spain, which was occupied by the moors, and preached Christ publicly. They were taken in front of the emir, who gave them freedom to proceed to North Africa. They crossed over to Morocco, and preached in front of the king himself. Pope Sixtus IV canonised them in 1481. The account of their martyrdom is found in Analecta Miramolin. The king expelled them from his country, but they returned in their resolve to preach the Christian faith. On 16 January 1220, after cruel torments, they were slain by the king." *Franciscana* III, pp. 579–96. The Franciscan Experience, Franciscan Saints and Mystics http://198.62.75.1/www1/ofm/ fra/FRAsnt03.html.

15. House, *Francis of Assisi,* 253.

16. Marion A. Habig, *St. Francis of Assisi: Writings and Early Biographies. English Omnibus of the Sources for the Life of St. Francis* (Chicago: Franciscan Herald Press, 1973), 1439. (References to the *Rules,* the *First and Second Lives of St. Francis* by Thomas of Celano, *The Little Flowers of St. Francis,* and the *Canticle of Brother Sun* are from this edition.), 1439.

17. House, *Francis of Assisi,* 258–64.

18. Cf. Joanne Schatzlein and Daniel Sulmasy, "The Diagnosis of St. Francis," *Franciscan Studies* 47 (1987): 181–217; the authors make a convincing case that Francis suffered and died from leprosy.

19. Habig, *St. Francis of Assisi,* 130.

20. House, *Francis of Assisi,* 267.

21. Ibid., 276–77.

22. Ibid., 280.

23. Roger D. Sorrell, *St. Francis of Assisi and Nature: Tradition and Innovation in Western Christian Attitudes toward the Environment* (New York, Oxford University Press: 1988), 69.

24. Ibid., 71.

25. Saint Bonaventura, *The Mind's Road to God,* trans. George Boas (Indianapolis: Bobbs-Merrill, 1953), 1.13 (p. 12).

FURTHER READING

Chesterton, G. K. *St. Francis of Assisi.* London: Hodder & Stoughton, 1923.

Francis of Assisi: Early Documents. Volumes I-III. Edited by Regis J. Armstrong, J. A. Wayne Hellmann, and William J. Short. New York: New City Press, 1999, 2001, 2002. (References to *The Legend of the Three Companions* and *The Assisi Compilation* are from vol. 2 of this edition.)

Habig, Marion A. *St. Francis of Assisi: Writings and Early Biographies. English Omnibus of the Sources for the Life of St. Francis.* Chicago: Franciscan Herald Press, 1973. (References to the *Rules,* the *First and Second Lives of St. Francis* by Thomas of Celano, *The Little Flowers of St. Francis,* and to the *Canticle of Brother Sun* are from this edition.)

House, Adrian. *Francis of Assisi.* Mahwah, NJ: Hiddenspring, 2001.

Moorman, J.R.H. *St. Francis of Assisi.* London: SCM Press, 1998.

Previté-Orton, C. W. *The Shorter Cambridge Medieval History.* Cambridge: Cambridge University Press, 1952.

Robinson, P. *St. Francis of Assisi. In The Catholic Encyclopedia.* New York: Robert Appleton Company, 1909. Retrieved November 17, 2010, from New Advent: http://www.newadvent.org/cathen/06221a.htm.

Sabatier, Paul. *St. Francis of Assisi.* New York: Charles Scribner's Sons, 1906.

Sorrell, Roger D. *St. Francis of Assisi and Nature: Tradition and Innovation in Western Christian Attitudes toward the Environment.* New York: Oxford University Press, 1988.

920
ICO

Icons of the Middle
Ages.

92538

$189.00

DATE			

Reference

Icons of the Middle Ages : rulers,

REF 909 ICO

92538

BRIDGEWATER-RARITAN
MIDDLE SCHOOL
LIBRARY   BAKER & TAYLOR